Literary Subterfuge and Contemporary Persian Fiction

The main focus of *Literary Subterfuge and Contemporary Persian Fiction: Who writes Iran?* is to identify components and elements which define Persian modernist fiction, placing an emphasis on literary concepts and devices which provide the dynamics of the evolutionary trajectory of this modernism.

The question of "*Who writes Iran?*" refers to a contested area which goes beyond the discipline of literary criticism. Non-literary discourses have made every effort to impose their "committed" readings on literary texts; they have even managed to exert influence on the process of literary creation. In this process, inevitably, many works, or segments of them, and many concepts which do not lend themselves to such readings have been ignored; at the same time, many of them have been appropriated by these discourses. Yet the components and elements of Persian literary tradition have persistently engaged in this discursive confrontation, mainly by insisting on literature's relative autonomy, so that at least concepts such as conformity and subterfuge, essential in terms of defining modern and modernist Persian fiction, could be defined in a literary manner.

Proffering an alternative in terms of literary historiography, this book supports a methodological approach that considers literary narratives which occur in the margins of dominant discourses, and indeed promote non-discursivity, as the main writers of Persian modernist fiction. It is an essential resource for scholars and researchers interested in Persian and comparative literature, as well as Middle Eastern Studies more broadly.

Mohammad Mehdi Khorrami is Professor of Persian language and literature at New York University. His research is focused on the literary characteristics of contemporary Persian fiction and classical Persian poetry. He has authored, translated and co-edited numerous books and articles. Among his book-length publications are *Modern Reflections of Classical Traditions in Persian Fiction*, and *Sohrab's Wars: Counter Discourses of Contemporary Persian Fiction*, which is a translated and edited collection of short stories; and the co-edited and co-translated *A Feast in the Mirror: A Collections of Short Stories by Iranian Women*. He is the founder of The Association for the Study of Persian Literature (www.persian-literature.org).

Iranian Studies

Edited by Homa Katouzian, *University of Oxford*
and Mohamad Tavakoli, *University of Toronto*

Since 1967 the International Society for Iranian Studies (ISIS) has been a leading learned society for the advancement of new approaches in the study of Iranian society, history, culture, and literature. The new ISIS Iranian Studies series published by Routledge will provide a venue for the publication of original and innovative scholarly works in all areas of Iranian and Persianate Studies.

Literary Subterfuge and Contemporary Persian Fiction

Who writes Iran?

Mohammad Mehdi Khorrami

Routledge
Taylor & Francis Group

LONDON AND NEW YORK

First published 2015 by Routledge

2 Park Square, Milton Park, Abingdon, Oxfordshire OX14 4RN

52 Vanderbilt Avenue, New York, NY 10017

Routledge is an imprint of the Taylor & Francis Group, an informa business

First issued in paperback 2019

British Library Cataloguing in Publication Data
A catalogue record for this book is available from the British Library

Library of Congress Cataloging in Publication Data
Khorrami, Mohammad Mehdi.
Literary subterfuge and contemporary Persian fiction : who writes Iran? / Mohammad Mehdi Khorrami.
pages cm. -- (Iranian studies)
Includes bibliographical references and index.
1. Persian fiction--20th century--History and criticism. 2. Discourse analysis, Narrative. I. Title.
PK6423.K46 2014
891'.553409--dc23
2014009244

ISBN: 978-1-138-78234-1 (hbk)
ISBN: 978-0-367-87000-3 (pbk)

Typeset in Times New Roman
by Taylor & Francis Books

For the memory of my mother, for my father,
For my sisters and brothers

Contents

Acknowledgments

In the introduction to this book I have allocated a rather large textual space to describing why, because of particular conditions imposed on Iran after the 1979 Revolution, conducting research on contemporary Persian cultural objects and topics does not follow conventional paths and processes. Interestingly, this unconventionality presents itself in a more pronounced manner when one writes acknowledgments. Undoubtedly, the main reason for this is the sudden nature of an event such as the Revolution and its unending consequences which have either eradicated most of the human sources who are used in such literary projects or have placed them in conditions which might make any acknowledgment of their contribution to this project dangerous to them. This is especially true in regard to Chapter 1 of this book, which owes a great deal to those who directly experienced prison and torture and brutal execution, as well as those who witnessed such atrocities. To spare further hardship to them and their families, many of whom are close friends and relatives of mine, I collectively, and anonymously, thank all of those who guided me to reliable sources of prison reports. I would further like to underline my appreciation to those who patiently and unselfishly answered questions which inevitably took them to times and places which they did not want to revisit. I am sure they know that this was as painful for me as it was for them. I thank them wholeheartedly.

Part of the work of researchers who cannot travel to Iran for obvious reasons but whose projects are about Iran, falls on the shoulders of family members, friends, and colleagues, who, among other things, play a crucial role in locating and sending unadulterated and uncensored primary sources. This project is not an exception. Nahid Khorrami, Zohreh Khorrami, Farzaneh Farahzad, Farkhondeh Hajizadeh, Ali Ma'sumi Hamadani, Marjan Riahi, as well as a number of other people who specifically asked me not to mention their names, have been extremely helpful in this regard. I am indebted to them.

There are also occasions when finding sources, even on this side of the ocean, is difficult. The story of production and distribution of exilic literature is one that requires a separate study, but suffice to say that were it not for the help of friends and colleagues such as the late Dariush Kargar, Reza

Daneshvar, Ali Erfan, Fahimeh Farsaei, Majid Roshangar, Masud Noqrehkar, Mahasti Shahrokhi, and a number of other friends and colleagues, the first part of this project would never have been completed. I am grateful.

Like any other book-length project, this study, too, has endured a long voyage during which variations of different sections were presented at various venues and benefited from the critique and feedback of wonderful friends and colleagues such Michael Beard, Peter Chelkowski, Farzaneh Farahzad, Faridoun Farrokh, M. R. Ghanoonparvar, Farkhondeh Hajizadeh, Ahmad Karimi-Hakkak, Franklin Lewis, Nasrin Rahimieh, and Shouleh Vatanabadi. I am absolutely convinced that without their comments and feedback, whether in formal conference sessions or in private conversations, this book could not have been completed. Indeed, when I think about the many hours of conversations with these colleagues and friends and their oral and written interactions with various parts of this study, I realize that such projects must always be defined in collective terms. I appreciate their ideas, and I cherish their friendship.

Perhaps, however, the most innovative comments and feedback come from my graduate students whose brightness is matched only by their literary seriousness. I strongly believe that all of us should not just acknowledge but even embrace the idea that it is the sharpness of our graduate students and their watchful eyes which prevent such projects from falling into the abyss of "academic jargonism". I cannot thank them enough.

To this list I should like to add Dr. Patia Yasin, my longtime friend and colleague, who read this text a number of times, and in addition to copy-editing, made invaluable suggestions. I am tremendously grateful to her.

Two short sections of this book were used in "Who Writes Iran? Prison Literature in the Islamic Republic: 'Les Damnées du paradis,'" and "The Aesthetics of Lone Moments in the Poetry of Forugh Farrokhzad." These articles were included in *Critical Encounters* and *Iranian Languages and Culture*. Both books are published by Mazda Publishers. I am grateful to Dr. Jabbari, the President of Mazda Publishers who graciously gave his permission for these sections to be included in this book.

I am also thankful to colleagues at Routledge. Suggestions made by Kathryn Rylance and Joe Whiting enriched this book, and the whole team made this process seamless. It has been a pleasure working with them.

And finally, my most heartfelt thanks goes to my partner, my friend, and my companion, Zari Asgari, whose contribution to this project goes far beyond simple support, encouragement, patience, suggestions and ideas; her presence gives meaning to my world.

Introduction

Overview

After the Iranian Revolution of 1979, the confrontation between competing discourses took new forms and assumed new depths. On the one hand, as usual, the official discourse tried to utilize tools which the newly-established political power had placed at its disposal in order to impose its narratives onto the various theoretical and practical spaces of Iranian society. On the other hand, contending discourses also attempted to choose some of these spaces as a field on which to wage this discursive battle. One of the natural sites on which to wage this battle was the arena of literature; primarily because this arena, at least over the past hundred years, has been one of the chief spheres where narratives of the official discourse have been consistently challenged and rejected.

In this steadily intensifying literary struggle, in addition to its propagandist devices and its unconditional support for its affiliated narratives, the official discourse has steadily increased its reliance on the apparatus of censorship and has formulated new measures to prevent competing discourses from even submitting their narratives. On many occasions, when such phenomena are examined, efforts are made to find in literary works examples of clear political confrontation with official measures, and to define such confrontations as indicatives of the influence of limiting policies on literature and art. But the issue goes far beyond a simple case of political confrontation. Indeed, once more, the experience of contemporary Persian literature has shown that literature is not a mere reflection of social issues, and that it is quite incorrect to define the dynamics between literature and other social realities through *obvious* examples of confrontation. With regard to contemporary Persian literature, the presence of competing and confrontational discourses contributes to the formation of a background against which literary discourses and narratives are constructed. Exploring different aspects of this discursive battle, in *Literary Subterfuge and Contemporary Persian Fiction* I identify and define different forms of reports and fictional narratives, with their specific devices and forms, which challenge the imposition of monologism by the dominant discourse.

The unconventional difficulties of doing research on contemporary Persian literature

About 30 years after the Revolution, the nature of problems facing those who are studying Iran has gone through transformations and created conditions which can only be described by adjectives such as extraordinary and even bizarre. I am of course limiting myself to issues and obstacles with which researchers working on contemporary Persian literature have to contend.

In ordinary situations when one wants to conduct a research project about driving forces and dynamics and/or literary circles, trends, what have you, of a particular literary tradition and in a given geography, one would probably start with academic institutions or entities specializing in the topic, and consult publications, libraries, archives, even bookstores and literary events to acquire not only information but necessary insights into the generalities and particularities related to the subject matter. In regard to Iran, however, if we followed this method, in effect, the major and probably the most important segments of what is taking place in modern Persian literature would remain completely hidden.

Like many other revolutionary/dictatorial governments, the Islamic Republic has defined a significant portion of its identity through the concept of "permanent revolution". To actualize this, the permanent revolution has been described to a large extent through continuous war with the enemies of the revolution, be they individuals, other governments, opposition entities, or other religions, without necessarily worrying whether these enemies were real or imaginary. And, like all wars executed and administered by revolutionary regimes, this war, too, is considered a "total war" which requires the mobilization of every aspect of the society and the employment of every tool and means at its disposal. Indeed, this is war conducted on every single front. Clearly, the field of culture, in its broadest sense, is one of these fronts. The Islamic Republic is not an exception to this rule by any stretch of imagination; yet the singularities to which this cultural confrontation has led are apexes, similar examples of which are extremely difficult to find, especially in societies with a literary tradition as ancient and monumental as that of Iran.

Describing these strange characteristics to those who have not experienced the extraordinary conditions of literary dynamics in Iran is a daunting task. At times, it even seems that the prerequisite of studying Persian literature is to live in Iran for a time. A colleague of mine used to go further than that and say that whoever wants to work on topics related to modern Persian literature should actually spend some time in the notorious Evin Prison because, she argued, in the past few decades, some of the best Iranian literary figures have been imprisoned there, and much new, avant-garde debate and at times even writing has taken place in the cells of that emblematic prison. Her more serious argument was that such an experience actually provides one with the necessary backdrops against which readings of many recent literary products could be, and perhaps should be constructed.

In any event, as mentioned above, with cultural revolutions following socio-political ones, in general measures taken by revolutionary governments, such as the imposition of unconditional control on academic environments and their production, as well as the establishment of a censorship apparatus, are designed to subjugate and manipulate the processes of literary production and distribution. Again, in ordinary situations, the researchers could rely on relating to circles which function on the margins, that is, outside the sphere of influence of the ruling power, to remedy this situation. This solution, however, is not all that appropriate when it comes to the specific case of Iran and its post-revolutionary governments. The total war initiated by the Islamic Republic is executed with such a degree of brutality and on such an expansive scale that this normal solution is not adequate; in fact, reacting to this total war requires new theoretical approaches.

I believe that over the past 100 years, the combination of censoring/eradicating the Other while promoting the Self has never been implemented with such a degree of ideological intensity. Because of the total war, the possibilities for relating to literary events which are not sanctioned by the regime have become extremely limited. It has been a long time since the censorship apparatus has gone beyond concentrating exclusively on topics; now, even single words and phrases are subject to scrutiny. Even quasi-independent publications are no longer tolerated; even when these publications make every effort not to enter "the forbidden zones," they are still closed down under fictitious pretexts, simply because "they are not with us." Non-governmental—and not necessarily anti-governmental—writers face constant threat. They are summoned to different security and prison offices; their non-commissioned books are covered with ever-accumulating dust in censorship bureaus. In the end, the personal and social cost of functioning independently becomes so unbearable that many simply abandon their work. Continuity, a fundamental requirement for creating meaningful research trends, is completely undermined; independent literary activities are conducted, more or less, like an underground movement. It is not an exaggeration to say that attending an independent literary event and interacting with literary figures known for their dissatisfaction with the government, and being identified with literary trends which do not follow the artistic agenda of the regime is as risky as going to a mixed party where alcohol is served! And still this is not the worst problem.

While working on this study, I have followed the macro-policies of the Islamic Republic in regard to the controlling of the processes of literary and, in general, cultural production and distribution. I am currently working on a short piece emphasizing the goals these policies are trying to achieve. The working title of this paper, I believe, summarizes these goals while referring to the predictable confrontation of competing discourses: "What kind of bastards are these people? They have let loose the dogs and made fast the stones." This is a line from a story in Sa'di's *Golestan* (Rose Garden). Here is the story:

A poet went to the Amir of a group of robbers and recited a panegyric for him. The Amir ordered that he be stripped of his robe and sent out of the village. The poor man was walking naked when he was attacked by dogs. He tried to pick up a stone and defend himself, but the stones were frozen to the ground and he was helpless. He cried out: "What kind of bastards are these people? They have let loose the dogs and made fast the stones."[1]

As mentioned above, I maintain that without directly experiencing literary and non-literary conditions in Iran, it is in effect impossible to acquire the necessary insights to form new, balanced methods essential for such studies. Examples of this situation may help to understand what I refer to as strange, extraordinary conditions.

Today in Iran, the most avant-garde, the newest, and I dare to say the most interesting literary events are taking place in half-covert, sometime completely covert margins and locations of the society.[2] To relate and connect with these circles, personal networks are indispensable as is the physical experience of being present at those sites. This is the only way to acquire the required insights. One might go even further and say that this is also a necessary prerequisite for the researcher to collect the required literary information. This is not easy, particularly for those who reside abroad. Throughout its life, with various levels of intensity during different periods, the Islamic Republic has made this presence conditional on what it calls respecting the red lines which often simply means avoiding certain areas and topics of study. For example, the examination of macro-policies governing censorship in post-revolutionary Iran, which has to begin with a series of speeches by Ruhollah Khomeini in 1358 (1979) with statements such as: "Corrupt pens should not be free," or "[People] should know poisoned pens. They should know those who use the pen against Islam, against clergy, against the nation. They should go and find out about their background … "[3] will clearly prevent the examiner from experiencing the site of research. Writing, again from a critical point of view, about the directives such as "One cannot leave the book market free because harmful books will enter the society"[4] issued by the current supreme leader, Ali Khamenei, and subsequent instructions by ministers of Culture and Islamic Guidance many of whom have honed their skills by having served in the Revolutionary Guards Corps inevitably problematizes the presence of the researcher in the site of research.

One very unfortunate yet predictable outcome of such policies is that many researchers end up accepting, albeit implicitly, the sacred and profane categories defined by the government, and simply avoid working on certain topics. More unfortunate is the fact that many students who are being trained in the field of Persian literature and are, in fact, the future generation of scholars of Persian literature, are also struggling with this predicament. I have been asked variations of this question by many students: "Will writing about this topic prevent me from going to Iran?" or "Isn't it better to remove this paragraph just to make sure that my next trip to Iran will not be intertwined with fear or at least with unpleasant complications?" One logical continuation of this process is that self-censorship becomes internalized. After a while we realize that the penchant for innocuous topics and methodologies gains strength in the scholarship of the field. This is still the less dangerous outcome. The catastrophe emerges when some scholars inadvertently or deliberately end up creating concepts which theorize the ignoring of certain topics and themes and use every conceivable verbal sophistication to justify this penchant. No doubt, the political position of many scholars about global issues and in terms of their definitions of global friends and foes only aggravates this problem. Researching such processes which, among other things, have led to the creation of theoretical concepts which do not refer to anything tangible or real could certainly be the subject of another study.

But let us continue with more examples of aberrant and indeed grotesque difficulties which in an ordinary situation might not even happen to a researcher. The Islamic Republic's claim that they should represent the divine on Earth, in all areas of human activity and that simultaneously they are duty-bound to stop the ungodly has reached ridiculous levels. For example, even books which have been published many times before are being censored when they are reprinted. Who would have thought that, in addition to training our students in using appropriate methods of research, we should also remind them that for example, if they are planning to work on Sadeq Hedayat, they should look for old editions because parts of his texts—and these are the texts which have received permission to be reprinted—are now judged to be un-Islamic and harmful by an employee of the censorship bureau and are thus removed from new editions. In many cases detective work is required to find that some words, or segments, have been eliminated. The following is a short segment from the original version of one the famous poems by Forugh Farrokhzad (1935–1967), "*Tanha Seda-st keh mi-manad*" (Only Voice Remains), which was published in her last collection:

> The end of all forces is union, union
> with the sun's luminous essence
> flowing into the intellect of light.
> It is only natural
> for wooden windmills to fall apart,
> why should I stop?
> I will hold a sheaf of unripe wheat
> Under my breasts
> And nurse it.[5]

About 15 years after the Revolution, the same poem was published in a study of Farrokhzad's poetry by one of the greatest experts in the field, Mohammad Hoquqi, and this poem was published as a good example of the poet's later works. This time, however, it was published with an ellipsis replacing the word "breasts":

> Why should I stop?
> I will hold a sheaf of unripe wheat
> Under ...
> And nurse it.[6]

One of my students who wrote her MA thesis on Farrokhzad was specifically using this poem. I vividly remember that her initial plan was to allocate a significant space to possible interpretations of the ellipsis in this passage!

Another amusing instance was the reprint of Nezami's twelfth-century masterpiece *Khosrow va Shirin* (Khosrow and Shirin), in which the love-making scene of Khosrow and Shirin, which, by the way, is told in such a convoluted manner that it needs a number of close readings for one to realize what the poet is writing about, was completely removed.[7] There are many examples of censorship applied to classical works of which many uncensored editions exist.

Obviously censorship is not performed only on Iranian writers; translations, too, go through the same process. Words, phrases, passages, even whole chapters are cut before a book can receive permission to be published.[8] And this is when the translators have not abandoned the whole idea and withdrawn their request to publish their work. Of course, there are also amusing cases of translators who volunteer to act as censors. By far the most famous example is the case of a relatively recent translation of Dante's *Divine Comedy* by Farideh Mahdavi Damghani. Shortly after its publication, some of the readers familiar with the text or who may well have read the original or its rendering in other languages realized that part of the book had not been translated. The omitted section describes Mohammad, the Prophet of Islam, and Ali, his cousin and the First Imam of the Shi'is. It is a very lurid and unsavory description of the two, who are in the Inferno because of their sins, especially their hypocrisy. Answering the question of why she has not included this part in her translation, the translator simply said that in the first place, she thought these sections were not that important, and in the second place, "No person of faith will ever translate such things"![9] Interestingly, this translator won the gold medal of the Italian city of Ravenna for her translation of Dante! One can only imagine how useful and reliable the literary debates and critiques would be, based on, as they are, false premises created through such truncated or even modified-from-the-original translations. This extends to theoretical works as well.

There is no need to say that the long arm of multi-layered censorship also reaches bookstores and book exhibits as well. In fact, it has become standard operating procedure for agents of the Ministry of Culture and Islamic Guidance to go to different booths during annual book exhibits, and order the selling of certain books or works by certain authors to be stopped. And these are books which have already received permission to be published![10]

While these efforts to remove the Other are being carried out, millions of dollars are spent on the promotion of "good literature," sometimes called "committed literature" or "values literature." The literary arm of the Islamic Republic does not shy away from rewriting the history of Persian literature and along the way defining new genres and sub-genres such as "literature of blasphemy," "literature of the Sacred Defense" (referring to the Iran–Iraq War), or "literature of the Ahl-e Beyt" (referring to works praising the life and works of Mohammad, the Prophet of Islam and his family members). And of course there are governmental literary prizes, most of which are designed with these innovative literary categorizations in mind. In addition, the task of presenting a particular image of Persian literature both inside and outside of Iran is carried out by promoting and fully supporting writings and translations which could help to achieve this goal. The idea behind "What kind of bastards are these people? They have let loose the dogs and made fast the stones" is now clearer.

These are just a few examples cited to make the point that those who do not acquaint themselves with the anomalous obstacles to the study of modern Persian literature and rely solely on traditional approaches and methodologies might buy into these misleading conditions and end up internalizing the official discourse's "permissible" as the only existing category. This is why I strongly believe that one of the major points one should keep in mind while studying modern Persian literature is to read ellipses—both in written texts and, more importantly, in social texts—and to look for these ellipses—silences—everywhere.

These particular conditions also have the potential of forcing the researcher to use approaches which might be considered unconventional by the traditional academic criteria. For example, in the process of rewriting history, many revolutionary/dictatorial regimes try to physically destroy documents which might refute their version of history. The Islamic Republic is a perfect example. Today, it is extremely difficult, if not impossible, to find some of the documents—in different forms of media—related to the first days and months of the Revolution. A serious purge has eliminated many documents which could potentially have repudiated the current official discourse of the Revolution. Even some of the speeches of the officials of the transitional government are hard to find. Many documents have even been removed from Iran's National Library. The result is that we have to rely on oral history and at times personal recollections. This is simply a fact that we need to accept and then try to incorporate it in our approach, and in our voice, in such a way that it would not undermine the integrity of the research. Obviously, such memories and oral histories need to superimpose the document-based narratives and discourses. Yet it should be acknowledged that the presence of an individual/personal voice in such studies is indispensable.

Then of course there are major questions about the impact of such a situation on the whole discipline. How do these conditions influence literary studies and scholarship in this field? How should the dialogues between scholarships produced on different sites be evaluated? How can these elements be incorporated into the training of the next generation of scholars of Persian literature? How far-reaching, temporally and spatially, are the dimensions of these macro-policies? And in a smaller context, how harmful is the unconditional promotion of government-prescribed trends and the corresponding atmosphere in which mediocre works could emerge and grow? Further, how one can measure the extent of the catastrophe wrought on Persian literature by silencing many voices and burying many works which will never play the role they were intended to play in the evolutionary process of Persian literature? Indeed, those who keep repeating the nonsensical cliché that censorship in the long run helps writers and artists hone their skills and come up with more innovations and thus, in the final analysis, might be considered a positive element are either ignorant or extremely biased.[11] In this study, I argue that in the final analysis, counter-discursive and non-discursive forces have certainly succeeded in writing Iran in the context of Persian literature, but I also maintain that this has been achieved despite constant limitations implemented by the prevalent official discourses. Indeed, taking into account the dimensions of the destructive consequences of the Islamic Republic's policies in various domains of literature—creative writing, literary criticism, literary studies, the future of the Persian literary tradition, the training of the next generation of writers and scholars, and so forth—it would not be unreasonable to add crimes against literature to the resume of the government.

To end this section, we should also mention difficulties related to the site where studies such as the present one are written. In other words, problems associated with conducting research about Iran (literary or otherwise) do not stem only from the current situation in Iran. There is another side to this story. These studies are written in an environment where calcified narratives and discourses have largely succeeded in defining the grounds of the debate, and where labels associated with those narratives and discourses are too easily used. For example, even the appearance of any critique of the "sacred narratives" could land one with the neo-con, native informant, sell-out label, or, conversely, pro-Islamic Republic, regime's crony, hanger-on, etc. Unfortunately, such discourses are all too often strong enough to divert the discussion from its logical path. Of course, similar dynamics exist in Iran as well, and any divergence from positions held sacred to the superficial progressives proves problematic. These considerations inevitably create forbidden zones and taboo topics which ordinarily should have no place in a scholarly work; yet it is clear that such reservations taint many otherwise valuable studies.

The conventional difficulties of doing research on contemporary Persian literature

One of the perennial theoretical challenges of such studies is the finding of a proper balance between content-oriented readings/analyses of literary works (with emphasis on socio-political discourses) and those which base themselves on the principle of the literariness of a given work. I discussed this matter in a previous monograph, arguing that during the roughly 100 years of modern literary criticism in Iran, in most periods, intellectuals active in the fields of politics and philosophy have succeeded in absorbing the intellectual energy of the society.[12] I further suggested that, subsequent to this fact, specifically in the field of literary criticism, it is necessary to concentrate on purely literary components—such purity existing only in theory—in the works of contemporary Persian literature. I have tried to follow the same directive in the present study. Yet because of the nature of the topic, especially the subject matter of Chapter 1, prison literature, extended references to historical, social and political backgrounds are also indispensable. These at times long descriptions are necessary because they function as the backdrops and backgrounds against which prison reports and stories are written. Furthermore, since the post-revolutionary government has always defined itself through what it considers to be religious and sacred texts, and has relied heavily on the notion of religious authority (legitimizing this authority again through the sacred texts of Islam/Shi'ism) to justify the behavior of the power apparatus in many spaces of the society, referring to these texts is equally unavoidable. The best instance of such a requirement is found in the last part of Chapter 1, where I present a reading of Ali Erfan's "Les Damnées du paradis" (The Damned Souls of Paradise) as an example of prison literature. I believe it is simply impossible to have a credible reading of this text without realizing its many direct references to some specific passages in the Qur'an. My effort, however, has been to stay as close as possible to the topic of the study which is the process of formation and evolution of literary counter-discourses, and to avoid theological or sociological discussions which clearly belong in a separate study.

I have organized this book with several criteria in mind. To define the direction of the progression of this study, I start with this hypothesis: that among the works in which emphasis on literariness is quite clear, the evolutionary process is defined by a decreasing presence of *direct* counter-discursivity to the point where, in the end, the indifference to dominant discourses is quite palpable. In other words, throughout this book I emphasize a trajectory of progression which begins with reports and descriptions challenging the narratives promoted or implied by the official discourse. This trajectory continues its path through works which attempt to add new dimensions to this challenge and establish defining elements of counter-discourses. The final stage of this progression is found in spaces and situations which are in fact individual/non-discursive definitions of different aspects of reality. In a sense, the organizing concept of this book is the distance of authors/narrators and narratives from definitions offered by official and prevalent discourses. Within this general approach, I have developed subcategories based on themes and literary devices and techniques which are created and employed by authors/narrators to materialize the creation of these new literary realities.

The increasing distance from the direct challenging of prevalent discourses is one of the major characteristics of Persian modernist writing—a topic which has been under-explored. This under-exploration is directly related to the lack of necessary foundations. Studies by scholars such as Ahmad Karimi-Hakkak, M. R. Ghanoonparvar, Farzaneh Milani, Michael Hillmann, Richard Davis, Michael Beard, Kamran Talattof, Nasrin Rahimieh, and Kamran Rastegar have made significant contributions to the field. Yet the discussion about literary modernism and its Persian version (or, for those who espouse the notion of a universal definition for literary modernism, the reflection of this universalist definition in the context of Persian literature) has continued to remain marginalized. Given the clear association of Persian modernist writing with the concepts of counter- and non-discursivity, I allocate a significant part of Chapter 3 to this topic. In particular, this approach has influenced my selection of certain texts which I have examined closely throughout the book.

This study is also informed by the *explication de texte* method which, as I have argued in my other works, is indispensable for refuting the imposed political readings which in many literary traditions of the South have turned literature into an extension of politics. This method not only demonstrates the flagrant aspect of the imposition of non-literary discourses especially on contemporary Persian fiction, it also contributes to a remedy for the problem. Furthermore, using this method provides a process of literary appreciation for a number of works which for various reasons have been neglected by traditional approaches; therefore such detailed explications could provide the bases for future studies. I should also add that language-based and stylistic approaches, specifically when they find kinship with the Russian Formalists' idea of "dominant technique," have influenced the manner in which I have constructed close readings of certain texts.[13]

Synopsis of the chapters

From prison reports to prison literature

Chapter 1 begins with a survey of prison reports, most of which are produced by the political prisoners themselves. This survey is by no means exhaustive. In fact, this is also true of topics mentioned in other chapters, such as contemporary Persian war literature. Of course, this is especially true in the case of prison reports and prison literature because, thanks to the Islamic Republic, this category has been one of the most prolific categories of documentary and literary production since the 1979 Revolution. As mentioned before, to refer to these categories is to provide signposts and contexts which unearth elements that constitute literary counter- and non-discursive productions, as well as their evolutionary trajectory.

To contextualize the main ideas of the chapter, the first part of the chapter provides a descriptive examination of the Islamic Republic's judiciary/penal system, which is characterized by its simultaneous kinship with pre-modern and modern systems of judgment and punishment; or, to use the Foucauldian term, the system of "*Surveiller et punir.*" In such a setting, contradictions are easily justified, and more importantly, this combination provides the official discourse with necessary narratives to define various social spaces, in this case prisons, in a positive manner. Prison reports must be examined, first of all, as representations of direct opposition to these narratives and their justifications. In other words, there is a discursive struggle to define prison spaces. This struggle is defined through the confrontation between narratives which rely on the falsification of history past and present, and are particular interpretations of religious sources to depict the Islamic Republic's prisons as "universities," and narratives which, by bringing to the fore facts of torture, summary trials and executions, directly challenge the official discourse's definitions.

While it is always difficult to impose fixed categories on individual works, it is not difficult to theoretically define a transition from prison reports to prison literature by emphasizing the component of literary imagination. Following the interactions between these two closely related areas, I try to identify components of prison literature—which has a rather long history in the Persian literary tradition—that function in the larger context of literary counter-discourses.

Literary rewrites of history

Chapter 2 begins with the assumption that "History is written by the victors." The themes of the falsification of history and the appropriation of myths, whether it is about the Iran–Iraq War, or the Battle of Karbala, or the *Shahnameh* story of Siyavash; and competing historiographies are functioning in the background throughout this chapter. The non-literary theoretical framework of Chapter 2 is informed by scholars of the New Historicism and alternative historiography such as Stephen Greenblatt, Catherine Gallagher and Hayden White. Within this framework, specific works are examined, but with less emphasis on particular spaces (such as prison). In other words, while opposing narratives are still competing to define existing spaces, many works of contemporary Persian fiction have gone beyond immediate spaces and have acquired historical and mythical dimensions. These works are not just rejecting the official discourse's re-definition of myths and histories; they are ridiculing icons used in opposing narratives. Once again, this confrontation has a long history in Persian literary tradition; therefore literary devices have reached a level of maturity which enables the work to accomplish this task with ease.

The general topic of the falsification of history has been discussed from a number of theoretical outlooks such as Orientalism, post-colonialism, and the critique of modern capitalism, to name a few. While I have drawn on a number of studies associated with these fields, I have also used them to develop and expand certain concepts originally introduced by Russian Formalists to approach some of the major works of contemporary Persian fiction. This eclectic methodology helps to anchor the analyses and readings in the field of literature, while never losing their contact with the topic of rewriting/remaking history and myths. Given the unprecedented number of works of contemporary Persian fiction which could easily be placed in this category, devising multi-purpose analytical tools is a necessity. Indeed, I believe that many works by authors such as Reza Baraheni, Simin Daneshvar, Hushang Golshiri, Mahmud Dowlatabadi, Shahrnush Parsipur, Amir Hassan Cheheltan, Reza Julai, and Bijan Najdi, for example, would remain mostly incomprehensible if analytical devices which can fluently travel within and through different disciplines are not used.

Individualistic literary spaces: non-discursive situations

"Any *petit récit* would puncture the historical *grand récit* into which it was inserted."[14] This process is seen in many modernist Persian works of fiction. The path of the increasing presence of individual/personal components in modernist narratives is parallel to the overall direction of the book: namely, the increasing dissociation of narratives from a direct confrontation with prevalent discourses, and indeed from discursivity. In other words, individual literary historiography is not aiming at refuting historical grand narratives; this is just a by-product of the evolutionary process of contemporary Persian fiction. The convergence of non-discursivity and emphasis on a Persian version of literariness is found in a large number of modernist writings in Iran; therefore a short discussion about Persian modernist writing occupies part of Chapter 3. In the same context, I also argue that elements of Persian literary modernism were not spontaneous generations. To understand, for example, why the Persian modernist *I* is different from its French or Russian counterpart, one needs to pay attention to a history of Persian literature to appreciate the evolution of devices, tropes, topoi, forms, etc. in the context of the Persian literary tradition. This is another area of scholarship which has not received enough attention because of traditional approaches to writing histories of literature. This means that the subordination of literary discourses to sociopolitical ones has led to a kind of literary historiography which, instead of explaining the history of development of devices and forms, and of literary trends and dynamics, has used literary events and developments to support its historical or political claims.

The three categories of modernist writings, history of literature, and personal historiography are crystallized in narratives which could be called non-discursive. Of course these non-discursive stories are not created in a vacuum; the genealogy of their production process is clearly marked by discursive confrontations. Subsequently, these stories, probably unintentionally, have a particular positionality vis-à-vis prevalent discourses, and thus are viewed as narratives of subversion and subterfuge.

Those who have experienced Iran's political prisons, both before and after the Revolution, know that interrogators/torturers always show particular sensitivity towards some of the books they find in the prisoner's house.[15] This sentiment could be understood when one deals with books which clearly debate and directly express political positions opposing those of the ruling discourse. But, in the case of texts such as, for example, *Buf-e Kur* (The Blind Owl), the logic of the interrogator's pathologically harsh reaction is at first not easy to understand, especially when this reaction comes from someone who does not even have the mental capability to impose a political reading on this text. The present study could be seen as an effort to find answers to such questions by situating them in a much larger context and then by referring to the formation processes of countering discourses and their subsequent mercurial penetration in most (literary) aspects of this context. It is my hope that this study will underline methodologies which, while informed by the dynamics of realities outside the text, approach modern Persian fiction, especially the modernist works, from a literary point of view.

Notes

1 Sa'di, *Golestan*, Chapter 4, Story 10. Throughout the book, all translations are mine unless otherwise indicated.
2 An excellent example of this situation in relation to music has been partially documented in Bahman Qobadi's film, *Kasi az Gorbehha-ye Irani Khabar Nadarad* (No One Knows About Persian Cats).
3 Ruhollah Khomeini, *Adabiyat-e Dastani*, no. 70, 2003, p. 30.
4 www.bbc.co.uk/persian/iran/2011/07/110720_l06_khamenei_book_limits.shtml (accessed May 5, 2014). During his reign as the Supreme Leader, Ali Khamenei has issued many such statements and edicts. I will refer to some of them throughout the book.
5 *Bargozideh-ye Ash'ar-e Forugh Farrokhzad* (A Selection from Forugh Farrokhzad Poems), 6th edition, Tehran: Morvarid, 1357/1978. The translation of this poem is taken from: *Remembering the Flight: Twenty Poems by Forugh Farrokhzad*, translated by Ahmad Karimi-Hakkak, (Port Coquitlam, BC, Nik Publishers, 1997), pp. 89–91.
6 This censored version of the poem was published in Mohammad Hoquqi's *She'r-e Zamān-e mā (4): Forugh Farrokhzad* (The Poetry of Our Time (4): Forugh Farrokhzad), Tehran: Negah, 1372/1993.
7 More recently, Nezami's *Khosrow and Shirin* once again became the subject of a more extensive censorship. This time it was argued that they were removing certain words and phrases from the text to make it more "refined for younger readers." Faraj Sarkuhi published a report on this matter on the BBC: www.bbc.co.uk/persian/arts/2011/08/110818_l41_book_classical_censorship_comment.shtml (accessed May 5, 2014).
8 One famous example is the translation of Milan Kundera's *The Joke* which was translated into Persian by Forugh Puryavari. In the introduction to the Persian edition, the translator specifically says that she had to remove a whole chapter from Part Five of the book so that it could receive permission to be published. This was when the censorship was much less brutal. To read more about this example, as well as the censored chapter, see www.khabgard.com/?id=438641374 (accessed May 5, 2014).
9 "Goft-o-gu ba Farideh Mahdavi Damghani" (A conversation with Farideh Mahdavi Damghani), Puriya Golmohammadi, http://isil.blogfa.com/post-3.aspx (accessed May 5, 2014).

10 In "Mojavvez-e Hezaran Ketab Batel Shod: Gozareshi az Siyahtarin Doran-e Ketab" (Permissions for Thousands of Books Annulled: A Report of the Darkest Time for Books), November 23, 2006, www.roozonline.com/persian/news/news item/archive/2006/november/23/article/-ccdbb5b06d.html (accessed May 5, 2014), Shahram Rafi'zadeh provides a number of examples of another method used by the government of President Mahmud Ahmadinejad. That is, since Ahmadinejad's government believed that previous governments had been too careless in allowing harmful, un-Islamic books to be published, a review process was established which led to the revocation of permission for a number of already-published books. Obviously these books had to be removed from bookstore shelves.

11 Even someone like Mohammad Ali Sepanlu, a contemporary poet, mentioned this idea in an interview: "Fortunately, the Islamic Revolution did not practice censorship in a way that would destroy Persian literature. Although there are people who oppose censorship, this censorship does not at all mean the uprooting of literature. In some cases we even see much progress being made." See: www.farsnews.com/newstext.php?nn=8411080498 (accessed May 5, 2014).

   Of course, early in 2011, Sepanlu, who had been waiting to receive permission to publish a few books, issued a statement expressing his dismay, saying that he knows the law and he has always respected the censorship laws "even if [he is] critical of them." He then added: "These days I am ill, and it no longer makes any difference to me whether or not my work gets published." See: www.khabar online.ir/detail/137600/culture/book (accessed May 5, 2014).

12 Khorrami, M. M. *Modern Reflections of Classical Traditions in Persian Fiction*, Lewiston, NY: Edwin Mellen, 2003, pp. 32–33.

13 I believe Kamran Rastegar's usage of Edward Sa'id's notion of "return to philology" and its development by Rastegar into "critical philology" invokes contextualization within which a text could be read. See Rastegar's *Literary Modernity Between the Middle East and Europe*, London: Routledge, 2007.

14 Joel Fineman, quoted from Catherine Gallagher and Stephen Greenblatt, *Practicing New Historicism*, Chicago, IL: University of Chicago Press, 2000, p. 49.

15 It has been a common practice before and after the Revolution to search the houses of political prisoners to find incriminating items, namely harmful books.

1 From prison reports to prison literature

Background

On the evening of the 22nd of Bahman, 1357/February 11, 1979, the taking of the National Iranian Television station was carried out by revolutionary forces who, at this point, did not meet with significant resistance from the pro-Shah forces. This was one of the most symbolically significant events and turning points which signaled the definitive victory of the Revolution. The first statements to be broadcast on the newly revolutionary television, as well as those read over the radio, were general congratulatory messages addressed to the Nation of Iran. More importantly, however, the broadcasters also took care to thank *all* political organizations, groups, and forces, which had participated in the Revolution. The acknowledgment of the fact that there were a number of political and ideological factions—whose differences were undoubtedly greater than their commonalities—which had contributed to the advancement of the Revolution and the destruction of the previous power structure did not seem to require any discussion. And in fact, until several months after the definitive victory of the Revolution, this was also part of the discourse and narratives of the new power structure. The general approach, devised and pushed forward by the now de facto leader of the Revolution—Ruhollah Khomeini and his cobbled-together organization—was to acknowledge the efforts of all who had taken part in the Revolution, regardless of their political and ideological positions, and to encourage them to accept the newly-established order for the sake of unity. However, it did not take long for the second part of this approach to metamorphose into attempts by the new power structure to wage war against all forms of the Other. Like many revolutionary governments, the Islamic regime employed all non-violent and violent means at its disposal to eradicate not only the discourses of the Other but the very possibility of the emergence of such discourses.[1]

The overt aspects of this strategic move can be divided in two major categories: the appropriation of cultural, ideological, and intellectual narratives, and the violent repression and silencing of those representing the discourses and narratives of the Other.

Non-violent cultural, ideological, and intellectual confrontations

The conscious efforts by Islamic forces and movements to eradicate the discourses and narratives of the Other were not apparent during and immediately after the 1979 Revolution—probably because of the non-violent appearance of their methods in the beginning. It took a while before the affinity was recognized between the intellectual–cultural operation and the functions of prison, torture, death squads, and other methods of physical elimination of individuals. It was not difficult for the opposition movement to comprehend the violent crusade which had begun against them, but until it was too late, they never grasped the significance of the "non-violent" campaign whose object was the total removal of their place (their voices and narratives)—not only from the history of the Revolution but from History—and they did not have many tools left with which to fight back. This is especially true with regard to movements with theoretical–ideological affiliations to the Left. A review of the activities of these organizations clearly reveals that their platforms and agendas had no goals or even preoccupations concerning subjects such as the definition of the Revolution—their recent history—or the definition of new, post-revolutionary spaces *from their own perspective*.

Those who experienced the days and months after the Revolution surely remember the innumerable, seemingly endless disputes in public places, particularly in the center of the capital, in front of Tehran University. Generally, these discussions took place between the political-intellectual movements which were beginning to oppose the creeping expansion of the new power structure and individuals who appeared to be not very educated or informed about socio-political matters.[2] In most cases, the principal argument repeated by these individuals was based on an exaggeration of the role of the political nouveau-arrivé, together with the denial of the role played by other factions. Such arguments were often received with supercilious sneers by intellectuals who considered profound ignorance to be the main reason for such utterances. It took a while before it became clear that these "ignorant people" and their "ignorance" were elements in a rather clever scheme contrived by the Islamic government to erase chapters of history together with their actors; at the same time, this new regime, like "all usurpers" tried "to make us forget that [it has] only just arrived."[3]

The real dimensions of the process of eradicating, silencing, and burying segments and voices of history, and then attempting to define all objective and subjective spaces according to the dominant discourse can be understood only when we define its position in a larger context which includes other social projects of the Islamic Republic's power structure. In future chapters I will discuss some reflections of this strategy, especially as it relates to cultural domains.

Spectacle, violence, compulsion

In 1967, in his now-classic text, *La Société du spectacle* (The Society of the Spectacle), Guy Debord placed the concept of "spectacle" at the center of his theory of the critique of modern societies.[4] He used this concept in a variety of situations and in a rather scattered manner; therefore it is not easy to offer a concise definition of it. In their analysis of Situationist theoreticians, and Debord in particular, Steven Best and Douglas Kellner have proposed the following definition:

"Spectacle" is a complex term which "unifies and explains a great diversity of apparent phenomena." In one sense, it refers to a media and consumer society, organized around the consumption of images, commodities, and spectacles, but it also refers to the vast institutional and technical apparatus of contemporary capitalism, to all the means and methods power employs, outside of direct force, to relegate subjects passive to societal manipulation and to obscure the nature and effects of capitalism's power and deprivations.[5]

With regard to social control, the aim of power structures in such societies is to impose the dominant discourse through "consensus rather than force." Of course not all dominant discourses succeed in this process to the same degree. Discussing this issue, Debord makes reference to the two main forms of spectacular power and calls them *concentrated* and *diffuse*.[6] Examples of the concentrated form are Fascism and Stalinism and totalitarian governments in general. The presence of these examples alongside those of diffuse form—for example, the United States—which try to achieve control through "consensus" emphasizes once more this fundamental point: whenever the power structure finds itself unable to impose its discourse nonviolently, it opts for the violent approach. The record of the Islamic Republic from the beginning of its coming to power in Iran provides a clear example of this. But before discussing the characteristics of this example, since the concept of discourse has been used in different senses and with a variety of implications, it is necessary to clarify this concept as used in this study.

I use the term "discourse" in its Foucauldian sense, specifically in regard to the relationship which exists between the establishing of the authority of the power structure and the presence of a discourse which defines the objective and subjective spaces of a society while producing secondary discourses—field-specific discourses—as well as its particular narratives. This approach is informed by mainly earlier works of Foucault such as *Folie et déraison* (Madness and Insanity, 1961), and *Naissance de la clinique* (The Birth of the Clinic, 1963), as well as *Surveiller et punir* (Discipline and Punish, 1975) where he examines the function of dominant discourse(s) with regard to potential threats to the authority of the dominant power structure.[7]

The juxtaposition of the Foucauldian idea of Discourse and Debord's concept of Spectacle creates a theoretical framework through which the secondary discourses and narratives of the dominant power structure in different fields—history, art (literature in particular), etc.—are examined not as accidental utterances but as facets of an operation to impose the dominant discourse. In future chapters I will discuss some historiographical and literary reflections of this project. Here I will mention a few examples which demonstrate the presence of this strategy.

One of the best instances which heralded the arrival of this strategy can be derived from a famous slogan that emerged in the final weeks of the Revolution during the last stages of the collapse of the Shah's regime and gained publicity in the street demonstrations. During this period the victory of the Revolution was considered a fait accompli. The Shah was going to leave the country; the increasing presence of people in the streets, the joining of the Army with the demonstrators, the general strikes, all pointed to the imminent triumph of the Revolution. It was during this period that, for the first time, the slogan *"Hezb faqat Hezbollah, Rahbar faqat Ruhollah"* (The only Party is the Party of God; the only Leader is Ruhollah) was promoted systematically and became the rallying cry at many demonstrations.

Obviously there were a number of competing narratives about the place and significance of various social forces during the Revolution and naturally the official discourse has always tried to belittle the role of other forces which did not succeed in sharing the post-revolutionary political power. Yet a passing review of the newspapers of the time demonstrates that even during these last stages of the Revolution, Khomeini and the Hezbollah (The Party of God), were not considered the main dynamics of the Revolution. And it was only towards the end—especially after Khomeini's move from Najaf (in Iraq) to France[8] and the formation of an ad hoc revolutionary headquarters around him—that a planned approach which aimed at the establishment of an Islamic government—and discourse—emerged on the scene of the Revolution. In *Dar Mehmani-ye Haji Aqa* (At Haji Aqa's Gathering), Farhad Behbahani, one of the co-authors writing their prison memoirs, refers to a conversation which documents this latter point:

> Ayatollah Golpaygani said: ... Ayatollah Haj Seyyed Reza Zanjani told me an interesting story. At a meeting he told me that when in the middle of 1357 (1978) it became clear that the Pahlavi regime had reached the nadir of its weakness and was reaching out to those whom it had suppressed until the previous day, I sent a message to Ayatollah Khomeini, saying, Now the time that we have been waiting for has arrived and the Shah is ready to listen to us and appoint people that we deem righteous to offices. Now we can do something so that the management of affairs falls into the hands of righteous and qualified people, and it would be proper if you were to introduce candidates whom you consider qualified for high positions in the country. Ayatollah Zanjani said that Ayatollah Khomeini did not answer my message for a long time; and when I inquired further, a message arrived from him saying: "I want an Islamic government formed in Iran."[9]

Let us return to the slogan "The only Party is the Party of God; the only Leader is Ruhollah." In this slogan, the key word is "only." It symbolizes an approach which attempts to efface the Other and any kind of discourse which might refer to it. It was during this period that the 1979 Revolution was gradually baptized "the Islamic Revolution" by the clerical leaders of the newly-established Islamic government. Shortly thereafter, hyperbolic, fabulous accounts of years of struggles by Khomeini and his entourage with the Shah's regime were fashioned. But the imposition of this "only" could not be realized in a vacuum by relying on fabrications of stories in regard to the current history; this process needed a context with historical and ideological dimensions.

Ideologically, this process began in the early days after the Revolution and the non-violent imposition of the Islamic discourse based on Islamic texts and extended propaganda with regard to the "righteousness of Islam." If slogans such as "The only Party is the Party of God; the only Leader is Ruhollah" and "theoretical debates" such as "Economy belongs to donkeys" (sic),[10] and historiographies-confabulations on the order of "Before Islam, Iranians were illiterate, uncultured, and generally uncivilized people who actually preferred to remain illiterate"[11] had any chance of being taken seriously, it was through their placement within an ideological, Islamic context. Of course, at the same time, such statements explain why it soon became obvious that in the discursive confrontation, the Islamic discourse of those newly arrived in power was not able to provide reliable arguments to convince opponents and to attract the undecided.

It was during that same time (the month of September 1980) that the Iran–Iraq War (1980–1988) began. This provided a suitable atmosphere for the power structure to propagate and enforce its discourse. The leaders of the Islamic government tried to carry out the conduct of the war against Iraq and the defense of the motherland within the Islamic discourse and thus weave together religious and patriotic symbols. In other words, the nationalistic sentiments which had been heightened because of war were effectively used by the ruling power to bolster the Islamic discourse. Khomeini in particular, in many of his speeches, attempted to merge patriotism and the Islamic discourse of the ruling power in order to create a kind of unity and between them and to identify them with each other.

> You have performed your duty to our dear Islam and to our noble homeland. You have cut off the greedy hand of the superpowers and their mercenaries from your country. You have courageously rebelled in the path of the nobility and honor of Islam. O how I wish I were with you, and I would have been graced with great blessing! Benedictions be upon the noble generals and warriors, and upon all those who fight for the glory of the country and of Islam![12]

Despite all this, the dominant discourse and its texts remained completely unsuccessful in the non-violent imposing or "convincing" process. The most obvious indication of this failure was the fact that the Islamic government decisively set foot on the path which had been paved by "concentrated spectacular forms of control" such as Fascism and Stalinism. Signs of such a shift, starting in 1980, are abundant. For example, realizing that universities in Iran had always been fertile ground for the emergence of alternative discourses, the Islamic government initiated a "Cultural Revolution" in 1980 which aimed to expand the presence of its discourse to universities. But the government officials in charge of this Cultural Revolution soon realized that this "convincing" would materialize only if it was accompanied by the expulsion and arrest of students and professors affiliated with alternative discourses. And indeed, this was the main outcome of the Cultural Revolution in Iranian universities.

Violent repression against any form of discourse or narrative of the Other was not to stop after the Other's defeat. The ultimate goal of this war was the complete eradication of rival discourses and narratives from every single subjective and objective space of current and historical time. Obviously, this war included not only their intellectual and ideological destruction but their physical eradication. From the very first days when this decision was adopted, some of those involved in this project who had understood its historical dimensions while unaware of the deep roots of many of these discourses and narratives especially in Iran's literary history, naively assumed that they could eliminate these signs swiftly by simply having their bureau of censorship issue an order. This led to rather ridiculous situations. According to a guideline which was never publicly announced, Ferdowsi's *Shahnameh* (The Book of Kings, *ca.* 980–1010), the most famous Persian epic, was considered a fallacious text because it evoked the memory of kings. In a few days it was removed from bookstores. Other fanatics decided to apply the same approach to other literary giants such as Hafez (*ca.* 1325–1390). For a few weeks, black markets for Ferdowsi's *Shahnameh* and Hafez's *Divan* (Collected Poems) flourished before overseers of the Islamic government realized that the roots of such signs of the discourses of the Other were so deep that they could not be removed by such methods. Indeed, the fact that copies of these texts are found in the homes of the majority of Iranians, together with the fact that many Iranians prefer to consult Hafez's *Divan* than the Qur'an for advice and counsel, encouragement and comfort is the most revealing indicator of the deep-rooted presence of these signs.

Of course, such policies represent only a small component of the project of the expunging of the Other's discourse. To repeat: the most important part of this project was the physical eradication of the human representatives of these discourses and narratives.

It is difficult to establish a specific date for the beginning of this course of action, particularly for those who were not privy to the discussions which took place during meetings of the leaders of the Islamic government about the ultimate future of the opposition. But the first clear and public reflections of this decision can be seen in 1981. It was exactly at this time that the Islamic Republic began not just receiving assistance from but completely relying on its armed forces, secret police, pressure groups, torture, prison and execution (mainly through the judiciary system) to advance its discursive war.

To understand the literary consequences of this approach an introduction is necessary. One of the significant aspects of any discursive war is to offer narratives capable of defining objective and subjective spaces. Primarily in their theoretical–ideological manifestations, discourses of dictatorships consume an enormous amount of energy for this purpose. In fact, allocating a huge amount of energy to impose guidelines such as covering one's hair, concealing the body's curves, not shaving one's beard, not wearing ties or short-sleeved shirts, as well as guidelines which sought to control even the most private spaces of one's life could be justified only through this discursive tendency.[13] But this energy is not infinite; therefore the founders of the dominant discourse are constantly trying to prevent the creation of any new space which is not native to their discourse. And that is precisely why any fresh experience which initiates new spaces is regarded negatively and with suspicion. The most recent example of this is the nervousness and even anger of the Islamic government at the Internet phenomenon, which has created a number of new spaces that need to be controlled and thus requires an allocation of energy.[14] The best example, however, is the seizing of the American Embassy in Tehran on November 4, 1979. Many have forgotten, if they knew it to begin with, that the original attack on the American Embassy was not the Islamic government's idea. As Suroosh Irfani has stated in *Iran's Islamic Revolution: Popular Liberation or Religious Dictatorship?*

> ... it was the *Fedayeen-e-Khalq* [sic] guerrillas who first occupied the American embassy in Tehran on 14 February 1979, only three days after the Pahlavi regime was overthrown. At that time the *Fedayeen*'s action was condemned by the clergy and the Revolutionary Council.[15]

This act by the *Fedaian*[16] had created a new space which had not been defined by the dominant discourse and was actually in the process of being defined by the Other. The *Fedayeen* were subsequently forced by the government to leave the US embassy. Nine months later, however, the clergy affiliated with the Islamic government plotted the seizure of the embassy by pro-regime university students.

There have been a number of explanations concerning the reasons for this action, including the argument that the leaders of the new government had no idea what kind of information could be found at the embassy and therefore wanted control over material possibly damaging to the members of the new government. Exploring these arguments is not within the scope of this study; suffice to say that the version of the concept of discourse used herein is broad enough to encompass such explanations. Therefore, such arguments do not undermine the main point, that mono-discursive governments are reluctant to expand the number of spaces which require definition and, consequently, room for discursive combat. And it is for this reason that I argue (from the point of view of the Islamic government and in the context of this discursive battle) the Islamic Republic's opting for the strategy of eradication of human signs and elements of the discourses of the Other was a grave mistake. This physical war and the subsequent use of prison, torture, and execution practically initiated and even rekindled the formation of a particular sign system—reflected in many narratives about such violent methods of discourse cleansing—whose mere presence signaled the emergence of narratives which, undoubtedly, would be identified with, and were indeed part of, discourses of the Other.

To understand the constituents of this space, we should begin once more from the first days of the Islamic government and its punitive-judiciary system. These days were filled with the continuous arrest and execution of the officials of the Shah's regime and of individuals accused of affiliation with that regime. The front pages of all the newspapers dating from this period were covered with pictures showing these individuals during their arrests and/or after their executions. A major portion of the programs on radio and television was allocated to the direct broadcasting of the trials of these individuals—trials which lasted a few days at most—in the "Revolutionary Tribunals." And of course, every day, as part of the daily news, the list of those who had been arrested and executed was read on radio and television.

It is difficult to find a comprehensive and logical explanation of the thoughts and goals behind this approach. The fact is that in the majority of revolutions such periods of violence have existed. One can think of many reasons for that. Perhaps the disarray and turmoil characteristic of leadership in these short, post-revolutionary periods could be considered the most significant reason. Usually, however, one cannot rely on these periods to examine the punitive-judiciary system of a given society. Indeed, even a cursory exploration of the few existing sources dealing with the punitive-judiciary system in Iran of this period demonstrates how the fate of many individuals was decided based on accidents, the ideological tendencies and the thoughtlessness of some of officials, or on ways of seeking revenge.[17] This might reinforce the idea that such an un-systemic basis for a judiciary could not but be temporary. Nonetheless, the reality is that in the case of the Islamic government of Iran, this period was never brought completely to an end. For example, the "Revolutionary Tribunals" which were supposed to be a temporary institution to deal with vestiges of the previous regime have continued to exist to this day. Therefore it is quite justifiable to consider this period as the beginning of the punitive-judiciary system of the Islamic government.

The Islamic punitive-judiciary system in Iran: a union of pre-modern and modern control systems

Michel Foucault begins *Discipline and Punish* with an account of several reports on the torture and execution of Robert-François Damiens (1757), a French officer who had attempted to assassinate Louis XV.[18] This account exemplifies one of the most barbarous punishment ceremonies ever recorded in history. The ceremonial took place in front of a large audience at the infamous execution ground, the Place de Grève, in Paris. The religious-judicial system had made extended efforts to prolong this show. At the beginning of the spectacle the hand which had attempted to take the life of the king was burnt. Then the main event began:

> "Then the executioner, his sleeves rolled up, took the steel pincers, which had been especially made for the occasion, and which were about a foot and a half long, and pulled first at the calf of the right leg, then at the thigh, and from there at the two fleshy parts of the right arm; then at the breasts. Though a strong, sturdy fellow, this executioner found it so difficult to tear away the pieces of flesh that he set about the same spot two or three times, twisting the pincers as he did, and what he took away formed at each part a wound about the size of a six-pound crown piece."[19]

Damiens' painful cries overwhelmed the Place de Grève; at the same time the executioner "'[dips] an iron [ladle] in the pot containing the boiling potion, which he [pours] liberally over each wound.'"[20] The show moves slowly on, with complete deliberation. After a while they tie Damiens' hands and legs to four horses. Four executioners try to pull the horses in opposite directions so that they can tear off the four limbs. After about fifteen minutes only two shoulder bones are broken. Efforts are doubled, still to no avail. Two more horses are brought and are added to the two already harnessed to the legs of the condemned man. Again no success. At first, the sponsors of the spectacle ignore the suggestion of the executioners who want to end Damiens' excruciating pain by killing him, but in the end the executioners are forced to help the horses so that this atrocious ritual will come to an end.

> "After two or three attempts, the executioner Samson and he who had used the pincers each drew out a knife from his pocket and cut the body at the thighs instead of severing the legs at the joints; the four horses gave a tug and carried off the two thighs after them ..."[21]

and then:

> "The same was done to the arms, the shoulders, the arm-pits and the four limbs; the flesh had to be cut almost to the bone, the horses pulling hard carried off the right arm first and the other afterwards."[22]

All this is taking place while the confessors and the parish priest of St Paul's who are also taking part in this theatrical production, keep going over to the condemned man and trying to comfort him. At the end, in accordance with the decree, Damiens' remains are given over to the fire.

This is only a short excerpt from the reports Foucault cites in his book. Foucault's purpose in alluding to these details is not to describe the indescribable savagery of this judicial system but to point out the relationship between the theatrical and spectacular characteristics of these ceremonies and the sovereign power.

After this section, Foucault discusses the emergence of "reformist" ideas in judicial systems and the transition from sovereign power to new frameworks of power in modern societies. Then, after examining some changes in the judiciary systems of societies such as France, the United States, and England, he concludes that in such societies "Punishment has gradually ceased to be a spectacle."[23] At this stage, forms of torture have changed, and, more significantly, if physical torture is taking place, it is carried out furtively. Foucault considers this kind of judiciary system representative of a disciplinary power which is applied in modern societies;

> ... it does so not for power itself, nor for the immediate salvation of a threatened society: its aim is to strengthen the social forces—to increase production, to develop the economy, spread education, raise the level of public morality; to increase and multiply.[24]

The case of the Islamic Republic, however, represents a merging of the two systems. Therefore, it would be problematic to examine the punitive-judiciary system of this regime through Foucault's theory alone. In *Torture and Modernity: Self, Society, and State in Modern Iran*, Darius Rejali argues that the experience of the Islamic Republic is one of the examples which stands in contradiction to Foucault's discussion, because this government represents a modern society where torture still exists.[25] In "Reflections on Cruelty and Torture," Talal Asad refutes this criticism and, after noting some of the shortcomings of Rejali's work, argues that Iran is not a modern society and should be called at best "a modernizing society."[26] This could be considered a valid point with regard to one aspect of Rejali's criticism of Foucault. The other point made by Asad, which is directly related to the subject of the present study, is that in many modern societies torture does exist, but it is surreptitious. Asad explains: "When torture carried out in secret is essentially connected with the extraction of information, it becomes an aspect of policing."[27] Talal Asad does not elaborate on the concept of "modernizing society" with regard to the forms of torture one can expect to see in such societies; indeed, the insinuation is that even if Iran is considered a modern society, "surreptitious torture" should be perceived as being completely different from the overt, medieval, ritualized torture. I do not want to concentrate on the discussion of whether Iran is modern or modernizing, and whether or not a "modernizing society" could be defined in such a way that it would include blatant torture. I only want to make it clear that in Iran, under the Islamic government, blatant torture and ritualized spectacles are part of the punitive-judiciary system. It is true that since the beginning of the Islamic Republic there has not been an exact replica of, for example, Damiens' execution in Iran, but the precisely-ritualized, theatrical ceremonies of stoning many condemned men and women to death are quite comparable to the savagery of Damiens' drawing and quartering. The following description is based on one of the clandestinely-videotaped stoning ceremonies.[28]

After reading the sentence aloud, those who have been sentenced to flogging for crimes in addition to those for which they are to be stoned to death—for example adultery—are taken to a spacious area. First, the condemned man is placed in front of a large wooden board set in the ground like a wall. The board almost reaches to his shoulders. His hands are bound to the two sides of the board; then the flogging begins. Once this prologue is completed, the main spectacle starts. The bloody body of the condemned man is placed inside a bag made of white cloth and the two ends of the bag are fastened securely with ropes. Then he is set in a hole in the ground and dirt is poured into the hole to render any movement virtually impossible. Condemned men are lowered down to their waists; women must be lowered further down so the dirt reaches above their breasts. According to the interpretation of the Islamic Republic of Shari'a law, if the condemned succeed in pulling themselves out of the hole and escaping during the stoning, they are to be saved, and the punishment may not be repeated. During the rule of the Islamic government, no one has ever been able to escape death, but the urge to live and the hope of being saved turn a stoning into a deadly, vicious, and "exciting" drama. In almost all cases, the hapless condemned man, seeing his death approaching, under a hail of stones succeeds in tearing open the cloth bag with a superhuman effort and pokes his head out. This only makes him a better target. It does not take long before his eyes are punctured, his teeth are cracked, and his face is torn as he is desperately trying to escape. The more he tries, the more the speed and force of the stone-throwing increases, as does the rhythm of the shouting of "Allah-o Akbar" (God is great). And at the end, the condemned man, only slightly out of the dirt hole, with a face and body which no longer look as if they belong to a human being, lies motionless in a pool of blood.

This is a spectacle, a theatre; next to these plays, of course, there are other shows such as public floggings; hanging from huge cranes in the great squares of big cities which can accommodate a large audience; cutting off of hands and arms;[29] ... These shows and rituals are not akin to surreptitious torture as an aspect of police work of modern control systems employed for the purpose of extracting information. These shows ought to be placed in precisely the same category as the torture and execution of Robert-François Damiens. Undoubtedly, this aspect of the penal code, similar to that of Damiens' time, aims to represent a sovereign power which, more than the many examples of absolute power which preceded it, defines its legitimacy and justification for such acts in terms of religion.

It would be a mistake if we considered the representation of sovereign power through this theatre to be the only fundamental characteristic of the control system of the Islamic Republic. As I said before, this system represents a combination of medieval/pre-modern and modern qualities. Once it decided to expand the category of opposition to include all those who did not embrace the dominant discourse, the Islamic government of Iran, which had begun in some confusion and disorientation, created a control system (a punitive-judiciary system) which is clearly a combination of the two forms. During the first days of the Revolution, the opposition and even some of the officials thought the chaotic and violent methods which carried many people indiscriminately to the gallows or before the firing squads, not to mention the presence of such spectacles, would not last long. But the decision of the Islamic Republic to go beyond those affiliated with the previous government did not leave any hope for those who tried to see this period as a passing phase.

Here, a comparison between two approaches, one represented by an event which took place towards the end of Shah's regime, the other introduced at the beginning of the Islamic revolutionary government, reveals the mentality behind the process which brought together the two control systems, pre-modern and modern. Five years before the collapse of the Shah's regime, a number of individuals were arrested. They were accused of "acting against national security"[30] by trying to kidnap the Queen and the Crown Prince. Many of these individuals were employees of the government-controlled Iranian Radio and Television. Among them there was a poet, Khosrow Golsorkhi, who had gained much popularity among young people because of the political/revolutionary allusions in his verse. A few days after his arrest, everyone found out that Golsorkhi had no relationship with the others and clearly the officials had decided to use this opportunity to silence him. Consequently this question was posed: Why did the Shah's regime, which had never hesitated to torture and imprison its opponents without ever feeling the need to offer any reason for their arrest or proof of their guilt, suddenly decide to use these means to silence and punish one of the narrators of the discourse of the Other? The answer shortly became evident. The Shah, for the first time, had decided to take a chance and effectively put his regime's legitimacy to a vote with regard to the suppression of the opposition. The trial was broadcast live on television. Only Golsorkhi and another defendant—Keramatollah Daneshiyan—were sentenced to death because they refused to repent and to ask for forgiveness. Others who recanted, repudiated their ideas and asked for pardon were granted life and shorter sentences. Of all these people, the name of Golsorkhi became the most famous. In the court of public opinion, this name represented the defeat of the Shah's regime in bringing out into the open the process of suppressing the opposition, a process which until then was being carried out in secret in prisons and torture chambers. In other words, the dominant discourse did not have the necessary tools to legitimize this suppression by actualizing its transition from a secretive and hidden process to a public and visible one. This was immediately understood by the regime, and it was the first and last such attempt. After that, the regime went back to its previous practices; namely, total reliance on the surreptitious use of prisons and torture chambers.[31]

During the early days of the Islamic government, too, a similar attempt took place. Having wiped out most of those affiliated with the previous regime, the revolutionary tribunals formed soon after the Revolution turned their attention to the opposition. At this point the number of arrests was so high and the pace of trials and executions was so fast that in practical terms it was not possible to mount shows exactly like Golsorkhi's trial. The important point, however, is that, like Golsorkhi's case during the Shah's regime, by posting the pictures of those executed by firing squad or the gallows, and by publishing reports about their "crimes" and their "trials," the new government counted on winning general approval for this process of elimination.

It should be noted that the social atmosphere within which these trials and executions were carried out was quite different from that of Golsorkhi's time. The Islamic government had been formed following a great revolution, and public opinion had not become distrustful of it to the same degree as it had of the previous regime. Despite this, like the trial and execution of Golsorkhi, these trials and executions underscored the same question: How is it possible to legitimize the open and visible suppression of those who oppose the dominant discourse? In other words, within the dominant discourse, is it possible to find elements which would have the theoretical–ideological capability of legitimizing and justifying such spectacles? Taking a different line from the Shah's regime, which, after the trial and execution of Golsorkhi, considered its decision a tactical mistake and returned to its previous course, the Islamic government opted for an eclectic approach. On the one hand, it tried in part to reduce the visibility of the most offensive aspects of the punitive-judiciary system; on the other hand it continued to insist on convincing the public of the righteousness of its practices. As we shall see, this "convincing" process very soon took a completely different form.

To justify and explain this policy, the Islamic government relied almost completely on the fundamental Islamic text, the Qur'an, and at times on secondary, mainly Shi'i, sources as well.[32] In using these texts the government pursued two goals: 1) By relying on the religious authority of these texts along with the regime's extensive propaganda to reintroduce and portray Islam as a kind and gracious religion, it sought to present its system of justice not just as a punitive system but also as a correctional one—something similar to a modern-disciplinary system; 2) By using some of these religious laws and rules, the government was also able to perpetuate spectacles and rituals representing the sovereign power and thus keeping the pre-modern aspect of this system intact.

Relying on these texts, phrases such as "corruptor on Earth," "fighters against God and his Prophet," "hypocrite," and "apostate" which had been forgotten for more than half a century once more became everyday expressions, and punishments such as cutting off the limbs and flogging, stoning, and other forms of execution, most of which were carried out in public, supposedly as a warning to others, became an essential component of the Islamic government's judiciary system. It is not difficult to find quotations from Islamic government officials citing these punishments in no uncertain terms as procedures established by God and his Prophet, and therefore irrevocable. For example, in an interview with the newspaper *Ettela'at* (Information), Ali-Akbar Hashemi-Rafsanjani, former president of Iran, the current head of the influential Expediency Council[33] and one of the most powerful figures in the Islamic government, specifically discussed these procedures and emphasized their Islamic nature, their unchangeability and their righteousness.

God's law prescribes four punishments for them [hypocrites]. 1- Kill them. 2- Hang them. 3- Cut off their hands and feet. 4- Banish them. If we had killed two hundred of them right after the Revolution, their numbers would not have mounted in this way. I say again: in accordance with the Qur'an, we are determined to destroy all who display enmity against Islam.[34]

Of course, by "God's law" he is referring to the following Qur'anic verses:

The punishment of those who wage war against Allah and His messenger and strive to make mischief in the land is only this, that they should be murdered or crucified or their hands and their feet should be cut off on opposite sides or they should be imprisoned; this shall be as a disgrace for them in this world, and in the hereafter they shall have a grievous chastisement. (5. 33)[35]

Remember thy Lord inspired the angels (with the message): "I am with you: give firmness to the Believers: I will instill terror into the hearts of the Unbelievers: smite ye above their necks and smite all their finger-tips off them." (8.12)

This because they contended against Allah and His Messenger: If any contend against Allah and His Messenger, Allah is strict in punishment. (8.13)

Rafsanjani referred to these laws in connection with a massacre which took place in 1988 in prisons run by the Islamic government. The story of this massacre is another example which contributes to a portrayal of the Islamic Republic's system of justice. That year, Khomeini issued a directive to those in charge of the judiciary branch which led to the execution of a large number of political prisoners. Much has been said about Khomeini's letter, and clearly many might have been motivated by their political agenda to depict this letter as worse than it was. But what Ayatollah Hosein-Ali Montazeri, a very high-ranking cleric who at one point was considered Khomeini's successor, has said about the letter can be trusted beyond a doubt. In one of the appendices to his *Memoirs*, Montazeri includes the letter, which reads as follows:

> Since *monafeqin* [hypocrites],[36] traitors to Islam, do not believe in Islam and whatever they say is because of their treachery and hypocrisy, and [since], according to the confession of their leaders, they have turned to apostasy, and considering the fact that they are Mohareb,[37] their taking up of arms in the North, West and South of the country, with the collaboration of the Baath party of Iraq, their espionage for Saddam against our Moslem nation, and further considering their connections to international oppressors and their cowardly strikes from the beginning of the Islamic Republic until now, those in prisons throughout the country who persist in their hypocritical position are considered Mohareb and are sentenced to death. The decision [as to whether these prisoners still hold to their positions or not] is based on the majority of votes by Hojjat-al Islam Nayyeri (the Shari'a judge), Mr. Eshraqi (Tehran's prosecuting attorney) and a representative from the Ministry of Information, although caution recommends that the vote be unanimous. Also in the prisons of provincial capitals, the vote of the majority of [a committee comprised of] the Shari'a judge, prosecutor [of the revolutionary court] or his assistant, and the representative from the Ministry of Information should be followed. Having mercy on Moharebs is naiveté; Islam's decisive action against the enemies of God is one of the unshakable principles of the Islamic system. I hope, with your revolutionary wrath and enmity towards the enemies of Islam, you will gain God's approbation. The gentlemen who are in charge of making these decisions should not hesitate or be in doubt and should strive to be unyielding against unbelievers.[38] To hesitate in judicial matters of Islam means to ignore the pure blood of the martyrs. I herewith conclude.
> Ruhollah al-Musavi Khomeini[39]

Using terms such as *ertedad* (apostasy), *Mohareb* (fighter/warrior [against God and his Prophet]) and *kafer* (infidel) was clearly intended to determine the fate of these prisoners; indeed in this letter Khomeini issued the death sentence for thousands of political prisoners.[40] After quoting this letter, Montazeri points to a letter addressed to Khomeini written by his (Khomeini's) son in which he passes along the questions asked by Ayatollah Musavi Ardebili (the head of the High Council of the Judiciary at the time) about Khomeini's order:

> Gracious father, honorable Imam, may you live long,
> Greetings. Ayatollah Musavi Ardebili has had some uncertainties about your Excellency's recent ruling concerning hypocrites [Mojahedin], which he has raised during a telephone conversation:

1- Is this ruling about those who are already in prison and have been tried and sentenced to death but have not changed their position and whose sentence has not yet been carried out, or are even those who have not even been tried condemned to execution?

2- Are those hypocrites who have been sentenced to a limited life sentence and have already served part of their sentence but are continuing to hold to their hypocrisy to be condemned to execution?

3- In reference to the situation of hypocrites: Should the cases of hypocrites in provinces which have judicial independence and are not subordinate to state capitals be sent to the state capital, or they can [the local authorities] act independently?

Your child, Ahmad

Underneath this letter is Khomeini's answer:

In the name of God,

In all the above mentioned cases, as concerns anyone who still maintains a position of hypocrisy, he is sentenced to execution. Destroy the enemies of Islam immediately. With regard to addressing the [above-mentioned] cases, [our] view is that whatever way expedites the carrying out of the ruling should be followed.[41]

Montazeri refers to these letters/fatwas from a critical standpoint, but his criticism was restricted to a concern that a three-member council might make mistakes in judgments taking place so rapidly, and that using such methods might hurt the image of the Islamic Republic on the international scene.[42] In fact, even a "liberal" Ayatollah such as Montazeri agrees in principle with these forms of punishment-justice. In his *Tawzih al-Masa'el*,[43] in the section about the punishment of the "*mohareb*" (fighter [against God and his Prophet]) and the "*mortad*" (apostate) he writes:

According to the Qur'an and related hadiths, the punishment for a mohareb is to kill him or to hang him (sic) or cut off his right hand and left leg, or exile him from his country. ... If a mohareb has plundered people's property and also committed murder, after taking his property, they should cut off his hand and leg and then kill him, or simply kill him.[44]

After describing different kinds of *mortads*, Montazeri writes:

As soon as he has become kafer (infidel [to Islam]) his property is divided among his heirs and he is sentenced to death by the Shari'a judge. ... A woman mortad [however] is not executed. She is to be jailed and be treated harshly. At the times of daily prayers [five times a day] she is beaten until she repents. If she repents she will be freed; if not, she will remain in jail until she dies.[45]

All these examples indicate the simultaneous presence of a dichotomy in the control/judiciary system which on the surface seems to have provided the Islamic government with a particular flexibility enabling it to use different methods under different conditions. In other words, given the fact that the Islamic government sees a direct relationship between consolidating and securing its existence on the one hand and the imposing of its discourse on the other, when this discourse succeeds in accomplishing the task through peaceful means, the need for using heavy sentences and medieval spectacles lessens, and the form and function of this control system become more like those of a disciplinary one without any need to revise the system's ideological–theoretical foundations. But if this discourse fails to impose itself by relying on peaceful methods, then it can take advantage of medieval punishments and rituals—representing the sovereign power—which have already been provided for in the same ideological–theoretical framework.

Probably the illusion existed among the leaders of the Islamic government that a simultaneous application of these two systems could suppress the voices of opposition much faster. But total reliance on religious texts—the only ideological–theoretical framework which could justify the simultaneous presence of the two systems—imposed limitations on the dominant discourse to the point where it was effectively stripped it of its abilities to absorb and assimilate many elements of the discourses of the Other. Paradoxically, a total reliance on these texts led to the isolation of the dominant discourse. This isolation—this defeat, in fact—is so obvious that the leaders of the Islamic government are not even trying to hide it. To demonstrate the extent of this defeat it is enough to consider what Ayatollah Mesbah Yazdi, one of the most conservative figures of the regime and one of its theoreticians, announced in a sermon during a Friday prayer in 2003. He admitted that 90 percent of educated people in Iran are moving away from religion; this while the Islamic government during its 24-year reign had used every conceivable tool and means at its disposal to impose its religious discourse.[46] This defeat, of course, was used as yet another justification for the increasing pressure by the power structure on the discourses of the Other.

Among numerous methods of repression and pressure, two strategies are particularly significant for the purpose of this study. The first was the creation of "pressure groups" managed and maintained by the leaders of the Islamic government. Of course the relationship between these groups and the leaders of the Islamic Republic has never been publicly acknowledged. Their main duty is to control the details of individuals' movements and their punishment in cases where their actions are perceived to be in opposition to the dominant discourse. The power of these pressure groups is such that their well-known leading figures have never been seriously questioned or investigated even when they have assassinated figures of the opposition.[47]

In the chapter "Panopticism" of *Discipline and Punish*, Foucault uses the allegories of the "plague-stricken city" and "Panopticon" to describe other aspects of differences between the two control systems representing sovereignty and discipline.

> The following, according to an order published at the end of the seventeenth century, were the measures to be taken when the plague appeared in a town.
>
> First, a strict spatial partitioning: the closing of the town and its outlying districts, a prohibition to leave the town on pain of death, the killing of all stray animals; the division of the town into distinct quarters, each governed by an intendant. Each street is placed under the authority of a syndic, who keeps it under surveillance; if he leaves the street, he will be condemned to death. On the appointed day, everyone is ordered to stay indoors: it is forbidden to leave on pain of death. ...
>
> Inspection functions ceaselessly. The gaze is alert everywhere; "A considerable body of militia, commanded by good officers and men of substance", guards at the gates, at the town hall and in every quarter to ensure the prompt obedience of the people and the most absolute authority of the magistrates ... [48]

In Iran under the Islamic government the presence of these methods is quite obvious. Not only are there the unofficial pressure groups but the official, militia-like entities such as the *Basij* (militia), *yegan-e vizheh* (special squad), and squads of *nahy-e az monkar* (preventing [people] from committing immoral, unreligious acts) and *amr-e beh ma'ruf* (encouraging good deeds), which are in charge of controlling the minutest details of behavior of every single citizen. These groups can stop men and women who are walking together in the streets and ask them to provide proof that they are related to each other either by marriage or family ties. They can stop women and issue warnings to those whose *hejab* is not perfect (meaning, for example, that a few strands of hair are seen from underneath their headscarves), etc. The creation of these groups displays the attempt of the Islamic government to expand its gaze to the smallest spaces in the public and private lives of every one of its citizens. The other system which Foucault calls the Panopticon, however, relies on another method.

> Panopticon is the architectural figure of this composition. We know the principle on which it was based: at the periphery, an annular building; at the centre, a tower; this tower is pierced with wide windows that open onto the inner side of the ring; the peripheric building is divided into cells, each of which extends the whole width of the building; they have two windows ... All that is needed, then, is to place a supervisor in a

central tower and shut up in each cell a madman, a patient, a condemned man, a worker or a school boy ...

Each individual, in his place, is securely confined to a cell from which he is seen from the front by the supervisor; but the side walls prevent him from coming into contact with his companions. He is seen but he does not see; he is the object of information, never a subject in communication.[49]

The similarity between this structure and the situation of political prisoners under the Islamic government—as well as under the Shah's regime—is undeniable. From the very first moment, political prisoners are required to wear a blindfold at all times, except when they are in their own cells or rooms. Even when they are supposed to go to the investigation room, or to torture chambers, they are not allowed to remove their blindfold. They are led by prison guards from one place to another. This rule is adhered to so strictly that many prisoners who have spent years in confinement still do not have the slightest idea about the architecture of their prisons.[50] But not only the prison, the whole society under the rule of the Islamic government could be allegorized as such. Indeed, in his *Behesht-e Khakestari* (The Grey Paradise), Ataollah Mohajerani, having been forced to resign his position as Minister of Culture and Islamic Guidance (1997–2000)—he was seen as too liberal—suggested as much. According to this semi-documentary novel, the ruling clergy of a fictional city decides to remove every conceivable sin from the city so that they can create the Paradise on earth. After much debate, they reach the conclusion that the only way to do this is by forcing the inhabitants to build their houses out of glass so that everything can be seen. Only the government buildings will be made of dark glass.[51] Foucault, however, uses these two previously-mentioned descriptions as allegories of the control systems of pre-modern and modern societies. While in a plague-stricken town, the disciplinary model, "absolutely violent," uses the "perpetual threat of death" and thus reduces life "to its simplest expression", the Panopticon model uses social institutions to "arrange power" and to make it more "economic and effective."[52]

As representations of the two above-mentioned control systems, the ensemble of these two images provides a precise portrait of the punitive-judiciary system of the Islamic government and the relationship between the dominant power and human elements of opposing discourses. Awareness of this portrait is essential in understanding the second strategy of suppression and pressure. Because of the presence of the two punitive-judiciary systems, this second strategy, which emphasizes the increasing role of prison and torture, creates a dichotomy in the functions of prison and torture. On the one hand the medieval, pre-modern aspect requires the existence of ritualized spectacles which would represent absolute power. In the following pages I will discuss samples of contemporary and televised versions of pre-modern tortures. On the other hand, the tendency of the modern aspect to hide this component has been reinforced because of the macro-policy of the Islamic Republic which has aimed to present a positive image of itself in international arena. As Ataollah Mohajerani indicated, spectacles such as stoning obviously damage this image and therefore "efforts should be made to stop the dissemination of the news of stoning and of filming the scenes."[53]

Because of these preoccupations and due to internal pressures, these spectacles—those initiated both inside and outside prisons—have not been performed as extensively as the proponents of the dominant discourse would have liked. In addition, for a number of reasons, these shows have acquired particularly discordant and incompatible characteristics. What makes this situation even more complex is that the Islamic government has always tried to present its system of punishment-justice within a particular framework of Islam which describes that religion as a religion of kindness and compassion, benevolence and peace—a description which highlights even more the incompatible aspects of the system.

To summarize, the two above-mentioned strategies are contradictory dynamisms which lead to the formation of dichotomous shows performed inside and outside prisons. The examination of these shows serves to explain a space within which the prison reports, and consequently the background against which prison literature should be read, are understood.

The "convincing" process in the Islamic Republic prisons

One of the most emblematic functions of the contradictory strategies is apparent in a show—it has had different names including *hoviyyat* (identity)—which started shortly after the Revolution on the Islamic government television and still continues, albeit with slightly modified goals. The majority of the episodes follow a simple outline. A number of prisoners, usually accompanied by a few prison officials, sit in front of a camera. An official would start with an introduction saying that these prisoners, after long "discussions and debates" with "brothers" and "sisters" who believe in true Islam and on whose hearts the light of Truth and Righteousness has shone, have realized their waywardness and darkness and have finally been "convinced" and have bowed their heads before the power of God's word and Islam and its teachings. Now they have come to share their experience with others who might still have tendencies towards un-Islamic and ungodly thoughts. Of course, in all these episodes it is emphasized that these prisoners have insisted repeatedly on sitting and speaking in front of the camera. Without exception, from the very first moment one can see the pain and torment on the faces of the prisoners. Seeing individuals who after many years of political activity and struggle appear on these shows and talk about their past mistakes leaves no doubt in the minds of the audience about the nature of the process of "convincing." One of the most famous examples was the episode on which Ehsan Tabari appeared. Ehsan Tabari was one of the founders and the main theoretician of

Iran's Communist Party (the Tudeh Party). During the Shah's regime he had spent 30 years of his life in exile, and he came back to Iran shortly after the Revolution. He was arrested a few months later. After a few years he was brought onto this show. "He began by explaining that he was reading his statement and speaking with a slur because he had recently suffered a stroke,"[54] and then he explained his conversion to Islam. At that time he was an old man of about 70, who had spent 55 years of his life promoting Marxist ideas, and through his books, articles and lectures was known as one of the most prominent thinkers of his time. He was now crying and talking about the days and years of his life he had squandered away from the true religion, Islam.[55] He finished a segment of his presentation by saying that "He now realized that his entire life's work was 'defective,' 'damaging,' and 'totally spurious'."[56] This was not a unique occurrence. Leaders and members of many political organizations were brought on this show, and every one of them repeated the same story of how they had come to understand that Islam was the only righteous religion and how much they regretted that they had passed many years of their lives in error. More interesting was the case of those who already believed in Islam, but an Islam different from what the dominant discourse required. They usually began by saying how Satanic ideas were presented to them in the guise of Islam and then reported their allegiance to the "true" Islam of the dominant discourse.

As mentioned above, as soon as an episode began, it was very easy to understand what a heavy price these prisoners had paid for these shows. And I argue that in fact the Islamic government knew very well that by observing the defeated faces of the confessors, people would immediately understand the nature of the "convincing" process. Indeed, this was one aspect of what the Islamic government intended to display: spectacles representing the absolute, sovereign power. The problem was that, through the same shows, the Islamic government also desired to present a modern image of Islam and its justice system. This was why, at the beginning of each episode, they had forced prisoners to declare that no torture or even pressure had been used to convince them to sit in front of the camera. This practically undermined the first goal. Of course, no one ever had any illusions about the nature of the confession process, not only because the defeated faces counteracted the idea of Islamic compassion and kindness but because the staggering number of those executed naturally called into question the efficacy and efficiency of the "convincing" process. Furthermore, reports on life in the prisons provided more precise accounts of this process.

One of the most famous reports is Shahrnush Parsipur's *Khaterat-e Zendan* (Prison Memoirs). Parsipur is the author of acclaimed literary works such as *Tuba va Ma'na-ye Shab* (Tuba and the Meaning of Night) and *Zanan Bedun-e Mardan* (Women without Men). She was in prison from 1981–1985. According to her own words, she never had any direct relationship with a specific political organization opposing the Islamic government;[57] therefore her report from prison was not informed or influenced by any specific political agenda. In this book, Parsipur describes one of the most terrible forms of "convincing." This method was used in Qezel Hasar, one of the prisons of the Islamic government. For a while, some prisoners who had not yet given in were sent to a special section of this prison so they "would become human." The phrase "becoming human" was in fact the inside-prison synonym for the outside-prison phrase "to be reformed" or "to be corrected." In this section, mock executions or being beaten by cables to the point where the prisoner's legs from feet to thighs[58] would be covered with infection and pus were not considered the worst forms of torture. According to all of those who have experienced this section, the "cage" or "doghouse" or "*dastgah*" (device) was the most savage, most horrible torture. All these three words refer to something for which "the word grave might be the most suitable one."[59]

> Using some pieces of wood, they had divided the space next to the walls into areas as small as a grave. In each grave sat a prisoner, in chador and blindfold. The first prisoner sat at a distance of twenty centimeters from the wall and the other prisoner was at the end of the grave ... The schedule was that each morning, when people woke up ... breakfast was placed in front of them ... After breakfast, they would take people, one by one to the bathroom, and they were all supposed to, in a very short time, use the toilet and also wash their plates. Then they had to remain seated until lunch. Lunch was placed in front of the prisoners in the same way [as breakfast]. ... Then they allowed the prisoners to lie down until three p.m. ... From three until dinner time the prisoners again had to sit and stare from underneath their blindfold at the blanket in front of them, in silence.[60]

Prisoners who were put in these cages were not allowed to read, speak, or even move. And this was not a matter of one or two days. There have been prisoners who spent months in these cages. Many prisoners, in order to end this maddening torture, had no solution but to speak and confess about their beliefs of yesterday and today in the following manner:

> While I was sitting in the "dastgah," I was gradually changing. New worlds were appearing to me. Little by little I felt that, as a communist, I was dirty. Finally, one day I found the Truth. I told the sister pasdars [revolutionary guards/prison guards]: "Bring me new clothes." I bathed and cleaned myself. I begged them to burn my old clothes because they were dirty. Then I prayed. I became fresh and new. I became a human being. Oh God, how wrong I had been. I told the sisters: "My name is filthy;[61] it should be changed. ... "[62]

Another prisoner describes her "reformation" process:

> Haj Aqa, I did a lot of thinking during this time. Believe me; I have
> absolutely no aptitude for political activity. God has created me so
> clumsy and hapless that I am only good for becoming a housemaid ... [63]

The Haj Aqa mentioned in this passage is Haj Davud Rahmani, one of
the most infamous and appalling figures of the prisons of the Islamic
government. It is difficult to find a prison report which does not mention
Haj Davud as one of the most "successful," "reforming" characters. According to these reports, Haji,[64] who had little literacy and less mercy, had been
given absolute power and freedom to manage the Qezel Hasar prison. Haji's
ultimate guiding principle was to drive prisoners to the point where they
would deny their past and confess to the righteousness of Islam. Above the
gates of the prison he caused the following to be written: "The Dumpster for
History's Garbage." For a time, Haji himself divided the prisoners sent to
Qezel Hasar into two groups: the "reformed" and the "not-yet-given-ups";
then began the process of "convincing" the latter. On many occasions
this process continued until the prisoners were ready to go "in front of other
prisoners, behind the microphone" and proclaim their abhorrence of their
past ideas.[65]

Quite possibly, it is not hard to find characters similar to Haji in Iran's
contemporary history or in history in general. But there is a particular
characteristic present in this Haji which establishes a link between him and
the dominant discourse. Of all the descriptions about him, the following one
given by a woman prisoner points to that characteristic:

> In Qezel [Hasar] the law was Haji's law. He would enter the ward at dif-
> ferent times without prior notice; he would set up rules; he would abolish
> rules; he would torture and he would pardon ... Haj Aqa did not care
> about the contents of our files. He did not care whether or not we were
> Mohareb [fighters against God and his Prophet] and Mofsed [corruptors
> on Earth], irreligious or religious, guilty or innocent. *Haji considered
> himself to be responsible for only one thing and that was to protect his
> Namus,*[66] *meaning us, the women prisoners. And if any of these Namuses
> made the slightest wrong move, Haji would teach her an unforgettable
> lesson.*[67]

This characteristic, which at first seems curious, is not necessarily strange
when it is looked at closely, because it underlines the fact that Haji and others
like him are created by ideological-historical thoughts and texts; and being in
a dominant position, they can now act upon these thoughts and texts. And it
is this characteristic which "promotes" Haji from being a simple jailor and
defines a kinship between him and many religious and unreligious myths of
real and fictional stories. Indeed, as we will see, it is this aspect of Haji's

personality which will be used to define a fictional character created based on his image.

In spite of all that, for many prisoners, Qezel Hasar was a pleasant prison compared to Evin. Evin is where the real torture took place. One of the most common forms of torture is to beat the prisoner with a cable, usually on the soles of their feet, but sometimes all over their bodies. The Islamic government has never denied this, but has argued that this punishment is not torture; it is *Ta'zir* (legal and indeed religiously-required punishment).[68]

Without exception, all prison reports have mentioned this form of torture, and I will cite only a few of them here. The first description is taken from Parsipur's *Khaterat-e Zandan* (Prison Memoirs):

> The Kurdish girl said: "Since you are a writer, it is not bad if you saw her so you would know what appearance a human being could have."
> I went towards the television room and, acting as if I wanted to watch television, I opened the door ... Razieh Al-e Taher was in bed. Her legs were bandaged from feet to thighs. Because of blood and purulent infection, the color of the bandages was like that of the Egyptian mummies. Razieh's eyes turned toward me. She lifted her hand as if she wanted to say something and she remained in that state for a while. There were blue smudges underneath her eyes.[69]

Throughout the beating process, and after it, the torturers/officials are careful that no important Islamic requirement is ignored by the prisoners. For example, in the case of women prisoners they are careful that the hair of a woman who is bleeding under the cable wire blows is not seen, and that her *hejab* is in order.

> They stood me up from the chair and made me lie down on the ground, on my stomach. Another man came and sat on my back, on my bound hands. With each blow my body reacted. I was retracting my legs and screaming ... They threw a blanket on my head and the man sitting on my head covered my mouth and nose over the blanket ...
> When I regained consciousness the blanket was no longer over my face and the interrogators had left. A voice shook me: "Cover yourself! Where is your shame?" I wanted to move my hands but they were still tied behind me. The interrogator came and untied my hands. My hands fell alongside of me, dead and motionless. I could not move them. The man repeated: "Cover yourself!"[70]

These are only a few examples of physical torture. Obviously there are many other forms.[71] All of them, in the majority of cases, pursue specific aims: either the physical and psychological eradication of those affiliated with counter-discourses or the forcing of them to reach the point where they will accept the dominant discourse "from the bottom of their hearts." This point has been explained in detail in *At Haji Aqa's Gathering*.[72] This book includes two prison memoirs: "At Haji Aqa's Gathering" by Habibollah Davaran and "Dastan-e Yek E'teraf" (The Story of a Confession) by Farhad Behbahani. Both authors, very religious and highly-educated men, belonged to a legal political organization named the Association for the Defense of Democracy. In 1990, when they were in their fifties, Davaran and Behbahani were arrested for having signed an open letter addressed to the President of the time, Ali-Akbar Hashemi-Rafsanjani. Of the two memoirs, "The Story of a Confession" is the more relevant because a few months after his arrest, the author, Behbahani, confessed to direct contact between their Association for the Defense of Democracy and the main enemy of the Islamic government, the United States of America. This confession was repeatedly broadcast on Iranian Television and printed in many government-controlled newspapers. In "The Story of a Confession," Behbahani explains how he reached the stage of making this baseless confession:

> We came to the first floor [in the prison]. Mr. 25 took a key out of his pocket and opened a door under the staircase. Then they pushed me inside a small basement which looked like a half-darkened hallway. There was a wooden bed. They sat me on it and ordered me to remove my socks. The strong interrogator put a rather thick wooden stick, about two inches diameter in my hand and said: "Do you see this? This is only number 3. Do something so you will be done with this and you don't get to numbers 2 and 1" ... I did my best to say whatever I could think of to change their minds but it was no use. They laid me down on the bed and chained my hands to a ring at the head of the bed and also tied my feet with ropes to the foot of the bed. Haji Aqa sat on the stairs and ordered Mr. 25: Strike! He first said "In the name of God, the most gracious and merciful" and then began hitting. I was in such pain and the chain and plastic ropes were pulling against my wrists and ankles so much that even without the blows I could not bear it.[73]

The beating continues until the prisoner is unconscious; when he regains consciousness, the standard procedure is to force the prisoner, whose feet have become so swollen that he cannot wear his sandals, to walk barefoot so the swelling will reduce and the blood gathered under the skin of his soles will flow out. This process is repeated once every few days. Behbahani, who has no special information, keeps begging his interrogator to at least tell him what he wants from him. Finally Haji Aqa explains:

> When someone is arrested and is brought here he gives in, but only outwardly. This is not enough; he must give in from the bottom of his heart so that he will let go of his previous ideas and allegiances. Only then do we understand that he is truly honest with us.

... Haji Aqa added: "Of course I find it improbable that you could reach this stage on your own. The ultimate solution is that I order them to beat you one hundred strokes in one single session. Then your soul will let go of all those interests and ideas ... "[74]

After a few months of undergoing different tortures, Behbahani was practically convinced that what he and other members of his organization did was in line with plots of the Great Satan against the Islamic Republic, and so confessed to their direct relationship with the United States.

Of course, this result is not achieved every time. When the persuasive power of absolute Truth does not seem to be working, the next stage is picturing the future that awaits unconvinced prisoners:

They moved all of us and made us enter Evin's courtyard. ... At this time they said, Remove your blindfolds and look straight in front of you. A gruesome scene appeared before tens of prisoners ... At the bottom of a rope which was hanging from a tall tree, the body of a young man was swinging. The arms of the young man were bandaged up to the elbows and his legs were torn because of cable blows. He was hardly twenty years old. His hair was short and he had a thin moustache. His thin face was blue because of the pressure of the noose; his head leaned calmly to one side.[75]

Parsipur recounts a similar experience:

That same day, or maybe the following day, a new group of prisoners was brought from Evin to Qezel Hasar ... Apparently, before putting them on the bus they had taken them to see the bodies. All of them were hysterical. One of them—I call her F.—in a state between laughing and screaming was explaining that the Revolutionary Guards took the hair of Rajavi's wife[76] and lifted the head so it could be seen better and then let it fall, and it hit the ground with a thud.[77]

This is the final stage of "convincing." Those who, according to the Shari'a judges, have not yet received the light of Truth and Righteousness will be subjected to the fatwa of the founders of the dominant discourse: "The ruling for whomever still maintains the position of hypocrisy is execution. Destroy the enemies of Islam, swiftly."[78]

It goes without saying that, in the process of imposing the dominant discourse, these tortures are only a fraction of the physical and psychological methods used in the prisons of the Islamic government. A detailed examination of these methods requires a separate, voluminous book. But to gain more insight into life in prison, it is useful to include a different perspective. Here again I will refer to Montazeri's *Memoirs*, mainly because he has always been part of the dominant discourse, and the veracity of his book has not been questioned even by the leaders of the Islamic government. In one section of the book, Montazeri recalls the time that, after receiving numerous complaints, he sent a committee to inspect the prisons and then sent a report to Khomeini. In this report, which had been prepared after inspecting some of the prisons in the provinces, he refers to prisoners with

> [b]roken arms, legs and fingers; pulled teeth; also those with wounds [of torture] on their bodies. A woman from Mashhad said that she was arrested during the month of Ramazan, and they beat her so much that she lost her unborn child. It was claimed that in two cases prisoners were beaten to death.[79] All of this was seen among ordinary prisoners of Bandar-Abbas, Sirjan, etc. who said the traces [on the bodies] were caused by beating with cable wire, kicking, burning with a lighter, tying prisoners to cars, burning them with kerosene and gas, and one of the prisoners said that they used a piece of wood covered with gasoline to burn his private parts.[80]

Montazeri also mentions Ayatollah Seyyed Ja'far Karimi who, apparently after Khomeini hears about tortures which exceed the imagination of even some prison officials, is asked to inspect the prisons. This individual recounts some of his report for Montazeri:

> "We went to Hasarak [Qezel Hasar] Prison, near Mardabad. There, we saw that there was a black blanket in front of a door, and inside it was so dark that day and night could not be distinguished; about ten people were imprisoned there." He then said: "We saw a girl who was eating her own filth. They had tortured her so much that she had gone mad and they still kept her there!"

Montazeri continues:

> I was very much touched by these matters and I went to the Imam [Khomeini] and said: "Sir, today, as opposed to other days, I have come to cause your Grace unhappiness and say distressing things! In our prisons they have kept a mad girl as a political prisoner; please do something about these things. What kind of prisons are these, in the Islamic Republic!"[81]

Montazeri's comments indicate that the events and conditions in the prisons of the Islamic government were not the result of the errors or overzealousness on the part of one or two prison officials, created without the knowledge and consent of the leaders of the dominant discourse. This environment and these methods were the inescapable consequences of strategies that the Islamic government had planned from the beginning in order to impose its discourse.

Of course it should be noted that the Islamic Republic's definition of this plan was different. The official narrative dealing with prisons was based on an order that Khomeini had issued shortly after the Revolution. According to this order, in a country where Islam and revolution rule, prisons must be centers of education.[82] The result of this order was that in all prisons, judges familiar with Shari'a laws were careful that no act which would undermine Islam and its justice system would be committed. Again, the important issue is who is narrating the stories of these Islamic approaches. For example, from the point of view of the dominant discourse, the story of torturing women while at the same time trying to cover their hair and make sure their *hejab* is in order would be a perfect example of unavoidable Islamic *ta'zir* combined with praiseworthy efforts to respect Islamic values. The same story, however, from the point of view of counter-discourses would be a ridiculous and painful tragedy which stems only from a sick imagination.

Children of prison

Another example which illustrates the confrontation of these discourses and contributes to the portrayal of life in the city of prison lies in the competing narratives about the Islamic treatment of children. The symbolic propaganda of the dominant discourse can be detected through the famous *hadith*, "Paradise lies at the feet of mothers." After the Revolution, this has become one of the favorite watchwords of the new power structure. It is attributed to the Prophet of Islam; to this day one can see that slogan written in countless places in many cities. Related to the same topic, there are other stories, including the story of the attack of the followers of the caliph of the time on Fatemeh—the Prophet's daughter and wife of Ali, the Prophet's nephew and the first Imam of the Shi'is—leading to a miscarriage, which has been told with a sensationalism (and every year, this story is repeated during the anniversaries of the deaths and births of Fatemeh and Ali) which attempts to leave no doubt about the special consideration that Islam holds for children, pregnant women, and mothers. Symbolically, however, one of the finest examples of the attempts of the dominant discourse to define the relationship between the Islamic government and children can be seen through one of the propaganda programs initiated by the government to describe Khomeini's special predilection for children.

> In early 1980s the unit for Literary Creativity of the Institute for the Intellectual Development of Children and Young Adults in Iran organized a national competition entitled "A Letter to Imam." ... On 23 Esfand 1362/14 March 1984, Ayatollah Khomeini received the organizers of this event and the twenty-nine finalists.[83]

And then the Imam's love and affection is described.

The children were waiting for the Imam's arrival impatiently. As soon as the Imam saw the children, a fatherly smile blossomed on his most gracious face. The children all broke into tears. We all cried. These were tears of joy. The Imam received the children with open arms. The children gave the Imam a book in memory of this occasion. They showered his hand with kisses. The Imam prayed for all the children, one by one. When we returned, the children were all silent in the minibus. Obviously, it was the impact of the Imam's visit. We felt we were washed by a bounteous rain of piety. The kind glances of the Imam had touched our souls. The children were in ecstasy as if they had just smelled the fragrance of a beautiful flower.[84]

But inhabitants of the city-prison have other narratives of the story of Islamic treatment of children (and mothers). During the first years after the Revolution, it was said that according to Islam, children should be with their mothers at least until the age of two, whether under the feet of these mothers lies paradise or prison ground. According to Sudabeh Ardavan, one of the political prisoners during 1981–1988, Asadollah Lajvardi, the notorious Director of Evin Prison, was actually proud of the fact that "Islamic kindness keeps children with their mothers."[85] Naturally prisoners considered the implementation of this Islamic principle yet another means of pressure.[86] Children who were brought into this environment (and this includes children who were born in prison) "learned how to walk and talk in prison"[87] and their first words were Revolutionary guard, *Khamushi* (lights out), *Havakhori* (recreation in open air) … These kids "had seen a car, a minibus, animals, a park, ice cream and a sandwich only on television."[88] In this strange city-prison, every morning, mothers had to leave their children and go to the interrogation room and at the end of the day, tired and worried, with injured legs, come back to the ward.

I saw a kid who had embraced the bandaged legs of her mother and kissed them. Many children, when they heard the names of their mothers from the loudspeakers, would turn pale and, crying and grabbing the legs of their mothers, try to prevent her from going to the interrogation room.[89]

And sometimes, when these mothers came back from interrogation, these children who were growing up too fast, rushed to help them:

Setareh usually did not talk about her memories, but one day she told us that at the time of her arrest, they also brought her son who was three years old. For months they kept them in the hallway, and the kid thought their home was the blanket on which he and his mother sat and slept. He did not have permission to set foot beyond the blanket. For long hours he would sit there without having a single toy to play with. His amusement was watching blindfolded prisoners passing by in the hallway. They had tortured Setareh, and for a long time she could not walk. When she wanted to go to the bathroom she had to drag herself on the floor, and the kid, who did not have a blindfold, was her guide. The mother would put her hand on his shoulder and he would show her the way.[90]

But without a doubt, the most heartbreaking moments of the life of these kids was when they were playing their well-known games:

One of the famous games of these little ones was bandaging legs. They would smear ointment on each other's feet and then bandage them. They would attend to each other and were busy for an hour. They had learned this from the grown-ups, since there were many wounded legs and dressings in the ward.[91]

According to all prison reports, the presence of children gave a human quality to the city-prison. Yet there is no doubt that these children were not those who deserved the warm glance of the leader of the Islamic government or his prayers; nor were these mothers those who were supposed to have Paradise under their feet. In fact, according to the prison officials of the Islamic government, the breasts of such mothers who would nurse their children with "milk of corruption" had to be torn from their bodies.[92]

Prison and prisoners' version of the Qur'an

Nevertheless, with regard to the formation of new counter-discourses and their prison version, the most significant element is the contradictory definition and place of the Qur'an, the most sacred text of Islam and Moslems, inside and outside prison. To summarize this contradiction, we could say that, while as part of the non-violent process of imposing the dominant discourse outside prison, this text was presented as a symbol not only of open-mindedness but of beneficence, mercy, kindness, and benevolence; inside prison this text became emblematic of intolerance, fanaticism, violence, torture, and even evildoing. In other words, the same "most gracious and merciful" God of outside-prison becomes a God inside the prison who is "severe in punishment"[93] and guides and encourages his followers to bring a horrible death to "the agitators in the city."[94] Indeed, at the same time people such as Khomeini described the Qur'an as a text which relied on the ultimate divine Truth and logic in order to convince people to accept divine laws—such as *hejab*—in prison other methods of convincing were applied.

Haji would knock and then immediately enter. As soon as he entered, he would kick and punch any prisoner who didn't have her chador on. He would keep on kicking as he moved onward. In this prison, which had only 12 individual cells, lived more than 180 prisoners. The running of those 180 women, overcome with terror and terror created an earthquake which is indescribable.[95]

And when after a while the prisoners "realized the importance and right-eousness of hejab," Haji used to come and look with disdain at those who, because of fear, had their black chadors on and say: "You black crows!"[96]

The issue was not just to implement the Islamic laws. At times, prisoners were forced to read the Qur'an under the threat of torture and in fact, after a while, the identification of the Qur'an with torture was so systematically achieved that one of the prisoners wrote in his prison memoirs: "Before prison, the sound of the Azan[97] for me was reminiscent of good childhood memories. But after prison it has become an evil sound, reminding me of human ugliness."[98] And that is not surprising, because, as we said, what happened in prison was an important part of the discourse of the Islamic government—the prison version of it. Indeed, this was not denied by the Islamic government and its prison officials. Quite the contrary, they empha-sized it. Many torturers "performed ablution before flogging because they considered it a religious duty."[99] Sometimes, while the prisoner was being tortured, the sound of the Qur'an recitation accompanied the blows of the cable wire. Even daily prayers which apparently include some of the most sacred verses of the Qur'an, were sometimes directly linked to pain and torture.

> The issue of not praying also was added to the pressures. In addition to flogging and torture during interrogation, every prisoner was beaten five times a day for not praying (instead of the five daily prayers). I was beaten for 40 days, each day five times, for not praying.[100]

> The news came to our ward with a woman who had been arrested for the accusation of being a Baha'i. We didn't believe it until another piece of news from Ward no. 2 confirmed it. This was the news: At dawn, around 4 in the morning, to the sound of the Azan, the door of the cell is opened. They take the prisoner out and lay him/her down on a bed in the middle of the hallway. They beat him, five times. They close the cell door and another door is opened. The second prisoner is laid on the bed, the third and fourth ... This lasts for about one hour. The second time is after the noon Azan. Another five blows. The third ration is around 4 p.m. The fourth, at the beginning of the night, around 8, and the last ration is before midnight. Twenty-five blows over five times.[101]

And even when, after being beaten for a long time, prisoners realized the greatness and sacredness of daily prayers, in order to prove that they have really and from the bottom of their hearts, understood the beneficial, salutary and salvational qualities of these methods, they were forced to play the role of the torturer and beat those friends who had yet to believe in the greatness of Islam and of the Qur'an and of prayer.[102]

These methods of "convincing" were used systematically. There have also been situations when prison officials, trying to impose the Qur'an, God and his representative on Earth, have gone so far as to brand the body of the executed prisoners with the slogan of "Allah-o Akbar, Khomeini Rahbar" (God is great, Khomeini is the leader).[103] But in this process of identification of the Qur'an—this most central text of the dominant discourse—with ruthlessness, torture and death, perhaps the most horrible of all, is the sound of the Qur'an recitation and the maddening shouting of *Allah-o Akbar* that those condemned to be stoned hear throughout the process, and with every bone that breaks and every new bloody wound these shouts grow louder and more ferocious. In such a composition there is not the slightest chance for assessing the Qur'an as a sacred text representing peace, tolerance, kindness, or benevolence.

Prison literature and its background

As mentioned in the Introduction to this chapter, my intention is not to present a comprehensive analysis of the Islamic government's political prisons and its numerous methods of torture and execution. Referring to these examples is intended first to demonstrate the contradictory process of the dominant discourse in the process of imposing itself within its punishing-judiciary system. Furthermore, and more importantly, these examples contribute to the sketch of a portrayal which functions as a *background* leading to a particular reading of prison literature—a reading which reveals the formation of one of Iran's contemporary literary counter-discourses.

To describe this process we should begin with an explanation about the two terms, "Prison Reports" and "Prison Literature." Throughout this study I have used these phrases to designate two different categories. The difference between the two is understood through the distances that each has from the *actual*. This approach once more evokes the well-known discussion of the relationship between reality and literature.

In *Modern Reflections of Classical Traditions in Persian Fiction*, I explored aspects of this topic in detail. I argued that if we accept the premise that the examination of a literary work should be based on its "literariness," then the distance between literary reality and the "everyday reality" should be one of our main foci. In *Russian Formalism: History-Doctrine*, Viktor Erlich refers to this point as one component of the Formalists' discussion about "divergence [of a given literary work] from non-literature."[104] According to Erlich, Formalists used the concept of *differenzqualität* in three different cases:

> ... on the level of representation of the reality, *differenzqualität* stood for the "divergence" from the actual, i.e., for creative deformation.

On the level of language it meant a departure from current linguistic usage. Finally, on the plane of literary dynamics, this catch-all term would imply a deviation from, or modification of, the prevailing artistic norm.[105]

For the purpose of this section of the present study, the first case, "the 'divergence' from the actual," is the most significant one because through this concept the difference between the two categories of "Prison Reports" and "Prison Literature" can be recognized. "Prison Reports" generally attempt to offer a precise picture of what has actually taken place, while the literariness of "Prison Literature" requires that these works stand at a distance from those actualities and, consequently, those reports. In an Introduction to *Zel Allah: She'r-ha-ye Zendan* (God's Shadow: Prison Poems), written about the prisons and political prisoners during the Shah's regime, Reza Baraheni expresses this quality of "Prison Reports"—its closeness to the actualities—in a poetic manner:

> The truth is that in these poems I did not try to use my imagination. Because the inferno in which the prisoner lives is the product of an evil and infernal imagination; the imagination of the Shah's executioners. There is no need for you to imagine. This inferno has been created in such a way that if you report its facts, you have made the greatest imaginations.[106]

Of course the word "distance" (i.e., "divergence from the actual") should not evoke "unrelatedness". Actually, since the word "distance" assumes a point of departure, the mere usage of this word suggests a relationship between Prison Literature and Prison Reports, between literariness and the factual. To describe this indirect relationship, in *Eisenstein's* Ivan the Terrible, Kristin Thompson uses her developed version of "background," another Formalist concept:

> For the Formalists, every work depends on its relations to other systems: nonpoetic language, other artworks, aspects of the everyday world. These external systems were referred to as *backgrounds*.[107]

In the present study, parts of these "external systems" have been referred to as secondary discourses and narratives controlled by the dominant discourse. I believe that with respect to prison literatures, one of the most important links between background and the literary work is that authors can select elements of this background—especially from dominant discourses and narratives—and use them in their literary works by making them "perceptible."[108] And as regards prison literature, the ensemble of perceptible components which have been created in this manner will assist the reader-critic to recognize the counter-discursive characteristic of these works.

The concept of background can be developed in another direction which recognizes the significance of a given background in creating a new system of signs and codes. With regard to prison literature, factual reports play the most important role in this process; indeed, for this reason, in examining prison literature, the concept of the city-prison is at the heart of the background. The semiological significance and richness of this city-prison—and consequently the new sign system—is rather for its novelty and difference with other systems which usually form the background. This city-prison is like an ancient city which has suddenly been discovered. It looks strange, incredible, even fictional. But it is quite tangible and real. This city has been formed under the influence of, or even because of, other systems such as the Islamic punitive-judiciary systems in Iran. Yet this city seems to be extremely self-contained. In previous pages I referred to some of the characteristics of this strange city and its people. Like fictional cities, the events and actualities of the city-prison and its inhabitants which at first seem strange are totally "reasonable" and "logical." The routine of being tortured and interrogated and insulted and threatened, the continuous efforts to find opportunities for everyday bare necessities, the constant remembering of those who have gone, the spending of part of every day blindfolded and in darkness, the learning how to walk in dark hallway-streets with wounded feet, the hearing of the children's happy voices as they play their prison games, the learning of ways to lessen pain, the being careful not to miss the daily bathroom calls or the weekly shower time, the learning how to decorate the small cell-homes with a torn piece of cloth or a statue made of left-over bread ... In this city such things are all considered "natural"; in fact they define this city and are understood only inside this city. This city even has its own language. Apart from the fact that any word or phrase pronounced in this city finds certain meaning because of the encompassing composition, there are specific expressions and phrases which make sense only in this environment.

After her release, Azam Kiakojouri, one of the inhabitants of this city, put together a small collection of these expressions. I cite only a few entries to emphasize the fact that this language is not limited to torture and death but covers many other "mundane" matters.

> **Picture Album of the Student's Life**: A Dossier which included names, pictures and reports on political activities of university students; prepared by Islamic Associations of universities and repentant prisoners.
>
> **Educational**: The closed-circuit prison television which broadcasts ideological programs and interviews with those who had repented. Watching this television was compulsory.
>
> **Testament Room**: The room to which prisoners were taken before their execution in order for them to write their last will and testament.
>
> **Emergency**: A person who needs to use the bathroom at a time other than the three or four times allowed per day.

Toilet Children: About ten female prisoners of Qezel Hasar who were forced to live in a toilet for several months.

Chicken Barbecue: Hitting a handcuffed prisoner hung by his hands while he is turned round and round.

Letter Day: The day on which prisoners were permitted to write letters. Usually the prison guard came with paper and pen; each prisoner was allowed to write five lines.

Store: A prison guard who would come round to the cells once a month with a list of food and items of clothing. Prisoners could use their money to buy some of these items.

Sleep Manager: The prisoner who was in charge of assigning the space for prisoners to sleep. When there was not enough room for all the prisoners to lie down, the Sleep Manager was in charge of designating their turn to sleep.[109]

This language and other aforementioned characteristics obviously indicate a kind of uniqueness about this city, but what gives richness and depth to this city-prison is the variety of unique voices. Quite possibly this is the result of feeling the constant presence of death close by. One of the best methods to describe the association of death and awareness is to remember a similar trope which is found in many literary traditions—especially in epic genres. In Persian literature, examples of the usage of this trope abound in Ferdowsi's *Shahnameh*. In many of the *Shahnameh*'s stories, once the heroes find death inevitable, they are suddenly distanced from the usual heroic-narrative style and find their own unique voices. One of the best, most famous examples is the story of Rostam and Sohrab. In this story, Rostam, the old hero of the *Shahnameh*, fights Sohrab, his twelve-year-old son. They do not know that they are related to one another. Throughout the fight, which lasts more than a day, Sohrab, who is still a child, acts and talks like a stereotypical mature hero: boasting, threatening, showing his manly skills and strength. But once Rostam, using his cunning and address, lays open his son's chest with a dagger and Sohrab realizes that he is going to die, he immediately finds his own voice. He becomes a 12-year-old boy who, defeated, threatens his foe with his father's revenge:

> Now should you, fishlike, plunge into the sea,
> Or cloak yourself in darkness like the night,
> Or like a star take refuge in the sky,
> And sever from the earth your shining light,
> Still when he learns that earth's my pillow now,
> My father will avenge my death on you.
> A hero from this noble band
> Will take this seal and show it to Rostam.
> "Sohrab's been slain, and humbled to the earth,"
> He'll say, "This happened while he searched for you."[110]

In the city-prison, death is always nearby and unique voices are abundant. Regrettably, numerous examples of such voices have reached us only through the last testaments of these prisoners. Many of these very short letters contain a few lines about the ideas and goals for which they are losing their lives, but the most effective moments are those in which the unique voice of the writer speaks in an unpredictable tone. Here are a few examples:

> ... I am writing these few lines as a happy farewell, with the expectation and desire that this is not really something important.
> First I start with the little ones, as usual. How is Ali, the little son of Hushang and my dearest sister? How is Olduz, that doll-like dancer? ... How about Ayla and Ayda? Are they still fighting or do they have a peaceful co-existence? How is my beloved Nazli? Is she still mesmerizing everyone with her cute speaking?
> Yusef[111]

> My dear father and mother, finally after ... days they handed down my sentence, and it seems that I am condemned to be executed.
> I have lots to say, but I cannot write anymore. I want to spend these moments with the happy memories we had together ...
> My Mojgan, my dear, my good sister,
> ... Tomorrow is your birthday and they will execute me in the morning. I don't know maybe even right now ...

> Dear Mersedeh,
> On the eve of your birthday I was tried, and on the eve of Mojgan's birthday they sentenced me. I really loved you and always thought about you. Mojgan, Mersedeh, don't let mom be too unhappy. Console her and tell her of other examples to calm her. Tell dad to forgive me. I really loved him.
> Manijeh[112]

> ... My dear ones, I am in a kind of state that I seriously don't know what to write ... As for the money you sent me, since I know you need it, I will send it back to you. It is about 1160 tomans. Dear mother, I am sending you the ring you had bought me. Please give my wedding ring to my mother-in-law. This is all I have, other than this shirt and pair of pants that I am wearing ...
> If my body does not reach Lahijan,[113] you can go to Golestan-e Choshal.[114] There is no time left. I don't know what else I would write ...
> I kiss you ...
> Hasan Jahangiri Lakani[115]

And there are countless such examples. When these voices are placed next to other characteristics of life in prison, gradually a surprisingly homogeneous architecture is formed; an architecture which is in fact a rich system of codes and signs.

Many works of prison literature contain references to the components of a background at the center of which this sign system is located. And indeed one of the possible readings of such texts is reading them against this background. Such a reading should not convey the idea that these literary works simply reflect the reality; nor should this reading be considered an example of a contextualist approach. As mentioned before, using the elements of this background helps in the making of perceptual effects in an autonomous literary reality. In fact, this is how "Whenever everyday life enters literature, it becomes itself literature, and should be evaluated as a literary fact."[116]

"Les Damnées du paradis": the emergence of a counter-discourse

Literary elements of a discursive transition

"Les Damnées du paradis"[117] (The Damned Souls of Paradise) opens with an explanation: One day, an exiled Iranian writer who lives in Paris receives an envelope which contains a story. It is the story of the life of a young woman in one of the prisons of the Islamic Republic. According to the author, the events "have taken place between 1360 and 1368, which correspond to 1981 to 1989 of the Gregorian calendar, in one of the prisons in the city of Tehran."[118] The appearance of the story is similar to other prison reports, but what places "Les Damnées du paradis" in the category of literature, as opposed to prison reports, is the situation-reality that is created at the end of the story, as well as the qualitative distance of this final situation-reality from the initial one.

The initial situation of the story as seen in the first few pages looks very simple. The narrator, along with her fellow inmates, has been in a prison which is called "school." This naming immediately reminds us of Khomeini's order that under the Islamic government prisons should become "education centers." The warden of this school is a man named Haji, and it is under his direction that all prisoners are required to spend their time learning the Qur'an. This character and his insistence on forcing the Qur'an are clearly reminiscent of the infamous "Haj Davud," the official in charge of Qezel Hasar prison. But this Haji is a "calm" and "quiet" man who tries not to use words related to "punishment," "vengeance," and "expiation." He even insists on calling this prison specifically a "religious school."[119] Of course, being in this religious school does not mean that prisoners have escaped the danger of execution. Not at all! The same Haji, as the master of the prison is responsible for letting the prisoners know of their death sentences. On many occasions, he is also the one who issues these death sentences, but he does so in the most "fatherly" manner.

> Haji was a calm and quiet man, whose most outrageous words were:
> — Be calm and have patience!
> With this phrase his interlocutor knew that it was time for her to write her testament. The following day she would leave this world.[120]

"Be calm and have patience!" This phrase immediately problematizes Haji's character; exactly like the parish priest of St Paul's who is present at the scene of the torture and death of Robert-François Damiens. When excessive pain "made [the condemned man] utter horrible cries," the priest "did not spare himself in offering consolation to the patient."[121] Indeed, the problematic character of Haji is displayed when we read that this absolute power, this promulgator of religious teachings and at the same time messenger of death and torture has also created a sense of gratitude among prisoners because of having founded such a school.

> He is our only hope. Throughout the time, we realized that a Qur'anic boarding school is better than a prison.[122]

Besides, Haji is the only one on whom prisoners can rely for different concerns, including the torment of not knowing about the future.

> We live in anxiety. We pin our last hope on the cold blood of Haji. We tell ourselves that if some danger threatens us, he will consult the Qur'an or will ask the opinion of God's representative [on Earth].[123]

With regard to the idea of background, previously discussed, the first implication of the phrase "God's representative," is the revival of the relationship between Khomeini and the absolute political power (sovereign) whose monarchist version (the Shah is the Shadow of God on Earth) is well known. As I have discussed in *Modern Reflections of Classical Traditions in Persian Fiction*, in the phrase "the Shah is the Shadow of God on Earth," in the post-revolution context, the word "Shah" became "*Velayat-e Faqih*" (Supreme Jurisprudence)—specifically, Khomeini. And indeed, Khomeini's first name, Ruhollah—breath of God—seems to have been made for facilitating this transition. Of course, besides this implication, the narrator, through specific allusions which we shall mention later, identifies the idea of God's representatives not only with Revolutionary guards in general but with the ugliest agents of this Qur'anic school.

In addition to mentioning the role and place of religion, specifically Islam and the Qur'an, in her description of this initial situation the narrator emphasizes the interdependent issues of obligatory *hejab*, love, sexuality, and consequently the position of women in these regards. When a man is about to enter the women's ward of this prison-religious school, Morad, one of the prison guards, who is also Haji's adopted son, shouts: "Cover your heads!"[124] Paying attention to the background connotes a context—for this statement—which is not necessarily limited, temporally and spatially, to the framework of the Islamic government and its prisons. This statement is also reminiscent of the Imperial guards who, especially during the reign of the Qajars, walked in front of the kings, and by shouting "Dur Sho, Kur Sho!" (Go away; Be blind!) announced the presence of the sovereign. Any contact or even a glance at the sovereign was considered insolence punishable by death, or at least by plucking the eyes from their sockets. The explanation by the narrator of "Les Damnées du paradis" of the prison guard's reason to shout "Cover your heads!" reveals the similarity between the functions of these two statements. "This was his way to announce the presence of the masculine."[125] This statement also reminds us of the famous slogan "Either a headscarf or a blow on the head"[126] used by pressure groups, shortly after the Revolution, to force women to cover their hair. Of course, this was one of the first, most significant projects of the Islamic government in the process of establishing and displaying its sovereignty. To disobey this order under the Islamic government had and has serious consequences. We have already read an example of such consequences: "Haji would knock and then immediately enter. As soon as he entered, he would kick and punch any prisoner who didn't have her chador on."[127] And the fear of such consequences imposes an abject surrender whose reflection in the prison-religious school is explicitly described: Hearing the order "Cover your heads!" and sensing men approaching,

> The experience has taught us to hide our hair and our faces as soon as possible and wrap our bodies in our chadors and sit in the hallway in a row against the wall, heads down and stuck to *harim*.[128]

As the writer explains in a footnote to the French text, the word *harim*—which means "wall" here—"refers to the women's quarters, but also to protection and protected women." This word could also symbolize the similarity between Haji's treatment of the women of the prison-school on the one hand and the relationship of Sultans and Caliphs with the women in their harems on the other. In one of the descriptions of the way Haji treats the prisoners, the narrator writes:

> When he [Haji] wanted to see one of us, a girl or a woman, he used the door at the end of his quarters which opens directly into our building. As the old woman who is our roommate says, he came to see us as if he was entering his *harem*. She is right. Haji is the only man who has the right to enter the "forbidden area" without notice.[129]

Even Haji acknowledges this relationship—"I consider you like my *harim*."[130] Of course, by using *harim* and not *harem*, he is trying to emphasize the protection aspect of this relationship. Yet the relationship between these two words is too obvious, and besides, by recounting the explanation of the teacher of Arabic, the narrator makes sure that the reader will not ignore this link:

> That morning, accidentally, our Arabic teacher had used this word to refer to the walls around us. He had explained that it was derived from the word "*harem*," and that it was applied also to a wife.[131]

Counter-interpretations of many of these elements play a decisive role in problematizing the initial situation and therefore the dominant discourse and narratives. One of the most revealing examples of these counter-interpretations is a discussion about a woman's sexual organ which undermines the place and function of sex and gender in the initial situation. A large textual space is allocated to this point, and as we will see, the treatment of this element by different techniques contributes greatly to the process of transition from the initial situation to the final situation. With regard to the initial situation, this point is referred to in a conversation between Haji and the narrator about the necessity of *mahrieh*[132] for girls before marriage. The narrator tells Haji:

— I don't want a *mahrieh*.
— That is impossible. It is as if you refuse to sleep with your husband. The *mahrieh* is the counterpart of the *boz*. And both are necessary conditions for a marriage to be legal.

I asked:

— What does *boz* mean?

Haji was so full of God's word that he explained without being embarrassed:

— The vessel of a woman's shame.[133]

This religious approach to a woman's sexual organ, which is clearly part of the narratives of the initial situation and in fact completes it, suddenly reminds the narrator of her conversations about the same topic with her mother. Her mother used to call this vessel of shame "caress," and continuously cautioned her: "Be careful about your caress!"[134] The narrator remembers that this phrase always "troubled her."

In "Les Damnées du paradis," these two episodes are juxtaposed. The first one—the narrator's conversation with Haji—belongs to the initial situation, but in the second one, the narrator reminisces about the narratives concerning this element—a woman's sexual organ—in a critical, even sarcastic manner. In addition, the narrator rejects the names given by the dominant discourse— whether through Haji's narrative or her mother's—to this organ, and in the process of making her own narrative, she calls it "there." This approach is indicative of the formation of a narrative-situation which, dissociated from the initial situation, is being created. Indeed, in the present reading of this story, the technique of juxtaposing the components representing the initial situation-dominant narratives on the one hand and the counter-interpretations of these components which are moving towards the creation of counter-narratives on the other, reveal the most recurrent literary technique of the story.[135] In the case of "Les Damnées du paradis," the dominant technique is the presentation of the story's elements in such a way that they provide the possibility of interpretations which would counter the "official" interpretations. In previous pages, I mentioned some of these elements and possibilities of interpreting them differently from the dominant interpretations. For example, the phrase "representatives of God on Earth," which posits a kind of legitimacy for these representatives, could also be reminiscent of the counter-narrative of "the Shah is the shadow of God," which effectively undermines this legitimacy. The shouting of "Cover your heads and face the walls" could also be read as the shouting of "Go away, be blind" of the warders of despotic kings or as the slogan of "Either a headscarf or a blow on the head" by the Whiteshirts[136] of the Islamic government. Prison which, from the point of view of the dominant narrative, is described as a religious and Qur'anic school could also be read as the harem of the legendary sultans of *A Thousand and One Nights.* And the Qur'anic narratives, those words of God uttered by Haji and other of God's representatives on Earth, which sometimes come upon strange similarities with religious-masculine narratives—for example in the case of the relationship between man and woman, specifically, the woman's sexual organ—could be ridiculed. Indeed, as we will see, the re-reading and counter-interpretation of the Qur'an has a seminal role in the formation of the counter-narrative of the final situation of "Les Damnées du paradis."

At this stage, however, new questions emerge: Why is it that despite the simultaneous presence of different interpretational possibilities from the very beginning of the story—suggesting the instability of the initial situation—is this situation described, even from the focal point of the mouthpieces of counter-narratives, as stable and unchangeable? Why do the narrator and her prison-mates "double their efforts" to memorize the word of God? Why is Haji—God's representative on Earth—who reads the Qur'an from beginning to end once a week, and at the same time easily issues death sentences, described as a father figure? Why is Morad the prison guard, and the adopted son of Haji and his likely successor, described in a rather positive manner? Why do not the narrator and other prisoners think about the deadly aspect of God's word, clearly one of the interpretational possibilities suggested by the narrator?

— Be calm and have patience!
With this phrase his interlocutor knew that the time had come for her to write her testament. The following day she would leave this world, because of a slight movement of Haji's lips, similar to one when he was reading the Qur'an. . . [137]

And why, in the initial situation, does not this interpretational possibility drive the narrator and her prison-mates away from God's word? How is it that they are quite aware of the stupidity of instructions and rules—as an interpretational possibility—which force them to cover themselves from head to toe and sit facing the wall, to even place their foreheads against the wall, yet this awareness has no outward indication? And in general, why is it that in this initial situation, counter-thoughts, counter-interpretations, and counter-discourses are not heard?

The answer is not difficult to find. It is clear that the dominant discourse always tries to control signs—which include the Qur'an, Shari'a laws, and characters such as the "*vali-ye amr*"[138] and Haji and Morad—and their interpretations. With regard to this control, once more the fundamental directive functions as the key dynamism: if peaceful means fail to achieve this control then by applying pressure, prison and torture, the process of "convincing" will be carried out successfully. And of course, at the end of this path, the ultimate solution is the physical eradication of creators of counter-interpretations. Obviously in the Qur'anic school of "Les Damnées du paradis," the second approach is being practiced. The narrator explains the beginning of this school and the prisoners' fondness for God's word:

> It has been a few years already; during the first months of residence here, some girls rejected the lessons of the Book. Haji firmly tried to send them back on the path of wisdom. Resistance on one side and insistence on another lasted until he ordered them one after another:
> — Be calm and have patience!
> Pale, horror-stricken we stared at the disobedient ones. The following day, they were not in class, nor did they return home. And we, we doubled our efforts, and "calmly" learned by heart the words of God.[139]

"Convincing" female prisoners to accept *hejab* and "convincing" them to accept the idea that looking at *na-mahram* men[140] is a grave sin is a similar process. In this regard the narrator recounts the story of a day when a religious judge came to their ward along with a few other men. As usual, the prisoners rapidly cover their bodies from head to toe and sit down, facing the wall,

> ... heads down, foreheads stuck to the *harim*. In this position we cannot see anything. And we have to be silent. We do not speak unless we are questioned. And without ever looking at men who are behind us. Apparently they are not *mahram*. Looking at them is a sin. Nevertheless, once, a tall, beautiful Kurd dared to turn her head; deliberately. She looked at the men one by one. She stared for a long time at the spiritual face of the religious judge. The sun had not set yet when Haji entered the harem:
> — Pack your suitcase. It is tomorrow. Have patience and be calm![141]

The violence that exists in this process of "convincing," in the universe of the text, becomes an element which functions against the dominant discourse. In other words, this violence becomes a textual violence which is indicative of sudden disruption and rupture in the course of the story.[142] This violence also functions as "the force that is necessary to set the narrative in motion."[143] As Thompson has argued, this term—violence—borrowed from Stephen Heath, is in direct relationship with the "traditional notion of *conflict*." She clarifies this "traditional notion of *conflict*" by alluding to Tomashevski's description of "conflict" which emphasizes the confronting interests and the "discord and struggle among characters."[144] I believe the concept of textual violence could also be developed, in a more literary fashion, in relation to the formation of countering narratives. In fact the fast pace of "Les Damnées du paradis" and the rapid formation of a counter-narrative which leads to the emergence of the final situation is due to the presence of various instances of violence. The most important of such examples is the reference to the 1988 executions of prisoners which I touched on in the previous segment.

As mentioned in 1988, a fatwa-instruction was issued by Khomeini according to which those prisoners who were judged by a three-member committee to be *mortad* (apostate) had to be immediately executed. Many prisoners were killed and buried in mass graves. During this process, it was said that many virgin girls were raped by prison guards/guardians of Islam and the Islamic Revolution before being executed. In this regard Montazeri reproduces a letter written to Khomeini which addresses the treatment of prisoners by the Islamic government. He writes:

> Do you know that in the prisons of the Islamic Republic, and in the name of Islam, such crimes have been committed that even during the evil Regime of the Shah, nothing similar to them was done?!
>
> Do you know that many have died under the torture of the inter-rogators? Do you know that in the Mashhad prison, because of the lack of a doctor and of treatment for young girls, they later had to remove the uteri of twenty-five girls, thus mutilating them?
>
> Do you know that in the Shiraz prison, a girl who was fasting was executed shortly after dinner for a minor offense?
>
> Do you know that in some of the prisons of the Islamic Republic, they raped young girls?[145]

In all these cases, they tried to find Islamic justifications for these acts. With regard to raping girls before executing them, some had actually relied on what Montazeri had said to come up with such a justification. Montazeri explains that in one of his letters he had mentioned that "girls should not be executed"; according to him, by using the word "girl" he meant all "female" prisoners, not just virgins But some interpreted this phrase differently and concluded that virgin prisoners should become *sigheh*[146] first, and then be executed.[147] The other argument heard concerning this act—the reflection of which is seen in "Les Damnées du paradis"—was that since it was said that virgins will go to paradise then it is necessary to first deflower these sinners—to prevent their entrance to paradise—and then execute them. Of course, this had to be done in an Islamic way: making them *sigheh*.[148] In "Les Damnées du paradis," one day a young judge comes to prison with an entourage and says: "Girls on one side and women on the other."[149] As soon as the prisoners find out that women are "going" and girls staying, thinking that the women are going to be released, they all try to place themselves in front of a midwife who has come with the judge and is in charge of separating the women from the girls. But before long, the reason for this separation is revealed by a new prisoner. According to her, prisoners are going to be executed. Women will be executed immediately, but the girls have a different fate. Prison guards are going to "marry" the girls before executing them. As a sign of "marriage," these "bridegrooms" even take sugar and sugar candy to the house of the prisoner's parents[150] to make everything Islamic and traditional. Then, two days later, usually the same bridegroom brings the news of the girl's death to the parents. Answering the question of the narrator about the reason of this act, the new prisoner says: "They say 'The virgin goes directly to heaven. We are heathens. By making a hole in our bodies, these gentlemen prevent us from entering Paradise.'"[151]

Thus the most violent moment of the text—and therefore of the narrative dynamic of the text—which began with a fatwa is defined through the violent acts of rape and inescapable death. When the narrator helps the new prisoner to commit suicide, this certitude is internalized. Responding to the request of the new prisoner, the narrator follows her to the toilet in the middle of the night and sees her standing on a trashcan. She has a noose made of pieces of her dress around her neck; she asks the narrator to tie her hands. It is from this moment on that it seems the certitude of death creates a kind of awareness and courage in the narrator's mind. This is another example of the association of death and awareness topos according to which heroes, as soon as they find death unavoidable, suddenly dissociate themselves from the dominant narrative style and find their own voices. In "Les Damnées du paradis," too, the story of the Kurdish girl is an example of the violence which, in its ultimate form—inescapable death—turns into a dynamic which actualizes the potential of the presence of counter-interpretations and counter-narratives. This is how the control of the signs and their interpretations is taken away from the officials of the dominant discourse. In this episode, after Haji condemns the Kurdish girl for the crime of staring at the face of the religious judge and at the other men:

> The Kurd, whose voice was even more beautiful than her face, offered us a recital of songs of her homeland, and her magnificent voice filled the hallways of all the buildings. When the call for prayer sounded, we all did our ablutions. She loosened her braids and her combed hair fell to her waist. She put on a sleeveless dress with a pattern of flowers. With the aid of a few things, she put on such makeup as if she had a magic pen in her hand. Smiling, she hugged each one of us. At the end, she read a Qur'anic story that she had copied into her notebook:
>
> *Holy Gabriel, peace be upon him, told Lot: "Go, and no one should turn or look back; except your wife." Lot's wife turned and looked. She committed the sin. A stone fell on her and killed her.*
>
> And the Kurd burst out laughing.
>
> The sun was rising. She was dancing towards the exit, her head and legs uncovered. In the room, we were crying.[152]

This episode is a wonderful example of the dominant technique of the story. The Kurdish girl is re-telling a story written based on the Qur'anic verses about Lot and his wife,[153] but her reading takes place in a composition which includes elements such as the girl's long braids, her sleeveless dress, her uncovered legs and head, her putting-on of makeup as the others are preparing themselves for prayers, and most importantly, laughing at the Qur'anic story. According to the prison officials all these things are clear violations of the Qur'anic teachings. Here, it is the positionality of the Qur'anic story in this composition which has a determining effect on the meaning of the words uttered. This composition and the specific places of its elements not only point to a different reading of the Qur'an and prayers but, in a broader context, represent a different narrative of what is taking place. The formation of this new composition which swiftly deconstructs the dominant narrative is above all else indebted to the change of the focal point through which the Qur'anic story is read/interpreted. Up to this point, the dominant discourse had forced the readers of the Qur'an and Qur'anic stories to read this episode from the viewpoint of Lot and other survivors; this is the first time that this part is read from the viewpoint of Lot's wife—the Kurdish girl. And suddenly the cruelty of the story becomes evident. Indeed, what would happen if the Qur'an, this central piece of the dominant discourse and its narratives, is read through the eyes of the victims?

At this point in the story, the text's strategy is to oust the dominant narratives of the Qur'an and of God and of his representatives on Earth by creating appropriate contexts and compositions and initiating counter-narratives. The fatwa of executing the apostates and then the ruling of the prison officials according to which girls should be subjected to "marriage" first and then be executed defines the framework within which this strategy is going to be represented. The key moment of the text which initiates the sudden move of the narrator—who, because of the textual (and meta-textual) violence of the certitude of death has grown rapidly and acquired instant awareness— towards this strategy begins with a description of the way these ceremonies are carried out:

> My companions have been taken to the bridal chamber, one after another, unconscious and involuntarily. Instead of tasting from the boiling fountain of milk and honey, they tasted dreadful lechery, the obligatory pleasure. They let out the first long, deafening, continuous cry.[154]

After a short time, the sound of firing of arms that men have aimed at sky is heard:

> They were firing to show their passion and pleasure, to cover the wailing of women which it is forbidden to hear.[155]

The Qur'anic paradise according to the narrator-huris

If these men are asked about their acts they will surely say that they are implementing divine-Islamic laws. Indeed these men exemplify the New Testament's premonition: "The time will come when whoever kills you will think he is doing a holy service for God."[156] It is at this juncture that the narrator places herself in a decisive manner against such a reading of the Book: " ... I will not allow [them] to treat me the same way."[157] Of course, even without this obvious rejection, the narrator's means to advance the strategy of the text are revealed through her characterization of the "wedding night." While the men name this relationship "wedding" and "marriage consummation," the narrator calls it "rape." Naming is a crucial component of the process of controlling and interpreting the signs, and plays a decisive role in defining the battlefield of countering narratives. The narrator's sarcastic and bitter reference to the reading of parts of the Qur'an by guardians of the dominant discourse clarifies this battlefield even more:

> Every guardian of the Revolution who has come back from the [Iran–Iraq] War knows [these verses]:
> *And the huris, who are like hidden pearls, are rewards for what they did. Immortal ephebes move about them.*
> *Virgins are there, the most excellent ones; huris are there, retired in their pavilions, never before deflowered by humans or jinns, sitting with their elbows on green cushions and beautiful carpets.*[158]

The reading of the Kurdish girl/Lot's wife of the Qur'anic story of the death of Lot's wife was undoubtedly educational for the narrator; and, following that principle, this time she looks at the Qur'anic description of Paradise through the eyes of the huris.

Indeed, who has talked about this Paradise from the viewpoint of huris? Devout Moslems have been promised that in Paradise they will have virgin girls—huris—in their arms. How would a huri feel when she finds out that she has been promised to a devout Moslem? When they are "given" to these pious ones and there is no mention of their consent, could any word other than "violated" characterize what happens to them? Worst of all, in this Paradise, so much emphasis is placed on virginity that one wonders what happens to huris when they lose their virginity. Are they going to be banished from Paradise? Are they going to be executed?

Having read the Qur'anic Paradise through the eyes of the huris, it is not difficult to find similarities between the treatment of the huris by devout Moslems/guardians of Islam and the Revolution on the one hand and the virgin prisoners by the same guardians/prison guards on the other. That is, the reading of huri-prisoners of the Qur'anic Paradise suggests that God's representatives on Earth are trying to create in this world the Paradise promised to them in the other world. At this point the structure of huri-prisoners' counter-narrative finds a precise strategy based on an "anti-utopian"[159] outlook. Based on this outlook, the fear is not that the promised Paradise might not be achieved; it is the thought of the realization of this Paradise which is horrible. To demonstrate this horror and as part of the overall counter-narrative, the main goal of this strategy is to superimpose the "bridal chamber" of the prison/ religious school on the heavenly Paradise. This strategy leads to the creation of the final situation. From this point on, the narrator takes the initiative and in each step exercises more control over the narrative devices and tools.

As the initial step in creating the final situation, the narrator asks Morad to marry her. This initiative is based on an assumption. Both the huri-prisoners and the prison guards know that what takes place on the eve of execution is outright rape, and that Morad's explanation (as well as that of Haji and other "brothers") "This has nothing to do with rape ... this is an imposed union, a religious duty; the 'brothers' say that this is making love without pleasure"[160] is a ridiculous argument and a justification which could be considered a "convincing" explanation only if it is backed up by torture and threat of guns and bullets. In fact, even these "brothers" know that their only motivation for spending an hour in the "bridal chamber" is to experience a brute pleasure tainted by the pain of the huri-prisoners. (And they are prepared to do anything to repeat this experience in the promised Paradise.) By proposing to Morad, the narrator attempts to change the nature of this experience and places herself in control. "I will not allow [them] to treat me the same way. I want to make love to Morad, the adopted son of Haji."[161]

In a larger context, this decision also confronts the shaming, degrading and even repulsive description by the dominant discourse of the place of woman and specifically of her sexual organ in a sexual relationship. In this regard, the dominant discourse not only includes the narratives of God's representatives but also the narratives of the masculine culture. In previous pages, I referred to one of the conversations of the narrator and her mother and the mother's abashed words about women's reproductive organs and her emphasis on their protection. In another conversation, the narrator asks her mother:

— How was making love with my father?

She answered bitterly:

— Like mourning!

And she added:

— I let him do his damn thing. And you?

— It was like "ashes poured on my head."[162]

And indeed, the presence of occasional erotic passages in the descriptions of the "wedding night" of the narrator and Morad,[163] by standing in direct contradiction to such examples of the dominant discourse of the initial situation, implies the creation of the antiutopia, the "Glass Paradise," of the final situation.

Once the marriage proposal is accepted by Morad and Haji, the rest is easy. The narrator has been reading the Qur'an so much, for many years, that she knows it by heart. Yet in order to make sure that in her satirical reconstruction of the heavenly Paradise even the smallest details are respected, she has a copy of the Qur'an in hand during this reconstruction process. And she recreates and decorates the "bridal chamber" exactly like the promised Paradise:

> Today, while waiting for him, I cut my dress and my clothes into pieces, as well as those of all of my companions who had been forced to get married before me. The fabrics are of different colors. I have set them on the floor, pasted them on the walls up to the sky. I have created this image of Eden that I have seen in the Book. For myself and Morad, I have created the Paradise …
>
> My husband enters the bridal chamber. He closes the door behind him. And I read, calmly, articulating properly:
>
> *And here they are in a safe refuge. They are lounged in gardens next to the fountains and creeks, dressed in delicate green-colored silk and brocade. We marry them to beautiful-eyed huris.*[164]

This counter-narrative is reminiscent of the court of Shahriyar, the Sultan in the tales of *A Thousand and One Nights*; the Sultan who, every night, sleeps with a virgin girl and in the morning kills her, and that is how he creates the promised Paradise on Earth. This counter-narrative image which owes its beauty to the colorful dresses of huris who have been killed after being violated needs one more component to complete the final image: the narrator's execution.

The morning after the "wedding night," Morad offers to help the narrator so that she can escape and then live with him. The narrator laughs at his stupidity. The construction of this counter-narrative has been her only goal, and it must be completed. If the narrator does not meet her death, a death similar to that of other huri-prisoners, the structure of the final situation and the counter-narrative will collapse. The narrator asks Morad for two things: first, she wants him to treat her exactly like others and be the one who will shoot her:

> In exchange for our last night's pleasure, I want you, Morad, to finish me off, tomorrow. Not in a chador; in a bag, like my companions.[165]

The other thing she asks him for is to give her time to write this story. At the end of the story, Morad comes back to perform his duty and provide the last piece of the counter-narrative of huri-prisoners:

> I hear Morad's steps.[166]

Notes

1 At this juncture, I am not including those affiliated with the Shah's regime as part of this discursive confrontation. The dominant discourse under the Shah had collapsed during the Revolution, and, in fact, the precondition for the inclusion of any discourse in the new scene was the total negation and even the denial of the existence of a pre-Revolutionary discourse. Of course, it did not take long before many people who considered the obliteration of those dependent on the Shah's regime to be "normal" realized the premonitory significance of this cleansing period, which was supposed to be temporary but never came to an end.

2 It was learned later that many individuals in this second group had been sent to these gatherings by the members of the new government. Some of these individuals became founders of infamous pressure groups which were directed and led (and are still led) by the most senior members of the Islamic regime.

3 Guy Debord, *Comments on the Society of the Spectacle*, translated by Malcolm Imrie, (1988) www.notbored.org/commentaires.html (accessed May 5, 2014).

4 In future chapters I will discuss this theory in detail.

5 Steven Best and Douglas Kellner, "Debord and the Postmodern Turn: New Stages of the Spectacle," 1999, www.uta.edu/huma/illuminations/kell17.htm (accessed May 5, 2014).

6 Debord, *Comments on the Society of the Spectacle*. It should be noted that in this text, Debord mentions that since the publication of *The Society of the Spectacle*, another form has been developed which is a combination of the two previous ones and has been pioneered in France and Italy.

7 For more on this subject, consult Hayden White, *The Content of the Form: Narrative Discourse and Historical Representation*, Baltimore, MD: Johns Hopkins University Press, 1987, Chapter 5.

8 One of the best analyses not influenced by a particular political organization is *Iran: Comment sortir d'une revolution religieuse* (How to Come Through a Religious Revolution) by Farhad Khosrokhavar and Olivier Roy (Editions du Seuil, 1999). Having discussed the underlying reasons for social unrest and the role of various political forces in the Revolution, the authors refer to Khomeini's reluctant move to France: "The forced departure of Khomeini from Najaf to France on October 16, 1978, made him the emblematic leader of the Revolution." (p. 23) And this was only a few months before the total collapse of the monarchy.

9 Habibollah Davaran and Farhad Behbahani, *Dar Mehmani-ye Haji Aqa* (At Haji Aqa's Gathering), Tehran: Omid-e Farda (1382/2003), pp. 191–192.

10 This is a famous statement by Khomeini from one of his speeches when he was speaking about Marxists; he was attempting to confront Marxism by rejecting the supposedly Marxist notion that everything is based on economics.

11 This is an excerpt from a speech by Dr. Ali Larijani, then head of the government-controlled Iranian National Radio and Television, on the occasion of Mohammad's birthday. Like those who deny the existence of Nazi Germany's death camps and the Holocaust, Larijani, in the same speech, added: "Unfortunately, today many lies are told about the Iranians before Islam and their level of civilization and culture, and also about the burning of libraries during the attack of Moslems [during the invasion of Iran by Moslems in 632]." www.balatarin.com/permlink/2009/9/30/1780356 (accessed May 5, 2014).

12 Peter Chelkowski and Hamid Dabashi, *Staging a Revolution: The Art of Persuasion in the Islamic Republic of Iran*, New York: New York University Press, 1999, p. 276.

13 Much energy has been devoted to such matters. For example, schoolchildren are bombarded with the importance of such "values" and the fear of ending up in

Hell to such an extent that it has sometimes happened that children have complained to their teachers and principals that their mothers do not follow these instructions properly, and that they are afraid that their mothers might end up in Hell! The Islamic government considers these events as the success stories of the dissemination of Islam.

14 The Iranian Government has been using different filtering and blocking methods to prevent free access to many websites they find objectionable. In addition to the Internet, the Islamic government has passed a law which prohibits the possession of satellite dishes because, through this technology, uncontrolled TV programs could be accessed.

15 Suroosh Irfani, *Iran's Islamic Revolution: Popular Liberation or Religious Dictatorship?* London: Zed Books, 1983, p. 191.

16 "Fedaian" is the more accepted transcription of the Persian word.

17 In a recent interview, Ebrahim Yazdi, one of Khomeini's advisors at the beginning of the Revolution as well as a Minister of Foreign Affairs in the transitional revolutionary government, speaks about the way in which Amir Abbas Hoveyda who had been Iran's Prime Minister for almost 14 years during the Shah's rule, and a few other officials were executed without being tried. Yazdi adds that in most cases, Khomeini personally issued the execution orders. This is only one example of such blind executions which took place after the Revolution. See www.khandaniha.eu/items.php?id=274 (accessed May 5, 2014).

18 In his very short essay "Taraj-e Tan, Jerahat-e Jan" (Raiding the Body, Injuring the Soul), Behruz Sheida alludes to the same scene of torture in Foucault's Discipline and Punish and to Foucauldian arguments about "pre-modern [system of] punishment" and the role of spectacle in that system. He then offers readings of three works of Persian prison fiction, including Ali Erfan's "Les Damnées du paradis", which, he considers as representation of simultaneous pre-modern and modern systems of punishment (http://asre-nou.net/1381/bahman/2/m-sheidai. html). While his readings of Foucault and Ali Erfan's work are vastly different from the ones offered in this text, I wish to fully acknowledge him and his "Taraj-e Tan, Jerahat-e Jan" (Raiding the Body, Injuring the Soul) as a source of inspiration for this section of the book.

19 Michel Foucault, *Discipline and Punish: The Birth of the Prison*, translated by Alan Sheridan, pp. 3–4.

20 Ibid., p. 4.

21 Ibid., p. 5.

22 Ibid., p. 5.

23 Michel Foucault, *Surveiller et punir*, Paris: Gallimard, 1975, p. 14. ("La punition a cessé peu à peu d'être une scène"). My translation. Obviously Foucault's use of the word "spectacle" is different from Debord's concept of spectacle.

24 Foucault, *Discipline and Punish*, p. 208.

25 Darius Rejali, *Torture and Modernity: Self, Society, and State in Modern Iran*, Boulder, CO: Westview Press, 1993, pp. 15–16.

26 Talal Asad, "Reflections on Cruelty and Torture," in *Formations of the Secular: Christianity, Islam, Modernity*, Stanford, CA: Stanford University Press, 2003, p. 105.

27 Ibid., p. 104.

28 See iran-e-azad.org. "Stoning to Death in Iran: A Crime Against Humanity Carried Out By the Mullahs' Regime", www.iran-e-azad.org/stoning/video.html (accessed May 5, 2014).

29 Usually the cutting off of different body parts does not take place in public, primarily because after the punishment is carried out, the condemned man needs medical attention. But the presence of his lynched body among the people is itself another spectacle.

30 Both during the Shah's regime and the Islamic government, all political prisoners have been accused of this generic "crime."
31 To hear the last defense of Khosrow Golsorkhi in its totality, 1973, see www.you tube.com/watch?v=buTlBLGdUfo (accessed May 5, 2014).
32 It is appropriate at this point to mention that, throughout this section, I am not trying to answer the question of whether this was true Islam or not. I am aware that not only the followers of Islam but also many academics in the West have always tried either to avoid taking a specific position on such matters or to attribute it to a particular reading of Islam. Precisely for this reason, I believe there is still a need to examine this issue from a "disinterested" standpoint.
33 Established by Khomeini, the Expediency Council is the final arbiter between the Parliament and the Council of the Guardians. When a legislation is passed by the Parliament, it is sent to the Council of the Guardians which is supposed to check the new law to make sure it is not against Islam and the Constitution. If there is disagreement between these two bodies, the case is sent to the Expediency Council. It should be noted that in recent years (after the election of Mahmud Ahmadinejad in 2005) Rafsanjani's clout has diminished significantly.
34 *Ettela'at*, October 31, 1981. This quote comes from People's Mojahedin Organization of Iran, *Crime against Humanity*, 2001, www.mojahedin.org/english/books/ Crime_Against_Humanity.pdf (accessed May 5, 2014), p. 52.
35 All translations of the Qur'anic verses are taken from www.biharanjuman.org/ Quran/quran_translation.html, which has three major translations done by Abdullah Yusuf Ali, Mohammed Habib Shakir, and William Pickthall.
36 This term was used by the Islamic government to refer to the Mojahedin (strugglers/ fighters); members of an opposition group involved in armed struggle against the government. Many of them were killed by the Islamic government; the rest had to flee the country. After a few years, they went to Iraq and remained there until 2004. A small group of them is still (2014) in Iraq.
37 Here, Khomeini refers to the crime of "*Mohareb ba khoda*" (one who fights against God).
38 Quite possibly he is referring to the following verse from the Qur'an: "Muhammad is the Messenger of Allah, and those with him are firm of heart against the unbelievers, compassionate among themselves." (48.29)
39 Hosein-Ali Montazeri, *Memoirs*, Appendix 152. Unless otherwise stated, translations are mine.
40 Montazeri uses the estimates of those who were involved in this process and puts the number of executed prisoners between 2,800 and 3,000. Many political organizations of opposition believe the number is much higher. Since the great majority of these victims are buried in mass graves, it is practically impossible at this point to arrive at a precise number.
41 Montazeri, *Memoirs*, Appendix 152.
42 Ibid.
43 *Tawzih al-Masa'el* is a text that high-ranking clerics write in order to answer common questions by ordinary people. It also contains principal legal issues, including punishments for different crimes.
44 Hosein-Ali Montazeri, *Tawzih al-Masa'el*, Qom: Markaz-e Entesharat-e Daftar-e Tablighat-e Eslami, 1984, p. 561.
45 Ibid., pp. 561–562.
46 In one of his articles, Masud Behnud, a veteran journalist, refers to Mesbah Yazdi's point:

> The fact that Mesbah and Jannati keep talking about bitter consequences and promise punishment in this world and have no solution other than making threats is indicative of a defeat which can no longer be hidden. If the fact that

after twenty-four years Mesbah Yazdi, who, according to the officials of the Friday prayer, does not speak without research and documentation, admits that ninety percent of educated people are moving away from religion and ignore the narratives that these gentlemen have brought does not signal bankruptcy, then what does?

www.pyknet.net/1382/page/09tir/p407jabari.htm
(accessed May 5, 2014)

47 On many occasions, these pressure groups, which are affiliated with the right wing of the Islamic government—the faction which wields the real power—have even attacked the opposition inside the government; but even when they have killed or tried to kill such figures, they have not received any significant punishment. One of the famous examples is the case of Said Hajjarian, a political activist and one of the main figures of the Reform Movement. In 1999 he was shot and wounded in an assassination attempt by Said Asgar. Hajjarian survived the attempt but he has since been confined to a wheelchair, and his speaking ability has been diminished significantly. Asgar was arrested shortly after the event. He was sentenced to fifteen years; then it was reduced to four years, and he was released after a very short time. See www.aswat.com/en/node/1926 (accessed May 5, 2014). What is even more comical is that Hajjarian was arrested after the uprising which took place after the 2009 presidential elections. He spent three months in prison and of course was brought on television recanting his words and actions and explaining why and how he had been deceived by the enemies of the Islamic government.

48 Foucault, *Discipline and Punish*, pp. 195–196.
49 Ibid., p. 200.
50 This treatment of political prisoners has been documented in many prison reports. In future pages of this chapter a number of these reports will be mentioned.
51 Ataollah Mohajerani, *Behesht-e Khakestari* (Grey Paradise), Tehran: Omid-e Iranian, 1382/2003, p. 54. The description of this paradise as well as the title of book are reminiscent of Zamyatin's description of a "glass paradise" in *We*, although the underpinnings are completely different. In *We*, Zamyatin "portrays a 'glass paradise' in which all men live in principled unprivacy, without a self to hide or a mood to indulge." Irving Howe, *Decline of the New*, New York: Harcourt, Brace & World, 1970, p. 67.
52 Foucault, *Discipline and Punish*, pp. 207–208.
53 www.iran-e-azad.org/stoning/women.html (accessed May 5, 2014).
54 Ervand Abrahamian, *Tortured Confessions: Prisons and Recantations in Modern Iran*, Berkeley and Los Angeles, CA: University of California Press, 1999, p. 204.
55 Mahmud Etemadzadeh (mostly known under his pen-name, M. A. Behazin, 1915–2006), who was also a member of the Tudeh Party and was also arrested during the same period, wrote about meeting his old friend, Tabari in prison. Although Behazin also went on television and recanted, he thought Tabari went too far. In his prison memoir, he writes about Tabari's willingness to collaborate with the regime and basically accuses him of selling himself out because "It is in his nature to think of himself and his wellbeing" in any and every situation. *Bar-e Digar va in Bar …* (Once Again and This Time …), 1370/1991. pp. 116–117. www.iranian.de/Main/khaterate%20be%20azin.pdf (Accessed May 5, 2014).
56 Abrahamian, *Tortured Confessions*, p. 204.
57 Parsipur has been living in the United States for many years now, and even during these years has never suggested that she is a political activist.
58 Shahrnush Parsipur, *Khaterat-e Zandan* (Prison Memoirs), p. 96.
59 Ibid., p. 297.

60 Ibid., pp. 297–298.
61 Here the prisoner refers to the fact that her name, "Azita" is not a religious name.
62 Parsipur, *Prison Memoirs*, p. 289.
63 Ibid., pp. 287–288.
    It should be added that in some cases even these confessions were not enough for the prison officials, and recanting prisoners had to participate in the execution of their friends in order to prove their allegiance to the true Islam and Islamic government.
64 *Haji* or its abbreviated form, *Haj*, is a title given to those who have performed the ritual of Islamic pilgrimage to Mecca.
65 Monireh Baradaran, *Haqiqat-e Sadeh* (Simple Truth), p. 89.
66 *Namus* means honor and also the women of a family under the protection of a man. In a traditional context, protecting Namus means preventing women of the family from behaving in such a way which would dishonor the family.
67 Parvaneh Alizadeh, *Khub Negah Konid, Rastaki Ast* (Look well; It is True), pp. 74–75. My emphasis.
68 *Ta'zir* is a religious punishment which is not specifically defined. In every case the kind and amount of *ta'zir* is decided by the Shari'a judge or the Imam.
69 Parsipur, *Prison Memoirs* p. 96.
70 Baradaran, *Simple Truth*, p. 24.
71 In addition to the many texts to which I have referred in this study, there are a number of other memoirs or descriptive analyses of the situation of Iranian political prisoners which are extremely helpful in terms of familiarizing the reader with various torture techniques used in the prisons of the Islamic government in Iran. Houshang Asadi's *Letters to My Torturer: Love, Revolution, and Imprisonment in Iran*, and Iraj Mesdaghi's *Nah Zistan nah Marg* (Neither Life nor Death) are among the noteworthy ones.
72 Here, the title "Haji," as in almost all prisons, is used generically and is not necessarily referring to the Haji, that is, Haj Davud Rahmani.
73 Davaran and Behbahani, *At Haji Aqa's Gathering*, pp. 104–105.
74 Ibid., pp. 115–117.
75 Alizadeh, *Look well; It is True*, pp. 19–20.
76 Masud Rajavi was (and still is) the leader of *Mojahedin-e Khalq*. In February 1982, his wife, Ashraf Rabi'i and a number of other *Mojahed*s were killed in a shootout with government agents.
77 Parsipur, *Prison Memoirs*, p. 183.
78 Montazeri, *Memoirs*, Appendix 152.
79 Even if some people had doubts about such reports, after the murder of Zahra Kazemi, an Iranian-Canadian journalist—her case received attention only because of the Canadian component of her citizenship—who died of the beating she received during interrogation, nobody doubts the routine usage of such methods in the prisons of the Islamic government.
80 Montazeri, *Memoirs*, Appendix 97.
81 Ibid., Appendix 97.
82 Rejali, *Torture and Modernity*, p. 118.
83 Chelkowski and Dabashi, *Staging a Revolution,* p. 232.
84 Ibid., p. 232.
85 www.equal-rights-now.com/April2011/sodabeh%20azadi-.htm (accessed May 5, 2014).
86 F. Azad, *Yadha-ye Zendan* (Prison Memories), p. 73.
    This pressure sometimes worked. In one of his lectures, Akbar Sarduzami, an author who has worked on prison memoirs, refers to this point and remembers a sentence, uttered by a woman prisoner, which is repeated obsessively in his mind: "Every morning, for the sake of one bottle of milk for my child, I said hello to

my interrogator." See Akbar Sarduzami, "A Simple Sentence," in *Ketab-e Zandan* (The Prison Book), ed. Naser Mohajer, vol. 2, p. 442.

87 Azad, *Prison Memories*, p. 83.
88 Ibid., p. 69.
89 Ibid., pp. 67–68.
90 Baradaran, *Simple Truth*, p. 265.
91 Azad, *Prison Memories*, p. 71.
92 Alizadeh, *Look well; It is true*, p. 53.
93 Qur'an (8.13).
94 "If the hypocrites and those in whose hearts is a disease and the agitators in the city do not desist, We shall most certainly set you over them, then they shall not be your neighbors in it but for a little while; Cursed: wherever they are found they shall be seized and murdered, a (horrible) murdering." (Qur'an, 8.60–61)
95 Parsipur, *Prison Memoirs*, p. 139.
96 Ibid., p. 215.
97 *Azan*; the call to prayer. It is recited in a loud voice to announce to the faithful that it is time for the obligatory prayer.
98 Farideh Zebarjad, "Az Band Rastegan ra Daryabim" (Let Us Care for Surviving Prisoners), in *Ketab-e Zendan*, vol. 2, p. 354.
99 Azad, *Prison Memories*, p. 15.
100 Ibid., p. 182.
101 Baradaran, *Simple Truth*, p. 391.
102 Azad, *Prison Memories*, p. 182.
103 Rejali, *Torture and Modernity*, p. 124.
104 Viktor Erlich, *Russian Formalism: History-Doctrine*, The Hague: Mouton and Co. 1965, p. 200.
105 Ibid., p. 252.
106 Reza Baraheni, *Zel Allah: She'r-ha-ye Zendan* (God's Shadow: Prison Poems), Tehran: Amir Kabir, 1358/1979), p. 38. Of course I do not believe that Baraheni has not used any "imagination" in producing those poems. What could be said about this collection of poems and a number of other prison-related works by Baraheni is that they always contain a meshing of the actual and the non-actual. This combination represents a type of literary production which could be called a "report-story." In the following chapters, I will discuss some of these works and their relationship to the emergence of the literary version of a historiographic counter-discourse in detail.
107 Kristin Thompson, *Eisenstein's* Ivan the Terrible: *A Neoformalist Analysis*, Princeton, NJ: Princeton University Press, 1981, p. 12.
108 The notion of "perceptibility" here draws on Viktor Shklovsky's doctrine of perceptibility versus automatism. In *Xod konja* he explained this doctrine in the context of "art form":

> Each art form travels down the inevitable road from birth to death; from seeing and sensory perception, when every detail in the object is savored and relished, to mere recognition, when the object or form becomes a dull epigone which our senses register mechanically, a piece of merchandise not visible even to the buyer. (Quoted from *Russian Formalism*, p. 252)

To read more about perceptibility and automatism, refer to the "Doctrine" section of Erlich's *Russian Formalism*.
109 http://iranian.com/BTW/2003/November/Prison/Images/farhang.pdf (accessed May 5, 2014).
110 Jerome Clinton, Translator, *The Tragedy of Sohrab and Rostam*, Seattle, WA: University of Washington Press, 1987, pp. 151–153.

111 Masud Noqreh-Kar, http://news.gooya.com/politics/archives/035235.php (accessed May 5, 2014).

112 Masud Noqreh-Kar, http://news.gooya.com/politics/archives/2006/03/045902print.php (accessed May 5, 2014).

113 Lahijan is a city in northern Iran.

114 Choshal is a very small village in northern Iran.

115 Shahla Shafiq, "Piruzi-ye Laisite bar Marg" (The Triumph of Secularism over Death), in *The Prison Book*, ed. Naser Mohajer, vol. 2, 2001, p. 442.

116 Juri Tynjanov, "Rhythm as the Constructive Factor of Verse," quoted in *Eisenstein's Ivan the Terrible*, p. 49.

117 This is the first story of a collection with the same name, Ali Erfan, *Les Damnées du paradis* (The Damned Souls of Paradise), Paris: Editions de l'aube, 1996.

118 Erfan, "Les Damnées du paradis," p. 10. Throughout this study, unless otherwise indicated, all quotations refer to the French text.

119 Ibid., p. 12.

120 Ibid., p. 11.

121 Foucault, *Discipline and Punish*, p. 3.

122 Erfan, *Les Damnées du paradis*, p. 12.

123 Ibid., p. 13.

124 Ibid.

125 Ibid., p. 14.

126 The Persian original is *Ya Rusari, Ya Tusari*, which was the shouting slogan of pressure groups who, backed by the government, attacked women who were not wearing *hejab* in the streets and finally managed to "convince" them to follow this rule.

127 Azad, *Prison Memories*, p. 139.

128 Erfan, "Les Damnées du paradis," p. 14.

129 Ibid., p. 13.

130 Ibid.

131 Ibid., p. 14.

132 The *Mahrieh* is a specified amount of money (or items of value) which the bridegroom promises to his future wife.

133 Erfan, "Les Damnées du paradis," p. 28.

134 Ibid.

135 Here I am referring to what Kristin Thompson, using Russian Formalists theories, calls the "*dominant* structuring principle" and alludes to Juri Tynjanov's description of this concept: "Every literary system is formed not by the peaceful interaction of all the factors, but by the supremacy, the foregrounding, of one factor (or group) that functionally subjugates and colors the rest." from Thompson, *Eisenstein's Ivan the Terrible*, p. 34.

136 Like the pressure groups of Mussolini's time, members of the pressure groups in Iran wear a uniform-like outfit. In the case of Iranian pressure groups, the members usually wear white shirts.

137 Erfan, "Les Damnées du paradis," p. 11.

138 *Vali-ye amr* (Guardian of the cause [of God]) or *Vali-ye faqih* (Supreme jurist) are terms used in Iran to refer to the highest ranking cleric who, in the absence of the Prophet or the Imams, represents God's will on earth.

139 Erfan, "Les Damnées du paradis," p. 12.

140 As mentioned in a footnote to the French text, the word *mahram* comes from the word "*harem*". It refers to men and women who are related either by marriage or through family ties. According to a strict interpretation of Islam, those who are not *mahram* (*na-mahram*) are not allowed to look at each other.

141 Erfan, "Les Damnées du paradis," pp. 14–15.

142   In literature, the term "violence" has also been defined by Juan Goytisolo and Bradley Epps as "the negation of an intellectually oppressive system [through] the negation of its semantic structure." For details, see Bradley Epps, *Significant Violence: Oppression and Resistance in the Narratives of Juan Goytisolo, 1970–1990*, New York: Clarendon Press, 1996.

143   Thompson, *Eisenstein's* Ivan the Terrible, p. 42.

144   Ibid.

145   Montazeri, *Memoirs*, Appendix 145.

146   *Sigheh* refers both to a temporary marriage and a temporary bride. According to the Shi'i version of Islam, a man may marry a woman for a short period of time (as short as an hour). Prison guards used this term to refer to the forcible "marriage" with virgin prisoners.

147   This is Montazeri's explanation:

> Here is the story: my utmost effort was to prevent them from executing women and girls because at that time many of those arrested in connection with the *Mojahedin-e Khalq* [People's Fighters] were girls, and they executed them as *mohareb*. One day I told the Imam: "Sir, as mentioned in the fatwas of jurisprudents, a woman *mortad* (apostate) should not be executed; some jurisprudents have said the same thing about a woman *mohareb*; and there is a debate among jurisprudents. Yes, if she is a murderer the ruling is execution whether the murderer is a man or a woman. But in cases other than murder, a woman *mortad* or *mohareb* is not treated like a man. [Please] order that they do not execute them. These [women] are usually deceived; they have been given a leaflet, they have been taught radical slogans, and most of them are not capable of distinguishing [between right and wrong]; they have been influenced. [Order] them to give them some prison time, perhaps they will realize their mistakes and then be released." The Imam said: "Well, tell the gentlemen not to execute girls." Citing the Imam, I told those in charge of the judiciary and those in charge of Evin [prison] and other places, do not execute the *monafeqin* [hypocrites] girls. I also told the judges, You are no longer allowed to write the writs of execution for girls. That was what I said. Then, here and there, they pretended that I said, Don't execute girls; first make them *sigheh* (temporary brides) and then execute them!
>
> *Memoirs*, Appendix 118.

148   Obviously since the Islamic government has never allowed any examination and research to be conducted about these years, it is almost impossible to know the extent to which this argument and this approach was used. However, the important point is the gradual formation of a counter-discourse (and in this case, a literary narrative) using the weakness of the dominant/official discourse to reject such statements.

149   Erfan, "Les Damnées du paradis," p. 17.

150   As mentioned in the French text, it is the custom for suitors to take such items to the homes of their future wives.

151   Erfan, "Les Damnées du paradis," p. 21.

152   Ibid., p. 15.

153   Here are a few examples from the Qur'an:

> And when Our messengers came to Lot he was grieved on account of them, and he felt powerless (to protect) them; and they said: Fear not, nor grieve; surely we will deliver you and your followers, except your wife; she shall be of those who remain behind. (29.33)

Surely We will cause to come down upon the people of this town a punishment from heaven, because they transgressed. (29.34)

And certainly We have left a clear sign of it for a people who understand. (29.35)

Surely We sent upon them a stonestorm, except Lot's followers; We saved them a little before daybreak, (54.34)

And certainly he warned them of Our violent seizure, but they obstinately disputed the warning. (54.36)

And certainly a lasting chastisement overtook them in the morning. (54.38)

So taste My chastisement and My warning. (54.39)

154 Erfan, "Les Damnées du paradis," p. 23.
155 Ibid.
156 The Gospel According to John, 16:2.
157 Erfan, "Les Damnées du paradis," p. 23.
158 Ibid., p. 22.

The following are some of the verses in the Qur'an which imply that for those who go to Paradise there are not only all kinds of fruit and meat and drinks but beautiful women:

And pure, beautiful ones, (56.22)
The like of the hidden pearls: (56.23)
A reward for what they used to do. (56.24)
Then We have made them virgins, (56.36)
Loving, equals in age, (56.37)
For the sake of the companions of the right hand. (56.38)
Reclining on thrones set in lines, and We will unite them to large-eyed beautiful ones. (52.20)
And We will aid them with fruit and flesh such as they desire. (52.22)
And round them shall go boys of theirs as if they were hidden pearls. (52.24)
And besides these two are two (other) gardens: (55.62)
In them are goodly things, beautiful ones. (55.70)
Pure ones confined to the pavilions. (55.72)
Man has not touched them before them nor jinni. (55.74)
Reclining on green cushions and beautiful carpets. (55.76)

159 In *Decline of the New*, Irving Howe used the term "anti-utopia" to describe a certain category of fiction in early twentieth-century Europe which rejected many assumptions of nineteenth-century philosophy of history. Describing the anti-utopian novel, Howe wrote:

Behind the anti-utopian novel lies not merely the frightful vision of a totalitarian world, but something that seems still more alarming. To minds raised on the assumption, whether liberal or Marxist, of nineteenth-century philosophy of history—assumptions that the human enterprise has a purposive direction, or *telos*, and an upward rhythm, or progress—there is also the fear that history itself has proved to be a cheat. And a cheat not because it has turned away from our expectations, but because it betrays our hopes precisely through an inverted fulfillment of those expectations. Not progress denied but progress realized, is the nightmare haunting the antiutopian novel.

Howe, 1970, p. 67.

160 Erfan, "Les Damnées du paradis," p. 24.
161 Ibid., p. 23.

162 Ibid., pp. 22–23.
163 Ibid., pp. 30–31.
164 Ibid., pp. 29–30.
165 Ibid., p. 36. According to some reports many women were placed in a bag before being executed so that the "brothers" who execute them and then carry their bodies would not see or touch a *na-mahram* woman.
166 Ibid.

2 Literary rewrites of history

In examining the aesthetics of literary production, the Russian Formalists defined the notion of *Differenzqualität* as one of the main explanatory concepts of these characteristics and described its function in three major contexts: divergence from the actual, from "current linguistic usage," and from "the prevailing artistic norm."[1]

The Russian Formalists correctly regard the "divergence from the actual" to be one of the aesthetic attributes of literary productions, and, while this theoretical approach makes reference of the non-literary realities, they ground the debate in the context of literature. But this idea was conceptualized at a time when the theories of Discourse and Power and Representation as well as the New Historicism had not yet been formulated, and therefore requires further development. The most significant component in this idea is the concept of the *actual*, whose definition, almost 100 years after its placement in the framework of these theories, has gone through a number of transformations and, at times, even revolutions. In the Formalists' conceptualization, the word *actual* is considered in its static sense, and the emphasis placed on distancing from the actual implies that there exists something unique, unchangeable, and generally accepted as Reality, that is, the actual. This approach does not take into account the fact that the definition of reality as part of history has always been—and will always be—influenced by different discourses, and that at various intervals it could have multiple, at times contradictory definitions. This is especially significant when the relationship of this changing definition with the Formalist understanding of background[2] is taken into account. From the point of view of Formalist aesthetics, the concept of background is directly related to the topic of *Differenzqualität*; therefore, it can be defined from linguistic, artistic (that is, artistic in relation to dominant artistic norms and forms), and historiographical perspectives. Thus, in works where divergence from historical background (the actual) is the main aesthetic dynamic of the work, the actual—the point of departure—together with its problematized definition assumes great importance.

In *Modern Reflections of Classical Traditions in Persian Fiction*, discussing the defining borders of the discipline of literary criticism and the notion of "literary reality," I argued that the definition of reality is specifically subordinated to the discursive requirements of different disciplines. If we apply the same approach to the countering discourses which function in regard to the same subjects, we will understand why countering elements of different discourses offer completely different images and narratives of the same phenomenon.

I would like to think that this is what Mahmoud Darwish had in mind when he said, "I am looking for the poet of Troy. Troy has not told its story yet." And indeed, although Homer wrote about "the Trojan War," his epics are above all the stories of Greece and the Greeks; not just because he chose the most magnificent heroes of his epics from among the Greeks, and not just because he allocated most of the textual space to the Greeks, but because he has imposed elements of a Greek discourse on the narrative, thus telling the story of the war and, more significantly, the story of the world after the war, from a, narratologically speaking, Greek perspective. This is always the outcome of a military defeat. The victorious side is not satisfied with smashing the opposition; it is not enough for the victor to put the enemy warriors in chains and even to execute them; the victor tries to eradicate the narrative existence of the vanquished as well. Truly, poets such as Ferdowsi,[3] who uncovered the hidden texts of the defeated Iranians and thus fought the narrative attack of the victorious Islamic Empire and incorporated the story of the defeated nation in the post-war history, are the exception rather than the rule.

In addition to the eradication of the narratives of the defeated in any post-war world, the dominance of the victors' discourse does not end here. Using its newly-found power, the victorious side delves into the history and attempts to rewrite the past so that it can create historical legitimacy for itself. This method has always been used. The example of Iran after the Arab conquest is a telling one. In a sense, the confrontation between the efforts of those defeated to form and offer their narratives and the aggression of the conquerors to keep these narratives silent is in fact the confrontation of two discourses, one of which, exaggerating the prowess of the defeated, proclaims Iranians the most technologically and artistically advanced people of their time and the second one, the victorious one, exaggerating the influence of the new discourse, describes every single achievements of that period through categories such as "Islamic art," "Islamic literature" and, by extension "Islamic scientific undertakings," etc. This confrontation has continued up to the present time. Interestingly enough, one of the loudest supporters of the latter group is the Orientalist discourse which, in concordance with the religious discourse, tries to rewrite history in such a way that it not only legitimizes the official discourse of the victors but makes certain that there will be no space left for the identity of the defeated to appear and develop.

A more recent example of such efforts to rewrite history in contemporary Iran was Mohammad Reza Shah's attempt to change the Iranian calendar. The Shah argued that the beginning of Iranian civilization had to be marked by the beginning of kingship in Iran more than 1,000 years before the Hijra from Mecca to Medina by Mohammad the Prophet of Islam, which was and is used as the beginning of the Iranian calendar.[4] This was an obvious effort to create a new vantage point from which a rewriting of the history of Iran could take place. The new beginning of Iran's civilization, reflected in the new calendar, was not at all akin to a multivocal historiography; instead it was intended to legitimize the official discourse by creating and centralizing a narrative link between Iran's history and the monarchy. From the point of view of such "historical robbery," quite possibly the best example of a theft of history in the twentieth century is to be found during Nazi Germany. In "Benjamin's Silence," referring to Walter Benjamin's famous article, "Theses on the Philosophy of History"[5] Shoshana Felman writes:

> History is now the property and the propriety of Nazis (of those who can control it and manipulate its discourse). It is by virtue of a loyalty to history that Hitler is proposing to avenge Germany from its defeat and its humiliation in the First World War ...
>
> History in Nazi Germany is Fascist. Fascism legitimizes itself in the name of national identity on the basis of a unity and of a continuity of history.[6]

More interesting is the similarity that this approach has with the treatment by the discourse in power of Arabs who live in Israel. The words of Mahmoud Darwish to which I referred at the beginning of this segment are in fact referring to this treatment. Currently about 20 percent of the Israeli population are Arabs who have Israeli citizenship. There is no doubt that the relationship between the Jews and Arabs of Israel is the relationship between the victor and the vanquished. And perhaps more so than other victors, many Israeli Jews have chosen an outright narrative onslaught against their Palestinian compatriots. Of course Palestinians have defined many narratives, but none of these narratives have been able to become part of or even play a role in the dominant discourse which, in Israel, has taken possession of history and, among other things, succeeded in producing and reproducing the Israeli identity. In fact, those in power in Israel have always tried to use all their cultural, economic, and military might to exclude the Palestinian narratives from the identity-making process and to turn these narratives into inessential elements of this identity. In "'Hidden Transcripts' Made Public: Israeli Arab Fiction and Its Reception," Rachel Feldhay Brenner explains this confrontation by referring to Homi Bhabha's characterization of this process:

> Israeli Arabs have turned into what Homi Bhabha calls colonized mimic people, "a subject of a difference that is almost the same, but not quite."[7] A process by which the colonized are accepted as "the same" up to a certain point and then disavowed as mimics, mimicry refracts the hypocrisy of the officially avowed morality and enlightenment of the colonizers.[8]

One of the most obvious contemporary examples in regard to the biased definition of the actual as part of history is the Islamic Republic of Iran, which, not satisfied with the mere recounting of past history, aggressively seeks to represent present history—the actual—from the viewpoint of its own discourse. Of course representing the actual in its own image is not exclusive to the Islamic government, but—to use Debord's terminology—the "concentrated" Islamic regime, by overly relying on force to impose its version of the actual has led to the creation of counter-narratives. In fact these imposed versions have become quite counter-productive. In "Comments on the Society of the Spectacle," Debord summarizes different forms of spectacular power:

> In 1967 I distinguished two rival and successive forms of spectacular power, the concentrated and the diffuse. Both of them floated above real society, as its goal and its lie. The former, favoring the ideology condensed around a dictatorial personality, had accomplished the totalitarian counter-revolution, fascist as well as Stalinist. The latter, driving wage-earners to apply their freedom of choice to the vast range of new commodities now on offer, had represented the Americanization of the world, a process which in some respects frightened but also successfully seduced those countries where it had been possible to maintain traditional forms of bourgeois democracy.[9]

As suggested in Debord's examples, the main difference between the two forms lies in the process of achieving the goals. The diffuse form bases itself on "convincing," and in this process presents its discourses and narratives to define every single space for social and individual life. These narratives and discourses, which can be categorized in the disciplines of history, sociology, economics, politics, etc., offer such portrayals of the existing subjective and objective spaces to the inhabitants of the society that, having voluntarily accepted these representations, they embrace the goals of the Society of the Spectacle. And indeed there have been many success stories of diffuse societies, and that explains why many societies have shifted away from the concentrated form of control. The concentrated form, however, opts for an authoritarian approach. Like the other form, this one, too, attempts to impose its discourses and narratives, but it appears that the central ideology of the Society of the Spectacle is not capable of offering convincing alternatives in regards to various social and individual spaces. This weakness leads to totalitarian apparatuses such as Fascism and Stalinism whose main convincing tool is sheer force.[10]

As previously mentioned, one of the essential narrative goals of these two forms is to offer a rewriting of history in general and of the actual in particular. Debord called this the most fundamental requirement for the Society of the Spectacle to establish itself. "Spectacular domination's first priority was to make historical knowledge in general disappear ... "[11] And the falsification of historical events is the chosen method. Occasionally this falsification is accomplished by ignoring events which cannot be contained within the framework of the official discourse. But for the most part, the official discourses simply ignore the evidence in order to fabricate their narratives. In the current history of Iran there are a number of events which the official discourse has tried to describe according to its patterns. The following is an emblematic example.

About two years after the 1979 Revolution, the Sazman-e Mojahedin-e Khalq (The People's Mojahedin Organization),[12] having realized that it could not be part of the new power structure in any way, decided to use different approaches to undermine the post-revolutionary government. Their most controversial method was the series of bombings of government offices, specifically intended to eliminate the officialdom of the Islamic Republic. The most famous and by far the most destructive attempt was the bombing of the headquarters of the Party of Islamic Republic of Iran in June 1981. A large number of people, mostly high-ranking party officials, were killed in this attack. Of course, as is the case in such events, it took about 24 hours until the exact number of people killed was determined. But right from the start, as soon as it was known that the number of people killed was about 70, state media used the number 72 to refer to the number of casualties. It was not and is not difficult to surmise why they did so. From the very beginning, a concerted effort was made to connect this incident to an iconic (for Shi'is) event which took place in Karbala in 680 CE. This event refers to the battle of Hosein, Shi'is' third Imam, and members of his family against the Omayyad Caliph Yazid. The battle took place in Karbala on the ninth and tenth days of the month of Moharram in 680 CE. According to most accounts, the number of people killed on Hosein's side was either 72 or 73. This was enough for the official discourse to identify the people killed in the desert of Karbala with those killed in the bombing of the headquarters of the Islamic Republic Party. The existence of undeniable differences between these two events gave rise to no hesitation in the minds of those in charge of the dominant discourse. Even today, after more than three decades, still on the anniversary of the bombing of the headquarters, this identification is stressed,[13] while at the time of the event even high-ranking officials such as Ali-Akbar Hashemi-Rafsanjani and Abolhassan Banisadr reported a different number.[14] What is extremely interesting is that Rafsanjani himself, less than 20 years after the event, in the first volume of his memoirs, *Obur az Bohran* (Traversing the Crisis) writes:

In the evening [of Thursday, 11 Tir 1360/1981] I went to the Central Office of the Islamic Republic Party, to attend the wake ceremony held for the explosion's martyrs. It was said that the number of martyrs was two or three people more than seventy-two but it was decided that [the number] does not change, because of the value of the number seventy-two and its similarity with the martyrs of the Karbala event which makes it easier to settle [in people's minds].[15]

This is while on the official site of Iran's State Radio and Television, in a short piece to memorialize this event, we read:

> 7th Tir (June 28, 1981) is the martyrdom anniversary of the martyrs of the June 28, 1981 bomb blast at the headquarters of the Islamic Republic Party in which the then Chief Justice of the Supreme Court Ayatollah Mohammad Hosein Beheshti and 72 officials of the Revolution were martyred.[16]

It is also noteworthy that those who believe the number of people killed at Karbala was 72 use the same number for the 1981 bombing.[17] Those who use another version of the battle of Karbala suggesting that there were 73 people change the number of dead from the bombing accordingly.[18] This is an obvious, and comic, interference in a measurable reality, the disjunction of which was undeniable even for the authorities, yet the dominant discourse was pursuing another goal which was not going to be disturbed by the consequences of such interference. The main goal which overruled the credibility issues resulting from such an approach was the creation of a sign system through which not only this but other events as well had to be observed. Such an approach of course is not exclusive to the Islamic Republic; dominant/official discourses have always realized that:

> It is by the power of sign that societies, despite their variations, process information so as to regulate and organize the manner in which individuals perceive and "know," the ways in which they interpret and map their environment prior to acting and as the basis for their actions.[19]

The main purpose of the official discourses is to colonize this system of signs and in this process the end justifies means which includes obvious falsification of well-known facts. The propagandist atmosphere of the Iran–Iraq War (1980–1988) was a great opportunity for the logical continuation of this method and for the expansion of this sign system. In this atmosphere words, phrases, symbols, and images, most of which are taken from periods of real or imaginary history about Islam, predominantly the Shi'i version, are used to define a prism through which people are encouraged or forced to observe the events of the War. In *Staging a Revolution: The Art of Persuasion in the Islamic Republic of Iran*, Peter Chelkowski and Hamid Dabashi directly discuss the formation process of this system. The authors have collected and analyzed a large number of semiotic elements which were consciously used by the Islamic government at different intervals and on various occasions so that they could mobilize the masses.[20] Inevitably, the authors allocate a significant part of the book to the images and symbols devised during the Iran–Iraq War. While some of the sign-codes used in this regard tended to engage patriotic emotions, the majority of the symbols were used to create a particular sign system at the center of which is placed the *lieu de mémoire* of

Karbala. Once again it is clear that the discourse in power is attempting to force people to approach the actual—whose center is the War—through the prism of Shi'i Islamic codes. One of the best examples of this is found in a speech by Khomeini about the War/Karbala in which he seeks to prove that:

> The righteousness of the Iranian cause against the Ba'athist Iraqis was rooted in the righteousness of Imam Hussein's cause against the Umayyad caliph: "If today all those who have power, and all those who simply talk gibberish, write, deliver speeches, or conspire against you and against the Islamic Republic, they would not be able to conceal the truth. You are right! Just as Imam [Hussein], the Prince of the Martyrs, was right. He put up a fight with a very small number [of supporters]. Although he was martyred, and his children were martyred, he still kept Islam alive, and he made a mockery of Yazid and of the Banu Umayyads. You too are the Shi'ites [that is, followers] of his Same Excellency. You too, in such battles as those of Abadan … [etc.], did something miraculous."[21]

These efforts are part of a much larger project of describing and interpreting past and contemporary history. At times, these efforts present themselves as the imposition of structures such as the prism of Karbala and sometimes as ignoring or silencing of the narratives and elements which are not compatible with the discourse in power and its understanding of history. The result is a system which has been formed for the purpose of imposing specific strategies about dealing with history/reality of the past and present. In so doing, the discourse in power has relied on methods such as biased inclusion, exclusion, appropriation, limitation, and restriction in regard to historical narratives.[22]

But these systemic efforts which aim to completely control the society's historical conscience, and are attempting to define it ideologically, are challenged by various currents of alternative narratives which want to be part of this historical conscience. A discursive/narrative confrontation has emerged where different discourses try to create history in their own image. One could imagine that the ideal situation for a healthy competition is when various discourses and their narratives can be present simultaneously but the fact of the matter is that discourses in power have always forced historiographers and historiography to, as Edward P. Thompson put it, see its subject "within expectations, the self-image, the apologetics, of a ruling class: 'the propaganda of the victors'"[23] while they have forcefully cracked down on alternative historiography and historiographers.

Collective narratives, individual stories

Against the relentless onslaught of the dominant discourse which has made it extremely difficult for any systematic presentation of the narratives of the Other, counter-discourses have opted to use individual/personal narratives. In a sense this has been the story of the critique of the modern consumer society in every system of power. The dominant discourse attempts to present an artificial and fabricated world to the member of the society to achieve its purpose.

> When the real world changes into simple images, simple images become real beings and effective motivations of a hypnotic behavior. The spectacle as a tendency *to make one see the world* by means of various specialized mediations (it can no longer be grasped directly), naturally finds vision to be the privileged human sense which the sense of touch was for other epochs ... [24]

One of the significant points in Debord's argument is his emphasis on the effort made by the dominant discourse to prevent the individual from experiencing history. Conversely, individual narratives challenge such attempts. In fact, as Steven Best and Douglas Kellner have demonstrated through their analyses of the Situationists, Debord and other Situationists were promoting a "radically democratic" approach which encouraged the individual to personally control his experience with the world around him.[25] Thus, individual narratives represent these experiences in the field of history and historiography.

Like the narratives of the dominant discourse, these individual narratives, too, choose their ingredients from contemporary events. In the terminology of New Historicists, these will create anecdotes, whose least effect is to "puncture the historical *grand récit*."[26] In contemporary Persian literature, the literary counterpart of what New Historicists call anecdote or *petit récit* is the "Report-Story."[27]

The Report-Story, which could be called an in-between or a transitional subgenre, is located between historiography and literature. Narratives which belong to this subgenre usually choose their "story stuff" from events familiar to the readers, but this familiarity is rather general, and on many occasions the information about these events—for example, the bombing of the headquarters of the Islamic Republic Party—is only a mutilated reflection which has reached the reader through the lens of the discourse in power. For various reasons, the narrators of Report-Stories are usually very knowledgeable with regard to the events which lie at the heart of the story. This fact strengthens the reportage aspect of the narrative and consequently provides the possibility of the reader's response; it also emphasizes the individualistic nature of the narrative and narration which will challenge the *grand-récit* and in general the historiography of the Society of the Spectacle.

One of the famous examples of this subgenre is *"Nakonad Pareh Konam Sineh-ye Sohrabam ra"* (Let Me Not Split Open the Breast of My Sohrab) from *Gozaresh-Qesseh-ye 1* (*Report-Story #1*) by Farkhondeh Hajizadeh (b. 1953). The materials of the story come from an event which took place in 1377/1998 in Iran in the city of Kerman. In the month of Mehr (September/ October) of that year, a young poet by the name of Hamid Hajizadeh along with his nine-year old son Karun, was attacked in their house; both were stabbed to death. This was only one of such assassinations which took place at that time. After a short period, these killings became known as the *Qatlha-ye Zanjireh-i*, ([Project of] Serial Murders). This project was specifically intended to arouse fear and intimidation by brutally killing known intellectuals, particularly writers and artists. After a while, the Islamic government declared that this project had been designed by one of the officials of the Ministry of Information and according to the government's spokesman, without the knowledge of the leaders of the Islamic Republic. Shortly after the arrest of this official—Sa'id Emami—it was announced that he had committed suicide by swallowing depilatory powder. Newspapers and reporters never received complete access to the relevant documents,[28] and the officials visibly scrambled to close the case as soon as possible. Naturally this situation led to the construction of numerous individual narratives about the Serial Murders which punctured the narratives affiliated with the official discourse. "Let Me Not Split Open the Breast of My Sohrab" should be read against this background.

The author is the sister of Hamid Hajizadeh and has detailed information about the murders of her brother and her nephew. Indeed, in some of her other works,[29] including some of the stories in the same *Report-Story #1*, she refers to these murders in minute details, but in "Let Me Not ... " her main concern is not with these details. In fact, throughout this short piece, it is evidently assumed that the reader is familiar with the general outline of the event. It is indicated in a footnote that the title of the story is taken from one of the poems by Hamid Hajizadeh. Throughout the story, the author has used real names; at times she also includes explanations which emphasize the non-fictional aspect of this work. Yet, as mentioned, furnishing the details of the incident is not her main concern.

The other assumption made by Hajizadeh is that the reader is familiar with the main stories of the *Shahnameh* specifically "Rostam and Sohrab" and "The Tale of Siyavash." In a nutshell, the story of "Rostam and Sohrab" is the account of the killing of a son (Sohrab) at the hands of his father (Rostam). Rostam, the main legendary hero of Persian mythology, is called upon to defend Iran against the Turanian (people of Turan), the epic antagonists of the Iranians. The circumstances place the young Sohrab, one of the leaders of Turan's army, face to face with Rostam. Unknown to one another, the son and the father join battle; in the end, Rostam splits open his son's breast. The title "Let Me Not Split Open the Breast of My Sohrab" refers directly to this part of the story.

Undoubtedly, the fact that Sohrab dies at the age of 12 before having a chance to experience life fully reminds the reader of Karun's age and untimely death. Some have maintained that the story of Rostam and Sohrab symbolizes a traditional patriarchal and gerontocratic society. This is obviously a topic which requires a separate study. Hajizadeh uses the adjective "patriarchal" to describe Kavus, the King of Iran and Siyavash's father, another *Shahnameh* character to whom the author refers in her text. Having rejected his stepmother Sudabeh's advances, Siyavash is accused by her, and although he proves his innocence by passing the test of fire, Kavus sends him to exile in Turan, and at the end he is slain in his innocence.

It is very telling that when the official discourse addressed the bombing of the headquarters of the Islamic Republic Party, it was making its utmost effort to identify it with the Karbala event, but by creating a link between the murders of a poet and his son with Sohrab and Siyavash, pre-Islamic mythic heroes, the storyteller-reporter of "Let Me Not … " clearly tries to provide a narrative affiliated with a counter-discourse. The main goal in this case and similar cases is to create a frame of reference, a window through which the interlocutor could experience the event in question. And indeed, this is why the term "Report-Story" is an accurate representation for describing such counter-discursive narratives. Explaining this choice, Farkhondeh Hajizadeh writes:

> Even if you decide to write a report of a moment, of a situation, of the life of someone or an event, you are drawn towards narration, and when you revisit what you have written you see that it is neither a story as you know it, nor is it a report according to conventional definitions. Therefore, and in order to give it an identity, you give it a name that you have made up; a name which is a combination of report and story, *Report-Story*.[30]

The reason for the distance between such writings and normal reports is an important issue to which I will return later. Before that, however, we should complete the structure of the frame of reference/the window which the author of "Let Me Not … " sets in front of the reader. An important part of this frame is designed by evoking Sohrab and Siyavash, in their representational capacities, symbolizing childhood and innocence as well as the victims of a gerontocratic-patriarchal society. The author leaves no room for doubt about this identification; she writes very clearly:

> You used to talk about the beauty of Siyavash who went through the redness of fire with his white horse. I felt sorry for Sudabeh, and your moon-like face was set on fire from anger. I pounded the ground with my feet, as I used to when we were fighting when we were kids. My hands combed through the hair of your Sohrab, and I considered the patriarchal Kavus the guilty one. We had experienced the bitter taste of patriarchy from our early years and the first years of school.[31]

In addition to contributing to the previously-mentioned window, the non-religious pre-Islamic myth into which the identity of the victims of these murders is collapsed, creates a relationship between the mythic narrative and current society by evoking the story of these two heroes who are killed by their fathers: Sohrab directly, Siyavash indirectly. The last sentence of the paragraph above functions as a hook which links the mythic narrative to the contemporary history. In this contemporary history, the reporter-storyteller, contrary to what might seem to be a normal reaction, does not issue a socio-political manifesto condemning officialdom; instead she uses the hook of the last sentence to reminisce about school years and the time when physical punishment still persisted.[32] She remembers a specific event from her brother's childhood and hers. The brother is being punished at school for some reason and the sister's cries of pain and protest are heard—cries which remind her of her mother's after the death of her son and grandson. "I was howling; like the howling of Mother after your death."[33]

The window placed in front of the reader progressively acquires a personal and individual side as well. The narration of these murders is gradually dissociated from the form of a report and follows the author's mental and psychological oscillations, and, contrary to the requirements of this form, seems to be approaching the stream of consciousness. Hajizadeh begins with the *Shahnameh* and its heroes; the unloving Rostam and Kavus remind her of the patriarchal society, and the memory of his brother being punished is revived. Then comes the memory of the howling of the mother and along this path personal memories appear one after another. It seems, however, that the predominant segment of these flashbacks is the memories of childhood punishments; the personal side of the window is constructed through the juxtaposition of these specific memories. At the center of this composition is the following story/memory: the narrator and her brother, mostly at the brother's suggestion, skip school for three days. The school officials are unaware of their absence until their mother finds out and reports it to them. The school officials decide to punish the brother with 80 blows of a wooden stick on his hands. As usual, the sister jumps in the middle and holds out her hands and asks them to punish her instead. This approach had always saved the brother—and of course the sister/narrator as well—but this time the crime is bigger than he could be pardoned. Towards the end of the story, at the wake for the murdered brother and his son, Mr. Afrasiabi, one of the teachers who had been present during that episode and had not been able to see and tolerate their punishment and had left school that day, comes to the narrator and stares into her eyes, "as if he wants to say: 'My daughter, where were your hands then?'"[34]

Because of its reliance on personal memories and because of its occasional following of the narrator's stream of consciousness, the account of these two murders is extremely personal and unreport-like. When this aspect of the narrative is placed next to the mythic link, the ensemble offers a reading of this event which clearly stands in opposition to the reading suggested by the dominant discourse. This counter-discursivity stems both from the selection of pre-Islamic myths, which the official discourse has always tried to ignore,[35] and from its reliance on the individuality of this historical narrative. This latter characteristic is a significant trait of many Persian contemporary works of literature which contribute to the formation of literary counter-discourses. I will discuss them in future sections. Here, it is necessary to mention one specific counter-discursive function of the individuality of the historical narrative in the context of the Report-Story. In Chapter 1, the examples of prison literature were all representative of narratives which directly challenged the narratives of the official discourse. The examples of the Report-Story do not necessarily follow this pattern. On many occasions, these examples choose their story material at the outset from spaces the official discourse has tried to silence. In fact, the imposition of silence on these spaces, which are usually filled with under-explored events, has always been, and still is, an important segment of the definition of the dominant discourse of the actual. The use of means such as the Ministry of Culture and Islamic Guidance, censorship, security forces, prison, and torture obviously makes any direct confrontation with this imposition difficult. Furthermore, the fact that the necessary tools and means for research and reportage about such events are only at the disposal of the dominant discourse makes it almost impossible for counter-discourses to offer their narratives of these events.

Consequently, the *report* aspect of the Report-Story cannot have the accuracy of an ordinary report. But the mere fact of giving voice to the silenced narratives undermines the attempts of the official discourse to offer its definition of the actual as the standard and generally accepted one. But, as mentioned at the beginning of this section, distancing from the generally accepted definition of the actual is one of the characteristics which define the literariness of a work of literature, and therefore the trait which I called the individuality of historical narrative contributes to the literariness of the work and simultaneously functions as an element of counter-discursivity.

There are many other examples of such works which oscillate between story and report. But probably the most famous one is Bahram Beyzai's *Majles-e Shabih dar Zekr-e Masaeb-e Ostad Navid Makan va Hamsarash Mohandes Rokhshid Farzin* (An Account of the Misfortunes of Master Navid Makan and Her Husband, the Engineer Rokhshid Farzin). This play has a longer story, to which I will return later.

The production of works defined under the subgenre of the Report-Story once more brings to the surface the relationship between literature and other disciplines—here, specifically, history. This is an old discussion, and I will just mention one point with regard to Persian literature. From the viewpoint of various disciplines, Iran's literary production of the past 100 years represents an ensemble of discordant/diverging experiences. On the one hand, since Iran's literary tradition in most periods has been at the center of the society and not its margins, certain unliterary responsibilities have been placed on its shoulders. One of them is the responsibility to dissent vis-à-vis the official discourse which has a representational value. On the other hand, and in contradiction to these unliterary responsibilities, at different intervals efforts have been made to prevent non-literary discourses from imposing themselves on the field of literature by emphasizing the literariness of the works. Clearly the presence of these contradictory components is not exclusive to Iran, but each example has its own particularities. In "Lyric and Public: The Case of Adam Zagajewski," Clare Cavanagh evokes one of these componentsby referring to an old essay by Czeslaw Milosz in which he writes: "In Central and Eastern Europe ... a poet does not merely arrange words in beautiful order. Tradition demands that he be a 'bard,' that his songs linger on many lips, that he speak in his poems of subjects of interest to all citizens."[36] As Cavanagh argues, this demand for being the collective voice of the poet's generation and its causes is clearly demonstrated in Zagajewski's early poems when he frequently speaks "In the First Person Plural."[37] Later on however, he rebels against this demand and famously writes: "I have the urge to become a dissident from dissidents."[38] This rebellion does not mean that he is forgoing dissidence; it is, rather, an effort to achieve a kind of individual lyricism. In the case of Zagajewski this individual lyricism is still informed by a dissident approach whose agencies could still function in the world of non-individual/collective events. Zagajewski's most famous poem in English is "Try to praise the mutilated world." It was written before September 11, 2001, and after that it was seen everywhere in New York City. The poem is particularly interesting because of its emphasis on personal lyricism, and curiously enough, line after line it gets closer to non-literary discourses through this same form of lyricism. This is how it manages to oscillate between a personal space made of the memories of "June's long days," "wild strawberries, drops of wine," and shared spaces of "the abandoned homesteads of exiles" and "the mutilated world."[39]

In Iran, too, at different intervals, efforts were made by the literary discourse to rebel against the imposed responsibility of being the public voice. After the 1979 Revolution many of these efforts were consolidated and, as in Zagajewski's experience, and that of many other writers and artists of similar societies, created different forms through which they could integrate various discourses. The Report-Story is only one of these forms. The outstanding characteristic of the report-story form is the obvious separation between its historical (report) and literary (story) aspects. Its counter-discursive characteristic is materialized both through the direct rejection of official narratives and the literary function of the work, that is, in the creation of a prism through which readers relate to the reported event. But this separation between these two aspects is not seen in other narrative forms whose structures include elements of historical and literary discourses. In addition, in many works which attempt to recount and rewrite history, the historical aspect does not necessarily follow the details of particular events, although in most cases reference to specific events can be detected. In other words, such works are attempting to rewrite history discursively, and not just rejecting certain narratives about certain events from a particular time and place. In Persian contemporary literature, the works of Reza Baraheni (b. 1935) offer the most persistent examples of such rewrites. Many of his works, placed on the historical-literary spectrum, with distinguishable trends of report-story form, represent one of the most ambitious projects of counter-historiography.

As mentioned in Chapter 1, some of Baraheni's works are directly and immediately related to specific segments of the current reality. The book *Zell Allah* (God's Shadow) is a collection of prison poems most of which have been informed by the author's direct experience of prison during the Shah's time. In the introduction to this text, Baraheni writes:

But the idea of this book was formed first in prison; because prison makes one's mind sharper about cruelty and every simple thing, with its image brutality is thrown in the middle and every image challenges the whole life with its cutting nakedness. In fact in these poems I did not try to use my imagination because the hell in which the prisoner lives is created by an evil infernal imagination, which is the imagination of the Shah's executioners. So there is no need for one to use imagination. This Inferno has been created with such an imagination that *if you report the reality of it* you have in fact made the greatest imaginations.[40]

Of course there is imagination in the poems of this collection, but the emphasis on reporting a particular reality—which clearly refers to a specific time and place—provides a kinship between this work and prison reports as well as Report-Stories. From a thematic point of view, this kinship is demonstrated through the direct rejection of narratives of dominant discourse about prison and political prisoners. At the same time, since the descriptive passages of many of these poems do not contain the information included in ordinary prison reports or follow the ordinary approaches of such reports, they have more of a resemblance to Report-Stories. The main point, however, is the goal that the author has prescribed for this work: reporting the reality. This same objective is defined in the majority of his other works as well, but in them a kind of progression is recognized which reveals the limits of this historiographical goal.

From a thematic point of view, Reza Baraheni's novel *Chah beh Chah* (Well to Well, 1983) is situated in the category of prison literature. It is the story of a political prisoner in one of the Shah's prisons who meets another prisoner; the latter tells him about the savage torture he has endured. He also tells him about the typical attributes of the overly-controlled and stifling society of that period, as well as the characteristics of prison guards. In *Ba'd az Arusi cheh Gozasht* (What Happened After the Wedding, 1982) and *Avaz-e Koshtegan* (The Song of Those Killed, 1983), similar themes appear. *What Happened After the Wedding* is the story of a teacher who ends up in prison because of his opposition to the Shah's regime; there he meets a prison guard. A significant part of the story is allocated to the confrontation between these two. Throughout the book, there are detailed descriptions of the unsavory characteristics of the prison guard, who is supposed to represent the Shah's regime in its totality. *The Song of Those Killed*, too, relies partially on prison themes. The central character of this novel is a university professor who rebels against the stifling conditions in the academic environment; he, too, confronts the regime by revealing its everyday atrocities. Similar to Baraheni's other works in this category, this novel includes episodes of arrest and torture, and descriptions of oppressive treatment by the Imperial regime and its agents.

As discussed before, there is a difference between prison reports and prison literature. In prison reports, specific experiences are described without any intermediary, and these experiences aim to give a description of the *actual* which stands in exact contrast to the descriptions of the official discourse. For example, the official narrative about prison as a place where prisoners are treated based on grace, kindness, and sympathy, and the main goal of this treatment is the rehabilitation and schooling of the prisoners, is refuted through the description of specific experiences such as torture, humiliation, injustice, rape, and summary executions. This new definition of the actual then is used in prison literature as a historical background. Works such as *Well to Well* and *The Song of Those Killed* function against backgrounds developed by prison reports and report-stories. In a sense, this background, whose main component is a particular definition of the actual, is taken for granted at this stage, and the novels' plots are defined against this background. This "being taken for granted" is an important step in the process of this definition and similar narratives becoming discursive.

An examination of these specific works of Baraheni is useful in that these works represent early steps in the creation of a counter-discourse based on historiography, or of a counter-history based on this background. At these early stages, the discursive confrontation is direct and takes the form of a "*thematic* contestation."[41] Examples of such direct confrontation are very easy to find in these three works—especially in *Well to Well*. In this novel, the narrator, Hamid, allots a large textual space to direct quotations from his cellmate, who is introduced only as "the Doctor." The Doctor is a very experienced political activist who has undergone a lot of torture; in the end these tortures cause his death. It is through these quotations that direct confrontation, which at times sounds like sloganeering or preaching, is seen. On many occasions, in order to underline the Doctor's discussions, and perhaps to indicate that these sections might be considered as metafiction, the narrator uses italicized font, and places them in parentheses.

> (*The Doctor used to say, People are like a forest. One could cut down one tree with an ax and fell it, one could cut down a hundred or a thousand trees, but no one can cut down the forest and fell it. No one has that ability. Then we must have the kind of power that a forest has.*)[42]

Or

> (*The Doctor said, Do not trust the regime, someone who is lying to you; someone who one moment calls you mother … ! and another moment, when you have trusted him out of fear, trusts you without any reason, never trust them. Someone who has two kinds of languages, two kinds of voice, with one language and one voice hits you and with another language and another voice, kisses you hypocritically to prepare you for the firing squad, never trust them!*)[43]

Or

> (*He said, In the government of the rich, when a worker becomes a police agent, he is no longer a worker; he is a police agent, the protector of*

money. He is the oppressor of workers. Then he would say, These are the
same police who arrest and imprison workers and students; hit
students over the head with their batons. Police, the army, the gendarmes,
the secret service, they are all police. The Shah's investigator orders the
young guard to violate a worker. And he does so. The police who used to
be workers are now the violator of the worker. Governments and states fall
but the police remain. An imprisoned worker is a prisoner, and a police
worker is a police agent. The first one is also a worker; the second
one is not.)[44]

Obviously there is not much literary value to these statements, but they serve
as very obvious examples which begin with the presumption that the official
narratives about prison have already been refuted and there is no further need
for documentation. This is a major step, because it is now assumed, and
indeed it seems, that, through prison reports, counter-discursive narratives
about prison have elevated themselves to the rank of almost generally accepted
"natural" narratives.

Next to this obvious confrontation, gradually other sections of a counter-
history are revealed. One of them is the description of new spheres—albeit
only literary spheres—based on this assumption, and this is the beginning of
a complex web of signs and codes; signs and codes whose relationship with
underlying counter-narratives and counter-discourses, after a while become so
organic that they become difficult to detect. So, it should be remembered
that they have been created in that context and have become an inseparable
part of the counter-discourse. Indeed, it is these signs and codes which
construct spectacles, countering the ones created by the official discourse.

In the previously-mentioned novels of Baraheni and other similar works,
the point is no longer whether the official discourse represents an undemocratic,
inhumane system which is fundamentally cruel; this has been established
through the naturalization of the counter-discourse narratives; merely repeating them does not add to the discussion. The interesting aspect of these works
is that they represent a movement beginning from established counter-narratives
towards the next stage which is looking at the rewriting of different subjective
and objective spaces through an eye informed by these narratives. This means
re-crossing and re-seeing times and places which up until then had been
defined solely by the dominant discourse.

In *Well to Well*, the narrator comes out of prison and passes through
places and memories when he is traveling to his birthplace in the north of
Iran, with a few guards, in order to find a pistol which he is accused of hiding
in his father's house. Thus the narrator's father enters the story indirectly, and
this becomes an opportunity for the narrator to mention the relationship
between his father and a famous historical revolutionary character, Mirza
Kuchek Khan-e Jangali.[45] Once again, it is obvious that, contrary to the
official discourse of the Shah's time, the identity of Mirza Kuchek Khan as a
revolutionary—and not as an insurgent incited by foreign powers—is treated

as an accepted fact; thus the only reason to refer to this character is the addition of a temporal-historical dimension to the narratives of a counter-discourse which, in each step, is trying to define new spaces in its own terms.

In *The Song of Those Killed*, too, this same approach has been used in a more elaborate manner. As Mirabedini has pointed out, "*The Song of Those Killed* is one of the few Iranian novels about the events of universities, professors and students."[46] In particular, the second and longest part of the novel defines the university environment and academicians as elements which, aside from a few exceptions, are serving the Shah's regime and its stability and, while carrying on their parasitic life, are not at all concerned with the real duties of educators and educational environments.

Before examining the significance of this approach in regard to the construction of a counter-history which is defined through the countering of the official discourse, another recurrent point in Baraheni's works needs to be addressed. Many of Baraheni's fictional characters, such as Hosein Qoli Mirza in *Razha-ye Sarzamin-e Man* (Secrets of my Homeland, 1987) or Mahmud Sharifi in *The Song of Those Killed* are defined as writer or university professor, or as being from Azerbaijan, or as spending time in the Shah's prison, all of which are traits of the author himself. Of course we can find similar examples in the works of other Iranian writers, and indeed part of what is called personal historiography is achieved through the reflection of such autobiographical elements. This is especially true in the case of Iran's post-revolutionary literature in which first-person narration has gained an unprecedented importance. However, what makes this element more significant in the works of Baraheni is the author's conscious approach to this personal historiography as one dimension of his larger historiographical project guided by a discourse which on the one hand seeks to counter the dominant discourse and on the other hand aims at creating an ensemble of "personal and collective history."[47] In this phrase, the meaning of collective history is beyond the idea of occasional reference to different historical periods and characters. This collective history very clearly has the signs of a developed counter-history, and one of these signs is the employment of a language and, in general, a system of codes which have always been rejected by the dominant discourse and narratives. In the introduction to *God's Shadow*, after a detailed description of the poverty, misery, and wretched situation of Iran under the leadership of Mohammad Reza Shah, and after referring to the officials' claims of Iran's long strides towards progress, Baraheni ridicules those claims by citing Iran's dependence on imperialism:

> The fact is that currently, Iran's sultanate is a phallus kept erected by the Pentagon and the CIA, so that it can rape the whole nation of Iran and its land and history; and this is what I have addressed in detail in *Ruzegar-e Duzakhi-ye Aqa-ye Ayaz* (The Infernal Times of Mr. Ayaz) and *Tarikh-e Mozakkar* (Masculine History), and we don't need to continue it here.[48]

This kind of language and imagery is not exceptional in Baraheni's work. In fact, in many of his works, Baraheni exemplifies the usage of words, phrases and, more importantly, images which are not acceptable to the dominant discourse. The exaggerated example of this technique is *Ruzegar-e Duzakhi-ye Aqa-ye Ayaz* (The Infernal Times of Mr. Ayaz). In the first section of the book, the main protagonists, Mahmud and Ayaz,[49] are cutting a crucified man into pieces and the details of this act are described with utmost precision. These two, slowly and with care, first saw off the right hand of the prisoner, and Ayaz describes: "The warm-odored blood of the one-armed man had spilled onto my knees and the apron of my winding sheet [shroud],"[50] And he hears the words "I am The Truth":[51] then "The people, the calamity-stricken dogs, wailed an answer in chorus: 'Now his left hand! Now his left hand!'"[52] After the horrifying description of the cutting-off of the left hand, it is the turn of the legs; at the end, the tongue of the condemned man is cut out and:

> Mahmud and I [Ayaz] had cut out his tongue and had thrown it into the middle of a tub full of coagulating throat's blood. And now his mouth full of blood, and Mahmud shouted, "Swallow it!" and he couldn't because his mouth was full of blood and Mahmud shouted for the last time, "Swallow it!" And giving me a piece of cloth, he said, "Wipe the blood off his mouth." And he couldn't swallow and the foaming blood flowed from his mouth and I wiped the vomited blood away from around his mouth with my cloth.[53]

In the first part of *The Infernal Times* ... there are many such repulsive descriptions, and on different occasions, the author also refers to the sexual pleasure that the executioners and the spectators feel while watching this ceremony. In other parts of the novel, also, there are references to sexual violations with disturbing details.[54] To be sure, the language used by Baraheni in this part of his novel is shocking, unconventional, peculiar. Examining this language, Mirabedini writes:

> The author's fearless realism contains his rebellion against the conformity of the deceived populace. Like Henry Miller, Baraheni wants, as a counter-conformist, to reveal the disgusting aspect of history and life, through naked descriptions. But he gets caught in writing obscenity.[55]

Taking into consideration the main traits of *The Infernal Times* ... the use of the word "realism" is not justifiable. This text has more affinity with the literature of the Fantastic than with Realism. In the context of this approach, these "obscenities" should be considered a contrasting language which has always been rejected and ostracized. In a sense this approach is reminiscent of a leftist historiography championed by E. P. Thompson, who tried to break with the conventional language of historians and the voices represented in their works. Catherine Gallagher and Stephen Greenblatt correctly refer to the importance of this approach to New Historicism:

> When the historian E. P. Thompson, for example, interspersed his prose with the putatively unprocessed "voices" of the lower classes, he was striving to present previously disregarded historical subjects, who could give access to a multiplicity of pasts.
>
> ... Since estrangement of the reader, the creation of surprise and conceptual dissonance, was the key to his method, he particularly relished marginal language that was dense, specific, misspelled, and ideologically irretrievable ... [56]

Using an "incorrect" language, Baraheni goes even further and at one point in *The Infernal Times* ..., referring indirectly to some of the famous inscriptions of the Achamenid Period (repeated mainly by Mohammad Reza Shah on many occasions, as a sign of his link to the ancient Persian Empire and kings), provides a mocking imitation of the language:

> My father Vishtasp, his father Arsham, his father Ariarman, his father Piss Royally on! ... Piss on, Xerxes I am, Erect, Rect, Rect (Hurrah!) I am a skilled archer whether on foot or horseback! Iyay amyay yrusCay, ahShay ofyay ethay orldway, eatGray ahSay, powerfulas the lion, ahSahy ofyay ebelBay ofyay umerSay ... Peace on Piss on Peace! ... a skillful man am I whether with two hands or two feet ... I am I am I am ... (Hurrah) ... [57]

As a point of reference, here is one example of such inscriptions:

> I am Cyrus, king of the world, great king, legitimate king, king of Babylon, king of Sumer and Akkad, king of the four rims [of the earth], son of Cambyses, great king, king of Anshan, grandson of Cyrus, great king, king of Anshan, descendant of Teispes, great king, king of Anshan, of a family [which] always [exercised] kingship; whose rule Bel [Marduk] and Nebo love, whom they want as king to please their hearts ... I did not allow anybody to terrorize [any place] of the [country of Sumer] and Akkad. I strove for peace in Babylon and in all his [other] sacred cities. As to the inhabitants of Babylon ... I abolished forced labour ... From Nineveh, Assur and Susa, Akkad, Eshnunna, Zamban, Me-Turnu and Der until the region of Gutium, I returned to these sacred cities on the other side of the Tigris, the sanctuaries of which have been ruins for a long time, the images which [used] to live therein and established for them permanent sanctuaries. I [also] gathered all their [former] inhabitants and returned [to them] their habitations.[58]

And Baraheni devotes a long passage to the representation of this reversal. Such ridicule and, in general, usage of such an unconventional language in the context of this novel reveals the more encompassing strategy of the writer—a strategy which he has directly addressed. In the introductory lines of *The Infernal Times* ... —which is part of the universe Romanesque—titled "*Qol-e Kateb*" (The Scribe's Words) the narrator writes:

> The scribe of this book narrates that when Abolfazl Mohammad-Ibn Hosein Kateb Beyhaqi sensed his death approaching, he confided in me a story which he had written very neatly in his own hand. In this clean manuscript he had mentioned here and there his name and the name of his country. The story was such that one would think that the adventures of Mahmud and Ayaz were narrated from the interior, as if it had been written by an internal eye.[59]

The scribe then adds that "Mahmud's spies or those of his son" seized the only copy of the book and washed down the characters "but the image that the scribe kept in his mind from the pages did not disappear."[60] And after a while he decides to present what he has in memory, once again, as a book. The author however, after a few lines, in a metafictional passage explains:

> Clearly, you know well that the link that the present scribe pretends to have with the original scribe is but a subterfuge. In fact, the present scribe cannot and does not even wish to have had a link with the original scribe. Consider the passing of centuries, of époques, and all this deep temporal distance, and realize that what was said about the relationship and link between these two scribes is only a pretext or justification used in front of actual possessors of power so that they would authorize and approve a *new historiography*.[61]

Before examining this new historiography a short description of *The Infernal Times* ... is necessary. This book was published in 1351/1973 but before being distributed, it was banned by the government of the Shah. All copies of the book were collected from the printing house and destroyed. However, according to Bahram Bahrami, a few copies were saved.[62] The book has not been published in its totality under the new regime either, but a large section of it was published in *Jonun-e Neveshtan* (The Madness of Writing), a collection of selected works by Baraheni. The whole novel was translated into French and published in France in 2000, and it is still awaiting its first complete publication in Persian.

As indicated in the "Scribe's Words" of the *The Infernal Times* ... the "story stuff" of the novel is "the story of Mahmud and Ayaz." According to clichés in traditional historical narratives in Iran, Mahmud Ghaznavi (r. 997–1030) was one of the most powerful kings of Iran whose military campaigns, especially to India—under the guise of religious wars—reflected and represented Iran's power. Through these campaigns and subsequent pillaging of the vanquished, he managed to gather enormous amounts of wealth.

In the world of literature, Mahmud, in his love with his slave, Ayaz, has a completely different reputation. This has been the subject of many classical poems as symbolizing one of the most romantic of attachments. Discussion about the creation this symbol is beyond the scope of this study, but awareness of this reading of the relationship between Mahmud and Ayaz is necessary for the understanding of the counter-discursive nature of *The Infernal Times* ... Of course the novel cannot be reduced to a single event or a single liaison or even a specific period of time. Indeed numerous characters, historical and fictional, as well as many events have been used so that the "scribe" could use the "story stuff" to react against historiographical techniques of the official discourse. References to literary narratives about Mahmud and Ayaz and different aspects of their relationship are also employed for the same purpose. Towards the end of "The Scribe's Words," the author/narrator mentions that what he has suggested about the fictional link between himself and Abu al-Fazl Beyhaqi[63] and the way he acquired the book are only "pretexts and justifications" for him to write this book in which he has attempted to "bring together all the events of the people of the past, present, and even future and set them before the mirror of words. In this process, he has used History more than any other discipline ... "[64]

Collecting the chronicles of "people of the past, present and perhaps even future," and in fact the rejection of historical time, is the first indication which demonstrates the incompatibility of this historiography with traditional historiography. In this regard, the most important tool used in the part of the book recounted by Ayaz is the technique of "history from below." I am borrowing this expression from Catherine Gallagher and Stephen Greenblatt who used it in the following context:

> Less structuralist was the host of feminist, anti-racist, working-class, and other radically revisionist, practitioners of "history from below" who professed to counter the history of the victors with that of the vanquished.[65]

"History from below" could include all silenced voices as well as those which have been purposely forgotten. From this point of view, Baraheni's effort has an obvious kinship with Ferdowsi's project to offer the narratives of the vanquished and silenced nation. In the final part of "*Golshiri va Moshkel-e Roman*" (Golshiri and the Problem of the Novel), and in the context of discussion about the dialogic characteristic of *The Infernal Times* ... Baraheni writes:

> In *The Infernal Times* ..., Ayaz is there, so is Mahmud, and Mansur, Amir Arsalan, Malek Mohammad, and Kurosh, as well as the boy who was buried in place of Kurosh. And Ayaz is that buried boy who, after 2,500 years, has opened his mouth and speaks out.[66]

According to legend, Astyages, Cyrus's maternal grandfather, and the king of Medes, dreamed that his daughter Mandana produced so much water that it swept over the whole world including his country. Fearing that this indicates that his grandchild would replace him, he married his daughter to a Persian who was not of the highest social rank. After less than a year, however, he dreamed this time that a vine grew out of the belly of his daughter. Then its branches and leaves expanded and took over the whole world. Dream interpreters of the court told him that his daughter would give birth to a son who would replace him and will conquer the world. Astyages ordered the child to be killed soon after he was born. After the birth, one of the courtiers took him to the royal shepherd and asked him to carry out the king's order. Incidentally, right at that time, the shepherd's wife had given birth to a dead son. They put Cyrus' clothes on the dead child and buried him instead; thus the name and memory of the shepherd's child were lost forever. This story, quite possibly untrue, nevertheless symbolizes those who have been silenced just so the narrative of the victors could be protected; this imposed silence has effectively led to the fading away of their identity. From this point of view, there is a strange similarity between Ayaz and the buried child. In official discourses of history and literature, Ayaz never has a voice and this silence is necessary for the dominance of Mahmud's voice, throughout ages and spaces.

Allowing a unique voice to Ayaz in the *The Infernal Times …* effectively functions against the direction of the official discourse. The presence of this voice in the novel is the precursor to a counter or at least alternate history which is based on counter-arguments about factual evidences. This expectation is of course fulfilled. In the narrative of Ayaz, we also come across the nature of the relationship between Mahmud and Ayaz, and this time when the story is told by Ayaz, and when we read that the young Ayaz was violated by the great Emir Mahmud,[67] it flies in the face of the dominant historical-literary narratives.

Yet these counter-interpretations of events, some of which, like the story of Ayaz and Mahmud and his mother, have a secondary role in the formation of the counter-discourse and the narrator/Ayaz, have other strategies in mind. Often, the object is to simply make perceptible facts which through the dominant discourses have become automatized.

The Persian version of the Ayaz narrative has the rather reductionist title of "dismemberment";[68] the first sentence is an order issued by Mahmud to Ayaz: "He said: 'Bring up the saw!'". In this section of the book, Mahmud and Ayaz are in the process of dismembering a man, and Mahmud calls for a saw so that they can cut off the convicted man's legs. As mentioned before, this process is described very methodically and in great detail in this first long part of the novel. The following lines are representative of such descriptions.

Mahmud shouted, "Begin!" and with a harmonious, rhythmical motion we began, Mahmud pulling the saw as I released it, I pulling the saw as Mahmud released it and the saw slipping and slicing through the flesh with the grating sound of a potter's wheel in a Ghaznayn or Ray or Baqdad [sic.] bazaar. With Mahmud pulling mightily upon the saw when

I released it and myself pulling mightily upon the saw when Mahmud
released it, the arm was soon severed, two hands-breadth lengths from
the wrist, just above the elbow, and Mahmud shouted, "Bring the oil!
Oil!" And from the foot of the ladder they handed me the bucket full of
boiling, steaming, fiery hot oil, and I handed it to Mahmud, and he
managed with agility to hold it and to twist the severed stump of the arm
into the oil and keep it until the blood coagulated.[69]

None of the narratives of the dominant discourses have ignored Mahmud's
cruelties, but the loci of emphases of these narratives are selected in such a
way that narratives about cruelties and misdeeds are represented in a cliché-like
manner and the uncontextualized repetitions have led to their automatization
and thus imperceptibility. The slow process of describing the dismembering of
the convicted man actually changes the location of emphasis and presents it
as one of the most, if not the most, significant segments of the narrative. At
the same time, the slow pace of the narrative makes this event perceptible.
This approach contradicts readings which consider these segments insig-
nificant details in the context of larger narratives aimed at justifying the existence
of leaders and their actions. Here this event functions like an anecdote
which punctures traditional *grand récits*. This also is reminiscent of Viktor
Shklovsky's famous example about the notion of perceptibility as an aesthetic
element in a work of art:

> Shklovsky starts with one of his favourite themes—the "conventionality"
> of art. He compares the well-known conventions of poetry ("oblique,
> difficult poetic speech, which makes the poet tongue-tied; strange, unusual
> vocabulary, unusual arrangement of words") with conventions of drama
> (Lear's failure to recognise Kent; Kent and Lear's failure to recognize
> Edgar, recognition scenes in last acts of classical dramas etc.), and even
> the formalities of dancing ("a walk which constructed to be felt"). Why,
> he asks, did Ovid, in creating as "Art of Love," recommend unhurried
> enjoyment? The answer to all these irrationalities lies in the very nature of
> art; art is: "the crooked road, the road on which the foot senses the
> stones, the road which turns back on itself—this is the road of art."[70]

In *The Infernal Times* ..., too, the deliberately slow process of description
achieves the same result, making the foot sense the stones.[71] Of course, this
slow pace slows down the action of the story considerably, but this is a side
effect of Ayaz's using this narrative podium to describe his mentality instead
of being mindful of the event-based progression of the narration.

This slow pace of narrative which serves to make the event more perceptible is a familiar technique used in modern Persian fiction and especially in
works which could be identified with counter-discourses.

The description of the dismembering of the convict in *The Infernal Times* ... is
also reminiscent of the torture spectacle of Robert-François Damiens which

Foucault reproduced at the beginning of his *Discipline and Punish*.[72] The difference, however, is that the victim of *The Infernal Times* ... functions beyond specific time and space. This convict sometimes shouts like Mansur-e Hallaj "I am The Truth," undergoes the same kind of mutilation that Ayn al-Qozat[73] underwent, and, like Hasanak-e Vizier,[74] is stoned. Indeed, such allusions suggest possible readings of this torture and mutilation process which has happened throughout Iran's history, including the tortures and stonings of recent periods. In this sense, such descriptions could be considered an example of the literarization process of a historical discourse which has been written in order to counter the official discourse.

This is only one of the characteristics of the project of producing a historical counter-discourse. Indeed, as previously mentioned, this book is one of the most ambitious of such projects. In the context of this work, the word *discourse* should be understood simply as "the complexes of signs and practices which organize social existence and social reproduction."[75] In the introduction to the third edition of *Qesseh Nevisi* (Fiction Writing), having mentioned many events which had happened to him and a number of his works, Baraheni summarizes his discussion about his works:

> I have reached this conclusion that what locates me in interaction with society and history, what digs in the depth of my psyche and connects to the psyche of others, what represents my individual defeat or blossoming in the guise of the defeat or blossoming of the others is the story; story is my private and public history.[76]

In comparison to works such as *Well to Well* and *The Song of Those Killed*, the novel *The Infernal Times of Mr. Ayaz* demonstrates the deliberate usage of literary devices to present a vast historical space which is not necessarily limited to the time of particular events of the narrative. In this regard there is a distance between this work and other works (Baraheni's and others') which are categorized as report-stories and have a strong emphasis on the journalistic duty of literature.

One of the literary techniques used in the *The Infernal Times* ... is designed to function against the internalization of the dominant discourse which is exhibited in the form of "naturalized habits and practices" by individuals.[77] This internalization process is, in fact, the logical continuation of the process of naturalization by the dominant discourse. In *The Infernal Times* ..., too, the same elements of creating a spectacle employed by the dominant discourse are used. But there is a twist which is achieved through emphasis on unnaturalness. In this spectacle, like its counterpart in the case of Robert-François Damiens, there is an audience, and these people are even involved in the stoning of the victim; in a rather predictable and unsurprising manner. But this time they are defined as "howling dogs," or "lambs," or "historically tame dogs," who have been deceived in such a way that they willingly accept the dominant discourse and its representatives. In one of his explanations about the howling of people who are enjoying the torture of the convicted man and demand that it continue, Ayaz says:

> In truth, between ourselves and the people, a question and answer exchange of a very particular nature had taken place; we had answered first and let them ask the question, and then we had given another answer and given them permission to ask another corresponding question, and they had imagined in this succession of questions and answers that they were asking us first and only then were we answering.[78]

Such an explanation, juxtaposed with the description of the savage torture applied, clearly challenges the "natural" behaviors which are the results of the internalization of the narratives of the dominant discourse. In this countering spectacle, there is another element which explains its exemplifying attribute. Although no exact description of the victim is given, there is no doubt that through his identification with historical characters such as Hallaj and Ayn al-Qozat, he is reminiscent of thinkers who belonged to a discourse of the Other. And indeed, with regard to Iran's recent history, the echo of this story is heard loudly and clearly in the context of the Serial Murders Project.

Bahram Beyzai: using the prism of modern events to read myths

In contemporary Persian fiction, there are numerous examples of works in which the authors have relied on epic or historical characters and events to represent aspects of modern history. In most cases, the writer selects characters and events which have a privileged position and importance in the collective memory; therefore any change in the commonly accepted version of their narratives is sufficient to suggest the emergence of different and possibly contrasting narratives. Predictably, and as mentioned above, one of the important sources which has provided many authors with a richness of such characters and events is the *Shahnameh. The Infernal Times* ..., too, although not directly, is linked to the historical time of this most important Iranian epic. The *Shahnameh* was completed during the rule of Sultan Mahmud Ghaznavi. Ferdowsi, after 30 years of working on his epic, dedicated it to Sultan Mahmud, hoping to receive a reward, but Mahmud rejected it.[79] This part of the story is known and is the commonly accepted account concerning this event. In one of his film scripts, *Dibacheh-ye Novin-e* Shahnameh (*A New Prologue to the* Shahnameh), Bahram Beyzai (b. 1938) has reconstructed and re-narrated this period in such a way that it can easily be interpreted from the point of view of modern history. Beyzai has written a number of works in which he has either been inspired by or directly used the characters and events of this epic, but none of them lends itself so readily to the notion of alternative historiography as the *New Prologue to the* Shahnameh.

The script opens with a scene in which "a group of twenty or thirty people in an alley is carrying a corpse on their shoulders."[80] This is Ferdowsi's body.

This procession is stopped by a "gownsman"[81] and a group of his followers who call Ferdowsi "the accursed one" and demand that those carrying the body change their path, "before the land is contaminated with blasphemy!"[82] When the savant/gownsman faces their consternation, inquiring about the reasons for this curse and anger, he replies:

> Oh the ignorance of you the unlearned! I will not allow you to take his corpse to the cemetery of the Muslims, for he has praised the infidels; with whom blasphemy thrives.[83]

Another one of the bearers very politely reminds the "master" that the man is dead and that final judgment will take place in another world and by the ultimate judge; but the master shouts:

> Do you yearn for the irreligious, you infidel? No wailing will I hear, no, never! May I be a fire worshiper if the invisible judge does not bestow upon me the first place in paradise for the passion I exalt on behalf of his religion. Quickly take away that accursed![84]

Clearly the image of this savant bears an uncanny resemblance to the typical portrait of religious fanatics, and in fact the word *molla* which is now occasionally used to refer to such fanatics means "educated" and undoubtedly the word "savant" (*daneshmand*) which is not usually used in such contexts, could legitimately be read as an attempt to indirectly refer to its religious counterpart, the molla. The behavior of this savant, too, is reminiscent of the negative description of the mollas, promoted by the contending discourses in Iran.

Not surprisingly, in this script, the symbolic figure of the dominant discourse of the time, Sultan Mahmud, is defined through the adjective *ghazi* (holy warrior) which is a clear underlining of his pretended religiosity, and even piety.[85] Of course, these are not the only characteristics which remind readers in a rather direct manner of the present times. Throughout the script, there is an obvious emphasis on the importance of language which is completely compatible with the traditional narrative of the *Shahnameh* and its significance in preserving the Persian language. According to this narrative, which is historically documented, Ferdowsi composed the *Shahnameh* at a time when the post-invasion Islamic government in Iran was gradually succeeding in imposing not only the new religion—Islam—but also the Arabic language. In a famous line attributed to him, he mentions his conscious effort to revitalize Persian. It reads: "I suffered during these thirty years, but I have revived the Iranians with the Persian language."

Since Muslims believe that the Qur'an is God's word which was revealed to the Prophet of Islam, Mohammad, in Arabic, Arabic has a particular sacred character; and during different periods of Islamic governments in Iran, this language has been promoted by the official discourse. The post-revolutionary governments of Iran are no exception to the rule, and it is not difficult to find such similarities between the conduct of these governments and that of the early period of invasion of Iran by the Muslim Arabs. In *A New Prologue to the Shahnameh*, Beyzai refers specifically to this Arabicism, and also Turkism (since Sultan Mahmud was originally a Turk), as examples of forgetting one's identity to the point of trying to please "the foreigners" at any cost, and emphasizes the relationship between these tendencies and loss of identity. In one of the scenes, an Arab comptroller, who is fed up with this kind of oppression and acceptance of this arabicization by those who try to please the invaders, refers to this confrontation by reproaching his Iranian assistants (accountants) who, in order to ingratiate themselves, exaggerate in their usage of Arabic language.

> Comptroller
> I do not understand your language. You Persians speak Arabic more than I, whose father and whose father's fathers were Arabs. At night when you are asleep, he is awake. And when you spit at your picture in the mirror, he records your genealogy. When you are serving the Turks and the Arabs, greasing your palms, he endures destitution in the service of the better among you. What should we tax him for? If we are not rewarding him, why must we despoil him?[86]

This last part, of course, is not just Ferdowsi's story; it is the story of numerous writers and artists who, because of their incompatibility with or dissent from the official discourse, have fallen from grace to the point where their very livelihoods have been threatened. Beyzai himself is one such example; during the Islamic government, his films either have not received permission to be made or have faced numerous problems after completion.[87] Of course, *A New Prologue to the Shahnameh* not only reflects its author's state of being, it has the potential of representing all current dissident writers and artists who are constantly being persecuted; this persecution going at times as far as attempts on their lives. The most famous example of such efforts is an event which took place in the summer of 1367/1997. As it was found out later on, this was part of the much larger project to which I have referred in previous pages, namely the Serial Murders. The details of this particular event have been documented by a number of writers who were supposed to be the first victims of this project. According to these accounts, in the summer of 1997 the Ministry of Information of the Islamic Republic planned the mass murder of a number of major Iranian writers. This is quite telling in the sense that the Islamic government has always considered non-official artists the most dangerous group of dissidents. Under the guise of an Iran–Armenia literary exchange conference, it was decided to send more than 20 writers from Iran to Armenia. A bus carrying the Iranian writers was driven by someone who was later determined to have been an agent of the Ministry of Information. During the trip, the driver tried to steer the bus towards a precipice while he jumped clear. It was sheer luck that the bus did not fall and the writers managed to save themselves. Interestingly enough, moments after the failed attempt by the driver, members of the Islamic Republic's Ministry of Information arrived and saved the driver, while they blatantly continued their verbal threats against the writers. This event has been documented by a number of writers who were on the bus.[88]

Incidentally, Beyzai recently wrote and directed a play which demonstrates his sensitivity to such issues. *Majles-e Shabih dar Zekr-e Masaeb-e Ostad Navid Makan va Hamsarash Mohandes Rokhshid Farzin* (An Account of the Misfortunes of Master Navid Makan and Her Husband, the Engineer Rokhshid Farzin) was one of Beyzai's few plays which received permission to be produced after a long time. The play deals vaguely with the Serial Murders. In one of the interviews he did after the play was premiered, Beyzai clearly said that one of his goals of writing this play was "to pay respect to those friends who are no longer among us." This was a rather direct reference to the victims of the Serial Murders.[89] The play was staged in 1385/2005 but after only 24 performances it was shut down. Obviously keeping the memory of the victims of the Serial Murders alive was not the only narrative strategy of the play. Beyzai can never be accused of writing one-dimensional works. Indeed, just the "non-Islamic" names of the main characters—Makan, Rokhshid, Farzin, Navid—show the playwright's effort to add historical-mythic dimensions to the play and taking it beyond a simple literarization of a particular event.

Reading such works with an eye on the idea of rewriting historical events reveals only one of their characteristics. Indeed, these works cannot be reduced to political manifestos about a particular situation or group of people. This point is amply clear in Beyzai's works in which he has employed mythic allusions, especially works such as *Siyavash-Khani* (Performing the Epic of Siyavash)[90] or *Azhdahak* and *Arash* which are derived from the stories of the *Shahnameh*. One of the strategies of such works is to create structures through which one could read or re-read history, be it ancient or modern, or, as in Baraheni's terms, private or collective. When juxtaposed, these structures constitute narratives of a discourse which is in contrast with the official discourse. *A New Prologue to the* Shahnameh is a perfect example.

In one of the few scenes in the script in which Sultan Mahmud is present, "The narrowed-eye Sultan of Ghazneh [is seated] on the throne and learned men and officials are standing around." Two of the learned men (gownsmen) are talking about Ferdowsi and the *Shahnameh* and, as usual, before anything else, they begin with his religion.

The First Learned Man
He has celebrated the former kings to shame the present Soltan. Tell me, what religion has he? Everyone must have the religion of the Soltan who follows that of the Caliph.

The Second Learned Man
What kind of religion does someone who praises the Zoroastrians have, except the religion of fire? He recounts many victories of Kavus,

Fereydun, and Kiumars, in order to disavow the victories of the leaders of the Ghaznavids. He praises the heroism of the Zal, Rostam, and Esfandiyar, to scorn the bravery of the Soltan and the leaders.[91]

This "critique" grows more precise; in fact, the problem is not just the fact that the poet has rendered pre-Islamic stories in verse and therefore, naturally, these poems could not have been in praise of "the religious campaigns of the great leaders." What these savants and their like have intuitively realized is that the *Shahnameh* was composed in order for history to be rewritten, and like all those works examined previously in the context of new historiography, it attempts to use specific myths and language to construct new prisms for readers to see the world and events and, in fact, to challenge the narratives of those who won the military battle. These savants have realized that the choice of language and myths has not been without purpose.

The First Learned Man

[Unrolls a scroll] Doldol (Ali's horse)[92] loses to Rakhsh (Rostam's horse), the Soltan's guard (*junds*) to the Persia troops (*sepah*); vengeance to blood; Arabic verses to Persian verses; Turban to the headgear (*dastar*) and the battle of Kheybar to the Castle of Bronze. Well, what is left? – A shrine to a temple, retaliation to rewards, Doomsday to Resurrection Day, and *ajal* (death in Arabic) [sic][93] to *marg* (death in Persian). If there is mourning, it is only for the death of Siyavash, or Sohrab, or Iraj. If there is any occasion for joy, it is for the Persian festivities. They call *alem* (Arabic for learned) *daneshmand* (Persian for learned), and *elm* (knowledge in Arabic) *danesh* (knowledge in Persian). Every Persian word they bring back is like a stone they throw at the *madraseh* (religious schools); and to virtue and excellence![94]

Such passages, because of their direct references, could be read with a particular time and space in mind, but because of their interpretive and suggestive nature, they cannot be reduced to simple political and social commentaries. Although such works point to specific times and events, they are not limited temporally or spatially. Indeed, by establishing delicate links between the *univers romanesque* and the present time, they suggest and provide and the opportunity for the reader to construct atemporal readings. This is how in *A New Prologue to the* Shahnameh, for example, the book-burnings initiated by Sultan Mahmud *ghazi* could well be reminiscent of policies of the Islamic Republic which led to many books being buried or burned because they were and are simply considered *zalleh* (misleading). Or the emphasis that Beyzai places on the catastrophic combination of ignorance and power when he describes in his script the making of the army of the official discourse could very well be related to the present time.[95] This is especially true, when Beyzai describes the times of Sultan Mahmud. He directly uses the *Shahnameh* and relies on verses which can easily be attributed to other times and periods. The backdrop of this description is provided through reference to Rostam Farrokhzad, the leader of the Iranian army during the Arab invasion. In this scene, Rostam Farrokhzad, having realized that the Iranian army has been defeated "is sitting on a bench and is writing his last testament."[96] And Ferdowsi, as if expressing his own ideas, in fact prophesizes a future which will come after the defeat of the Iranians and the supremacy of the Islamic government.

> When four hundred years have passed and gone,
> Then shall this world see wisdom undone.
> They shall turn from their sacred vows and from the truth:
> Mendacity and error will be held dear for sooth.
> ...
> Out of the Turks, the Arabs, and the dehqan[97]
> Shall be formed a new race, and three merges into one.
> He who is not a Turk, an Arab or a dehqan
> Shall speak the jargon of deception.
> ...
> That one this one robs; this one robs that;
> Curses and praise are one; they cannot discriminate.
> ...
> What concealed is worse than what men see
> No one will care for justice and generosity.
> The people's hearts will turn as hard as granite;
> Some men will suffer, others will benefit.
> ...
> For their own gain, they seek to harm the rest;
> In the end a religion will rise at their behest![98]

Tackling the taboos: direct confrontation and grinding struggle

One of the methods employed by the official discourse to guarantee its permanence is to define cultural concepts and phenomena as unchangeable and perennial. Informed by an underlying ideology, these definitions suggest an artificial stability for the existing conditions and reduce the possibility of change. In a sense, this approach creates fixed patterns for subjective and objective activities which, after stabilization, lead to semantic and conceptual limitations. In other words, the fixity of the contours of these patterns removes the possibility of interaction of these concepts with the world beyond them. One of the consequences of such fixed patterns is "the coercive taboo upon the forbidden, the irrational, the mad, and the false."[99] In case of the success of the official discourse, the natural continuation of this trajectory will be "the internalization by individuals of such outward authority in the form of 'naturalized' habits and practices."[100] Conversely, the attempts by individuals to reject this internalization and naturalization and then to challenge the constants in order to increase the number of variables, is another site of the counter-discourse's struggle against the discourse in power.

The first, most simple route for this struggle is the overt confrontation with the taboos through the direct use of subjects forbidden either by law or by convention. Defining many of these taboos in terms of religious sanctity, the official discourse of the Islamic Republic has tried to prevent everyone, especially writers and artists, from using many subjects to shape this confrontation. Nonetheless, examples of such efforts do exist.

In *Jensiyat-e Gomshodeh* (Lost Sexuality), Farkhondeh Aqai takes on one of these taboos. In her introduction to this novel, the author writes that the idea of writing this book was engendered after she read in a newspaper about a young man who undergoes a sex change and, after a short while, regrets his decision. The author adds that she has used elements of this true story and tried to produce an entertaining book in order to attract readers to a social problem.[101] She does not elaborate but it is clear that her main point is the difficulty of expressing various aspects of different sexual behaviors in present-day Iran. In every society such reluctance has its own causes, but undoubtedly in the context of the current discursive confrontation in Iran, one of the major reasons for this reluctance is the reaction of the discourse in power to such matters. From this point of view, *Lost Sexuality* could be placed in the category of taboo-breaking literary works, mainly because the Islamic-based official discourse has always been apprehensive about openly discussing the issue of possible sexual identities. Of course, this issue and similar ones have not been defined by the official discourse as absolute taboos either; therefore there have been brief windows of opportunity to bring them up, and even to offer a different outlook towards them. The presence of undeniable realities has secured these opportune moments.

The addressing of taboos and the pointing to the existence of different viewpoints triggers the immediate and natural reaction of the official discourse to control and limit these activities. The most elementary and primitive reaction is to rely on the apparatus of censorship. Reviewing literary works of pre- and post-1979 periods which included references to such topics reveals the enormous dimensions that this particular category of censorship has acquired during the post-revolutionary decades. To have a point of reference, one can examine Persian literary production of much older periods. Many Iranian poets and writers, from the time of classics such as Fakhr al-Din As'ad-e Gorgani (eleventh century), Nezami (twelfth century), Sa'di (thirteenth century), Molavi (Rumi) (thirteenth century), Obeyd Zakani (fourteenth century), and Hafez (fourteenth century) to literary figures of the late Qajar period such as Iraj Mirza (1874–1926) and Aref Qazvini (*c.* 1883–1933), and then the pre-Revolution contemporaries such as Sadeq Hedayat (1903–1951), Forugh Farrokhzad (1935–1966) and Sadeq Chubak (1916–1998) have addressed directly or indirectly topics related to sexual identity and desire, and for the most part managed to avoid the sword of censorship. In *Shahed Bazi dar Adabiyat-e Farsi* (Pederasty in Persian Literature),[102] Sirus Shamisa has collected a large number of examples about homosexual love and relationships in the Persian classical literature. This book was published in 2002 during one of the most "liberal" periods of the Islamic Republic; after less than six months, still in the same liberal period, it was banned and taken off the bookstore shelves and distribution centers, and recycled. *Pederasty in Persian Literature* is simply a collection of examples which aims to represent various approaches in Persian literary tradition in expressing the notion of love and sexuality, with an emphasis on the same-sex relationship. The fact that this text was removed from circulation demonstrated clearly how much the official discourse had lost its capacity to tolerate different narratives about such topics, and how seriously it was relying on traditional methods to fight the production and propagation of counter-discourses. By "traditional methods" I mean the misuse of the official discourse of its position of power to throw obstacles in front of contending discourses.[103] When such a scholarly study, written by one of the most respected academic figures, is treated in this manner, one can easily imagine what fate awaits writers and artists who include references to such subject matters in their creative works.

In addition to such stifling of counter-narratives, the official discourse also exploits the notion of the sacred to define many spaces of subjective and objective activities as sacrosanct and thus effectively prohibits non-official discourses from dwelling in these spaces. Examples are truly numerous, and I will refer only to two non-literary events which underline this point.

In the summer of 1999, at a student demonstration in Tehran, for the first time the Supreme Leader (Ali Khamenei) was directly and systematically criticized; in slogans he was even likened to famous dictatorial figures. Students who were arrested, in addition to the usual accusation of "acting against national security" were also accused of "insulting the sacred office of the Supreme Leader." From that day on, the word "sacred" in the phrase "sacred office of the Supreme Leader" was effectively declared a code word which signified that it is absolutely forbidden to criticize Khamenei in any way, shape, or form.

A second event took place in 2002, when Hashem Aqajari, a university professor and a devout Muslim, who had lost a leg during the Iran–Iraq War, in one of his lectures talked about the Shi'i concept of *taqlid* (imitation)[104] and criticized those who follow religious leaders blindly. At first he was accused of apostasy and sentenced to death, but after demonstrations in a number of cities against the verdict, the charge was changed to "insulting the sacred Islamic concepts." In the end, his sentence was commuted to five years' imprisonment and five years' deprivation of civil rights, including teaching.

These examples not only demonstrate the limitations caused by the sanctification of various fields of human activities, but underline the difficulties of direct confrontation and direct desanctification efforts, which in many cases are easily fought against and prevented by the dominant discourse.

Next to direct confrontation and prevention, some of the more moderate segments of the official discourse have tried to use appropriation methods to effectively undermine contending discourses and narratives. Of course the increasing inflexibility of this discourse has not left much room for that approach to be carried out. But there are representative efforts, the most famous of which is Mohajerani's *Behesht-e Khakestari* (Grey Paradise), to which I referred in Chapter 1. The main subject of the book is about members of a religious government which seems to have the praiseworthy goal of preventing any member of the society from committing any kind of sin. However, according to the text, the methods used by this government are at times incorrect and even inhumane. The author implies that these rulers, through extremist interpretation of Islamic instructions, in actuality justify imprisonment and torture. In the end, still trying to remove any kind of possibility for committing a sin, they force people to build their houses out of glass so that the leaders can watch every minute of their lives. Describing this situation, Mohajerani employs a very simple language and attempts to provide an allegoric as well as ironic effect.

> Vaezi shook his head: …
> – It is necessary to have guarantees … How can we be sure that people truly believe in carrying out their duties? The society should be transparent and limpid. We need an exceptional transparency. Listen well; open your eyes; take a deep breath; swallow the water in your mouth; pause. Pay close attention: I suggest that we make all walls made of glass so that no action or reaction remains hidden from our eyes. Think about how to make walls and ceilings out of glass. Come with proposals; define priorities. Also, be really and deeply careful not to ask any questions.[105]

Soon after, they realize that there are areas which cannot be transparent, so they decide to exclude places such as prisons, government buildings, the houses of members of the secret police and intelligence services from being built with glass.

Both the title of Mohajerani's book and the description of the "Grey Paradise" made of glass are reminiscent of Yevgeny Zamyatin's *We*. In Zamyatin's novel, too, we have a "Glass Paradise" which is designed in the name of the Benefactor to remove every kind of private space and individual choice and freedom.[106] There is, however, a fundamental discursive difference between the two texts. While Zamyatin is moving in the direction of complete disengagement from the discourse in power, Mohajerani, by agreeing to the ideological foundations of the official discourse, moves in the direction of appropriating discourses and narratives of contention and dissent. In Mohajerani's *Grey Paradise*, the ultimate goals of the official discourse are never questioned; indeed, the rulers and their behavior are not situated in the context of power relationships. Instead, the impression is given that this is simply a misguided approach by some officials, who might even have good intentions. Overall it seems that the author, who looks more like a father advising his children, is trying to warn those in power to beware of extremism, while not challenging the ideological fundamentals of their course. That is why, for example, he criticizes the official discourse not for using torture in general but for using it against "decent people." All examples of torture in the book happen to good and decent people, as if to say that torture is acceptable in other cases.

Of course, no matter how much the author tried to appease the official discourse and not challenge it, and no matter how much he tried to show himself as a member of its proponents, this discourse was more inflexible than being able to tolerate even such superficial and occasional criticism. This lack of flexibility shows one of the most significant characteristics of the official discourse: its emphasis on reducing the possibility of change. In previous pages, I referred to this characteristic as emphasis on increasing the constants and as reducing the variables. This feature plays a crucial role in the context of art and literature because such emphasis on rigid and unchangeable components impedes the process of creation. To understand the extent of this rigidity, we need only review some of the instructions and directives issued by major figures of power of the Islamic Republic. One of the sources through which these instructions are publicized is *Adabiyat-e Dastani* (Fiction),[107] a journal considered the literary and artistic organ of the official discourse. Every once in a while this journal offers a collection of such instructions to its readers. The overarching directive, taken from Khomeini's "message to committed writers," published in issue 69 of the journal, summarizes this ideological approach:

> The only art acceptable by the Qur'an is the one which burnishes the pure Islam of Mohammad, peace be upon him, the Islam of the Imams, peace be upon them, the Islam of the pain-stricken poor, the Islam of the wretched, the Islam of those who have been whipped by bitter and shameful history [sic].
>
> ... Art in its real place describes the image of bloodsuckers who enjoy sucking the blood of the pure Islamic culture, the culture of justice and kindness. We should pursue only the kind of art which teaches the way to fight Eastern and Western Imperialists, at the top of which are America and the Soviet Union ... [108]

This approach has been carried on by Khomeini's successor Ali Khamenei, and his instructions are simply specific examples of those same directives:

> I believe that at this point, for one specific cultural task, we should go and find three or four committed and artistic writers and ask them to write ten books of stories and novels for the martyrs ... [109]
>
> My only point is this: I say if you want the art in this country to grow, you should rely on the pious young artist. He can defend Islam and the Revolution and this country. If a director or a producer who, while making a movie, thinks "I am going to include this point in the movie so that I can target one of the ideological foundations of this regime," then he is not defending Islam and the Revolution![110]

These crude instructions are not the exception; they are the rule. Reliance on ideological goals in order to offer opinions without any particular expertise or knowledge is one of the common characteristics of such official discourses. The same approach is used when this discourse attempts to defend its practice of censorship. Khomeini and Khamenei have both emphasized the necessity of such "supervision" and have argued that any text or work of art which depicts the "values" contrary to those promoted by the regime must be stopped, because one of the "rights" and "responsibilities" of the government is "to prevent the dissemination of corruption in the body and soul of each and every citizen."[111] Khomeini had argued for this same approach.

> We should recognize the poison pens; those who pick up a pen and write against Islam, against the clergy, against the direction of the nation; we should know them and find out about their backgrounds.
> …
> A pen is free; a pen which does not conspire. A pen, a newspaper, is free only when it doesn't seek to take the nation backward. This pen is the same old bayonet, which seeks to bring devastation to the nation [sic.]. Of course the nation will not tolerate that; [a nation] which has lost its young people [in the Revolution] does not tolerate four bureaucrats coming and plotting and saying, "The pen is not free." What is not free? Which pens are not free? Corrupted pens should not be free. Even now there are corrupt pens which are free, including these very pens which say "Why don't you leave [pens] free?" These, too, are conspirators.[112]

A common denominator of these directives is their completely stagnant nature. These statements also encourage a certain kind of reading of literary works. Indeed, *Adabiyat-e Dastani* is filled with critiques which are based on these instructions; predictably, according to this approach, the best works of literature are those which follow these static directives and contain no variable agent. The impediments thus created in the path of literary production become quite significant in the case of Persian literature. In the post-revolutionary period, one of the most predominant literary trends has been characterized by its pronounced dissociation from constants and consequently by its increasing association with fluidity and instability. This trend has been directly confronted by the official discourse; this is quite understandable because in dealing with the discourses of the Other, ideological discourses have always preferred a defined and stable opposition to fluid, unstable, and changeable ones.

More than trying to control subject matter, the ideological police seek absolute control over the treatment of subject matter; more so in the case of sensitive issues, the number of which is increasing. From this point of view, a book such as *Lost Sexuality* is problematic for the official discourse, not only because of its topic but because of the way the author treats it. The book deals with the question of sex change, but the author does not consider the sexual duality of the protagonist a contagious illness; rather, she uses it as a defining element of a character for whom this attribute points to the presence of different levels of consciousness. This story clearly reflects the difference between examining this issue from a religious/ideological viewpoint and an approach which at least does not negate the possibility of the existence of other viewpoints and, more importantly, the acknowledgment that there could even be positive aspects in such cases.

In the Persian literary tradition, there are also instances of works which, in the category of sexually-defined subject matter, for example, go beyond the limits accepted by the Islamic/ideological definitions of the official discourse and thus cross the red lines drawn to separate the sacred, taboos, etc. The official discourse's confrontation with these transgressions has been difficult yet decisive. "Difficult" because Persian literary tradition is filled with such examples, and many of them in the classic works are very well known. Part of the confrontation with these transgressions is accomplished through old-fashioned censorship (as in the case of Shamisa's *Pederasty in Persian Literature*, or similar studies, as previously mentioned), but the official discourse has concentrated on more modern works which contain such "subversive" components. In fact, in the case of authors such as Sadeq Hedayat or Forugh Farrokhzad whose works include such components, or those whose works include even indirect references to such components, the literary arms of the current power apparatus have initiated a full-scale campaign to discredit them by projecting them as sick creatures with identity problems. Here are some examples:

> In some of these [feminist] works, there are cases of indirect promotion of prostitution, for example, under this argument that reaching the ultimate level of decadence and dirt will lead to intuition and revelation. In the novel *Women Without Men*, we are confronted by such an approach with regard to the prostitute protagonist of the work. This is while, parallel to her, the pious girl of the story, covered in the Islamic hejab, is depicted as truly a hypocrite and corrupt.[113]

Or

> Basically it seems that Sadeq Chubak's imagination knows only one way to function and produce images, and that is through a lustful and instinctive approach.[114]

Or

> Using the criteria and measures of pathological psychology and clinical psychology, Hedayat was certainly depressed, and this depression of his caused him to have illusory melancholic illusions [sic]. From the viewpoint of spiritual psychology, too, Hedayat was a sick and deeply depressed person.[115]

In June of 2006, an interview was published in the journal *Adabiyat-e Dastani* (Fiction) which symbolizes the importance of the ideological approach to everything, including art and literature. Ahmad Shakeri, one of the editors-in-chief of *Adabiyat-e Dastani*, did this interview with Mostafa Mastur, a very religious writer whose most famous novella is entitled *Ruy-e Mah-e Khodavand ra Bebus* (Kiss the Beautiful Face of God, 1379/2000). The main point of this novella is to provide reasons for the existence of God, yet apparently this is not enough for the official discourse. After arguing against this work, mainly because while proving the existence of God, it does not specifically emphasize the only way to reach God namely Islam and probably its Shi'i sect, Ahmad Shakeri, who is criticized by the interviewee because of his ideological approach which will lead to the complete stoppage of the work of art and literature, says:

> No, it will not lead to the complete stoppage. But if not producing unhealthy art means the limitation of the field of production, why do you insist that these works should not be stopped? When we have accepted the basics of the religion, what is wrong with sacrificing these things for religion?[116]

And when Mastur reminds him that this is too ideological an outlook from which to judge literature, Shakeri says:

> What is wrong with the ideological approach? ... You are saying that since you have accepted a phenomenon called story, you are required to accept its [artistic] necessities. But I am saying that literary necessities are subordinate to the religion's imperatives. It means that first I consider my religion's imperatives and only if the story structure fits these imperatives will I use it.[117]

This is ideological policing in action par excellence. This ideological policing does not stop at simply controlling the circulation of raw materials needed for the development of any counter-discourse; it goes beyond that and defines all the red lines in every field of human activity. Of course, such decisive-ideological reactions effectively situate many narratives in the position of the Other and thus provide them with a positional value which facilitates counter-discursive readings.[118]

Direct confrontations and attempts to step over red lines have never been very successful. Their positionality provides them with counter-discursive value, but that same positionality makes them easy targets for the dominant discourse. Iran's post-revolutionary literature is a case in point. It was very easy for the official discourse to identify and violently challenge literary expressions of such confrontations and their representatives. The more effective style for counter-discourses has always been indirect approaches. This method begins with the assumption that discourses, in order to impose themselves, try to define everything according to their own terms and frame them in structures made from their own concepts, languages, and narratives. In other words, official discourses—especially those which rely on ideology—are effectively trying to protect an ensemble of calcified perceptions and consequently calcified expressions. Assuming that "A Dominant discourse is the imposition, not so much of certain truths ... as of a certain language,"[119] this approach begins its challenge by modifying fixed languages through subtle and gradual changes. Modifying a fixed language is a grinding process which relies more on language than the subject matter; therefore both identifying it and relating to it are difficult.

In the case of Iran's recent fiction, many works representing this trend undermine specific relationships between signifiers and signified established by the official discourse and its fixed and established languages. This way, an aleatory aspect is created for these works which is unpredictable and has volatile consequences. And it is exactly this indeterminacy which worries the ideological/unchangeable discourses. At the same time, censorship, this most reliable tool of the official discourse to cleanse the fields of art and literature from narratives of the Other, has difficulty with these works whose common denominator is simply dissent from traditions and stability.

Mohammad Rahim Okhovvat's novella *Ta'liq* (Ta'liq)[120] is one such work, and, because of its emphasis on the ways transformation could be generated in established vernacular and, in general, semiotics, exemplifies this grinding linguistic contention.

The narrative movement of the story begins with a young man, the narrator, who goes to the house of Hajieh Khanom[121] (whose real name is Shirin-Banu). The young man, who works in the miniature shop of Mosavvar, has come to Shirin-Banu's house at her invitation to choose some of her antique objects in lieu of some of her debts. The old woman takes him to the basement of the house. There the presence of various paintings, calligraphy, and other objects evokes different time periods and events from the past.

At the heart of the text is the account of an incident involving one of the Qajar princes who has killed the son of one of his senior courtiers. The narrator begins by suggesting that apparently at the court of this prince, there had been a tradition that if any courtier wanted to have a mistress, he had to take the woman first to the prince and after he spent some time with her then, once he got tired of her, he would pass her on to the courtier. The son of the senior courtier however, falls in love with a woman and imprudently does not follow this tradition. Although this imprudence does not last long and the young man sends the woman to the prince as a gift, he still becomes the target of his rage, and the prince, in one of his many moments of revelry, shoots the young man and "hunts the one who had stolen his prey."[122] As was customary in such situations, on behalf of the prince, a letter is written to the father saying that his son's death was due to an unfortunate accident, that the prince is sad, and the father should hope to receive the favors of the court. According to the rules of the game, during a period when the sovereign is the uncontestable master of the life and wealth of his subjects, the father should humbly accept this fictitious explanation and should express his utmost appreciation for the royal robe of honor that the court has sent, as well as for possible future favors. The father seems to be doing that and sends a letter to the court.

> The noble epistle was received when the fire of the scourge was aflame in the solitary heart. Its contents were revealed. The royal robe trampled the flame of the heart and hid the fire of [the loss] of the light of [my] eyes in the bosom under the ashes; maybe until such time as a breeze pushes away the ashes of time and the old fire rises anew.
>   The least of the humble servants of your threshold, Enayat-Allah.[123]

Deviation from the servant's idiom is obvious. The narrator, just to make sure, explains: "its appearance is servant-like. Inwardly, it is another story. Why didn't he write to soothe the flame of the heart? You understand the difference. What did he mean by that breeze?"[124] It is precisely these seemingly small differences and others such as the hiding of the pain under the ashes, and the expression of the lasting rage of the father which distinguish this letter from the established language of a servant. It is not important whether or not the author has tried to use a particular syntactic and rhetorical methodology of subversion, but there is no doubt that this passage and its deviation from customary language, which from a narratological point of view destabilizes the calcified, is the microcosm of the story, as well as its dominant technique.

The novella is organized through a series of seemingly traditional descriptions of events, objects, and different time periods. The narrator has tried to reproduce the old atmosphere by including old expressions and syntax. Yet from the very beginning, divergences from ordinary descriptions are seen. Many of these descriptions are based on the paintings and engraved writing cases which the narrator has found in the basement of Shirin-Banu's house. At times the narrator presents with deliberation the details of nude bodies of women seen in these pictures and creates subtle erotic atmospheres which are not customarily part of such descriptions. In fact, at one point, one of the characters defines these scenes as shameless.[125] On another occasion, the narrator directly reminds the reader of the unconventional nature of such scenes. "Why did they draw so many nude women? Or why were only women drawn nude? I thought only the Europeans used to draw nude bodies; but they, too, have done so."[126]

Under the pretext of describing writing cases and paintings, there are other digressions such as detailed descriptions of using opium, and gatherings for revelry and carousal. But more significant is the fact that this time these paintings, most of which depict royal or princely courts and courtiers and are commissioned by them, are described/read by their subordinates. This is another effort to construct the silenced narratives.

In addition to the dominant technique of the novella, namely the delicate diversions on the level of word, phrase, and syntax, the general structure of the work emphasizes a kind of transitionality and instability which are obviously incompatible with the permanency of concepts and values usually promoted by ideological/religious notions and the fixed images of different times and spaces created, based on these concepts and values. From the very beginning of *Ta'liq*, the narrator goes to the basement of Shirin-Banu's house and wanders in the middle of forgotten, lost, dust-covered times and spaces. Each painting and writing case and example of calligraphy reminds him of a forgotten time period which had quite possibly been considered eternal and unchangeable, even sacred by the official discourse of that time. Faces, clothes, and customs seem quite strange; indeed, the objects and events which are reconstructed in the imagination of the narrator after he sees the pile of old items are described by another character in the story as objects and people which no longer exist. The end of the story is a reiteration of the transitional and temporary nature of time periods and corresponding discourses which have all considered themselves eternal. This last part is narrated by Mosavvar, the owner of the miniature-making shop who also, throughout the story, provides many descriptions of the objets d'art. Mosavvar begins this segment by referring to the end of the story of Nasr-Allah Khan, the son of Enayat-Allah Khan. The first was killed by the bullet of the Prince because he had kept a mistress to himself; the second (the father), for the crime of having written that letter, showing impertinence towards the Prince, was strangled.

> [Nasr-Allah Khan's] grave was in Takht-e Pulad. It is still there, next to the Bakhtiari plot. Amongst all those large gravestones with carvings, this one is very poor. At the foot of the wall. They said even the choice of that place for the grave had made the prince angry. I think Enayat-Allah had called it the place of sacrifice. Maybe he had not actually said it, and people said he did. And after that, of course, their official establishment had collapsed.
> Amidst the opium smoke, the words had a choked, heavy resonance.
> – The time of the strong and distinguished people had come to an end. It was the turn of rootless people to settle. Laymen were replacing the clerics, and who knows when they would change their places again.[127]

The question of "When will they (laymen and clerics) change places?" was asked at a time when this prediction had actually come true. *Ta'liq* was written almost 20 years after the 1979 Revolution, after the replacement of the laymen by the clerics. But this question is more general, and its significance lies in stressing the notion of transition with regard to the official discourse, whether it is constructed by the laymen or by the clerics.

Ta'liq is one of many examples in which an antiquated language is used, and at the same time the signifieds to which this language ordinarily refers are undermined, and thus different narrative potentials are brought out. Such a language, especially when it is juxtaposed with religious contexts and references, given the religious characteristics of the official discourse, finds even more significance. Naturally, the official discourse is more sensitive towards works which include such references and contexts.

In *"Ma'sum-e Panjom ya Hadis-e Mordeh bar Dar Kardan-e an Savar keh Khahad Amad"* (The Fifth Innocent, or the Story of Hanging the Dead Body of that Rider Who Will Come), the last story he wrote using the title of "Innocent," Hushang Golshiri used such a language. This short story was written in 1355/1976 but did not receive permission to be published. Shortly after the Revolution, in 1358/1979, when the newly-formed power apparatus had not yet created its administrative arms in different fields, including censorship, this book was published in limited circulation. After a short time, it went out of print. This was the first and last edition of the book. At the beginning of the text, Golshiri attributes the story to a character named Abu al-Majd Ravaq who, according to Golshiri's text, had heard it from someone else. Like the narrator of *The Infernal Times of Mr. Ayaz*, and like Baraheni, Golshiri attempts to expand the temporal dimensions of his narrative. The language of "The Fifth Innocent" is very old and extremely difficult. In an interview, Golshiri said about this story: "I wrote 'The Fifth Innocent' for five people."[128] The main subject of this short story is that the people of a fictional city are waiting for the arrival of the Shi'i Messiah, the Imam of the Age, and so every day they take a saddled horse to the city gate so that in case the Messiah comes, he could ride it and enter the city. At the end of the year the horse is stoned to death, and each person takes a piece of the horse's flesh for a blessing. On the other hand, the rulers are trying to fight the people's belief in the coming of a Messiah by means of prison, torture, and death; of course they are not successful. In the context of this study, the importance of this story lies in its use of linguistic and conceptual characteristics such as *Mahdaviyyat* (Shi'i messianism) which, whether because of their antiquity or their relationship with the official discourse, are identified with unchangeable or even sacred traditions. However, by attributing a brutal behavior—stoning an animal to death—as well as also by referring to the illogical and futile nature of this wait, and more importantly by construing these issues as part of the dynamics of relationship between the rulers and subjects, Golshiri's narrative dissociates itself from the traditional semiotics and provides the possibility for a different reading of such concepts.

In *"Ostureh va Khorafat: Talashi baray-e Tafsir-e 'Ma'sum-ha' az Hushang Golshiri"* (Myth and Superstition: An Attempt to Interpret Hushang Golshiri's Innocents), having argued that Iranian myths under the influence of monotheistic religions have been contaminated with superstition, Kazem Amiri attempts to show Golshiri's fight against these superstitions and illusions. He especially uses "The Fifth Innocent" as one such example. To be sure, this intention of Golshiri is obvious, but the literary point of "The Fifth Innocent" is more a linguistic one and thus more similar to that of Okhovvat's novella *Ta'liq*, that is, the use of a particular language/parole to suggest potential narratives which are in contrast to or different from discursive implications of that language/parole. The particular characteristics of these potential narratives are not known, but the mere reference to the possibility of their existence shifts the religious/antiquated language from its fixed status and adds an aleatory aspect to it; this creates a new site for confrontation.

Dominant discourses have always tried to control the aleatory aspect of the language; conversely, counter-discourses have always attempted to undermine the predetermined boundaries. In this sense, authors such as Okhovvat and Golshiri who attempt to destabilize fixed systems of linguistic signs and codes, as Julio Cortazar puts it, "work the limits,"[129] or more precisely, they work the limits of the language.

There is not much distance from the undermining of stability and stabilization, and therefore of calcified expressions and perceptions, to parody. But since, according to definition, parody has a specific target (to parody), it cannot be used easily, especially when it directly targets the official discourse and narratives identified with it. Censorship and suppression make it impossible for this technique to be used effectively; even if in particular cases such works get through the censorship, they are confronted as soon as they are identified as parodies. Obviously the closer these parodies are to the subject matter and themes, and even words considered sacred, the harsher and more inexorable this confrontation is. Therefore, obvious or exaggerated examples of works which directly parody the "sacred" foundations of official discourse can present themselves only when the levers of the power apparatus do not have access to authors or their works.

One of the most exaggerated contemporary examples is Sadeq Hedayat's *Karvan-e Eslam: Al-Be'sat Al-Islamiah Il-Al-Belad Al-Afranjiah* (The Caravan of Islam: The Emergence of Islam in European Countries), 1309/1930. The few main characters of the text, which looks more like a pamphlet than a short story, are superficial caricatures based on negative clichés of Muslim clerics (which at times are referred to in Hedayat's text as the representatives of Islamic nations [Umma]). Almost the whole text is designed to ridicule Islam and its teachings in a very superficial, too-obvious manner. The text consists of three parts: the first part is the description of these Muslim leaders discussing their intent to travel to European countries and convert people forcibly to Islam. The second part is a description of their train travels in Europe, and the last part is an account of them in Paris, two and a half years later. At the beginning of the text it says that this text was written in Arabic by a news writer who worked for a magazine called *Almanjilab* (Vile), and that the author has just translated it.

Throughout the book, in addition to sneering at Islam and its teachings, the author constantly refers in a very direct way to hypocrisy, avarice, and lustfulness, and many other unsavory qualities as ordinary attributes of Muslim clergy.

Mr. Andalib al-Islam: "According to my son, Mr. Sokan al-Shari'a, who despite his youth is quite knowledgeable about religious matters and has spent five years in infidel countries and written a book called Zobdat al-Nijasat [Selected Filth], there is a lot of money in the 'New World'."

Mr. Sokan al-Shari'a: "Yes, there are many rich people in that part of the world, and each one of them who converts to Islam should then go on Hajj. Therefore we can place a group of highway robbers on the road to Mecca to take their belongings, and we should also have some agents who will place fleas on their bodies, because then for every flea they kill they will have to sacrifice a sheep to God. Of course it is preferable for them to kill two sheep, because they are newly-converted and their ancestors have been cross-worshippers. Those who don't convert to Islam should pay a special tax to the Muslim treasury, otherwise their possessions will be confiscated; they cannot have a wife, and they could be killed." (Those present applaud.)[130]

Clearly this book is in such opposition to Islam that in post-revolutionary Iran—even owning it, is a punishable offense.

Perhaps the only important point of *The Caravan of Islam* is found in those rare moments in the text when the anger of the author/narrator against Islam goes beyond the superficial ridicule of Muslim clerics and leaders and targets the whole religion of Islam (still in a superficial manner). The significant aspect of these outbursts is the questioning of the unquestionable and the suggestion of a *reversal of the source of authority* which, in the context of the religious official discourse is considered non-negotiable and sacred. These instances are found in the third part of the text which begins with the narrator's description of the fate of these Muslim leaders and their plans. Most of them have ended up in Paris working in bars, or as pimps, or as a doorman at the *Folies Bergère*, and in general are involved with the lowest of the low. The narrator asks Mr. Sonnat al-Aqtab, who had been introduced as a professor of *feqh* (Islamic jurisprudence) and now is operating a bar with a woman, a number of questions to find out what happened to his beliefs. The main point of his answers is simply that they were promoting those issues because they were thinking of their own interests and nothing else. The narrator asks him specifically:

"Then what about religion? What about Islam?"

What religion? What nonsense! Is Islam anything other than robbing and killing people? All its rules and instructions are designed for a couple of small areas in front and back of the man. Have you forgotten how Qut-e Layamut described the main Islamic conduct, saying that either you should convert to Islam and follow the instructions of Zobdat al-Nijasat or we will kill you, or that you should pay a special tax? This is the only logic of Islam ... [131]

In *Islam and Postcolonial Narrative*, Erickson refers to the notion of reversal as one of the main characteristics of Salman Rushdie's *The Satanic Verses* and defines it as a phenomenon which "conjures up the opposing concepts of truth." This is what "Mikhail Bakhtin finds in the contrast between the official feast of the Middle Ages that sanctioned a 'truth' that was considered as timeless and invariable, and carnivalesque 'truth' that opposed all that was predetermined and considered as unchanging or absolute."[132]

It is difficult to say with certainty which part of *The Satanic Verses* was presented to Khomeini which made him issue the fatwa for the assassination of the author, but undoubtedly the reversal of the ultimate source of authority or at least the providing of legitimacy for other readings of truth and equating it with The Truth reflected in the divine verses (the accepted version of the Qur'an), was one of the main reasons for the fatwa. Describing *The Satanic Verses*, having mentioned that there are verses which are not included in the authorized version of the Qur'an and are called "the Satanic verses,"[133] Erickson refers to certain chapters of the novel which are "involved in counter-dialogue against the authorized version of the Qur'an."[134] This I believe defines the internal structure of Rushdie's novel. The religious characteristic of the discourse in power, or in Erickson's terms, the magisterial discourse, is its exclusivity and can in no way accept the legitimacy of any reversal of the source of authority because such a reversal has the potential to create a rival in regard to the absolute Truth and, in some cases, including the *The Caravan of Islam*, end in complete transposition of sacred and the profane.

Indeed, the campaign of magisterial discourse against these works is not for their ridicule and even insult of Islam; this confrontation before anything else is against a literary device which, by giving voice to those who have been silenced through a discursive dominance, provides the possibility for the emergence of a new source of authority. This device at times functions by giving voice to Ayaz (in Baraheni's *The Infernal Times of Mr. Ayaz*) in the context of an alternative historiography, and at other times, by giving voice to Satan, projects the sacred as profane. It therefore stands to reason that writers who rely on this technique are detested by such magisterial discourses. Discussing Rushdie's usage of this technique, Erickson points to an episode in *The Satanic Verses* which depicts this hatred. In this episode a brothel is described in which there are 12 women who have some similarities to the wives of Mohammad, the Prophet of Islam. Baal,[135] "the writer-adversary of Mahound,"[136] after being arrested by Mahound, who represents Mohammad, explains the reason he is going to be killed by Mahound: "Whores and writers, Mahound. We are the people you can't forgive." And Mahound's reply is probably the representative voice of all official and magisterial discourses: "Writers and whores, I see no difference here."[137]

The formation of a literary counter-discourse on the site of magic realism

Reza Julai's "Purple Hills"

In the battle of discourses, the victorious discourse is the one which succeeds in projecting itself as normal.[138] In this chapter I selected and referred to works which directly countered the narratives of the official discourse; I have also pointed to the fact that many elements of this counter-discourse succeeded in gradually expanding their temporal and narrative presence until they established themselves as normal. Following this stage, many such established elements were used as backgrounds against which other narratives are formed. These do not challenge the narratives of the official discourse explicitly; so, in order to discuss their strategies new sites of counter-discursivity need to be explored.

In "Magic Realism as Post-Colonial Discourse," Stephen Slemon suggests a post-colonial reading of some literary works based on characteristics of magic realism. Slemon's encompassing idea is that the style of magic realism questions the fixity of borders and the limits of defined and determined spaces. He argues that binarisms such as "Europe and its other, colonizer and colonized, and the West and the rest"[139] and fixed borders, are all defined by colonialism.[140] I believe this issue can be posited on a larger scale and in relation to official and dominant discourses in the sense that any discourse naturally tries to define objective and subjective spaces through its elements.

In previous pages I referred to a number of examples depicting the resulting discursive clash. In this process, some fundamental elements of counter-discourses succeed in establishing themselves as widely accepted code words or signs. They provide the possibility for creating narratives which, by including these elements, even as secondary and non-essential elements of the story, will belong within a counter-discourse without necessarily engaging in a *direct* clash with the official discourse and its fixed, opposing components. Iran's post-revolutionary fiction provides many examples of works whose imaginary atmospheres possess a kind of fluidity which carries this discursive battle through its challenge of fixity of time and space.

"*Tappeh-ha-ye Kabud*" (Purple Hills)[141] is the tale of a non-descript archeologist in an unidentified region in search of the remains of fortresses and towers belonging to a time "about fifteen centuries ago."[142] In this story, past and present have been interwoven through temporal oscillations as well as a mixing of historical events and characters, to the point where past and present cannot be distinguished from one another. Next to the atmospheres with unstable and unfixed borders, this intertextuality is the most important narrative achievement of the story. The ensemble leads to the creation of spaces which are incompatible with spaces defined by the official discourse, without this incompatibility necessarily being the determining factor of the author's strategy at every moment.

The first two pages of this 30-page story are largely allocated to the description of the place where the protagonist begins his journey/search. There are no specific details or signs which could remind readers of a particular geography. On the contrary, it is clear that the narrator is consciously trying to use phrases and images which present the environment as unnatural and magical. Indeed, even the title of the story functions along the same lines.

The story opens with the following paragraph:

The tall green bushes, the desert plants in spring, the swelling silence and the purple of the horizon. There was a slight fear in this purple which he could not detect in that half-blue, dusty sky over his head. He was on the trail of this fear. On the trail of this fear, he had strayed many parasangs away from the main road and was walking down a gentle slope. The variety of plants and the virgin colors of the stones: ruby, ochre, blue, and the color of granite, the hard color of lead which melted into the fear of the purple horizon; all had absorbed him. And now there was certainly something behind those green bushes which was moving their branches. He had to approach them cautiously. Wolf? Cheetah? Hyena? Or maybe Death itself, dark and cloaked.[143]

Then the barren desert is described, and bushes, which are moving without a wind or a breeze. When the protagonist searches through the bushes, he does not find anyone or anything which could explain their movement. In this environment, descriptive elements have been carefully selected to instill an amalgam of unfamiliarity—of unnaturalness and buoyancy. Phrases such as "the dusty sky," "dread of the purple horizon," the ambiguity which exists in the description of "behind the mass of green bushes," the presence of "the scent of a strange plant whose name he couldn't remember,"[144] the feeling of presence of an invisible creature who is watching him,[145] all contribute to this unnatural, unfamiliar space. Because of its distance from customary and "realist" definitions, such a macabre environment gains the capability to slide and transfer itself into different times and places.

To state the obvious, in general, instability, fluidity, slipperiness, and the absence of fixity, function against the desire and will of the discourse being promoted by Iran's current political/military source of power. The most exaggerated form of this emphasis on fixity and unchangeability is seen in the political prisons owned by this discourse. In the prison report *At Haji Aqa's Gathering* which consists of two reports by two prisoners, Farhad Behbahani, one of the authors, describes one of his torture sessions during which he thought he was no longer able to endure the sheer pain. He pleads with his "interrogator" (Haji Aqa), asking him to tell him whatever he wants him to confess; he hears that what they are looking for is not just for him to give in; they want him to be changed internally and truly; to become one of them; and this is not possible without outside "help."[146] The official discourse wants everything according to its image; thus, according to this approach, any Other is part of a counter-discourse.

In a large number of recent works of Persian fiction there is a clear distance between created literary realities and ordinarily-defined everyday realities. One of the major reasons for this is the fact that, because of their personal nature and self-referentiality, as well as their fluidity, such literary realities cannot easily be pressured by the official discourse, simply because this discourse is not equipped to deal with constantly changing entities. I will discuss this issue in Chapter 3 in more detail.

In "Purple Hills" however, counter-discursivity is not limited to spatial instability; through the story's characters it reveals a historical dimension as well. Moreover, in the spatially and temporally fluid spaces of the story, specific binarisms are formed which indirectly reject the official discourse.

At the beginning of the story the author mentions that, entering the search area, the archeologist encounters a "dark-complexioned, swarthy gendarme" who, having examined his documents and his permits, tries to discourage him from continuing his search.

> There are no ancient buildings in these parts. Other than this stark and, of course … dangerous salt marsh …
>
> Even if there is something … considering the things I have seen … it is not worth getting into … [147]

When the gendarme realizes that these indirect suggestions do not seem to be working,

> In a dry voice, the gendarme said: "When you pass the dry river the slope will become steeper. The lake begins there. If it rains the river will become the path of a flood. Don't expect us to help." His voice had changed: "Do not disturb the sleep of the dead."[148]

The gendarme's last sentence is out of context and out of character. Yet these are not the only characteristics which question his link to the real, natural, tangible world. That is done more clearly when a historical counterpart is created for the gendarme.

When the gendarme says "Do not disturb the sleep of the dead," it seems that he is warning the protagonist not to pursue a path which leads to a past, to a different world to which the gendarme may somehow be linked. But of course the archeologist continues his work. In fact the circular structure of the story begins with the gendarme's warning, after which the protagonist plunges into the past/history/imagination and then returns to the present/"reality."

The archeologist enters a blue fog which seems to suggest an unaccustomed world. Suddenly, "he saw familiar signs … This was that very land of the final battle. Blood in plenty had been shed on that ground."[149] A few pages later, this battle and the two sides are described: "It seemed that a wave of mail-clad riders was standing on one side; facing them was another group of riders with black headgear and cloaks and crescent swords and surcoats of leather."[150] It is almost clear that the narrator is referring to the decisive battle of Qadesieh (635–636 AD) when the Arabs defeated the Iranian Sassanian Empire, which led to the Islamization of Iran. Later, the narrator offers a more precise description of the fictional context of this battle which, according to this story, "was the description of the historic battle between the Sassanian Queen and the Arab army." The narrator is actually reading a book which describes this battle:

The young Farahshid [the Queen] *assembled a small army and repelled the attacks of the Arab army. When the news reached the Sardar of the Arab army, he went into deep thought. He assembled a large army and himself went to the battlefield.*[151]

Then he goes on to recount the rest of the story which describes the defeat of the Iranians and the falling in love of the Arab Sardar with the Iranian Queen.

The historical background of "Purple Hills" is a familiar and more or less widely accepted counter-narrative according to which Islam and the Arabs came to Iran relying solely on force. Many consider this event so negative that they dwell on the impossible wish to change history. It is practically impossible to read this story and not think about a reading in the context of the present time and the formation of the Islamic government in Iran. In other words, it is quite legitimate to identify the current official discourse in Iran with a colonizer discourse which has rewritten history—especially about the way Iran and the Iranians "accepted" Islam. It therefore makes sense to think that refuting this rewrite, to use Stephen Slemon's argument, is done by creating a counter-colonialist discourse.

Having arrived at that bygone battlefield, the narrator of "Purple Hills" writes:

This was that very land of the final battle. Blood in plenty had been shed on that ground. But now, a green tranquility was hidden in the moist dirt, and there was no sign of savagery and animosity. Time had placed a veil on the face of the world; it would take him a mighty effort to remove this veil. He had come for this purpose.[152]

In this passage, the word "time" could be replaced with a colonizer/official discourse. To form the counter-colonial discourse, the author defines binarisms which have acquired their opposing characteristics through reference to a new rewrite of the history. In the context of the general binary of the Iranians and the Arabs, the counter-narrative, which posits the invasion of Iran by Arabs as a completely negative phenomenon, is reinforced through the description of the pain and torment of those on whom the war has been imposed:

Once because of fire or heavy catapults these walls had collapsed on the heads of warriors who were fighting in their shelter; warriors whose wives and children had hidden in the catacombs in fear. Death, dark death, had crept inside. The sound of the groaning and moaning of those who were half-alive beneath the rubble went through his mind.[153]

Based on the new, microcosmic narrative of this battle, the barbarism of this massacre was imposed on the Iranians because the Arab Sardar was rejected by the Queen. According to the story, once he hears the description of the Queen, the Sardar falls in love with her and asks for her hand. The Queen replies to this proposal—which is reminiscent of colonial symbolic narratives—in a most insulting and decisive manner; she orders her guards to cut off the ears and nose of the messenger.[154] The Sardar defeats the Queen with his huge army; the Queen, who prefers to die rather than fall into the hands of the Sardar, orders the head of her personal guard to kill her and bury her in an unmarked tomb. The Sardar, indignant because he has not been able to attain his goal of possessing the Queen—the new country—orders "the slaying of the Queen's entourage and in particular ... he tortured to death a young man who had been the object of the Queen's grace and favor."[155]

The savagery of this Arab Sardar is contrasted with the elegance of the Iranians; especially with the Queen's tenderness, which is found not only in the remains of the old fortress and tower but in her tomb. This narrative obviously functions against an implied background which considers the coming of the Arabs to Iran not the beginning of a divine religion but as an assault of barbarianism, backwardness, and lack of humanity and civilization. Considering this background, even the slightest narrative indication, such as the efforts of the Sardar to possess the Queen despite her desire, or the brutal destruction of the Iranians' citadel, is sufficient to form a series of parallel binaries—Iranians–Arabs, civilized–uncivilized, love–force—in the reader's mind.

The next structural stage of the story is to create a link between the recounting of this quasi-historical event and discourses which can be identified with the present time. From the beginning, the protagonist attempts to remove the veil of time (i.e. the official discourse) in order to regain elements of his existence and identity as a historical being. Having found vestiges of this past symbolic event, he dwells on the details. He hears the pounding of horses' hooves on the ground—a woman crying. He sees the battlefield and the spectres of soldiers, who "with drawn blades finished off those who were wounded and removed their armour and swords from them as booty."[156] One could read this kind of involvement of the narrator as a simple plunge in the world of imagination. But the relationship between present and past is much closer and more complicated than could simply be explained and justified by a mere function of the imagination.

When the archeologist enters the tomb of the Queen for the first time and sees her coffin, he tries for a while to open it. Unsuccessful, he comes out of the tomb and listens to the rainfall. A number of "old memories" rush to his mind; among them is the memory of "a girl whom he loved in the past ... and she had committed suicide ... "[157] This reference suddenly adds a personal and contemporary aspect to the narration of the historical event. The protagonist attributes the link between the Queen and this girl from the present time to simple nostalgia and attempts to forget it. Once again he tries to open the coffin. This time he is successful. Once the coffin is opened, the familiar strange scent that he had felt after entering the tomb permeates the atmosphere. "He smelled that strange scent again, and memories emerged. It was as if he had lived in the distant past and experienced this event many centuries ago."[158] This time he cannot ignore the similarity between the Queen and "the girl he loved at one time." He lifts the hand of the skeleton, and on its finger he sees a familiar jewel on a ring.

> Slowly he pulled the ring off the bone. He heard a sigh. Now he was sure this was not an illusion. It was the same ring. He had searched for days until he had found something that he liked in a corner of a goldsmith's shop, and he had paid his price without haggling. He had known the girl would like it, and that is what had happened.[159]

At this point, the discursive transition from past to present and vice versa goes beyond mere imagination. In the *univers romanesque* of the story, this decisive moment is referred to right after the episode of the ring. "A wheel had turned time and space and carried them back many centuries."[160] One of the suggestions contained in this statement is what the members of opposition to the post-revolutionary official discourse have argued: that the official discourse is seeking to recreate the world of 14 centuries ago: the beginning of Islam. Julai however seems to be more preoccupied with intertwining the elements of the past and the present, and identifying them with each other. Along this path, having superimposed the character of the Queen of the past with the girl of today, he continues with the archeologist's story. He pulls the sword by which the Queen had met her voluntary death out of her skeleton and leaves the tomb. Now he is certain that he *really*, not just in his imagination, is in the midst of the historic attack of the Arabs against the Iranians. Shortly after staring at the blue fog, he hears the commotion of the troops and finds himself, sword in hand, among the Queen's guards who are blocking the enemy warriors. He is the leader of the guardsmen. During the fight he sees the Sardar, a thin man with a dark complexion, riding a white horse with a crescent-shaped sword in hand and somber eyes.[161] Once again, in the context of Iranian history, this description is reminiscent of the warriors from the early days of Islam. The narrator, however, is consistently trying to superimpose specific elements of past and present. The Arab Sardar arrives. The archeologist/leader of the guardsmen cuts off the legs of his horse, and when they face each other he lowers his sword at the Arab. The Sardar draws back, but "the edge of the sword cut his face near his mouth."[162] From the literary point of view, this is a very carefully designed stroke. In the beginning of the story, when the protagonist meets the gendarme for the first time, we read in his description:

> The gendarme faced him and stared at his eyes. He had an unpleasant feeling. The gendarme's pupils were black, black, and dark. There was something in that unpleasant darkness which frightened him. There was also a scar from a deep cut on the left side of his mouth.[163]

This is a cut caused by a historical wound which has scarred the face of the gendarme, the representative of the official discourse and system. Indeed, this wound, contrary to the narrative of the current official discourse in Iran, suggests, almost explicitly, that the coming of the Arabs and, consequently, of Islam to Iran did not meet with the open arms of the Iranians but faced their resistance to the last breath. The final episode of the story reinforces this reading. After wounding the Sardar, the leader of the guardsmen hesitates for a moment, and the Sardar seizes the opportunity and flees. He then comes back with his soldiers and kills the Queen's guards one after another.

The archeologist leaves the tomb. The circular structure of the narrative has brought him back to the present time, but he carries with him a real and tangible experience in the context of the literary reality of the story: an experience which includes his memory of hesitating to kill the Sardar and consequently the thought of what would have happened if he had killed him. The archeologist/leader, even after leaving the tomb, roaring, still continues his fight. Suddenly he feels an arrow pierce his shoulder from behind. "He stopped and turned to face the enemy. He took the tip of the arrow and in one movement broke it and threw it to the ground. Blood gushed from his shoulder."[164] Then, moving to the parallel universe, he sees the gendarme who is standing in front of him with a rifle in hand. The gendarme aims and fires. A bullet penetrates his left shoulder. After firing his gun, the gendarme says: "I told you not to disturb the sleep of the dead."[165] Once again the phrase "sleep of the dead" can easily be replaced with "the narrative of the official discourse." This time, the archeologist, having learned from his historical experience, doesn't hesitate; before the gendarme can reload his rifle, he pulls out his hunting knife and goes towards him. He looks at the scar on his face and "this time, without hesitation, plunged the knife into his chest and grasped his collar in his other hand so he could see the shivering of death in his eyes."[166]

What Julai creates in this story is a combination of event-based and atmospheric literatures. I am using the term "atmospheric" to refer to unstable spaces which, in an indirect manner, primarily through their positional value, create a series of countering effects such as counter-thoughts, counter-movements, counter-interpretations, counter-convention, and counter-conventionalities. This combination is one of the most significant trends in contemporary Persian fiction. Many writers, stylist writers in particular, have experimented with this combination by creating works which resist simple identification with any given discourse. This is especially true in the case of contemporary Persian war literature. Exploring this genre obviously requires a separate study, but one point needs to be made: because of the significance of the Iran–Iraq War within the ideological thoughts of the Islamic government and because of its sensitive nature, such literary constructions became even more remarkable. Indeed, by pushing the main event (the War) to the margins and creating extremely personal atmospheres, many works of war literature could represent the multivocality of interpretations about this event. And I maintain that it is the emergence of the individual/personal voice which indicates the resistance of many contemporary works of Persian fiction against the imposition of positionality.

Julai's "Munes and Mordekhai": resisting positionality

In my reading of "Purple Hills," I have underlined elements which illustrate the circular structure of the story as well as the binaries representing the official and counter-discourses. There is, though, another pivotal literary device in this work of Julai and in some of his other works which cannot be easily situated in the context of a dualism created by the oppositionality of discourses and counter-discourses whose main narratives are informed by political-ideological concepts and opinions. Julai ends the story with this sentence: "The Queen belonged to him now."[167] This closure points to the narrator's emphasis on the importance of an extremely personal relationship (in this case his relationship with the Queen/the girl), and consequently of the personal/individual life in the context of the main narratives of established discourses. At first, given the fact that one of the passages in the story refers to the Sardar's lack of understanding of love, it seems that the story's closure seeks to reinforce this idea and thus still remain within the previously-mentioned binaries. This is *partly* true. In fact the post-revolutionary official discourse has been challenged before from the point of view of lack of understanding of such matters as love. This confrontation has been emblematized and immortalized in one of Ahmad Shamlu's famous post-revolutionary poems. The poem opens with these somber lines:

> They smell your breath.
> You had better not have said, "I love you."
> They smell your heart.
> These are strange times, darling ... [168]

This direct challenge to the official discourse is clearly reflected in Julai's story as well, but I believe the full impact of the romantic component of "Purple Hills" is appreciated only when it is placed in the context of new historiography and the role of anecdotes in puncturing the *grand récit* of dominant and official discourses.

In Iran's post-revolutionary fiction, the anecdotal approach based on personal/individual issues has been one of the most dominant trends. Undoubtedly, this is one major reason for the presence of a large number of first-person narratives in contemporary Persian fiction. In the short stories of Julai, most of which are in third-person narration, the strategy of such romantic episodes with extremely personal/individualistic elements is to question the widely-accepted narratives of official discourses of different periods and their established counter-discourses, as well as to proffer narrative components for a discourse of the Other. In addition, such works demonstrate the existence and function of an autonomous literary discipline and space. One such work by Julai is his short story "*Munes-o Mordekhai*" (Munes and Mordekhai). As in many of his other works, the story begins towards the end of the Qajar period and during the tumultuous era of the Constitutional Revolution

(1905–1911). In such works Julai usually evokes the period and its main discourses and narratives with a few general strokes of his narrative paintbrush. Here I do not want to enter into the details of the discourses of Constitutionalists, religious, and monarchist opposition, but one point bears repeating: the fact that these discourses relied heavily on political-ideological narratives, and intellectuals active in these fields began absorbing most of the intellectual energy of this period until the 1979 Revolution. It was only in the post-revolutionary decades that challenges made to them found an established discursive form. The domination of political-ideological discourses in major fields of intellectual and artistic arenas resulted in narratives about different periods which ignored many aspects of those times—aspects which were incompatible with these grand narratives. Through their focus on these silenced aspects, "Munes and Mordekhai" and other Julai stories set in the Constitutional Revolution period demonstrate examples of works which go beyond established discourses and counter-discourses. In a sense, they can be identified with a general counter-discursive mood, whose narratives do not share elements of a single historical, sociological, political, or ideological outlook. They have only one common denominator: they are personal. This feature has proved to be one of the most effective characteristics which places the narrative outside the domain of the established discourses. And this is how it deserves the wrath of the official discourse.

"Munes and Mordekhai" begins with direct references to the time of the Constitutional Revolution but immediately concentrates on the characters of Munes and Mordekhai. Munes is a young singer and musician, who after many years of adversity and poverty and hardship, has succeeded in having a comfortable and pleasant life by performing with her troupe for the members of the Royal court and other prominent people. Mordekhai is a businessman who used to have a small shop in one of Tehran's oldest neighborhoods, but with cleverness and through timely speculations has accumulated sizeable wealth. Munes' life passes in luxury and hedonism, while Mordekhai lives a life of utmost frugality. Munes loves sumptuous dresses, expensive perfumes, and jewels, and Mordekhai is so unrefined that "even muleteers who came to his shop to buy used harness and trappings, [seeing the way he ate] would shake their heads and smile."[169] Munes and Mordekhai are both Jewish, and this is intriguing because in the widespread grand narratives of different periods in Iran the prevailing image of Jews and Judaism has been generally negative, but in this story these two characters are defined through their mutual love. It should be noted that the negative image of Jews and Judaism has also been predominant in Iran's literary discourses, and that there are many examples of this, especially in classical Persian works. From this point of view, Julai's writing functions against the stereotypical and fixed literary images as well.[170] Obviously, however, the positive treatment of two Jewish characters shows its significant counter-effect even more in relation to the current official-Islamic discourse. But the love story of these two characters produces a more far-reaching effect.

The love of Munes and Mordekhai for each other does not follow any usual or ordinary path. In fact, the narrator suggests that his only reason for telling the story is its difference from the "customary" and "natural."

> I talked too much about secondary details and the main point was left untold. My main point was to talk about love between two people; one delicate and seductive, the other rough and abrasive. I am certain that these two, despite all the interpretations and explanations that people offered about their relationship, were in love with each other. Why are you smiling? You don't believe me? People usually evaluate the behavior of lovers from the way they talk or act and look, and in general from their appearance. But all these things could be misleading. The appearance of these two people was completely different from other lovers; like day and night.[171]

Munes and Mordekhai get married, and although they are so dissimilar, they prize their love and what they have.

> These two had seen so much adversity; therefore they valued what they had. They bought a big house in Zargandeh[172] with many servants and maids. They spent their honeymoon in the same house. According to one maid, their confidante, at night, after dinner, they sat on the veranda. They always had a bouquet of pink flowers, in front of them, Munes' favorite color. They turned on the fountains of the small pool, and sometimes when Munes was in high spirits she would murmur a ghazal.[173]

Next to the significance given to this different narrative of love, the narrator, occasionally and through various methods, trivializes the Constitutional Revolution and revolutionaries. Sometimes, he terms their activities "playing the game of revolution";[174] at other times, he recalls some of the revolutionaries as people "who became pro-revolution because they had to."[175] The most important component of this trivialization, which functions in relation to the main subject matter of the story, is reference to a true event of this period when three of the main leaders of the Revolution tangled with each other. The narrator begins his description of this event with an introduction concerning one of Mordekhai's transactions. Having realized that a period of fighting will follow the unrest, and so that there will be a market for weapons and ammunitions, Mordekhai buys a large quantity of cartridges in exchange for some of his old wine from some of the officials of the Qajar ruling state. After the triumph of the Revolution, he sells these cartridges to a group of revolutionaries headed by Yaprem Khan.[176] Soon a confrontation transpires between this group and another group headed by Sattar Khan and Baqer Khan,[177] two other famous leaders of the Revolution. It is at this point that the narrator uses the term "playing the game of revolution."

Look how this world maneuvers; the cartridges bought from government ministers were used in the Park-e Atabak affair[178] against the constitutionalists by another group of constitutionalists. When I said "the game of the Constitutional Revolution" I was thinking about this tale.[179]

Yaprem Khan and his warriors try to use the cartridges Mordekhai has sold them, but they are defective; this becomes the first source of animosity between Yaprem Khan and the couple.

The narrator refers to these events in a nonchalant tone, as if to suggest the insignificance of the widely-accepted heroic accounts of this Revolution. And indeed, he makes one wonder how much importance should be given to such discourses when they are compared to personal/individual stories and histories.

Any discourse founded on an ideology, precisely because of its reliance on mutualities (or because of the invention of such mutualities) stands to some extent in opposition to individuality. According to such discourses, characters, events, ideals and ideas should serve the absolute truth advocated by the ideological discourse, and any deviation from that absolute truth is conceived of as being in line with counter-discourses. In "Munes and Mordekhai," the first section of the story itself undermines the established ideological narratives about the Revolution and revolutionaries of the period and conversely emphasizes the presence of silenced narratives. But the strategy of the story goes beyond this.

The enmity of Yaprem Khan against Munes and Mordekhai continues, and the decisive victory of the revolutionaries provides Yaprem with favorable conditions to take his revenge. He tightens his grip around Mordekhai's business; so much so that they finally lose everything. Their debts increase, and after a short time the only thing they have left is a car they had bought some time ago and kept in their house without using it. Of course, according to their old maid, the only servant who at this time is still with them, their life is not totally devoid of happiness. Every once in a while, Munes still brings out her tar,[180] plays a little and whispers a song. In the meantime, their efforts to appease Yaprem Khan lead nowhere. The only solution Yaprem suggests through his people is that if Munes agrees to sing for a banquet at his house, then he might forgive them. "Munes was ready to die but not to accept such a shame."[181] The events of the last night they are seen are told by their old maid.

The maid had said that on that night they sat next to the pool and whispered with each other; maybe they were making their last calculations. The following day they were going to lose their house and end up wandering in the streets. Munes goes to her tar and embraces it; she plays softly and sings:
I used drunkenness as an excuse to cry.
And how much I complained of this world.[182]

They go to bed very late. In the middle of the night, the old woman thinks that the lights on the upper floor are lit. In the morning she finds above her head a sum of money and a letter. From the contents of the letter it becomes clear that those two, after thanking her for her service, were planning to travel to a faraway place so that no one can reach them.[183]

This is the last time they are seen. The narrator works as a collector at a firm which, years after the time of Munes and Mordekhai, has acquired at an auction a caravansary previously belonging to the couple and located near their house. One of the secretaries of the firm has told the narrator the story of Munes and Mordekhai. In fact, the narrator is drawn to their story when the firm decides to use the caravansary and sends him there to measure its different cubicles.

In the context of literary historiography this structure of the story provides numerous reading possibilities for the author/narrator and the reader. In his review of the past, the narrator confronts various stereotypical thoughts and accounts which promote preconceived and established narratives. The first thing is the choice of two Jews for this love story. As mentioned above, it would be quite difficult to find another such example in Persian literature. More important than this, is the narrator's confrontation with grand narratives. With each step of the story, the narrator trivializes the grand narratives of the Constitutional Revolution and conversely increases the emphasis on the completely unique and non-collective love story of Munes and Mordekhai. The uniqueness and being personal as part of the narrative strategy are reflected even in the increasingly smaller, more private spaces and settings of the story as the narration concentrates more and more on Munes and Mordekhai and their love.

Having arrived at the caravansary and inspected it, the narrator goes to their old house, which is almost in ruins, in order to find some sign of their different version, their unique anecdote, of love. He finds nothing. Suddenly, in the middle of the night he wakes up, as if he has remembered something. In the morning he goes back to the firm and reviews his measurements of the caravansary and realizes that "the length of one of the sides of the caravansary from outside was more than the length of the same side from inside!"[184] He convinces his boss that this is worth further investigation. They go there together, and after making a hole in the wall, they find a hidden compartment. They enter and find a car covered with heavy dust, with construction tools next to it. All these details lead to the final scene of the story which is completely in line with the progressive trajectory of the narrative. The powerful closure of the story provides the ultimate point of this direction, completely effacing the idea of grand narratives and celebrating the unmistakable and unqualified triumph of personal/individual anecdotes. It emphasizes once again the narrative strategy of the author who, having moved away from the counter-discursive historical contexts created by previous literary efforts of writers such as Hajizadeh, Aqai, Baraheni and Beyzai, goes towards the construction of fluid (literary) realities within which unique, individual voices can emerge.

> I went ahead and opened the back door and took the lamp forward. I saw the strange scene, that other anecdote. I saw the skeletons of a woman and a man in old-style clothing, sitting next to each other on the back seat. Their faces had turned to dust, but their hair was still in place. The man had his head on the woman's shoulder and they were holding hands. There was a small black glass container in one of his hands and a pink bouquet of dried flowers on the woman's skirt. There was also a lantern and a *tar* next to them.
>
> I stood there and stared at them for as long as they gave me time. Then I took the bouquet of flowers and came out. The image of those two was before me, those faces now turned to dust, and that amorous posture they had, clinging to each other's hands. Before me I was seeing the other face of love. I am certain that with their love for each other they had cared nothing for the fear of the final moment.[185]

Notes

1 See Chapter 1 for more discussion on *differenzqualität*.

2 For more details on the Formalist definition of historical background, consult Kristin Thompson, *Eisenstein's* Ivan the Terrible, p. 12.

3 Abolqasem Ferdowsi (*c.* 935–*c.* 1020) was one of the most significant epic poets of Iran. By collecting Iran's ancient mythic stories, then versifying them in his life's work, the *Shahnameh*, he played a major role in revitalizing Persian language and culture at a time when conquerers were making conscious essays to rid that conquered society of its history.

4 Iran's calendar was, and is, called *Hijri Shamsi*. The calendar begins with the *Noruz* (first day of spring) of the year of the Hijra of Mohammad from Mecca to Medina (622 CE). The Shahanshahi (Shahanshah means King of Kings) calendar begins with the *Noruz* of the year that Cyrus the Great founded the Achamenid dynasty. At the order of Shah Mohammad Reza Pahlavi and the predictable approval of the bicameral parliament in 1975, all government offices and publications, textbooks, and official correspondence started using this new calendar, but the Shahanshahi calendar was never accepted by the people, and after a few years it was effectively discarded.

5 Walter Benjamin, "Theses on the Philosophy of History" has been published in different collections, including *Illuminations*, Hannah Arendt (ed.), Harry Zohn (tr.), New York: Schocken Books, 1979.

6 Shoshana Felman, "Benjamin's Silence," *Critical Inquiry*, Winter 1999, vol. 25, pp. 208–209.

7 Homi K. Bhabha, "Of mimicry and man: The ambivalence of colonial discourse," in *The Location of Culture*, London: Routledge, 1994, p. 86.

8 Rachel Feldhay Brenner, "'Hidden Transcripts' Made Public: Israeli Arab Fiction and Its Reception," *Critical Inquiry*. Autumn 1999, vol. 26, p. 88.

9 Guy Debord, "Comments on the Society of the Spectacle," translated by Malcolm Imrie, (1988) www.notbored.org/commentaires.html (accessed May 5, 2014), p. 3 of 30. It should be noted that in this text Debord mentions that since the

publication of *The Society of the Spectacle*, another form has been developed which is a combination of the two previous ones. He writes: "Since then, a third form has been established, through the rational combination of these two, and on the basis of a general victory of the form which had showed itself stronger; the diffuse. This is the integrated spectacle, which has since tended to impose itself globally." (Ibid.)

10 For more details on this concept, refer to Chapter 1 of the present study. To read more about this differentiation consult the following articles: Debord, "Comments on the Society of the Spectacle,"; and Steven Best and Douglass Kellner, "Debord and the Postmodern Turn: New Stages of the Spectacle" 1999, www.uta. edu/huma/illuminations/kell17.htm (accessed May 5, 2014).

11 See Debord, "Comments on the Society of the Spectacle." Debord mentions this in his discussion about the Integrated Form of the Society of the Spectacle, specifically in relation to France. Obviously though, this characteristic can be attributed to all "societies of spectacle."

12 Sazman-e Mojahedin-e Khalq-e Iran (People's Mojahedin of Iran), MKO, is a Muslim militant-political organization which opposes the Islamic government of Iran. This organization was active before the 1979 Revolution as well. www. mojahedin.org/pages/index.aspx (accessed May 5, 2014).

13 For one such example, consult the following website: www.tebyan.net/newindex. aspx?pid=128459&Keyword=%D8%A8%D9%85%D8%A8+%DA%AF%D8%B0 %D8%A7%D8%B1%DB%8C+%D9%85%D8%AC%D8%A7%D9%87%D8%AF %DB%8C%D9%86+%D8%AC%D9%85%D9%87%D9%88%D8%B1%DB%8C+% D8%A7%D8%B3%D9%84%D8%A7%D9%85%DB%8C+%D9%87%D9%81%D8 %AA+%D8%AA%DB%8C%D8%B1+%DA%A9%D8%B1%D8%A8%D9%84% D8%A7 (accessed May 5, 2014).

14 On the 30th anniversary of the bombing of the Islamic Republic Party's head-quarters, BBC produced a report which contained different narratives of these officials.

www.bbc.co.uk/persian/iran/2011/06/110628_l10_30khordad60_7tir.shtml (accessed May 5, 2014). The following site also has useful information about this event, including data about the number of people killed: http://didban.ir/images/content image/278/1077.pdf (accessed May 5, 2014).

15 Hashemi-Rafsanjani, *Karnameh va Khaterat-e 1360: Obur az Bohran* (Records and Memoirs of 1360: Traversing the Crisis), Tehran: Daftar-e Nashr-e Ma'aref-e Enqelab, 1378/1999, p. 186.

16 www.irib.ir/occasions/Ghoveh-qazaei/Ghoveh-qazaeiEN.HTM (accessed April 21, 2009).

17 "The nation of Iran lost seventy-two innocent people, the same as the number of the martyrs of Karbala."

www.tebyan.net/newindex.aspx?pid=128459&Keyword=%D8%A8%D9%85%D8 %A8+%DA%AF%D8%B0%D8%A7%D8%B1%DB%8C+%D9%85%D8%AC% D8%A7%D9%87%D8%AF%DB%8C%D9%86+%D8%AC%D9%85%D9%87%D 9%88%D8%B1%DB%8C+%D8%A7%D8%B3%D9%84%D8%A7%D9%85%DB %8C+%D9%87%D9%81%D8%AA+%D8%AA%DB%8C%D8%B1+%DA%A9% D8%B1%D8%A8%D9%84%D8%A7 (accessed May 5, 2014).

18 Of course there is still a huge debate about the number of people killed at the Karbala event.

19 John Erickson, *Islam and Postcolonial Narrative*, Cambridge: Cambridge University Press, 1998, p. 9.

20 Peter Chelkowski and Hamid Dabashi, *Staging a Revolution: The Art of Persuasion in the Islamic Republic of Iran*, New York: New York University Press, 1999, p. 9.

21 Ibid., p. 274.

22 For more on how these techniques are used to serve specific discursive purposes, consult *Islam and Postcolonial Narrative*, John Erickson's reference to Michel Foucault's discussion of this matter, p. 9.

23 E. P. Thompson interviewed by Mike Merrill in *Visions of History*, Interviews, edited by Henry Abelove, Betsy Blackmar, Peter Dimock, and Jonathan Schneer, New York: Pantheon Books, 1984, p. 8.

24 Guy Debord, *Society of the Spectacle*, quoted from "Debord and the Postmodern Turn: New Stages of the Spectacle," Steven Best and Douglas Kellner, 1999, www.uta.edu/huma/illuminations/kell17.htm (accessed May 5, 2014).

25 Steven Best and Douglas Kellner, "Debord and the Postmodern Turn: New Stages of the Spectacle," 1999, www.uta.edu/huma/illuminations/kell17.htm (accessed May 5, 2014).

26 "Indeed, the anecdote as a form has often been counterpoised against more ambitiously comprehensive historical narratives. Our late colleague Joel Fineman, for example, claimed that *any petit récit* would puncture the historical *grand récit* into which it was inserted. All anecdotes, simply as complete little stories in themselves, perforate the context of narrative explanation." See Joel Fineman, "The History of the Anecdote," in *The New Historicism*, ed. H. Aram Veeser. New York: Routledge, 1989, p. 49.

27 The Persian term is "Gozaresh-Qesseh." The term was first coined by Farkhondeh Hajizadeh, one of Iran's contemporary authors.

28 Akbar Ganji, the famous Iranian journalist, published some of his findings in regard to Sa'd Emami's death and the Serial Murders in *Alijenab-e Sorkhpush va Alijenaban-e Khakesetari* (His Eminence in a Red Cloak and The Gray Eminences) (1999). In these articles, Ganji named a number of public officials. Quite possibly, if this story could have been researched further there would have been more revelations, but the author was arrested on 2001 and spent six years in prison. Others, such as family members of the victims and their legal representatives, who were also pursuing these murders through the legal system, were silenced, either by being threatened or by imprisonment.

29 Farkhondeh Hajizadeh has recently published a novel titled *Man, Mansur va Albright* (Mansur, Albright and I) (Paris: Khavaran, 2006) in which she refers to many details of the murders of her brother and her nephew.

30 Farkhondeh Hajizadeh, *Report-Story #1*, Tehran: Vistar, 1380/2001, p. 11.

31 Ibid., p. 14.

32 Interestingly, in the past few years at many anti-government demonstrations, physical and psychological punishments from one's school years are used as a metaphor for the pains of living under undemocratic societies. There is in fact a very famous song, "*Yar-e Dabestani-e Man*" (My Grade School Friend), which has become the song always sung at anti-government demonstrations.

33 Hajizadeh, *Report-Story #1*, p. 14.

34 Ibid., p. 19.

35 In general, the Islamic Republic has always had the project of imposing its myths. This project, for example, attempts to compare Khomeini with the twelve Imams, the 1979 Revolution to Hosein's uprising against Yazid, and so on. Pre-Islamic references are practically positioned against this project.

36 Czeslaw Milosz, *The Captive Mind*, quoted from: Clare Cavanagh, "Lyric and Public: The Case of Adam Zagajewski," *World Literature Today*, vol. 79, no. 2, May–August 2005, p. 16

37 Ibid.

38 Adam Zagajewski, *Solidarity, Solitude*, quoted from Clare Cavanagh's "Lyric and Public," p. 16.

39 To read the English translation of the poem, see Clare Cavanagh's "Lyric and Public".

40 Reza Baraheni, *Jonun-e Neveshtan* (The Madness of Writing), Tehran: Rasam, 1980, p. 725. My emphasis.
41 Richard Terdiman, *Discourse/Counter-Discourse: The Theory and Practice of Symbolic Resistance in Nineteenth-Century France*, Ithaca, NY: Cornell University Press, 1985, p. 63.
42 Reza Baraheni, *Chah beh Chah* (Well to Well), Tehran: Nashr-e no, 1362/1983, p. 23.
43 Ibid., p. 40.
44 Ibid., p. 49.
45 Mirza Kuchak Khan was the leader of an uprising in Iran in 1914. His revolutionary movement was based in the province of Gilan, and he declared this province independent. The movement was defeated in 1921.
46 Hasan Mirabedini, *Sad Sal Dastan Nevisi-ye Iran* (One Hundred Years of Fiction-Writing in Iran), vol. 3, Tehran: Cheshmeh, 1377/1998, p. 814.
47 Baraheni, *The Madness of Writing*, p. 743.
48 Ibid., p. 709. In the post-1979 censored reprint of this piece, the word phallus has been replaced by ellipsis.
49 Sultan Mahmud (971–1030) was the ruler of the Ghaznavid Empire, and Ayaz was his favorite slave/lover. In a historical contex Sultan Mahmud is known to have been an unforgiving warrior, but in the context of love stories, his romance with Ayaz has often been referred to as an example of devotion in love.
50 Carter Harrison Bryant II, *Rezá Baráheni's The Infernal Days of Áqá-ye Ayáz: A Translation and Critical Introduction*, Diss., The University of Texas at Austin, 1982. vol. 1, p. 123.
51 *Ana al-Haq* (I am The Truth) is the famous saying of Mansur Hallaj (858–922), a Sufi who was executed because he was accused of blasphemy.
52 Bryant, *Rezá Baráheni's The Infernal Days*, p. 122.
53 Ibid., p. 166.
54 One such very long passage pertains to a scene in which Mahmud leads Ayaz to the chamber of the Queen Mother, and Baraheni describes the seduction process of Ayaz by the Queen. However, at the end of this process he is violated by the Sultan, and this identity-making moment for Ayaz is described in detail by Baraheni. (Bryant, *Rezá Baráheni's The Infernal Days*, pp. 246–286).
55 Mirabedini, *One Hundred Years of Fiction-Writing in Iran*, vols 1 and 2, p. 433.
56 Catherine Gallagher and Stephen Greenblatt, *Practicing New Historicism*, Chicago, IL: University of Chicago Press, 2000, pp. 54, 55.
57 Bryant, *Rezá Baráheni's The Infernal Days*, pp. 403–405. This section in Persian included sentences which are directly taken from famous inscriptions, but the order of letters in each word has been changed. Obviously this cannot be translated, but both English and French translators have tried to reproduce a similar experience for the reader.
58 Josef Wisehöfer, *Ancient Persia from 550 BC to 650 AD*, translated by Azizeh Azodi, London: I.B. Tauris, 2001, p. 45.
59 Baraheni, *The Madness of Writing*, p. 690.
60 Ibid., p. 690.
61 Ibid., pp. 690, 691. My emphasis.
62 Bahram Bahrami, "Daramadi bar *Ruzegar-e Duzakhi-ye Aqa-ye Ayaz*" (A Prologue to *Les Saisons en enfer du jeune Ayyaz*), on the occasion of its publication in French, www.vazhe.com/ayaz101.htm, June 2000 (accessed May 5, 2014).
63 Abu al-Fazl Beyhaqi (995–1077) is the most famous Persian historian. His most famous book, *Tarikh-e Beyhaqi* [Beyhaqi's History], is about the rule of the Ghaznavid dynasty. There is only one section left from this book.
64 Baraheni, *The Madness of Writing*, p. 691.
65 Gallagher and Greenblatt, *Practicing New Historicism*, p. 53.

66 Reza Baraheni, "Golshiri va Moshkel-e Roman" (Golshiri and the Problem of the Novel), in *Royay-e Bidar*, Tehran: Qatreh, 1373/1994. pp. 224, 225.
67 Reza Baraheni, *Les Saisons en enfer du jeune Ayyaz*, translated from Persian by Katayoun Shahpar-Rad, Paris: Pauvert, 2000, pp. 123–125.
68 Throughout the French version there is no title.
69 Bryant, *Rezá Baráheni's The Infernal Days*, p. 122.
70 Richard Sherwood, "Viktor Shklovsky and the development of early Formalist Theory on Prose Literature," in *Russian Formalism: A Collection of Articles and Texts in Translation*, eds Stephen Bann and John Bowlt, New York: Barnes & Noble, 1973, p. 30.
71 In one of his poems, "The Footsteps of Water," Sohrab Sepehri (1928–1980), has the following memorable line: "Sometimes the wounds on my feet / Have taught me the ups and downs of the soil."
72 Foucault, *Discipline and Punish*, pp. 3–5.
73 Ayn al-Qozat Hamadani (1097–1131) was a Sufi philosopher, a follower of Mohammad Ghazali and then his younger brother, Ahmad Ghazali. He was killed because of his unconventional thoughts and interpretations of the tenets of Islam and thus accused of blasphemy.
74 Hasanak was the last Vizier of Sultan Mahmud who, after the death of Mahmud and during the reign of Masud, his son, was accused of having religious convictions different from the version of Islam promoted by the Caliph; he was hanged and stoned.
75 Terdiman, *Discourse/Counter-Discourse*, p. 54.
76 Baraheni, *The Madness of Writing*, p. 743.
77 In *Discourse/Counter-Discourse*, Terdiman discusses this point in detail, as it was conceptualized by Foucault, p. 56.
78 Bryant, *Rezá Baráheni's The Infernal Days*, p. 154.
79 The most common story about this rejection is that when Sultan Mahmud saw this work he said: "Why should I value a work which is about someone (Rostam) the like of whom I have many in my own army!"
80 Bahram Beyzai, *Dibacheh-ye Novin-e* Shahnameh (A New Prologue to the *Shahnameh*). All translations are form Pari Shirazi's *Filmnameh or Mental Cinema: A New Literary Genre in Persian Literature*, Dissertation, 2001, p. 351.

   Pari Shirazi's Dissertation is a noteworthy contribution to the argument that many of these screenplays have been written to be read and not necessarily to be turned into films—a modern version of "closet drama."
81 "Literal translation of the word is learned man [daneshmand]. However, because it has a political and religious connotation the word gownsman seems more appropriate." (Shirazi, p. 351)
82 Beyzai, *A New Prologue to the* Shahnameh, p. 351.
83 Ibid., p. 352.
84 Ibid.
85 The adjective *ghazi* (holy warrior) was given to Sultan Mahmud because of his numerous military campaigns to India which, he claimed, were to disseminate Islam.
86 Beyzai, *A New Prologue to the* Shahnameh, p. 410.
87 One famous example is *Bashu, Gharibeh-ye Kuchak* (Bashu, the Little Stranger, 1986). After a few years, Beyzai received the permission to make the movie. But after its completion, the government did not give him permission to screen the film, and Beyzai lost so much money that for a long time he could not possibly work on new projects. Also, producers became extremely hesitant to back a film-maker whose works could be banned from movie theatres.
88 To read more about this, November 25, 2005, see www.nourizadeh.com/archives/001485.php (accessed May 5, 2014) and www.radiofarda.com/content/backgrounderembedded/313765.html (accessed December 12, 2012).
89 See http://news.gooya.com/culture/archives/033485.php (accessed May 5, 2014).

90 Siyavash-Khani is a very old tradition during which the story of Siyavash is re-played. According to Beyzai, the myth of Siyavash has very old Indo-Iranian roots, and this tradition, which is still performed in many places, has acquired many different forms. To read more about this, see "Siyavash-Khani: Az Jahan-e Pakan dar pey-e Asl-e gomshodeh" (Siyavash-Khani: From the World of the Pure, in Search of the Lost Origin), Hamid Amjad's interview with Bahram Beyzai, *Simia*, no. 2, 1386/2007: 136–163.

91 Beyzai, *A New Prologue to the* Shahnameh, pp. 438, 439.

92 Ali is the fourth Caliph who succeeded Mohammad. He is also the first Shi'i Imam.

93 While the meaning of the word is not death, this Arabic word is used in Persian to refer to death.

94 Beyzai, *A New Prologue to the* Shahnameh, p. 439.

95 Beyzai, *A New Prologue to the* Shahnameh. Persian version, p. 110

96 Beyzai, *A New Prologue to the* Shahnameh, p. 459.

97 "Persian land owners were called dehqan" (Shirazi, fn. p. 459). The word *dehqan* has also been used to refer to "an Iranian" and to one protecting Iranian customs and traditions.

98 Beyzai, *A New Prologue to the* Shahnameh, pp. 459, 460.

99 Foucault, quoted from Terdiman, *Discourse/Counter-discourse*, p. 56.

100 Ibid.

101 Farkhondeh Aqai, *Jensiyat-e Gomshodeh* (Lost Sexuality), Tehran: Alborz, 1990. "Introduction," pp. 9–11.

102 Sirus Shamisa, *Shahed Bazi dar Adabiyat-e Farsi* (Pederasty in Persian Literature), Tehran: Ferdows, 1381/2002. On the last page of the book, the author has translated the title as: *Sodomy Based on Persian Literature*, which is a very inaccurate translation of the title.

103 Of course the misuse of the position of power not only means direct reliance on censorship and imprisonment and torture and threat, it also means using its "material control over access to production of discourse." (Foucault, quoted from Terdiman, *Discourse/Counter-discourse*, p. 56.)

104 *Taqlid* means imitation; it refers to the notion that a Shi'i Muslim needs to be the follower of a jurisprudent.

105 Ataollah Mohajerani, *Behesht-e Khakestari* (Grey Paradise), Tehran: Omid-e Iranian, 1382/2003, p. 39.

106 Yevgeny Ivanovich Zamyatin, *We* (1921); translated by Clarence Brown, New York: Penguin, 1993.

107 This monthly journal was first published in 1371/1992. Since then it has gone through a number of changes in the composition of its editors and many of these changes were decisions made by Hozeh-ye Honari (The Arts Center), one of the major organizations in charge of literary and artistic policies of the Islamic Republic and the major patron of *Adabiyat-e Dastani*. With the coming of the last group of editors (Mohammad Reza Sarshar and Ahmad Shakeri), the direction of the journal has become completely ideological. Its main efforts are to propagate the Islamic Republic's objectives in the field of art and literature. Apparently, the last issue of the journal was published in 1387/2008.

108 Ruhollah Khomeini, *Adabiyat-e Dastani*, no. 69, 2003, p. 16.

109 Ali Khamenei, *Adabiyat-e Dastani*, no. 61, 2003, p. 64.

110 Ali Khamenei, *Adabiyat-e Dastani*, no. 101, 2006, p. 17.

111 Ali Khamenei, *Adabiyat-e Dastani*, no. 100, 2006, p. 31.

112 Ruhollah Khomeini, *Adabiyat-e Dastani*, no. 70, 2003, p. 30.

113 Shahryar Zarshenas, "*Feminism va Barkhi Nomudha-ye an dar Adabiyat-e Dastani*" (Feminism and its Reflections in Fiction), *Adabiyat-e Dastani*, no. 72, 2003, p. 41.

114 Shahryar Zarshenas, "*Sadeq Chubak va Naturalism-e Freud Zadey-e Lompani*" (Sadeq Chubak and his Vulgar Freud-Stricken Naturalism), *Adabiyat-e Dastani*, no. 86, 2004, p. 41.

115 Shahryar Zarshenas, "*Adabiyat-e Ya's va Bimari-ye Sadeq Hedayat*" (Literature of Despair and Sadeq Hedayat's Sickness), *Adabiyat-e Dastani*, no. 60, 2003, p. 6

116 Ahmad Shakeri, "*Goft-o-gu ba Mostafa Mastur*" (Conversation with Mostafa Mastur), *Adabiyat-e Dastani*, no. 101, 2005, p. 50.

117 Ibid., p. 49.

118 Jean François Lyotard has used the phrase "positional value" when discussing "marginal discourses." To read more about this notion and its usage in post-colonial theory, see John Erickson's *Islam and Postcolonial Narrative*, Cambridge: Cambridge University Press, 1998, pp. 18, 19.

119 Descombes, *Modern French Philosophy*, p. 108. Quoted from Terdiman, *Discourse/Counter-Discourse*, p. 62.

120 *Ta'liq* is the name of a particular style of calligraphy. The word also means "suspension."

121 A title usually used to refer to women who have performed the Hajj pilgrimage. It could also be used only as a sign of respect.

122 Mohammad Rahim Okhovvat *Ta'liq*, Esfahan: Naqsh-e Khorshid, 1378/1999, p. 63.

123 Ibid., p. 68.

124 Ibid.

125 Ibid., p. 8.

126 Ibid., p. 55.

127 Ibid., p. 82.

128 Interview with Mitra Shoja'i, *Dena* Magazine, no. 8, Mehr 1379/2000. http://www.golshirifoundation.org/interview_MitraSchojai.htm (accessed May 5, 2014).

129 Julio Cortazar, "To Reach Lezama Lima," *Around the Day in Eighty Worlds*, San Francisco, CA: North Point Press, 1986, p. 85. Quoted from Erickson, *Islam and Postcolonial Narrative*, p. 8.

130 Sadeq Hedayat, *Karvan-e Eslam: Al-Be'sat Al-Islamiah Il-Al-Belad Al-Afranjiah* (The Caravan of Islam: The Emergence of Islam in European Countries), Irvine, CA: Iran Zamin, 1985, p. 7. This book was originally written in 1930. It should be noted that all names and titles in the text used to refer to Muslim characters are constructed in such a way as to be particularly pejorative.

131 Hedayat, *The Caravan of Islam*, p. 27.

132 Erickson, *Islam and Postcolonial Narrative*, p. 150.

133 Ibid., p. 140.

134 Ibid., p. 152.

135 Baal is a pre-Islamic deity.

136 Erickson, *Islam and Postcolonial Narrative*, p. 152.

137 Quoted from Erickson, *Islam and Postcolonial Narrative*, p. 152.

138 The concept of normalization as an ensemble of social processes which promote certain values and actions as normal and natural has been discussed in many works by Foucault, especially in *Discipline and Punish*.

139 Suzanne Baker, "Binarisms and Duality: Magic Realism and Postcolonialism," *Journal of the South Pacific Association for Commonwealth Literature and Language Studies*, No. 36, 1993. See http://literarystudies.wordpress.com/2007/08/07/binarisms-and-duality-magic-realism-and-postcolonialism/ (accessed May 5, 2014).

140 Stephen Slemon, "Magic Realism as Post-Colonial Discourse," *Canadian Literature*, No. 166 (Spring 1988): 9–24.

141 Reza Julai, "*Tappeh-ha-ye Kabud*" (Purple Hills) in *Baran-ha-ye Sabz* (Green Rain), collection of short stories, Tehran: Juya, 2001.

142 Ibid., p. 107.

143 Ibid., p. 105.

144 Ibid., p. 106.
145 Ibid., p. 108.
146 Habibollah Davaran and Farhad Behbahani, *Dar Mehmani-ye Haji Aqa* (At Haji Aqa's Gathering), Tehran: Omid-e Farda, 1382/2003, pp. 115–117.
147 Julai, "Purple Hills," p. 107.
148 Ibid.
149 Ibid., p. 111.
150 Ibid., p. 116.
151 Ibid., p. 117. In the original, this part is distinguished by being in bold font.
152 Ibid., p. 111.
153 Ibid.
154 Ibid., p. 117.
155 Ibid., p. 118.
156 Ibid., p. 125.
157 Ibid., p. 122.
158 Ibid., p. 128.
159 Ibid., p. 129.
160 Ibid.
161 Ibid., p. 131.
162 Ibid.
163 Ibid., p. 107.
164 Ibid., p. 133.
165 Ibid.
166 Ibid., p. 134.
167 Ibid.
168 These are the opening lines of Shamlu's famous poem, *"Dar in Bonbast"* (In this dead end).
169 Reza Julai, *"Munes-o Mordekhai"* (Munes and Mordekhai), in *Nastaran-ha-ye Surati* (Pink Sweetbriers), Tehran: Markaz, 1998. p. 36.
170 The negative depiction of Iranian Jews is not of course limited to Classical Persian literature. To read more about this topos-like treatment, see Jaleh Pirnazar's "The Image of the Iranian Jew in the Writings of Three Modernist Writers," *Iran Nameh*, Vol. XIII, no. 4, 1995.
171 Julai, "Munes and Mordekhai," p. 40.
172 A rich neighborhood in Tehran.
173 Julai, *Pink Sweetbriers*, p. 41.
174 Ibid., p. 35.
175 Ibid., p. 38.
176 Yeprem (Yaprem) Khan, an Armenian born in Azerbaijan, Iran, was one of the leaders of Iran's Constitutional Revolution.
177 Sattar Khan and Baqer Khan were the two of the most famous leaders of Iran's Constitutional Revolution.
178 The Park-e Atabak affair was one of the significant incidents of the Constitutional Revolution during which different groups of constitutionalists confronted each other and defined differences among the revolutionaries.
179 Julai, "Munes and Mordekhai," p. 35.
180 The *tar* is a long-necked stringed instrument.
181 Julai, "Munes and Mordekhai," p. 45.
182 The poem is by Aref Qazvini (*c.* 1883–1933).
183 Julai, "Munes and Mordekhai," pp. 45, 46.
184 Ibid., p. 48.
185 Ibid., pp. 48, 49.

3 Individualistic literary spaces: non-discursive situations

Using the concept of colonialist discourse and post-colonial theories in general to discuss and examine the interactions and interconnectedness of prevalent discourses could be useful up to a point. Indeed, research conducted in the field of literary counter-discourses in relation to colonial dominant discourses could help shed light on aspects of many contemporary works of Persian literature. As suggested in Chapter 2, I believe John Erickson's *Islam and Postcolonial Narrative* is a good example of such research. One could even argue that in the field of Middle Eastern literatures, among works written in the North, it is one of the most pertinent ones because of its emphasis on literary techniques and devices and not a rewrite of the idea that these literary productions represent "national allegories."[1] Through an analysis of works by Assia Djebar, Abdelkebir Khatibi, Tahar Ben Jelloun, and Salman Rushdie, Erickson attempts to find narrative characteristics for literary works belonging to the "post-colonial discourse." In doing so and with an eye on the significance of the relationship between the textual and beyond-textual realities (this distinction is crucial from the point of view of describing a counter-discourse), Erickson maintains, "The discourses I study tend also to emphasize a dialogic relationship outside the text ... "[2] He then identifies a number of sites on which this dialogism functions:

> This dialogic operation reverses the conventional direction of narration by producing narration as an outcome of dialogic exchange in lieu of the imposition of narrative structures fixed in advance that determine the direction to be taken by specific event.[3]

The specific narrative consequence of such an approach is the undermining, or to use Erickson's term, the "detotalizing" of the structures of conventional narratives. Conversely, this dialogic operation creates narrative structures which do not allow for closure and finality. This dialogic operation is atemporal and multivocal; and it "presents propositions and understandings in essentially non-linear, synthesizing sequences."[4]

As mentioned before, these concepts could be used in an analysis of many contemporary Persian works of fiction, primarily because many literary atmospheres created in such works, before taking form and in order to take form, are obligated first of all to reject the colonizing official discourse. However, there are also many contemporary works of Persian fiction which cannot be explained and analyzed through post-colonial concepts and theories. The central reason for that is, once again, the relationship between the textual and beyond-textual realities. Concepts such as "dialogic relationship" and "dialogic operation" are too general and in many cases cannot be sufficiently effective. In the context of this study, these concepts—and post-colonial theories in general, when they engage the narrative characteristics of post-colonial literary discourses—provide only one of the dimensions of the context within which certain contemporary works of Persian fiction will be discussed.

In recent decades, many Iranian writers have adopted the first-person narrative style. Any attempt to find a simple, short answer to explain this phenomenon is futile. Even a quick review of the material of such stories indicates that some of them could be considered efforts to carve out a space for an individual voice as part of a reconstruction of collective history. There are other works which reflect attempts to simply define a socio-political identity; still others could be categorized as fictionalized autobiography. In addition to these categories, because of what I call "emphasis on everyday life," there are works which, in spite of their affinities with these sub-directories, could be put in a separate category. I use the phrase "everyday life" in the sense that was defined and developed by Henri Lefebvre and, after him, the Situationists.

Influenced by Existentialism and Marxism, Henri Lefebvre (1901–1991) expanded and developed his Marxist understanding of the notion of aliena-tion which had been defined in the context of social relations of production. But he located this alienation in "everyday life" and defined the latter as epitomizing the alienation of and in a capitalist society. In the definition of everyday life, which according to Lefebvre is "whatever remains after one has eliminated all specialized activities," the emphasis is placed on the extremely limited roles the dominant discourse has ascribed to individuals. In new forms of capitalist societies, individuals spend a specific amount of time in specific spaces in order to perform those assigned roles. According to this definition, the remaining time and activities constitute everyday life. Domi-nant discourses, however, have tried to colonize even the remaining time and spaces in order to coordinate everyday lives with their own imperatives. Lefebvre specifically discusses the needs of the new capitalist/spectacular society. His main point is that the discourse in power has depleted even this aspect of life, and that this depletion is a prerequisite for directing individuals towards using spectacular goods—not just materialistic goods, but narrative items which strengthen various aspects of the Society of the Spectacle, whether economic or ideological.

Rob Shields describes the position of individuals in this condition very succinctly when he writes: "Rather than resolving alienation, consumption is part of the mis-recognition of their alienated state by modern consumers, in a cycle which Lefebvre and Guterman referred to as the 'mystification' of consciousness."[5] In this context, Lefebvre's definition of modern consumer (the consumer of spectacle) sheds light on one of the most important projects of such societies. The implementation of this project, especially in totalitarian or, as Debord puts it, "concentrated," societies, requires both violent and non-violent approaches. For example, the official discourse of the Islamic Republic, especially because of its emphasis on religion, has been able to use this combination to establish its dominance. Understanding this point is crucial, because in many cases it is extremely difficult to recognize how, and to what degree, spaces of everyday lives have been influenced and defined by the official discourse on the one hand and individual identities on the other.

The smallest component constructing everyday life is the moment; indeed the confrontation with and repelling of the insidious *coup d'état* of the official discourse which attempts to control all spaces by defining them begins with moments. But which moments? With what characteristics? In his review of Lefebvre's work about his *Critique of Everyday Life* and then his suggestions for revolutionizing everyday life, Shields writes:

> Against "mystification", against the banality of the *"metro-bulot-dodo"* life of the suburban commuter, Lefebvre proposes that we seize and act on all "Moments" of revelation, emotional clarity and self-presence as the basis for becoming more self-fulfilled (*l'homme totale* – see 1959). This concept of "Moments" reappears throughout his work as a theory of presence and the foundation of a practice of emancipation.[6]

Explaining the ways to recognize such moments, Shields gives examples such as revelation, déjà-vu sensations, love, and committed struggle. Lefebvre's emphasis here is on pointing out moments which cannot easily be appropriated by the dominant discourse, and he also seems to be underlining the instantaneity of these moments as well. But we should go further than that, because the issue is not just recognizing these moments but finding ways through which they might be fully experienced. In this study I only follow this examination in its literary context. In this regard I will examine pitfalls which could prevent the finding and experiencing of such moments in literature.

At first it may seem that finding works which register such moments should not be that difficult. Many writers, especially writers of short stories, have been praised for their skill in capturing moments. But in actuality, finding moments which reflect dissociation from prevalent discourses in the context of everyday life is not so simple. Because the process of literary registration of moments—putting them down on paper and giving them a literary quality— effectively introduces new elements into the process which not only question the instantaneity of these moments but lays the groundwork for conditions in which some of the narratives of the dominant discourses can penetrate the literary-structured moments and attempt to undermine the counter-discursivity of these moments. Sadeq Chubak's *"Dozd-e Qalpaq"* (The Hubcap Stealer) is a good case in point.

"The Hubcap Stealer" is a short story in the collection *Cheragh-e Akhar* (The Last Alms) which Chubak published in 1344/1965. At the center of this very short story (it is less than 1,000 words long), there is a striking image which, at first, seems to convey the narrator's attempt to register precisely a moment and his experience of and reaction to that moment. It shows a 13-year-old boy who, having been caught while stealing a hubcap and having been punched, kicked, and slapped, is lying on the ground writhing in pain. Around the boy there is a "circle of miserable feet," a circle full of "heavy, menacing and bitter words ... which wouldn't let his pain go away."[7] Chubak constructs this image in the first section of the story through unmediated emphasis on a few simple events. The precise description of the blows on the boy by the people of the neighborhood and the passers-by, without any words being put in their mouths, along with a few interpretive interpolations on the part of the author, provides the possibility for readers to establish an unmediated link with the text. This immediacy gives the impression that the narrator has suspended the usual filters by means of which relating to literary moments materializes and has tried to record this unadulterated experience. The story begins here:

> People captured the thief when he was removing the second hubcap from the tire. He held the first one under his arm and with a screwdriver he was taking a whack at the second one, when a bitter hard blow on his head threw him on the ground. Then a kick landed on his side and he immediately felt griping. Everything became dark before his eyes; he retched and peed on himself.
>
> People gathered around him. The hubcap under his arm fell to the ground and rolled further away, then lay flat on the ground. Someone took his arm and stood him up. He couldn't stand straight. Another heavy blow to his head and a few slaps once again threw him to the ground. His face was shrinking with a crying pain. His face was wincing. He was thirteen and barefoot.[8]

This description, which bears Chubak's trademark of describing precise details, and which is a complete story in itself,[9] arrests the ideological, even theoretical filters, and allows the reader to write this scriptable text in a variety of ways.[10] But in the paragraph that follows this passage, this quality is gradually challenged through the introduction of superfluous descriptions. At the beginning of the paragraph, the car, a "shiny Cadillac with black fenders," is described as a "gadfly [which] had fallen asleep in the crowd and had not been annoyed in the least that its hubcap had been removed."[11] Using the metaphor of gadfly (out of place, a pest) is the narrator's first step in constructing a filter through which readers are invited to judge the situation. The narrator goes on to tell us that this event has taken place in a very poor neighborhood, thus emphasizing the anomaly of such an expensive car being in such a place. But this is just the beginning of the narrator's process of creating numerous filters and positioning them in front of the direct experience of the moment and its transference to readers. The car belongs to the head of the butchers' union, and the cruel behavior of the butcher towards a boy who is rolling in his own blood and urine is reminiscent of the superficial identification of the butchers' profession with cruelty and insensitivity.

> People opened a way, and Haji [the head of the butchers' union] came to the street and stood over the head of the little boy who had his hand on his belly. The asphalt was wet with his urine and blood. Haji kicked him in his flank as soon as he arrived. It was so hard that the boy's face turned blue; he stopped breathing and fell into a convulsion.[12]

We see the same cruelty and insensitivity in the people of the neighborhood who shower the boy with the most vulgar curses while continuing to beat him. And after reading fewer than 500 words, the filter to invite readers to judge between good and evil effectively tarnishes, even undermines the unmediated relationship with the earlier image.

In addition to that, there is another layer of filtering which has been in the process of taking form from the start. Quite possibly, when we read at the beginning of the story that the car was a Cadillac, we do not consider this piece of information particularly important. A few paragraphs later, however, this detail becomes significant. When the people of the neighborhood inform the butcher that they have captured a thief while he was removing the hubcap of his car:

> Haji came to the door wearing baggy, dirty underpants and undershirt. He looked like a village yokel. He was bald. Under his eyes puffy wrinkles had opened their mouths. His belly was huge. His son, in an American cowboy outfit, a toy gun in his hand, came to the door and planted himself in front of his father . . . [13]

This passage contains very clear references to established revolutionary narratives from the Mohammad Reza Shah period. References to the fact that the car is made in America and to the Americanization of Haji's son are obvious attempts to construct another layer of identity for "the villainous side." Elsewhere, I have referred to the powerful presence of this discourse (which counters the official one) in Iran's literary scene over the past 100 years. "The Hubcap Stealer" exemplifies how the influence of this discourse's narratives takes away from readers the possibility of relating directly to the moment and forces them to look at this moment and other, similar moments from an ideological viewpoint. At this point in the story, the focus of the narrator and readers is shifted towards the presence and significance of such catalysts. The Cadillac is no longer just a Cadillac; it is a synecdoche for

American Imperialism; Haji the butcher, "a village yokel" and his son who is wearing a cowboy outfit, may represent the "cultureless, arriviste America," and, like America, Haji has filled his coffers by exploiting others and stripping them of what they have (hence the poverty of the people around him). Moreover, this is not a one-time phenomenon; indeed, future generations are being formed. The narrator remembers to emphasize this point by saying directly that Haji's son "was the same age as the boy who was writhing around himself on the ground with his hand over his belly, his urine mixed with his blood."[14]

On top of that, we have the wretched people surrounding the poor kid, beating, cursing, and spitting on him. According to the established counter-discourse, those wretches are in fact deceived souls who have been brainwashed to the point that they defend those who are actually sucking their blood. At this point, readers are far removed from the direct experience of the moment, they only have a discursive description based on a particular ideology. In fact, other than the first part of the story in which the central image of the narrative is set out, the rest serves to describe an ideological confrontation. The device is quite predictable; a number of contrasts are defined; each of them has antagonistic sides belonging to the ideologically-opposed factions. Familiar metaphors and symbols representing repetitive, well-known narratives belonging to these two factions, and, more importantly, representing a superficial, linear logic, have been used to create a space within which the experience of the moment takes place. This space, because of unnecessary descriptions—in relation to the experience of the moment—is contaminated by the prevalent discourses. Before anything else, such an approach reduces the place and importance of the instantaneity of the experience. At the end, that central image, which had been constructed ever so skillfully, becomes part of the confrontation of the well-known discourses of the past 100 years of Persian literature and thus loses all its kinship with unique moments which function beyond these discourses.

About 50 years ago, Ahmad Shamlu composed a poem called "*Negah kon*" (Look!), which was published in the collection *Havay-e Tazeh* (Fresh Air). It began:

> The bad year
> The windy year
> The year of tears
> The year of doubts.
> The year of long days and little endurances
> The year when pride begged.
> The year of the abject
> > The year of pain
> > The year of mourning ... [15]

When the poet Mehdi Akhavan-Sales, Shamlu's contemporary, read this part of the poem for the first time, he wrote: "I shivered all over with excitement.

The first time I heard it, I cried. Nothing more delicate, more painful, more riveting has been written this year. It is excellent; it should be praised. ... "[16] Akhavan-Sales continues with the rest of the poem:

> Life is not a trap
> Love is not a trap
> Even death is not a trap
> Because *the lost friends are free*
> Free and pure ... [17]

In this section, once again familiar discourses begin to penetrate the poem and stain its authenticity, individuality, and sensibility which were at the core of its first part. Akhavan-Sales reacted:

> Well, it is not that bad. It has descended from that apogee of sensitivity and tenderness; still it has something to say; at least I hear it. I think the effect of the previous part is still within me, and he [Shamlu], cleverly, *is using poetry as a weapon and has ascended the pulpit. He is trying to instill ideas.*[18]

What Akhavan-Sales calls preaching and the instillation of ideas is nothing but the retelling of the well-known narratives which gradually impose their presence on this poem. It reaches the point where, having read the rest of the poem, Akhavan-Sales remarks regretfully: "The poem which had started so beautifully ... what a pity ... see where that poem has gone; that poem, that feeling, they were betrayed ... "[19]

Akhavan-Sales criticizes the poem above all because of its slogan-like utterances, which, in his opinion, have to do with the poet's conscious efforts to define an identity for himself. I believe this is not a very precise way of describing "poetic betrayal." The "Betrayal" should be defined as a transition from a moment enriched with individuality to one of cliché statements tainted with the usual discourses which, by prescribing a particular path to experiencing the moment, effectively erase its richness, authenticity, and individual quality. This is exactly what happens in Chubak's story.

One of the best examples in recent Persian fiction which demonstrates the use of literary devices to create unique moments and their spontaneous experience is the very short story "*Beh Donbal-e yek Buseh*" (After a Kiss) by Marjan Riahi. It is the story of a young woman who in the transitional space of an airport reproduces the moment of saying goodbye to her friends and family members. She reconstructs this moment with a temporal dimension construed through explaining the meaning of different kisses she receives. The way she treats these kisses becomes a symbolic motif in the story which serves to demonstrate the narrator's rejection of the prevalent discourses and leads to the establishing of the independence and originality of the moment.

I didn't expect so many people to come see me off. My kisses were duti-ful; the kisses I received spoke volumes. My aunt's kiss was saying that all her wonderful words came from the bottom of her heart, and my cousin's kiss was saying that she hoped to goodness she would never see my face again. My older sister's kiss was full of hopes of marriage, as if I could find a great husband in a few hours. My sister-in-law's kiss was full of special effort, and a sickening magnanimity that was meant to show that the grave family problems were less than they seemed.[20]

Each one of these indulgences where the narrator allows her imagination to freely move about within familiar narratives carries a potential danger for the unmediated experience of the moment. This potential danger, however, never materializes because each time, after spending a few short lines inside a familiar narrative, the leitmotif of a kiss interrupts and dismisses these nar-ratives and brings the narrator back to the airport space, and the immediacy of the moment remains intact. There are many such examples in this two-page story:

My best friend's kiss revived the memory of a year in political prison. That year had happened ten years ago. The moment I wanted to say goodbye to my prison mate and kiss her, she just shrugged her shoulders. Kissing? What for? Not kissing was a sign of strength.

Or

My niece's kiss was full of the wishes of a seventeen-year-old, and maybe they could be realized through me. Her kiss was depressed because of wearing a long dress and headscarf every day and wanted to ride a bicycle under a sun that caressed her hair.[21]

The last moment before take-off with its transient nature is a wonderful device. It functions as a centripetal force and creates narrative imperatives which force the narrator to bring all the digressions and descriptions—the best outlets for prevalent discourses to penetrate the story—back to the moment. In addition, the locations of the story, the airport, then the plane, are com-pletely unstable, unfixed environments which provide the narrator with the possibility of dissociating herself from established descriptions and definitions, always part of dominant discourses. Thus, another component which has the potential of undermining the moment-centered narration is neutralized.

Another technique which functions on the sentence and phrase level and indirectly prevents the influence of these discourses is the use of a very simple language, one almost completely devoid of any embellishment as well as the most common figures of speech such as metaphors, or allegories, or even symbols. These figures without exception create a certain intertextuality which could be a channel for the presence of elements of prevalent discourses. The narrator of "After a Kiss" has consciously chosen this approach. Indeed, this is seen in many works by Marjan Riahi. No doubt this has been one of the main reasons why many of her stories have succeeded in capturing exceptional moments or short slices of time, without linking them to other spaces.[22] In this sense, "After a Kiss" has created a self-referential text which is reminiscent of the self-referentiality of modernist authors when their modern sensibilities are used in relation to the description of a moment without any link to its historical, social, political, or other expected dimensions. Of course, I am not arguing that this story and similar ones are examples of "modern fiction" in the sense that this phrase has been used to describe the works of writers such as Joyce or Proust. This concept, which has been defined in regard to a stage in the history of some Western literary traditions, cannot be used in the case of a completely different literary tradition such as Persian. In those cases the modern sensibility was defined in relation to self-referentiality through statements such as "There is no outer reality." I suggest that with regard to works such as "After a Kiss," this should be modified, and the originality and authenticity of the self should be replaced with the originality and authenticity of the moment. In that case, it would be much easier to understand the two-dimensional/flat language of such stories, which, in the context of capturing the unique experience of the moment, should be considered a positive characteristic.

In *Decline of the New*, explaining the importance of subjectivity in the modernist outlook, Irving Howe refers to Gottfried Benn, the German poet, and his famous statement: "There is no outer reality, there is only human consciousness, constantly building, modifying, rebuilding new worlds out of its own creativity."[23] In future pages I will refer to examples of modernist Persian fiction which, from the viewpoint of self-based structures, have a kinship of sorts with this subjectivity, but in moment-centered structures there is no such emphasis on "building new worlds." Precisely for this reason, for example in "After a Kiss," Riahi employs devices and techniques which do not use the capturing of the moment as the beginning of the construction of an individualistic world, or even simply as part of a larger context. Indeed, for this reason, the shortness of the story is quite appropriate.[24] The closure of the story is also quite fitting, in that, once again, it emphasizes the centrality of the moment which ends once the plane lands.

> The sky behind the airplane window curves and reaches the ground. I have not started yet, but many things have already ended.[25]

This does not mean that the memory of the moment has been forgotten, because reminiscing about the events which took place during this moment will effectively transform it into a *lieu de mémoire*, but the unique and unmediated experience of the moment has ended.

I called the structure of this Riahi's story a centripetal one. Comparing this story with Chubak's "The Hubcap Stealer" could clarify the usage of this metaphor. In "The Hubcap Stealer," the central moment of the story fades before the powers of prevalent discourses. This strategy is clear from the very beginning: the narrator chooses a particular moment, and a particular event and space which lend themselves very easily to discursive digressions. Conversely, from the beginning, Riahi's story distances itself from familiar, ideologically-based literary environments which lend themselves easily to prefabricated definitions of prevalent discourses. Here, the author/narrator chooses the simple yet effective approach of selecting the unstable, unfixed atmosphere of transition. This approach is not uncommon in Persian fiction of recent decades. For example, in "*Halat-e Avval*" (Original Position),[26] Tahereh Alavi, relies on an environment which is very similar to that of "After a Kiss." This story is about a young Iranian woman who, having lived in Paris for a short period of time, is now returning to Iran. The first paragraph of the story describes the long moment of flight, specifically from the point of view of transition between two locations which, according to the narrator, are worlds apart in terms of values and judgments.

> But the basic problem lies in these few hours of flight, which makes what was good up until last night turn bad, and make what was bad become good and praiseworthy. Especially the efforts of most of the girls on board Flight Number 733 to preserve their chastity. Those efforts will turn into smoke and vanish into thin air at one in the afternoon Paris time.[27]

Referring not just to their relative appropriateness but rather to the idiocy of values considered absolute, this paragraph by itself deflates all moral grand narratives. The rest of the story, an account of the narrator's brief residence in Paris and her internal struggle concerning the relationships between men and women and the moralities of different societies, accentuates the experiencing of the moment of suspension which takes place in the transient space of the flight.[28] Once again, the transient, unfixed nature of such spaces makes it possible for them to maintain their independence by remaining outside the pre-defined locations and thus outside prevalent discursive narratives.

This is, of course, only one way of setting up a distance from familiar discourses. Another approach is the deliberate, overt rejection of familiar discursive atmospheres, followed by creating environments within which the presence of such unique moments and their unmediated experience becomes possible. One of the most creative examples of such a stylistic approach in modern Persian fiction is "*Sarasar Hadeseh*" (Action-Packed) by Bahram Sadeqi, whose body of work represents one of the most consistent proponents of literary counter-discourses in contemporary Persian fiction.

Bahram Sadeqi and Mohammad Asef Soltanzadeh: using irony to explain tragedy

Undoubtedly, Bahram Sadeqi is the most significant ironist in Iran's twentieth-century fiction. He was writing and publishing during the period of 1957–1972, but it took a long time for his works to receive appropriate readings and analyses and to find their proper place in Iran's history of contemporary literature. Still, Sadeqi's work has not been analyzed sufficiently from the point of view of his literary techniques and merits. There are two main reasons for this. As I will comment later, the significance of Sadeqi's work lies in its crafting of an extremely effective system to reject prevalent discourses and narratives in their various forms. These forms refer not only to the discourse in power but also to familiar discourses which challenge the existing political power apparatus. In situations where narrative catalysts belonging to these discourses have been contrived and installed in all fields of human activities (including literary production), it is very difficult to relate to works such as those by Sadeqi, because once they are put through such filters, not much will be left of them. In other words, for those whose readings are based on such discourses, a great part of these works should be ignored so that they may be reduced to the level of familiar narratives. Or, they will be regarded as intellectual nonsense which have nothing much to say. The second reason which explains the difficulty of relating to such works is their technical characteristics. In these works, instead of being contextualized in a lighthearted atmosphere, the ironies are presented in a dark sarcasm which encompasses even the reader and the author/narrator. Bahram Sadeqi's "Action-Packed" is one such example.

All of the events of this "eventless" story, as Gholam-Hosein Sa'edi put it,[29] take place in a three-storey house owned by a widow and her three sons. They live on the third floor and have five tenants on the other two. The eldest son, who has practically replaced their dead father, is employed by a drug company. The middle son is a doctor's aide, and the youngest one is a high-school senior. The tenants include an ailing young man who lives in a room on the same floor. He has been studying languages at the university for many years. He has covered the glass door of his room with black paper, and the door is always locked. On the first floor live two brothers with strange names, Darvish and Bolbol (nightingale). Darvish behaves like a sufi and is constantly reading Rumi's *Masnavi*. He has only one follower: the middle brother from the third floor. Bolbol is a young man who believes he is a very good singer. In the rooms on the second floor live a 50-year-old man and his 35-year-old wife; their only problem seems to be that they have no children.

"Action-Packed" begins with the following suggestion by the older brother:

> In the morning, when the older brother wanted to go to work he said, "Tonight we should invite all the tenants and, following the perennial old custom, give them dinner. Because in addition to the fact that *Yalda*[30] is a historic night, this is an occasion for us to get together."[31]

The younger brother's reaction to his brother's suggestion to have a party demonstrates, from that very first moment, the author's strategy in using irony as the dominant technique of the story.

– Then what will become of my studies? Every night we have the same story! You are just looking for a pretext to set up the same situation. At the beginning of the night there is a heated political discussion. To hell with it, I say; let them scream as much as they like and hit each other over the head. Then you end up fighting each other. Again I say, to hell with it. Then Mr. Mohajer, who is dying to do so, comes down and makes peace between you. Very well! But this is only the beginning of the scene: Mr. Behruz Khan recites the *Masnavi* in the unrefined voice of his and you, Your Highness ... begin playing the *tar* with your mouth. Our poor mother falls asleep, and I ... I remain helpless like a donkey in the mud, trying to solve a simple two-variable equation; such a minor problem.[32]

To recognize the dramatic irony in this scene, we should comprehend the subtle exaggeration located at the end of Masud's speech. The emphasis on the "two-variable equation" is rather peculiar and out of place; naturally the reader, instead of empathizing with Masud, finds him strange and even a bit comic. Since throughout the story, in order to define the existing situation through their points of view, the characters persist in their ironic expressions, this subtlety is gradually replaced with free-rein utterances whose kinship and incompatibility with familiar narratives and discourses are quite clear.

When after their discussion the elder brother pokes fun at Masud, his studies and talents, and when their mother asks Masud not to quarrel with his elder brother, Masud,

... as if he wanted to confide in an unbiased onlooker assigned to solve their problem, with those same movements of head and hands answered:
– Fairness, justice, humanity, democracy, socialism, whatever you think ... just for one minute think about me. None of you has any studying to do; you have no problem to solve. ... Behruz is a doctor's assistant, it doesn't make any difference to him whether the room is quiet or not. As for Your Majesty, you go to the firm in the morning and sit behind the medicine-making machine; you come back at noon and go out again in the afternoon. You don't have to answer to the roll call. There is no teacher to call on you and your exams are not approaching. And you, dear mother, who are issuing instructions, you tell me: do you think being a math major, in the last year of high school is a joke? No, seriously, you answer me! Here you go, here is a physics problem: please determine the density of ... do you really think it is easy to find the density? And here is a chemistry one: write down the expanded resulting formula. How can I write that?[33]

This is an excellent example of unusual synthesis of words and of the caricaturistic hyperbolization of familiar narratives and phrases, done to discredit them. In other words, if this discussion was to follow its "ordinary" path, it should not have juxtaposed the idea of determining the density and socialism and democracy and the teacher's calling the roll. Clearly the juxtaposition of these subjects is carried out in order to ironize narratives whose basic concepts are construed based on these terms and phrases. The continued usage of this technique heightens the narrative and linguistic frenzy. Along this same line, a few pages further, explaining the strange name of one of the brothers who lives on the first floor, we read:

> Of course, for a modern Iranian youth, "Bolbol" is a ridiculous, comical, strange name. But why blame us? His name was Bolbol maybe because he had a loud voice, and he always sang and always participated in the radio's artistic tryouts. He always swore that next Friday, at such an hour, after the historical play, they would broadcast the tape of his song. And every Friday, after the historical play, the religious play would start immediately and consequently Bolbol and others cursed this breaking of the promise and lack of artistic connoisseurship.[34]

The tone employed here is a combination of caricaturization and sarcasm which debilitates the cliché narratives.[35] The other example in "Action-Packed" of utilizing this technique against an ironic background is found in the description of Maziyar, the university student who studies languages:

> But poor Maziyar .. although his body was ailing, he had a pure soul. Since his father had promised to provide him with his education expenses, he, very coolly, took two years to go through each year of coursework. In the letters he wrote to his father, after the usual greetings, and having asked him about the state of his beloved province and its hardworking people, he explained that in order to reform the important matter of education and in order to bring up skilled young people so that they could properly direct the great and shining future of the country, a surprising revolution in all cultural and academic fields has taken place. That is, from now on the number of years of study will be determined by the students themselves. And since he would like to be at the top of this promising future, he has come to the conclusion that he has to study language for many, many years to come … [36]

In this short paragraph, many familiar clichés are first evoked, then quickly discredited—in various ways. The sentence "Although his body was sick [he] had a pure soul" has been seen, heard, and read in many newspaper serial romance novels.[37] Once this phrase is placed next to the one in which the narrator talks about Maziyar's "coolness" in taking advantage of his father's money by taking two years to go through one year's worth of coursework, it is immediately ridiculed. Similarly, all stereotypical phrases and sentences such as "his beloved province and its hardworking people," "the important matter of education," and "bringing up skilled young people," and "revolution in all cultural and academic fields," which are all reminiscent of the cliché propaganda of the discourses in power, when they are placed in the context of Maziyar's plan "to study languages for many, many years to come," and in general the incompatible nature of the juxtaposition of these phrases, creates a comic and unstable ensemble which discredits all familiar narratives one by one.

The term "irony" is, I believe, suitable to describe Sadeqi's technique, because it materializes the most important function of irony, which is to create inconsistency between customary words, definitions, and narratives on the one hand, and tangible realities on the other. The phrase "dramatic irony," which in many cases defines Sadeqi's technique, is used to underline the fact that it seems only the audience (narrator/author and readers) is aware of this inconsistency. The actors (the story's characters) are behaving "naturally" towards each other—and it seems their story and all the events have been repeated so many times—as if there is nothing odd in their statements and conduct, and in the environment surrounding them.

Each line of this story is an example of the process of ironizing narratives associated with customary discourses. This process reaches its apogee when the guests arrive for *Yalda* and begin their conversations and discussions. The radio is broadcasting a report about a soccer match between "the two great teams of America and the Soviet Union" which for some reason has been postponed. Discussing this, quite simply leads to ridiculing communists, revolutionaries, "God-worshiping materialists," such as Behruz and his pir, Darvish, as well as America and Imperialism. Of course, Behruz's Sufism is not spared by any means; this is not because of his not-all-that-wise comments on various issues but rather because his pir, Darvish, has already talked about Behruz and his Sufism, saying:

> But as for Behruz, it is not clear; it seems that for all his cool and scholarly appearance, he still needs the guidance of an older person. Otherwise why has he believed what I say and taken it so seriously? It seems that he cannot live without a guardian. Maybe this is why he is imitating what I do, though I don't know why, for example, I smoke *bhang*; why I read the *Masnavi* although I don't understand it; why I am taking everything so trivially; why I go to the *khaneqah*, as I call it, every night.[38]

Amidst all the ridiculous noise and discussions of the evening, and next to the loud radio, Masud's opening his heart to Mr. Mohajer is a mournful masterpiece of irony:

> – Mr. Mohajer, you are like my father ... I am becoming miserable in this house; I cannot do anything. Please look at this: This is the blueprint to invent a car which runs on kerosene. (He held out his notebook, flipped through it and showed it.) I am thinking all the time, without any means or tools and without any encouragement ... This is the chauffeur's seat; right here is the place for the engine. Underneath it there is a barrel in

which water is boiling. When we want the car to go faster, turn up the wick; when we want to stop it we blow out the flame ... You can go to Khorasan on ten liters of kerosene. You don't want that; you can go to Shah Abdolazim on half a liter of kerosene, or wherever you want ... But what is the use? It is stupid of me to do this ... I built a sleeve camera with these few tools. But it can't take any pictures. You know why? Because I don't have a darkroom, because my tripod is wobbly ... [39]

This is an extraordinary example of a ridiculous hyperbole which has totally lost its kinship with customary definitions of reality and has reached a level of idiocy. This exaggeration, caricaturization, and ironization, is not gratuitous; the narrator employs this device to build a space unadulterated by the (familiar) discursive effects The important point is the taking form of this space which is created based on the negation of dominant discourses, and it does not necessarily contain or offer an alternative viewpoint.[40] In this environment the moments are authentic and original simply because they are related to a unique space which is completely removed from the customary discourses.

The main point about these moments is that they are not necessarily representative of "real" events which have occurred outside the text; yet, in the context of a literary reality, they are quite real. Understanding this point is crucial because it underlines that life, real life, can take place through art and literature; especially when literary and artistic situations ignore or confront prevalent discourses, interaction of the writer, narrator and readers with such situations define an aspect of their lives which is quite tangible.

The moments created in the unique atmosphere of "Action-Packed" could be interpreted both as beyond-textual or simply as textual reality, but in both cases they provide readers with the conditions needed to experience them independent from filters of the dominant discourses. One of the most powerful moments, in many ways a moment unequaled in modern Persian fiction, comes towards the end of the story.

The *Yalda* party continues, and after a while the elder brother, unbeknownst to the mother, suggests that they start drinking. They all agree. Masud goes to the kitchen; the others somehow provide the mother and Mrs. Mohajer with excuses and send them to the kitchen as well, and the drinking begins. Mr. Mohajer, apparently, at the time of his marriage, had promised Mrs. Mohajer's father, who was a *Hojjat al-Islam*,[41] to give up drinking; apparently he had forgotten his promise from the start. Moreover, according to Mrs. Mohajer, from the time the couple realized they could not have children, Mr. Mohajer, on one of their pilgrimages, repented drinking and in exchange asked God to give him a child. Naturally Mrs. Mohajer believes she has not gotten pregnant because he has broken his pledge. The situation grows more and more convoluted, and on the same pages we read that Mrs. Mohajer's extremely religious father was also extremely in love with music, which, according to the story, was considered forbidden in Islam.

Being a *Hojjat al-Islam*, therefore, "He issues a fatwa that just for himself music is permitted." Mrs. Mohajer then tells how each one of the six brothers and sisters learned to play an instrument and every evening, after the father finished his prayers "They gathered and played and sang."[42] There is no end to these paradoxical statements, and in fact, these are all part of the strategy of destabilizing the accepted narratives and discourses.

Then, as if this confusion is not enough, drunkenness is added. Intoxicated, the characters, one after another, deny what they have said before, to the point that the readers cannot rely on anything. In a strange way, the resulting chaos, described in detail, seems to be in harmony with the non-discursive anarchy of the situation.

The culmination of undermining and mistrusting everything emerges when Mr. Mohajer persistently asks Maziyar to open the door to his room and for once shows them what is inside. Completely intoxicated, Maziyar accepts and invites them to his room. Mr. Mohajer and Darvish follow him. He opens the door and once he turns on the light they see a most strange scene.

> At the end of the electricity wire, near the lamp, there was a thread tied to the tail of a skinny, dirty mouse. The hanging mouse was struggling, with amusement. With his fingertip Maziyar tickled the mouse and then clapped his hand happily and like a kid jumped up and down ... [43]

Maziyar's explanation of the reason for this act is completely incomprehensible and does not follow any particular logic. He says that, three nights ago, this mouse had come to his room from the lower floor in order to harass him! But he does not follow this path of reasoning and does not reach any conclusion. Everything he says thereafter is unintelligible. Among these utterances, he says:

> I believe in the mouse. I tell myself: this mouse, too, is a living being; he is also skinny and sickly-yellowish looking ... so far, exactly like myself. I am sure he studies language, maybe for years. How and where? Of course we don't know where. Then I say: Maybe he, too, is alone ... [44]

It seems he is trying to identify himself with the mouse. Maziyar explains that he caught the mouse the night before "because in the next week or the next year I might be able to understand the meaning of life ... "[45] And then,

> Maziyar sighed and, with a sadness which had replaced the happiness of a moment ago, continued:
> – Anyone in my place would have killed him or would have given him to a cat to swallow. But I thought he should be tormented, tortured ... At the end of the night I woke up and burned his whiskers with a lighter. Poor thing, in the process, a little of his lips got roasted and in the morning after I woke up I felt pity for him and I treated him with

mercurochrome. This is why, this is why I say one should believe in many things ... [46]

This is the height of cruelty, a sad, villainous perversion which, in a direct and yet strange way, contradicts the way Maziyar was previously described, especially his "pure soul." However, it is incorrect to consider this specific contradiction as the main element of this scene. Other elements, including the totally irrelevant last sentence, "This is why, this is why I say one should believe in many things ... " do not allow for such a limiting interpretation. What is even more bizarre, none of Maziyar's companions show any reaction, as if nothing out of ordinary has happened. Darvish is sitting in a corner crying and lamenting, wishing his mother was there so that he could put his head on her lap and go to sleep. This is the same Darvish who makes fun of Behruz because he thinks "[Behruz] needs an older person." Meanwhile, Mr. Mohajer keeps talking about the fact that he does not even know whether or not he wants to have any children with his wife, whom at this point he detests.

This scene is the technical emblem of the whole story, creating an environment in which dramatic irony is constantly being reproduced, thus an environment in which no grand narrative can survive. That is why the efforts of some critics who have tried to read Sadeqi's work through the lenses of prevalent discourses seem particularly reductionist, simply because the effectiveness of such scenes is created against the backdrop of the weakening of grand narratives and discourses. This is reminiscent of Debord's statement about the construction process of "situations": "The construction of situations begins beyond the ruins of the modern spectacle." As regards modern Persian fiction, that statement could take the following form: the originality of these works is formed on the ruins of prevalent discourses and narratives. The previously-mentioned scene is an excellent example of such originality. In this scene, different sentiments are conveyed in a pure form: pure cruelty, pure sadness, pure sensitivity, and so on. I am using the adjective "pure" in the sense that these sentiments are not contaminated by conventional discourses and narratives. This is achieved through a conscious use of irony which leads to situations such as Maziyar's room with the mouse hanging from the ceiling, and this irony represents something quite different from what the characters of the story were attempting to present. Such usage of dramatic irony, which I do not believe was ever used in such a systemic manner after Sadeqi, nevertheless established a key principle, that the prerequisite for creating pure moments and situations is the total disengagement from realities defined by established narratives and discourses.

These situations and their internal, unique logic owe their self-existent quality to the narrator's understanding of the fact that his literary reality is a reflection of modern mass society[47] in which individuals, as soon as they are placed next to each other regardless of their individual limitations, feel empowered; and they could be mobilized. Therefore, undermining them cannot and should not stop at the level of just parodying characters and satirizing their idiotic beliefs and statements. In fact, in this work of Bahram Sadeqi, one of the most significant methods of undermining a mass society whose main characteristic is the eradication of true individuality, the function of parody and satire takes place in the context of a discursive irony which challenges conventional discourses on both individual and collective levels.

These examples also demonstrate that there is a tight link between literary representation of a unique moment and the space within which this representation is materialized. This link underlines the fact that one cannot remain at the level of moment and expect a revolution in everyday life. Indeed, in his theoretical discussions concerning spaces, Henri Lefebvre begins with a categorization which I believe is directly connected to his critique of everyday life. According to him, there are, theoretically, three main categories of spaces. In reality, of course, spaces contain elements of all three categories. He names these three types as: *"le perçu," "le conçu,"* and *"le vécu"*. In *"le perçu"* the emphasis is placed on the materiality of spatial forms, and on the ordinary and popular understanding of spaces. On the other hand, *"le conçu"* is the representation of space through ideas and concepts; therefore it emphasizes an abstract/professional/theoretical approach to spaces. The third type, *"le vécu"* represents space as it is *really* experienced by an individual.[48]

At the risk of a gross simplification, according to this categorization, the individual, in order to increase the individualistic aspect of his life, should expand *"le vécu"* and it is precisely here that the link between this categorization and Lefebvre's discussion about everyday life crystallizes.

If we pay close attention to these categories, we realize that the central issue concerns the individual's experience (in the most encompassing sense of the word) of his environment; it also involves the question of the degree to which this experience stems from the individual himself (as opposed to having been influenced by imposed elements of prevalent discourses) and can therefore be a representative of an individual's life. These statements are supported by assumptions which are drawn first on Lefebvre's critique, on the Situationists' critique of capitalist societies, and then on the discursive critique of these societies. According to these assumptions, the imagined and abstract spaces (the first and second categories) have been constructed based on the specific needs of the dominant discourses of these societies; therefore, in most cases, the category of experienced space is forced to neutralize the other two categories in order to materialize itself. A more precise discussion, especially about the first category of spaces, is found in the studies done by sociologists specializing in urban spaces. Many of these studies attempt to demonstrate the link between requirements of dominant discourses and the process of the formation of urban spaces.[49]

Following this categorization, many critics have described the characteristics of these spaces, especially those related to the third category and they have also tried to offer guidelines as to how moments which form these spaces are created. Some have pointed to the importance of using the imagined and abstract spaces and then going beyond them. Soja, for example, defines an experienced space as one that "draws upon the material and mental spaces [Firstspace and Secondspace] of the traditional dualism but extends well beyond them in scope, substance, and meaning";[50] while Shields, following Lefebvre, places the emphasis on imagination and the creation of moments uninfluenced by prevalent discourses.[51] The Situationists, too, after their critique of the Surrealist approaches, offered their own guidelines for creating such moments and ensembles of moments. In the context of this study, however, the main point is the analysis of the process of literary creation of these moments in modern Persian fiction. In the following pages, I will explore instances of different approaches to create and present the experienced space (*le vécu*).

The first method, and probably the most common one, is to begin with established, familiar situations and then gradually to distance oneself from them in order to create new environments which would have the potential to accept the presence of such moments, and even to aid in their formation. One of the best such examples is the short story *"Damad-e Kabol"* (The Bridegroom of Kabul) by Mohammad Asef Soltanzadeh, an Afghan writer who came to Iran as a refugee during the civil war. He lived in Tehran for a period of time. There he published one of his collections of short stories, *Dar Goriz Gom Mishavim* (We Disappear in Flight). The experiences of life in exile, and of confrontation with a new world which provides the exile with the possibility of going beyond both familiar worlds, have undoubtedly helped Soltanzadeh in the defining of moments whose experience does not have to pass through the filters of dominant discourses. Such moments are found in almost all of the stories in this collection; one of the most extraordinary of such moments arises at the end of "The Bridegroom of Kabul."

Like the majority of the stories of this collection, "The Bridegroom of Kabul" begins simply, with an ordinary sentence, "The Bridegroom should dance!" The bridegroom, who is also the narrator, is describing his wedding day. Occasionally, throughout the description, he remembers past events and offers a very stereotypical description of the civil war period, the absurdity of war, and the idiotic ideological beliefs of different groups involved in that civil war. At times these descriptions look like bumper stickers, and, especially when the narrator talks about contradictions between ordinary lives and ideological battles, his statements sound more and more like worn-out slogans. Yet it seems that these descriptions, which are presented at a rather slow pace, have an aim which is not limited to the juxtaposition of ideological battles and ordinary life in order to condemn the former.

At the beginning of the story, there is a description of the wedding day. The house is decorated from top to bottom. The sound of occasional bullets and missiles is heard. The sound of music comes from inside the house. Suddenly a mortar shell explodes near the house, and the host asks the guests, who are quite used to such situations, to take shelter in the basement. The party is continued there, however, and the narrator skillfully uses the half-dark basement as the setting for a dance scene which at first reading appears to be at once indicative of the continuity of life despite the civil war and a refutation of sorts of the dominant ideology.

> The women had begun to strike the tambourine and dance, and from this side we could see their shadows on the curtain. The shadow would sit, then rise and bend and turn. Then she would raise her arms and move her waist. ...
>
> A wave began from the legs of the woman behind the curtain and rose; it moved her hips, waved her breasts, and left the body through the hands, and again. ...
>
> The shadow was turning around behind the curtain. Hair was flying about in the air and the flared skirt was turning like a circulating dome and turning again and again, and my head was spinning.[52]

This description, although quite skillful, is still in the context of the familiar contrast between the pleasant and natural, ordinary life, and the unjustified war. It does not advance this contrast and does not add anything new. Yet, at the end, all these ordinaries suddenly turn into points of references through which the story arrives at an extraordinary uniqueness.

All are gathered in the bridegroom's house except the narrator's paternal uncle who, because of a falling-out with his brother, has not come. Traditions, as well as the narrator's aunts, insist that he be present; the only one who can force him to come is the bridegroom/narrator, because "nobody can reject a bridegroom's request on his wedding day." The bridegroom and his best man, the Shah Vala,[53] get into the car and cross the war-stricken city to get to the uncle's house. Inevitably, they have to go through the checkpoints of confronting rival bands. At one of those checkpoints they encounter a commander who arrests them as enemies simply because they do not belong to his tribe. He scolds them for having come to the war-torn streets in such elaborate wedding dress and sarcastically repeats the first sentence of the story: "The bridegroom should dance." But this familiar sentence takes on another meaning in the final moment of the story. The image described in that last moment is astonishing; its positionality, along with all those seemingly ordinary, undramatic moments and images, described earlier, register its uniqueness in a stunning, awe-inspiring fashion. This moment arrives when one of the fighters, after a few minutes of making fun of them and chanting "The bridegroom should dance" suddenly and without warning cuts the narrator's head from his body; the final scene is described through the eyes of the still-living head which has fallen to the ground.

> Ahhh! What happened to me? I did not understand how all of a sudden my eyes, looking at the dirt and gravel fall on the ground and then they roll and remain looking at the sky. I hear the Shah Vala's voice: No, I told you; first me ...
>
> From down here, from the ground, I look up and I see a body without a head, standing. A man with a large knife from which blood is dripping

is standing behind him. The headless body takes a few steps and next to a flower-bedecked car, slowly bends on his knees. Red blood pours from the cut neck onto the white clothes. Red runs into the white. How beautiful! I never knew that someone could be this beautiful, red and white. A fountain of blood pours on the white flower-bedecked car and makes the red paper flowers and ribbons even redder. Someone that I don't see gives a red-hot shovel to the one who has the knife in his hand. I try to turn my eyes so that I can see him better, my eyes don't turn. The man drops the knife and places the red-hot shovel on the cut neck. The body stands straight and begins moving his hands. I see people are crooked; they are clapping and the body keeps turning around himself and runs every-where. He doesn't have eyes to see where to go. The voice of the commander is heard: the Shah Vala, too, should dance!

The Shah Vala enters the frame of my vision, with a burning fuse that they have wrapped around his body. The spiral of fire runs around the legs, the waist and the whole body of the Shah Vala and lights the lead-color air. The Shah Vala goes to the headless body and takes his hands and brings him to the middle of the scene. Now the Shah Vala was the eyes for both of them, and slowly he was creating a rhythm in the move-ments of their legs and arms. Now it seems that the Shah Damad is no longer shy and puts his hand around the waist of his Shah Vala, and both raise their legs and take steps. They shake their chests, turn their waist, then take steps. They are turning around me, again and again. And I see that the whole world has begun turning with them. From down here, in the middle of the clapping of the armed men and the echo of the wedding music which is ringing in my ears and the congratulation song that the woman behind the curtain sings and the striking of the tambourine which has filled the whole world, I see the Shah and I see the Shah Vala, whose hair is now in fire, and both of them are dancing against the dark, tar-like sky.

As everything is fading away in my eyes, their movements, too, become slower and slower. Gently, they fall on their knees, right in front of me. The Shah Vala, whose face is burned with nothing left but two eyes sticking out of their sockets, stares at me.[54]

Such an image is not sustainable by itself; it needs to be built up gradually in the course of the story. Throughout the story the author/narrator creates a situation and then quickly goes beyond its normal contours. This process reaches its apogee at the end, where the scene cannot be explained through customary discourses and, more importantly, cannot be experienced through them. And this experience is unique.

Soltanzadeh follows a similar method in many of his stories. Another one of these very unbelievable yet completely logical and acceptable and thus believable images is found at the end of the story "… ta Mazar" (… to Mazar).[55] The *fabula* here is completely different from that of "The Bridegroom of Kabul," yet the approach is similar. This time it is about the transfer of a corpse from Kabul to Mazar-e Sharif for burial. The dead man's two sons and the brother are taking him there in a car. Once again they have to go through multiple checkpoints; once again, the slow pace of the story provides the opportunity for the creation of familiar situations and references to known discourses and various groups and well-known critiques of their absurd extremism. And once again, at the end of the story, all these idiocies crystallize in an image and a unique experience of the moment.

At a cemetery in Mazar, the sons and the brother watch a grave-digger working. Then a small truck with a few armed men approaches. The grave-digger tells them:

> Since yesterday the city has changed hands. New armed men have replaced the old armed men. They are different. They wear shirts and pants and instead of hats they wrap turbans around their heads, with their hair sticking out, and long beards ... [56]

The armed men riding in the truck arrive, and, in addition to ordinary questions, their leader's first reaction is to reproach them for not having completely respected the Islamic rules and regulations. The main issue over which they are criticized is that some of them have apparently shaved off their beards. An argument follows; in the end, the leader decides to carry out what he considers Islamic punishment of the travelers. He tells them:

> It is everybody's duty to guide his brother in religion and punish them for their wrongdoings; this will cause their sins to be removed. Know this: all people should continuously answer [for their wrongdoings] so that they can get ready for the Day of Judgment.
>   Osman said: Well, how are we going to be punished?
>   – Each one of you is going to receive ten lashes; may God forgive our sins.[57]

But the story does not end here, and the armed guards at the checkpoint who consider the precise implementation of Islamic laws their sacred duty, pursue their obligation to a rather ridiculous degree and decide to punish even the dead man. This is how the hysterical final scene is played out.

> Molavi[58] untied a lash from his waist. It had a leather handle with thin strands of leather woven together. He looked carefully at everyone. The uncle had a long, white beard; he was saved. Faruq, a very young man whose upper lip had just begun to darken; not yet in his majority. The grave-digger, a man who has probably seen thirty springs but in this unfriendly time, he has seen so many dead and has buried so many people that he has many wrinkles and only a few soft, thin hairs on his face.
>   – Why did you shave?

– I swear to God I never had a beard; I am thin-bearded.

– Ah! God has forgiven you my son.

The grave-digger breathed a sigh of relief. Osman, proud and angry, with his face covered in the dust of the road …

– You should receive the Shari'a punishment of ten lashes.

Before he could move, two men took his arms and pulled his shirt up. Osman took the ten lashes. The blood had rushed to his face, from shame or anger, or perhaps both; and ready-to-fire weapons forced him back.

Now Molavi had gone to check the dead man, Gholam Omar, with his closed eyes and white, thin beard which had given him a spiritual aura.

– This one, too, has a beard which is shorter than a handful … [59]

And then with his hand he measured his own beard.

– This one, too, should receive the Shari'a punishment. Maybe God will forgive his sins … May God forgive him.

And then he faced the sky. They don't know what to do. Should they object or remain silent. Ashamed of the fact that they weren't able to do anything, they couldn't look at each other; as if they had committed a collective sin and now, ashamed of it, they are silent. They didn't see how, but Molavi and his men pulled the hands of Gholam Omar out of the shroud's slit and Molavi whipped his hands, ten lashes, and … They just saw that they left by the same way they had come, quiet and calm, and disappeared into the thick fog.[60]

It is necessary to underline the relationship of the prevalent discourses with the characteristics of these two specific images: the dance of the headless body as well as the body twisting, set on fire, and the caning of the hands of a dead man whose beard is not long enough—to which I referred as the creation and, indeed, the registering of unique moments. At first there might seem to be many similar examples of such images and moments in literature. The fact is that if we look at these images as a tourist who glances at the contextless paintings in museums for a moment and moves on, then there are similar moments. But this is precisely the point. These two images should be read in a context formed after having gone through the prevalent discourses. Indeed, it is the un-discursive nature of these images—their experiences—which emphasizes their uniqueness. For another point of reference, we can compare this approach to the French Romantics' imagery which has undoubtedly created some of the most effective images in their works. The main difference between these two approaches is that the Romantics' images are situated inside a discursive context which claims to be able to find an ultimate truth. And in fact, the discursive element of these romantic images actually questions the possibility of the individualistic experience of moments on which the French Romantics placed such emphasis. It is only in exceptional masterpieces of the Romantic Movement, for example, the episode of the death of Gavroche in *Les Misérables*, that we find the process of creating and registering moments which go beyond discursive and delimiting frames. In fact, because of their un-discursive nature, the two previously-described images in Soltanzadeh's stories cannot be placed in the category of images and defini- tions which are created to rouse emotions and sensitivities alone. In other words, the purpose here is not to create a traditional emotionalization through "non-artistic exaggeration." In *Lectures on Russian Literature*, in the chapter devoted to Fyodor Dostoevski, Vladimir Nabokov writes about sen- timentalists: "Remember that when we speak of sentimentalists, among them Richardson, Rousseau, Dostoevski, we mean the non-artistic exaggeration of familiar emotions meant to provoke automatically traditional compassion in the reader."[61] Nobokov attributes Dostoevski's sentimentalism to "the influence which the European mystery novel and the sentimental novel made upon him."[62] Elaborating this idea, he implies that the presence of familiar/ prevalent discourses (literary and otherwise) provided a suitable seedbed for this emotionalism. Conversely, therefore, I argue that in order to create sensitive, and not sentimental,[63] moments, it is necessary to go beyond those familiar dis- courses which could become carriers of generic moments. The two examples from Soltanzadeh demonstrate how such an approach leads to sensitized, yet unsentimentalized depiction of Authentic Moments and their unmediated experience by the narrators.

Linguistic divergence, discursive subterfuge

Reading "The Bridegroom of Kabul" and "... to Mazar," I argued that the method employed by the narrators of these stories was to create or evoke, at different intervals, atmospheres compatible with familiar discourses and then, after the realization of these atmospheres to bypass them, as if to demonstrate their inefficiency. This is what Russian Formalists would call divergence from the ordinary description of the environment ("divergence from the actual").

As I mentioned at the beginning of Chapter 2, the Russian Formalists used three categories of divergence to describe their idea of literariness: divergence from the actual, divergence from ordinary language, and divergence from commonplace literary dynamics. In contemporary Persian fiction, for reasons some of which will be discussed later, there are many examples of divergence from linguistic norms. In some of these works, this method has been used to establish authentic moments.

In 1382/2003, Shahriyar Mandanipur published *Abi-ye Mavara'e Behar* (The Blue Beyond the Seas), a collection of short stories which, as the author conveyed to me in one of our conversations, were written after he saw the scenes of the September 11, 2001 attack on New York's Twin Towers on tele- vision. There are 11 stories in the collection, and their unifying parameter is the narrator's effort to understand this event and/or to find an explanation for it. In some of the stories this search is conducted in a historical/mythic context; others have approached the event in the context of individual and collective emotions. In almost all the stories an unordinary language has been used. This is in part because of the many independent dynamics of Persian fiction (its literary trends and movements) of the past few decades and in part because of inefficacy of standardized and conventional methods in describing September 11, the main pretext of this collection. The unordinary language—which at times renders parts of the stories quite inaccessible—could be explained either as part of the effort to understand and explain this event or as indicative of the futility of such efforts, and in fact the impossibility of any such explanations. The first story in the collection "*Chakavak-e Aseman Kharash*" (The Skyscraping Lark), however, does not fit this characterization. In this story, the narrator's main preoccupation is the description of a moment and the experiencing of it. All the elements of the story, including its unordinary language, serve this purpose. In fact, the linguistic digressions of this story are different from those of other stories. Here, these digressions are not limited to the undermining of the linear logic of the narrative and the occasional syntactic and grammatical tumult; they even reach the limits of fragmentation of words. These are all efforts to find a unique expression for an individualist experience of a particular moment, a completely unmediated expression.

"The Skyscraping Lark" begins with these lines:

- This is our son.
- No, he is not.
- I am ready to swear that he is certainly our son.
- And I said that this person I say is not our son is not our son, and that's it. So stop talking about it when I say he is not our son.

A dark body diving down from the building stopped somewhere between the 20th and 30th floors. Then with a speed faster that his fall he went back up, maybe up to the 100th floor, or maybe even higher ... [64]

The whole story is structured around a conversation between an old couple about whether or not their son had been among those who threw themselves down from the burning towers. It seems their conversation has been going on for a while, and the narrator uses this mechanism to bring up various narratives about September 11. And yet, it seems the explanations are not that relevant to the main event.

The old man "had recorded the jumping down from the tower hastily on the first tape he had found."[65] Apparently he has nothing to do except sit in front of the television and continuously watch that scene in which a young man wearing dark clothes is leaping from the building. Every time, after watching this scene, an argument follows and the old woman tries her best to convince the old man that he is not their son. Indeed, the old woman is still waiting for their son to drop by on the last Saturday of the month, as he has always done, and stay overnight.

Of course, this information has to be extracted from the text. Sentences are in disarray, as if an idea is tried in one segment of the paragraph and then abandoned and another one is tried in another segment. Sometimes this disarray reaches the level of the sentence. No particular line of thought can be discerned, and it is only rarely that we have a passage with connected sentences. On one such occasion, we learn that the son was a ventilation repairman and used to go from one tower to the other.

- How old do you think he was? My son, other mothers don't do that, with my own milk, pampering him, caressing him, I raised him, so delicate, so beautiful. And you, with his broken leg, say it, how you forced him to walk on it and so it never healed. He, if he had not become lame, my son, with all that talent, certainly he could have become exactly what he wanted ...
- Don't say he could. Don't do this.
- So valiant, if he could, being a pilot ...
- No ... I carried him in my arms.

The old woman shouted:

- Becoming a repairman, anybody's son can do that. His workplace, from one tower to another, with that lame leg of his ... When you were forcing my poor son to walk on his broken leg to find those damned snails of yours, yes, you were writing (marking?) his destiny ...
- I didn't know you were so cruel ... Destiny always remains. Even if he had become a pilot his destiny would have become like that of the pilot who went into the tower.

The old woman moaned from her old, weak throat:

- I tell you he wasn't there. You keep trying to say that he has been there. If you are saying he was there then you should say also that many people could escape with their healthy legs. They could run down the stairs and save their lives. But that lame son of yours, how could he escape, with a leg gifted to him by his father.[66]

Once again we are faced with a textual preparation which makes the ordinarily unbelievable ending "logical" and thus believable. This preparation, however, is more of a linguistic nature. In other words, this syntactically and grammatically scattered language becomes an accepted fact, and against this background the ending of the story is heard: the last phone message from the son to his father before he jumps from the tower. Continuing their argument, the old man says:

- I didn't want to shatter you. You asked for it. Listen then!

Strange, never-before-heard sounds twisted under the ceiling: the pouring down, the barking of the flames, the laughing of twisting irons; and in the midst of them there was the wailing of men and women. And then, suddenly, the voice of the son, or ... it was not clear whether it was the scratching of a shout, a lament, a laughter or a never-before-experienced cataclysmic state of being ... and some of the words were missing:

– ... if my mobile disconnect, my goodbye to ... don't, at all, tell mom this telephone ... kind to her ... love her ... if I say these things in the middle of the air, then no one will have ... you will get rich ... my leg ... burni ... it is getting clo ... hot, burning ... blist ... it is burning, very close ... blisters on my hand ... my clothes, smoke ... dad ... are you ... are you sure you are recording this? I am burning dad ... oh ... ah, my fa, face ... this is me crying, this man in this corner ... in my eye, broken glass ... they are exploding ... Oh, I want to ... do you hear me? Down there dad ... no, don't say anything! I want to ... the water cooler was boiling ... nothing. ... just say something, give me courage ... Are you quiet because you are crying? I cannot take it any more ... I should jump. Fire in my chest ... you will have ... whatever you want ... courage to me ... When I am in the air I will tell you how ... maybe pleasure ... I should also tell you ... I always wanted tell you ... the snails ... do you hear? ... I ... from snails ... like ... do you hear? This is the sound of the wind, on this edge ... make sure you record ... I want say how it feels in the air ... you must be the only dad in the world whose son in the middle of the air ... honors ... don't let them deceive ... cheap ... sell it, my voice, very expensively to ... Ahhh, dad I am burning! Listen! You always wanted it. This is your son who is laughing. En ... enjoy it! Don't let mom ... don't mention this phone call, at all ... now ... now, I will jump ...

The son shouts from the bottom of his throat. The sound of exploding of the glass and stones gets further and further. The sounds of howling, water's thirsty boiling, volcanic commotion, all get further in the middle of the splitting air ... the grey eyes of the old woman, staring at the door ... the sounds of the inferno up there are fading ... the wind, the swift vicious wind, waving and splitting, hooting, blows.

The tower collapsed.

And nothing, the son hasn't said even a word ... [67]

Against tabooization of spaces

The theoreticians of the concept of the critique of the everyday life considered everyday life a component of the society under the dominance of the capitalist discourse. They suggested that reforming and revolutionizing this component is the only solution to materialize the true individual/personal life. Their most fundamental instruction was to create conditions which would have the potential to include authentic moments and their complete and unmediated experience by individuals. In fact, this was the reason for the Situationists to choose their name; at the most fundamental level, creating situations which are not influenced by the Society of the Spectacle is the most crucial weapon Situationists have against the discourse of such societies. Of course, like many other theoretical concepts of this movement, the process of how such situations could be created was never precisely defined, however, in early writings by the founders of the movement, instructions are suggested in this regard which could be used in the study of some of the contemporary works of Persian fiction.[68]

The most significant success of the Society of the Spectacle is that it has turned individuals into spectators who are not truly involved in every single moment of their lives. This is true even when the individual believes that he has the initiative; namely, when he *decides* to use yet another spectacle product. In order to turn the individual into a pure spectator, the Society of the Spectacle presents its members with both objective and subjective collective paths, cleverly calling them "natural" paths along which every "ordinary" individual should travel. Thus every move or step incompatible with these paths is considered unnatural, out of the ordinary and, according to the definitions of the official and dominant discourses, deviant. The project of naturalizing these paths is quite extensive and includes many sub-projects such as daily propaganda to create a collective identity, defining extremely specialized fields in order to impose particular discursive definitions of different spaces, and to disseminate stereotypical definitions of the most important concepts such as family, love, tradition, taboos—concepts which regulate interpersonal relationships and are designed to control even the most personal and private human relationships. Conversely, it seems it should not be that difficult to define methods which could disrupt the function of the Society of the Spectacle, because simply by "deviating" from these paths one can undermine the strategies of such societies. In fact, through the concept of *dérive*, Situationists have pointed to the importance of deviating from these paths. But the issue is much more complex, because these paths are so internalized that in most cases their preconceived, collective nature is not recognizable. In addition, dominant discourses, especially in the "diffuse" societies of spectacle, have become so adept that they have managed to appropriate the opposition; meaning that they have created frameworks within which opposition is presented in a controlled manner.[69] Yet the most effective weapon of prevalent discourses is the peaceful imposition of values which control the individual's behavior at every moment with no need for these discourses to manifest their violent, blatant presence.

In different fields of art and literature there are abundant examples of confrontation with such values and regulations, particularly when the focus is interpersonal relationships. But every once in a while, the structure and devices used to construct this confrontation are so novel and unique that they lead to the examination of unexplored components of aspects of the Society of the Spectacle and the means by which it executes its control. Such works remind us once again that in any work of art, the process of treating the subject matter is more consequential than the subject itself.

David Lean's film, *Brief Encounter* (1945), is a rare example which indirectly leads to the examination of one of these unexplored aspects. Lean made this film long before he turned to subject-centered, expensive, Hollywood spectacular projects. The story of the film, which is based on Noel Coward's play *Still Life*, is extremely simple. An English man and woman, both middle-aged, middle-class, and both married, meet by chance and fall in love. In the end, after a few weeks, distressed about the difficulties of continuing such a relationship, they decide to separate.

What turns the treatment of this hackneyed subject into an original work is, first, the emphasis on the contrast between the existing order, precise planning, and routine on the one hand, and deeply individual/personal life based on truly individualistic decisions on the other. The second reason, probably the more important one, is the idea, conveyed implicitly by David Lean to the audience, that there are undeniable interconnections between the imposed routine and physical spaces. It is from this point of view that I would like to focus on *Brief Encounter*.

The first scene shows a train which rapidly goes through a station. The railroad agent looks at his watch; apparently everything has gone according to schedule. His smile shows his complete satisfaction. This precision, this planning, these predetermined commutes are emphasized in a deliberate manner throughout *Brief Encounter*. Laura Jason is a homemaker who lives with her husband and two children in a house in a suburb. Every Thursday, she comes to the town near their suburb and goes through the routine of a bit of shopping, a short promenade, going to see a movie ... returning to the refreshment room of the train station at Milford Junction, having a cup of tea, then taking the train home. Alec Harvey, a medical doctor, also has his own routine of working in the hospital, coming to the same refreshment room, waiting for his train and then going through the unchangeable underground pathway to take the train home. All these repetitions, as well as the emphases on the exact times of the trains' arrivals and departures and commuter schedules, symbolize the institutionalization of completely pre-structured lives.

Yet from the very beginning, the seeds of an opposing discourse are planted in the mind of the spectator. As we find out at the end of the film, the first long scene is in fact the end of the narrative and the end of their story. This familiar device is quite meaningful, in that it suggests that the traditional beginning, middle, and end points are not that important, and that it is the process on which one needs to concentrate. In this scene, Laura and Alec are sitting at a table, with sad, serious faces, talking. Suddenly Dolly, one of Laura's friends, enters; a chatty, noisy woman, who comes directly to their table, she sits down and begins talking and thus takes away their final moments alone with each other. The gossipy attitude attributed to Laura's friend subtly but positively demonstrates Laura's and Alec's difference in relation to this woman (and others), and very quickly the reason for this difference is revealed.

A few moments later Alec's train arrives; inevitably, he leaves the room. Shortly after that, Laura's and her friend's train comes and they, too, set out. While they are walking from the refreshment room to the train platform, Laura, answering her friend's question about Alec says he is going to South Africa, with his family, for a long time. Hearing this, Dolly says:

Well I suppose it's sensible in a way, rushing off to start anew in the wide open spaces and all that sort of thing. But, ha, ha, wild horses wouldn't drag me away from England and home and all the things I'm used to.

The difference between Laura (and Alec) and Dolly (and people like her) lies exactly in their thinking about the possibility of challenging these routines and habits which have been construed and promoted for specific reasons and goals. When they are on the train, by closing her eyes, Laura has forced her companion to be quiet, and she is deep in thought. Her voice-over clearly and succinctly expresses the confrontation between the compliance with pre-packaged rituals of society and its systems and the cherishing of experiences which take place outside these routines. The end of one of these experiences is hurting her profoundly:

> This can't last. This misery can't last. I must remember that and try to control myself ... There'll come a time in the future when I shan't mind about this anymore. But I can look back and say quite peacefully and cheerfully how silly I was. No, no I don't want that time to come hither. I want to remember every minute, always, always to the end of my days.

In this clash, the procrustean prevalent discourse relentlessly tries to revive its narratives in Laura's consciousness. In one of the movie's scenes, when Laura imagines herself telling everything to her husband, she keeps reminding herself:

> You see, we're a happily married couple and let's never forget that. This is my home. You're my husband. And my children are upstairs in bed. I'm a happily-married woman ...

In this situation, not only does she not celebrate her love for Alec but con-siders it a "violent" event: "I've fallen in love. I'm an ordinary woman. I didn't think such violent things could happen to ordinary people."

Clearly the idea of violence is defined in relation to the "ordinariness." The concept of ordinariness is repeated constantly throughout the movie by means of images and words. In fact Laura begins her story with this sentence: "It all started on an ordinary day in the most ordinary place in the world—the refreshment room at Milford Junction." This love is violent because it breaks the ordinary.

The uniqueness of this film is in its reflecting this contrast in the context of the architectures and locations of the film and in its challenging the ordinary function of these spaces. The most important location of the film is the station at Milford Junction. This location and its architecture have been carefully designed to serve specific goals. Early in the film, Lean takes pains to make sure that all the actions correspond to the goals of that architecture. In the refreshment room, waiting for their trains, everyone is trying to busy themselves, mechanically, reading a book, drinking tea, carrying on pre-dictable conversations. Milford Junction has two tracks, and some of the passengers have to go through an underground passageway to reach the plat-form on the other side. The behavior and actions of passengers are completely in accord with what is expected of them in these spaces, to the point that it seems that the passengers on one platform are not even aware of the other platform and the track in front of them. The first time this preconceived path is challenged occurs after Laura has met Alec a few times, accidentally—and after their second chance meeting, these meetings are rather the results of conscious decisions, with the appearance of accident. One day when her customary routine lasts a little longer than usual and she has to run to the Milford Junction, the train on the other track, Alec's train which has just started to move and Laura, with a waiting and expecting eye, looks at the passing train and its windows. This action indicates the using of the spaces in ways not intended by the architecture of the prevalent discourse. A few weeks later Alec asks Laura directly to come next week—to eliminate the accidental appearance of their meetings—and Laura promises to do so. Because of this conversation, Alec is about to miss his train, and he runs through the underground passageway, and Laura, for the first time, before her train arrives, leaves the refreshment room and stares, with a smile, at the opposite platform and Alec getting on the train. Gradually, these paths and these platforms and tracks are coming upon different, new meanings and functions.

In the first half of the movie there are many similar scenes. Laura and Alec are shown repeatedly in familiar, regular, and ordinary locations; yet they are attempting to use these structures differently. Sometimes they walk next to each other in the underground passageway, although their trains are on opposite tracks and only one of them is supposed to go through; they even hug each other surreptitiously. In the refreshment room, they sit opposite each other and enjoy their conversation enormously, while at the same time, they are very careful lest their actions reveal their challenging of the routine and ordinary, or attract the attention and trigger the reactions of the guardians of the existing order.

Depicting the limitations they have in letting themselves go freely in these spaces is done particularly through the lighting of scenes, which is reminiscent of *film noir*. This device—particular usage of lighting in different spaces—clearly delineates the limitations that individuals have to overcome in order to experience their personal and individual lives completely. It underlines that, for example, on a path built to move the individual from home to work, it is very difficult to contradict this collective goal (going from home to the workplace) and instead pursue a different, individual goal. It does not take long before Laura and Alec realize that there is a limit to using existing atmospheres and architecture in a way different from that intended by the dominant discourses. They make plans to create their own atmospheres.

In the scenes that follow, they are seen walking in a park. Then they rent a rowboat and spend some time on the river. A couple of times they rent a car and leave the city. In most of these scenes, David Lean has used medium shots to emphasize the locations more than the protagonists. These sequences are crucial, because these brightly-lit, varied locations are in complete contrast to the dimly-lit, ordinary, repetitious locations. In her description of these times, Laura, declaring "I was enjoying every single minute," expresses another aspect of the contrast between the deeply individual life and the routines which are designed to serve discursive goals.

Towards the end of the film, Alec borrows his friend's car. Once again they go somewhere new. After they return, Alec tells Laura that he has decided to spend the night at the house of his friend, who is out of town. All the scenes in this segment are full of the sense of sin and guilt, as if the narratives and values of the dominant discourse have employed all their might to inform and warn them—and the spectators—about the "falsehood" of their actions. Nonetheless, Laura decides to miss her train and spend the night with Alec. But his friend returns unexpectedly, and Laura runs away. Her walking in the rain in deep distress, through empty, almost frightening streets, warns of dangers which are the consequences of deviation from predetermined routes. While Laura is sitting on a bench to catch her breath, a policeman approaches her and in a suspicious way asks if she is all right. The reading of this scene, based on the idea that the policeman, too, is programmed to be part of the dominant discourse and to discourage such behavior, is irresistible. Indeed, discouraging such behavior sometimes is implemented through punishments such as lashing and stoning to death, sometimes through milder and more indirect approaches. After this event, Laura's voice is heard saying that she is walking towards the usual station; this undoubtedly recreates the untroubled state, the peacefulness of repetition, of routine, of being safe. The end of this sequence is a great example of "disintegration of personal identity" and the impoverishment of everyday life.

The traditional critique considers *Brief Encounter* a typical story about the boring life of the middle-class woman. This subject-oriented critique effectively ignores the large section of the film which is about digression from routine activities. The roughness and lack of sophistication in the function of the characters represents the novel, experimental mode of their behavior. This is how the main characters reject the imposed functionalism of paths, spaces and in general, existing architecture. If we expand this notion and think about the physical paths we go through every day, and why, then it would be easy to understand the discussion about how the dominant discourse imposes itself through its architecture and functionalist urban design. The Situationists' emphasis on the significance of this subject also stems from the allegorical importance which the dominant discourse forces the individual to undergo, and represents precisely the individual's lack of involvement in his own path of life. Using the existing paths in a way contrary to the predetermined goals, the protagonists of *Brief Encounter* constitute the effort to actualize transition from being a spectator and involuntary participant to being conscious and constructive of the moments of their lives.

It is interesting that none of these "deviations" are explained through a defect in the personality of the characters, and from this point of view there are kinships with both the surrealists' automatism and Situationists' *dérive*, although the Situationists argued vehemently that their concept was completely different from that of the Surrealists.

The way the grey ("five pm") lighting, normally associated with *genre noir*, is used in *Brief Encounter* also provides the opportunity for different readings which are quite suggestive with regard to concepts such as sin; and it is the allusion to such concepts which undermines in part the notion of *dérive* because according to definition, such a deviation is a *conscious* disorienting in order to suggest a different path leading to the evolution of emotions which could influence a variety of fields in one's life.

Finding similar examples in Persian fiction of recent years is not that easy, mainly because of the current situation in Iran and the increasing limitations imposed on different fields of arts and literature. Some examples have gotten through, possibly because there are times when censors are not patient enough to contemplate ambivalent spaces in stories, and their possible readings. Tahereh Alavi's "*Mesl-e Hamisheh*" (As Always)[70] is one such work. This story with its ambivalent atmosphere, exemplifies modes of expressions which, while expressing a unique and individual experiment to capturing a moment and its experience, also express an "unrefined" behavior and function, quite indirectly, against the prevalent discourse and its definitions of the normal, the natural, and the accepted.

"As Always" is only five pages long and this limited textual space is compatible with the description of the moment situated at the center of the narrative. The story begins with a very vague, indirect description of "after sex":

> When the woman got up, the man felt weird; it was rather a feeling of fatigue. A kind of psychological and spiritual fatigue. And he was feeling disheveled. Like a newborn, be became more and more bunched up; almost crumpled. He closed his eyes. He didn't want to see the woman even accidentally; or even her shadow. There was a rustling sound coming from inside the room. Then the sound of a zipper being pulled up. It was surely a pants zipper. The man had noticed that the woman was wearing a black pair of pants. A black bell-bottom pair of pants. Whether the top of the pants was as tight as other bell-bottom pants, he didn't know. He had not looked. Or, if he had, he had not paid any attention. He was still lying down on his side. Then he felt he had to get over his fatigue somehow and get up. He had to collect himself. Before anything else he had to put on his clothes. He tried to crawl toward his undergarments, each of which had been thrown in a corner. Then, taking advantage of the woman's absence, he put them on. He was buttoning his shirt when the woman came back into the room. The man turned his face toward the wall. His hands were shaking, and the buttons were slipping from between his thin, boney fingers. He abandoned the idea of buttoning his sleeves altogether; they were not cooperating. He swiftly tucked his shirt into his pants. This time the sound of pulling up his own zipper twisted in the room. He immediately coughed a few times; but it was too late. Then he paused. He was waiting for the woman to decide what to do with him. He didn't know whether he had to leave by himself or if she

would give him a ride. This time the blackness of the woman's manteau[71] passed by him. While leaving, she left the door open and from the doorway turned back and glanced at him. He felt that he should follow her, and he did.[72]

The reader soon finds out that the man and the woman had not known each other before that day. The woman sees the man in the street when his car is broken, and she brings him to her house, and after they have sex she drives him back to where his car was, and:

Without even a word he got out of the woman's car. She didn't say anything, either. Only when he was closing the door she said: "Don't worry; I will call a mobile auto repair." The man automatically said: "Thank you." A moment later, the woman's car disappeared in the midst of all those cars which were moving so close to each other.[73]

And the man, whose being married is casually mentioned, is left with the regret that he did not say a word or even looked at the woman's face more attentively, and the story ends.

There is a peculiar nonchalance in the way the story is told. This sense is also felt in Alavi's "Original Position," which I mentioned at the beginning of this chapter. There, too, the basic material of the story concerns a sexual relationship. Having lived in Paris for a short period of time, while on an airplane flying back to Tehran, the protagonist of "Original Position" is thinking about the relationship she had in Paris, and specifically about the fact that this relationship came to an end because she refused to have sex with her boyfriend, and he left her for someone else. The protagonist uses this simple point to *implicitly* refer to the controlling taboos which function inside the mind of individuals. Indeed, Alavi, contrary to the writers discussed in Chapter 2, does not attempt to convince or incite; her fight does not seem to be a philosophical or ideological one.

There is a similarity between "As Always" and *Brief Encounter*; the protagonists follow, more or less, the same path. The case of Tahereh Alavi's protagonist is a little different in that she acts on her impulses and does not necessarily express the feeling of guilt, or of being sinful. But the atmosphere created in the story is far from being joyous and cheerful. The language is very indirect (and of course we should not forget the presence of censorship as one strong reason for this), the lighting of the scenes is again reminiscent of *film noir*, and it seems that a conscious effort has been made to veil the central event of the story. Still, this is an artistic production which expresses a "clandestine [problem] of everyday life, albeit in a veiled, deformed, and partially illusory manner."[74]

In addition, it is clearly a step in the direction of "the free creation of events,"[75] as opposed to staying on the discursively-prepared paths. And finally, this is a good example of an effort "to emancipate pleasure"[76] in order to create a situation within which a "momentary ambience of life" is constructed even if it is not yet transformed "into a superior passional quality."[77]

Whether we consider the background of such modes of expression the ubiquity of censorship or the internalization of cultural and social taboos, the presence of an embarrassed language is quite detectable. There are many such examples in contemporary Persian literature which begin with an embarrassed, bashful, and unusual mode of expression but end by appearing and indeed becoming ordinary and customary definitions. Of course, examples of official and prevalent discourses confronting new narratives and definitions are equally numerous.

The work of Forugh Farrokhzad, the most famous female poet of twentieth-century Iran, is certainly one of the best examples of trajectories informed by concepts of sin, taboos, shame, etc. depicted, for instance in *Brief Encounter* and Alavi's "As Always." Perhaps Farrokhzad's work is distinguished from these two simply through the fact that in her poetry she crosses the boundaries more frequently and more specifically than others. Also, an evolutionary process in dealing with these boundaries is particularly distinct in Farrokhzad's poetry. In one of her famous early works, she wrote the following poem which could be considered an emblematic start of this trajectory:

I sinned, a sin all filled with pleasure
wrapped in an embrace, warm and fiery
I sinned in a pair of arms
that were vibrant, virile, violent.[78]

This feeling of guilt is quite pronounced in Farrokhzad's early work and many scholars have made note of that. In *She'r-e Zaman-e ma (4): Forugh Farrokhzad*, Mohammad Hoquqi has done a study which draws on the frequency of words in Farrokhzad's poems of different periods. According to his study, words referring directly or indirectly to the concept of sin are found very frequently in her early poems.[79] Such a usage could be interpreted as rebellion against a somewhat internalized and conformity-seeking official discourse. To be sure, this rebellion and rebellious language were attacked by many including even artists and intellectuals. One famous instance is when Mohammad Hosein Behjat Tabrizi (1906–1988), the most prominent Azeri poet who wrote under the penname Shahriyar uttered the following judgment about Farrokhzad, both as a poet and as a woman: "At the beginning Forugh was imitating me. She had the soul of a poet but they corrupted her, both in terms of her poetry as well as her morality."[80] Nonetheless, this rebellion continued to be a crucial component of her work which at times took clear aim at masculine history or patriarchal/religious/traditional system and of course at what she had previously called sin. In fact, in one of her later poems, "*Fath-e Bagh*" (Conquering the Garden), the triumphant tone against the discourse of sacred taboos is quite clear and even provocative:

Everyone knows
everyone knows
that you and I peered into the garden
through that cold, captious casement
and picked the apple
from that playful, out-of-reach branch.
...
I speak not of flimsy bond between two names
or union somewhere inside the pulping pages of an
                                             ancient ledger
I speak of my happy hair
touched by the burning peonies of your kisses
and the defiant intimacy of our bodies
and the brilliance of our nakedness
like the scale of a fish under water.
I speak of the life in a silvery tune
the little jetting spring murmurs at dawn.[81]

In "The Aesthetics of Lone Moments in the Poetry of Forugh Farrokhzad,"[82] I have argued that being provocative was an important component of Farrokhzad's poetry at a particular stage of her creative production; yet her most linguistically stellar poems—her very last poems—are those in which one can see a complete insouciance about her environment and the grand narratives defining them. In other words, towards the end, more than anything else, she was after creating a personal language, without even trying to relate to her surrounding by repeating pre-packaged meanings. The following is her last poem:

My heart is pressed
my heart is pressed

I walk to the balcony and move my fingers
along the stretched skin of the night
Connecting lights are off
connecting lights are off

No one will introduce me
to the sun
no one will take me to the feast of sparrows
Remember the flight
the bird is a dying thing.[83]

Reading this poem it is difficult to speak about authorial intention and, in general, the production of meaning. This poem is an excellent example of performativity while transferring the agency to the reader. But the most important aspect of it is its depiction of a complete indifference to prevalent discourses. This indifference is an important element of Persian modernist writing, and of course it took a while for it to become considered an acceptable feature of this trend. Many works which opted to reject clear identification with prevalent discourses were accused of irrelevance or uselessness. A famous example is Ahmad Shamlu's criticism of Sohrab Sepehri's work. In an interview with Naser Hariri, Shamlu was asked about Sepehri's work and he said:

> Unfortunately at this point I have a hazy image of them [Sepehri's poems] in mind. You know? It is difficult for me to believe that untimely mysticism (*erfan*). [Imagine], they are cutting off the heads of innocent people at the edge of a stream and I am standing a few steps down and making the recommendation: "Don't muddy the water!" I suppose one of us was completely off, either me or him.[84]

Here Shamlu is referring to Sepehri's famous poem, part of which reads: "Let's not muddy the water / Down the river, perhaps, a dove is drinking water."

Another author who I believe was in part ignored or accused of including many gratuitous descriptions in her works was Ghazaleh Alizadeh. This criticism was levied especially on parts of her most famous novel, *Khaneh-ye Edrisi-ha* (The House of the Edrisis, 1370/1991). This component, "gratuitous description," which is a significant trademark of Persian modernist writing, is actually where, as Roland Barthes would put it, "There is Text in it."[85] In this sentence the word Text should be understood in terms of "indeterminate functioning of language" and "its force of subversion with regard to the old classifications."[86] I would further suggest that the ambiguity of the term as it has been defined by Barthes in "From Work to Text" allows for multiple interpretations of this term, including one which could relate it to Barthes' discussion about "The Reality Effect." According to him, in any given work of fiction there might be a "class of useless objects whose function is merely to say: we are reality, reality is real."[87] Or as Culler puts it, "The more meaningless the details, Barthes concludes, the more vigorously they signify, 'we are the real.'"[88] These concepts are quite important in understanding a trend in contemporary Persian fiction, what I have called non-discursive fiction. This phrase—non-discursive—is inspired by what Reza Ghassemi has called "*jarian goriz*" (escaping [literary] movements) which refers to works that cannot be identified with a particular literary movement of their time.[89] The term non-discursive, however, defines such works as perhaps the most important part of Persian modernist writing. In the following part of this chapter, I will return to these concepts while discussing representative examples of contemporary Persian non-discursive fiction.

Counter-discursive impulses in Persian literary tradition

Are major literary changes the results of inner dynamics of different literary traditions or historical events which have taken place outside the autonomous framework of literature? For literary historians as well as literary critics this has always been a point of contention. The correct answer is probably a combination of both. Indeed, even schools of literary criticism such as Russian Formalism which emphasize that works of art and literature should be analyzed using the elements taken from the work itself, introduced concepts such as "deviation" from existing reality as a feature contributing to the literariness of the work and thus involved the non-literary reality in describing literary events. What is missing in these studies is the way in which this influence is materialized, which is more important than accepting the presence of the elements of both realms. Of course, it should be noted that the Structuralist project paid specific attention to the underlying contexts and systems and relations within which meaning(s) could be created. This is what Jonathan Culler called "conditions of meaning."[90] Still, many of them—certainly with the exception of Roland Barthes—including Culler, who articulated the *Structuralist Poetics*, stopped at the level of defining those underlining environments. This section of the present study is based on the argument that even in their evolutionary forms, social changes could at best affect the literary evolution by creating new potentials within the existing literary traditions. Understanding this point is essential to the understanding of many works of contemporary Persian fiction, especially those which have been designated with the adjective "inaccessible."

The adjective, "inaccessible," has been used about many works which largely ignore the prevalent familiar discourses. In regard to the literary production of the post-1979 Revolution, this inaccessibility at times has been explained as a result of the search by the author to define himself/herself after such a fundamental change. This is partially true, but, as we will see, such inaccessibility has existed in many works produced long before the Revolution, albeit the number of them has increased exponentially. In fact, it is because of this increase in numbers that they should be considered as representing a significant aspect of contemporary Persian fiction, and therefore it is no longer possible to simply use this adjective—and other adjectives such as "experimental"—to brush them off.

In various literary traditions, the adjective "inaccessible" has been used as an epithet to approach works which give the impression that they are diverging from the normal path of literary evolution. In the case of modern Persian fiction, this label has been very harmful as regards the presentation of a complete image of this literature both inside and outside Iran; meaning that, for example, many of these works have been dismissed by being placed in the category of "formal experiments." Examples are innumerable and include contemporary writers such as Abbas Na'lbandian, Shamim Bahar, Alimorad Fadainia, Bahman Forsi, whose works have been more or less ignored, and others such as Sadeq Hedayat, Bahram Sadeqi, Hushang Golshiri, Bijan Najdi, Mohammad Rahim Okhovvat, and Reza Julai, whose "inaccessible" works have not received much attention.

Outside Iran, the roots of this approach should be sought in neo-Orientalist methods which, while acknowledging superficially that there are Other literary traditions, in practice however, believe that there is only one path for literary evolution—their own—and other traditions are measured against this path. In fact, I use the term neo-Orientalist to underline the discrepancy between what is said and what is done.

Of course, neo-Orientalism is one of the reasons which explain why some of these works are deemed inaccessible and are dismissed.[91] There is also the universal, perennial fact that it is difficult to relate to new, different, and Other forms. Conversely, the tendency towards traditional, habitual forms has also functioned as a force to repel the New.

To make works of Persian modernist writing more accessible, I believe an understanding of a history of Persian literary backdrops and devices is necessary. Such an understanding actually demonstrates why many character-istics of these supposedly inaccessible works are rather normal and natural outcomes of the evolution of Persian literary tradition.

Along the same lines, I further argue that an ensemble of literary and non-literary events and changes has provided conditions for the formation of elements which, with regard to the individual sensibility they are presenting, could be considered representative of the Persian version of literary modernism. In the following section, I will refer to components of this history and discuss the reflections of these elements in some of the works of contemporary Persian fiction.

In previous pages I mentioned the famous story of Sultan Mahmud's reaction to Ferdowsi and his *Shahnameh*, a story which provides an emblematic image of the confrontational characteristic of this literary tradition. According to legendary/historical accounts, when after 30 years of work, Ferdowsi presented Sultan Mahmud with his epic work, the *Shahnameh*, the Sultan rejected the work; his critique was that Ferdowsi had not offered a realistic or appropriate depiction of pre-Islamic Iranian myths. He is said to have for-mulated his criticism in the following manner: "The *Shahnameh* is nothing but the story of Rostam, and in my army there are thousands like Rostam."[92] This is understandable. Sultan Mahmud's government defined its official identity through its Islamic nature and consequently through Islamic myths. It follows that identity-making concepts had to be defined through these myths and not through the pre-Islamic ones. This was not limited to the political apparatus. A review of Persian poetry from this period shows that poets, for the first time, began consistently replacing Iranian myths with Arab-Islamic ones. In *Sovar-e Khial dar She'r-e Farsi* (Imagery in Persian Poetry), through a meticulous study of Persian classical poetry of different periods, Mohammad Reza Shafi'i Kadkani points out that in this period (starting in the early tenth century), "The Islamic color of poetic images is very strong, and the influence of Semitic and Islamic myths on these images is clearly seen."[93] In any case, the Ferdowsi-Mahmud story, together with its continuous presence in historical surveys, identifies it as a source on which the sensibility of a large part of Persian literature feeds to define its confrontational characteristic. It should be said, however, that this characteristic shows itself more in the reading process than in the production of the work. Another example underscoring this point is the collective, and not necessarily the professional, approach to the poetry of Hafez, the fourteenth-century Iranian poet. According to this approach, the uniqueness of Hafez is not in the literariness of his work and his place in defining the apogee of the Persian ghazal, but in his fight against the hypocrisy of rulers and ascetics. Obviously, judging the veracity of such statements is not the goal of this study; I merely point this out to underline the function of the counter-discursive impulse within Persian literature. Quite possibly, one can find many examples of incompatibility between literature and official discourses in a number of literary traditions, but in the Persian tradition, on many occasions, this incompatibility reaches the stage of antagonism and confrontation which have been institutionalized through influencing literary devices, techniques, and forms.

The mark of this characteristic is seen in many periods, but the most pronounced and documented periods are the Safavid and the Islamic Republic periods, wherein the ideological nature of the official discourse is quite visible. Interestingly enough, during the Safavid period (1501–1736), we also witnessed official policies which pursued goals such as "uniformization of thought, banishing of different aspirations and beliefs, preventing the exchange and interaction of ideas, and lack of freedom of thought."[94] It would be very interesting to examine the similarities and differences between these two periods in terms of their official discourses and their literary productions, as well as the official policies designed by them to regulate cultural production. Mohammad Fotuhi's book, *Naqd-e Khial: Naqd-e Adabi dar Sabk-e Hendi* (The Critique of Imagination: Literary Criticism in Indian Style) has undoubtedly prepared the ground for such a study.

It should be noted that this confrontational characteristic is by no means the only significant element explaining the atmosphere within which the sensibility of the Persian literary tradition has grown. My emphasis on this point is simply because of this characteristic's place in the context of the discussion of Persian literary counter-discourses. I argue that this feature, which has existed to different degrees in most periods of the history of Persian literature, has effectively produced one of the most important conditions for the creation of narratives which belong to counter-discourses, as well as narratives which operate beyond confrontational discourses.

The most important trait of ideologically-defined discourses is their procrustean nature, which explains why they are incapable of appropriating elements of the Other. It is enough to look at the post-1979-Revolution version of this discourse to realize the extent of this incapability. Even those who in general had no problem with the dominant discourse, and at times even worked hard to found and expand it, fell from grace as soon as they showed signs of a non-collective identity; some of them even endured prison and torture.[95] The same approach has been used in the realm of literature; the best examples are found among government-sanctioned literary critiques, especially those regarding the literature of the Iran–Iraq War. Reviewing these critiques, it is not necessary to read between the lines or look for statements with double entendres; ideologically-defined views have been expressed in a most clear fashion. The story of Ahmad Dehqan—very similar to that of Mostafa Mastur[96]— one of the most famous writers of the war is a point in case.

Ahmad Dehqan is a war veteran who started his writing career after he came back from the front. His early collection of short stories which were basically rewrites of the official narratives of the war with the usual emphasis on us versus them, the battle of Right against Wrong, glorification of martyrdom, etc. were praised unconditionally. Then he published a collection of short stories called *Man Qatel-e Pesaretan Hastam* (I Killed Your Son, 1387/2008) in which signs of dissent from the official discourse could be detected. Ahmad Shakeri, one of the prominent critics representing the literary arm of the Islamic Republic reproached the writer for not having respected the "Islamic worldview" and "divine justice":

> In his recent collection of stories, Ahmad Dehqan claims that he has depicted the reality. Even if we assume that he has told the realities, has he been able to function properly in his selection process? In his selections, Dehqan has not been just. Besides that, someone who is a Muslim and espouses the Islamic worldview, and accepts God's fairness and adheres to it as one of the principles of this religion cannot write a story in which there is no "divine justice" and in which the existence of God and Godly religions are meaningless. It is improbable for such a thing to come out of a Muslim's mind, unless it is someone who has been assimilated; someone who has reached the conclusion that the world has become completely dark and gloomy. One must not talk about realities from a materialistic viewpoint.[97]

Naturally, Dehqan, who by the way is considered a "values-writer,"[98] tried to defend his allegiance to the values of the Sacred Defense. He further demonstrated his loyalty to the official ideology by rejecting an invitation from the Golshiri Foundation which had selected *I Killed Your Son* as a candidate for the Golshiri Foundation prize. Dehqan refused to participate in a clip which the Foundation made of the candidates reading their stories. To explain this, it should be said that the Golshiri Foundation is one of the Organizations where "non-values writers" congregate.[99] The *Adabiyat-e Dastani* was so ecstatic about Dehqan's decision that it reported the event and wrote:

> Before presenting the prizes, in each section a clip of the writers reading their stories was played. According to Ahmad Dehqan, the author of the collection *Man Qatel-e Pesareten Hastam* (I Killed Your Son) had decided not to take part in this film. Furthermore, in a laudable act, he did not even attend the award ceremonies of this Foundation.[100]

The story did not end there. A few years later, Dehqan published *Safar beh Geray-e 270 Darejeh* (Journey to Heading 270 Degrees), which was translated into English by Paul Sprachman. When Sprachman went to Iran, he was asked to attend "the unveiling ceremony of the translation of this book,"[101] after which he was interviewed by Ahmad Shakeri and Kamran Parsinejad, an *Adabiyat-e Dastani* critic. He was virtually investigated about his reasons for choosing this book[102] and effectively chastised for having translated a book which is not representative of the Iran–Iraq War. This is Shakeri's argument:

> If in the Iranian culture there are millions who believe in martyrdom, then how could a work which does not believe in martyrdom be written about this culture? Then the war described in this book is not the Iran war. It is a war of some other place![103]

Almost the whole conversation is based on the idea that since at the end of this book the protagonist is not "martyred," it is therefore not a realistic book about the war, and thus is not worth translating. Once again, this is said about the likes of Ahmad Dehqan who has not only been in the war but considers himself one of the "values writers"; and; to be sure, *Journey to Heading 270 Degrees* is clearly in line with the official version of the war, its narratives and even its terminology. The only "problem" is that there are faint signs of non-collective identity which at times emerge through the behavior or the fate of the protagonist.[104]

This example and other, similar ones—one needs only flip through the government's literary organs (such as the journal *Adabiyat-e Dastani*) and read these "literary critiques" to find other examples of those who have fallen from favor—are indicative of the official discourse's inability to deal with even a pseudo-Other. This situation has deteriorated so comically that even the novel written by an ex-Minister of Culture and Islamic Guidance, Ataollah Mohajerani, was considered a "misleading book"! Where the official discourse is concerned, the drawback of this intolerance, and indeed this lack of desire to include new spaces and structures, has been that it has effectively yielded many arenas to the narratives produced by the Other. Considering the fact that this situation has existed for many centuries in the history of Persian literature, it is not difficult to realize how powerful the non-official discourses and narratives of this literary tradition have always been. In other words, the official discourse, which has been following the extremely constricting motto, "Those who are not with us are against us," has ignored the fact that a limited "us" means an expanded "against us/Other," which can then produce its own independent mechanisms and dynamics, and consequently its autonomous movements. At best the official discourse—even relying on its armed forces—can only slow these movements down.

Another point which needs to be underscored: In the process of creating narratives, literary techniques, devices and forms incompatible with the official discourses, there have been periods defined by competitions among counter-discourses to control the domain of the Other. The most recent and obvious example is the particular brand of critical thinking which began to form around the period of the Constitutional Revolution (1905–1911) and very soon took over many disciplines, including literary criticism.[105] This brand which, following the traditional dichotomy of form and content, emphasized the content of literary works and argued for the utilitarian function of literature in regard to social issues, greatly influenced the field of literature, and even imposed its readings on different literary works;[106] but its reach on the creative process was not equally far. This is especially visible when non-discursive works are taken into account. These works, which were either dismissed by content-oriented criticism or were simply ignored, continued to play their role in the evolutionary process of Persian literature. They persistently continued their presence, and actually moved from being isolated examples into a non-discursive literary trend. Here, I am using the term *non-discursive* to refer to works which, because of their techniques and narrative logic, are so different, or so unique, that they cannot be essentialized or be mutilated by reductionist approaches. Indeed, in terms of their usage of language, these works sometimes go so far as to create a kind of suspension of meaning. In *The Literary in Theory*, discussing Roland Barthes' notion of reality, Jonathan Culler refers to a similar idea:

> Barthes concludes that in modern literature there is an opposition between meaning or function on the one hand and reality on the other. There is an assumption, deeply ingrained in Western culture, that the world—reality—is what is simply there, prior to our perception of it or interpretation of it. What does not bear meaning or is not being interpreted may thus stand for real. When there occur items that have no role in the plot and do not tell us anything about the character, this very absence of meaning enables them to anchor the story in the real but, Barthes emphasizes, not by denoting reality but by connoting it.[107]

Such an approach to language unavoidably places stylists in a unique position; meaning that it is no longer possible to ignore them or to brush them aside by using clichés of content-oriented literary criticism. Of course, that does not mean that such efforts have not been and are not being made. The most common method was to label them as imitations of the literature of decadence or as expressions of the despair of a newly-formed middle class in Iran.

But, as we shall see, the *stylistically-defining elements* of these works (both modernist and non-discursive) had started to develop long before this period.[108] This is especially true when we think of Persian poetry, both by classical as well modern poets, such as Nima Yushij (1897–1960). The causal logic of traditional narratives is not used in these works, narrative congruity and harmony is not seen in many of their segments. It appears that the narrators in these works are merely trying to create literary spaces to be experienced by readers, as well as by the narrators, without necessarily making any attempt to establish any links between these spaces.[109] Reading these works is not easy and requires a minimum of familiarity with technical and formal elements of the Persian literary tradition. As an example, we can think once again about the place and importance of the poetry of Hafez—the apex of Persian lyric poetry. Hafez's ghazals are literary expressions without much thematic unity;[110] content (in its traditional sense) is used as an excuse to create literary spaces rather than to offer a message. In many cases there is no logical link between the different verses of a ghazal, so much so that sometimes it is possible to change the order of verses—and indeed this is seen in different manuscripts—without creating any obstacle for the reader to experience the poem. Throughout centuries, this Persian poetic logic has influenced the linguistic and narrative and formal aspects of Persian literature, and this characteristic, even after poetry has lost its prevalent position—starting before the Constitutional Revolution—has continued its presence. It is for this reason that I maintain that relating to non-discursive works is less difficult for those who are familiar with this logic.

A formalist historical context

As with all literary traditions with long histories, Persian literary tradition has been the subject of many studies which have attempted to provide an overview of its evolutionary trajectory. Among the most famous examples are: Edward Browne's A *Literary History of Persia* (1902–1924), Jan Rypka's *History of Iranian Literature* (1968)[111] and Safa's *Tarikh-e Adabiyat dar Iran* (History of Literature in Iran, 1953–1979).[112] At one point or another, all these works begin with the earliest Persian literary production and continue up to the period of the Constitutional Revolution and shortly thereafter. Safa's book ends with an earlier period (before the Constitutional Revolution Period). Although these studies bear different titles, they have a number of elements in common, including the fact that they do not necessarily differentiate between the history of literature and literarized history. The historicity of these studies is achieved through a similar approach, namely, treating literary works and figures in a chronological order. Of course, each one of these studies is informed by the author's philosophical outlook and the resulting context within which the study is presented; but in fact none of these perspectives has much effect on the nature of their definition of the literary historicity embedded in them. The chronological structures of these books and the direct relationships they see between literary production and socio-historical events make them good examples of literarized histories, not of history of literature.

Of course, this does not mean that these texts do not offer any literary analysis; indeed, there are many occasions when, especially in Safa's work, we see descriptions of samples of literary innovations and influences of a given period and their effects on the trajectory of the evolution of Persian literature.

Or, in Rypka's case, there are numerous examples of literary analysis based on a Marxian approach whereby the contributors attempt to describe a work of literature based on the author's background and his socio-political standings and positions. Amin Banani's short review of Rypka's *History of Iranian Literature* precisely refers to this aspect of the book and correctly concludes that this approach has resulted in neglecting many major literary figures at the expense of those whose political positions were more in tune with that of Rypka.[113] Still, the common denominator of all these texts is that the fact that they rely on a chronology of non-literary events to define the historicity of their work and to contextualize those rare cases where literary concepts and their evolutions are alluded to, places them in a secondary and subordinate position.

If we consider the concept of evolution—without it necessarily containing a positive connotation—as an essential component of historiography, then we will realize that we do not have a comprehensive history of Persian literature, one which would describe the evolution of forms. Here the word "form" is used in its Russian Formalist meaning, with particular emphasis on "rhetorical codes, narrative techniques, narrative structures, and poetic structures."[114] In *Figures III*, describing a similar lacuna in French literature, Gérard Genette writes:

> It seems to me, therefore, that in literature, the historical object, that is the object which is durable and variable, is not the work: they are [rather] these elements which transcend the work and are constituents of the literary game which, to expediate [the discussion], we call *forms*: for example, the rhetorical codes, the narrative techniques, the poetic structures, etc. There exists a history of literary forms, of all aesthetic forms and all techniques, based on the fact that throughout ages these forms modify themselves and continue to exist. The unfortunate thing, here again, is that this history, essentially, remains to be written.[115]

Genette then argues, convincingly, that one of the reasons for this is that "even the objects of the history of forms have not yet been sufficiently identified by the literary 'theory.'"[116]

Figures III was published in 1972, and since that time this theoretical lacuna has not been addressed in a comprehensive manner. Perhaps it could be said that for different reasons—including the fact that theoretical structures used to read and interpret literary works are not very mindful of the literariness of these works—many critics and historians of literary works have not placed this need high on their agenda.

With regard to the Persian literary tradition, however, it should be said that while it is true that there is not a comprehensive Formalist history of literature, there are also a number of studies which, while including a historical aspect, have prioritized a literary discourse and have thus contributed greatly to the definition of research topics (*"l'objet historique"*) whose examination and evolutionary processes contribute to such a Formalist history. Among the studies which have addressed Persian literature of the classical period are the works of Mohammad Reza Shafi'i Kadkani—in particular his *Musiqi-ye She'r* (The Music of Poetry) and *Sovar-e Khial dar She'r-e Farsi* (Imagery in Persian Poetry). While structuring his works in a very general chronological order (especially in *Imagery in Persian Poetry*), Shafi'i Kadkani has achieved the historicity of his works by emphasizing the evolutionary processes of poetic objects, whose transformation trajectories do not necessarily coincide with the beginning or end of a century or the reign of a king. In his introduction to *The Music of Poetry*, he states emphatically:

> In no way does this book claim to have entered discussions related to form and structure. But practically it reveals small aspects of some of those perspectives; meaning that it is an effort to examine some of the issues concerning form in Persian poetry.[117]

This work and Shafi'i Kadkani's other similar studies are informed by a brand of literary criticism which has fallen out of favor with many Iranian literary critics of the past 100 years. I refer to traditional/pre-modern Persian literary criticism, which was formed on the shoulders of very early critics, philosophers, and poet/critics such as Avicenna, Khajeh Nasir-e Tusi, Abd al-Qader Jorjani, Shams-e Qeys Razi, Raduyani, Rashid Vatvat, and Nezami Aruzi to more recent ones, particularly those who were involved in the critique of *Sabk-e Hendi* (Indian Style)[118] to still more contemporary ones such as Malek al-Sho'ara Bahar, Foruzanfar, Qazvini, and Safa.[119] To this list we can add the names of many *Tazkereh* writers who have chiefly compiled biographical information about poets who wrote in Persian. Of course, these *tazkereh*s usually include comments, mostly of a short and general nature, about the quality of the poems and their authors referred to in their compilations. What all these categories have in common, however, is their contribution to the identification and definition of poetic subjects and concepts. It is from the same perspective that, I believe, the most significant contribution of studies such as *Imagery in Persian Poetry* is in the field of identification of subject matters which need to be examined in the literary studies which have a historical dimension as well—the same topic whose need has been underlined by Genette.

Shafi'i Kadkani has done this mostly about Persian classical poetry. Among the very few works which have emphasized the contemporary period and modern poetry (though not necessarily modernist) Ahmad Karimi-Hakkak's *Recasting Persian Poetry: Scenarios of Poetic Modernity in Iran* is a good example. While being quite conscious of the historical dimension of his work, he creates this dimension by tracing the evolutionary process of concepts and literary topics for study. And, while aware of the interaction and interplay between different disciplines, this methodology, which challenges narratives, insufficient at best, on the order of "the Constitutional Revolution was the main source of modern Persian poetry" or "Nima's acquaintance with French poetry led to the emergence of modern Persian poetry" underlines the transformation process of literary characteristics which gradually produced modern and modernist Persian poetry.

Methodologically, studies such as Shafi'i Kadkani's on classical poetry and Karimi-Hakkak's on modern poetry could play a significant role in explicating and describing the emergence and formation of non-discursive works which constitute one of the most significant categories of Persian modernist writing. By this I mean that in order to understand that such non-discursive works are not examples of heterogenesis or spontaneous generation, one should examine the trajectory of the evolution of literary and linguistic possibilities and then examine these works as the materialization of one of the potentials of this trajectory.[120] This approach is vaguely reminiscent of what Jonathan Culler has called "conditions of meaning." In the preface to *Structuralist Poetics* he writes:

> The type of literary study which structuralism helps one to envisage would not be primarily interpretive; it would not offer a method which, when applied to literary works, produced new and hitherto unexpected meanings. Rather than a criticism which discovers or assigns meanings, it would be a poetics which strives to define conditions of meaning.[121]

The structuralist understanding of this concept is important in that it emphasizes the significance of "various semiotic conventions,"[122] but to that, a Formalist emphasis on the work as well as focus on the process of creation of the linguistic-literary architecture of the work need to be added.

Buf-e Kur *and Persian modernist writing*

Buf-e Kur was published in India in 1936. Only 50 mimeographed copies of the handwritten text were produced.[123] Chronologically speaking, this work was an anomaly for its time. Most of the works which were published roughly around the same time, in terms of form and content, could easily be indentified with the main conventionalized trends of or before their time. This suffices for us to consider *Buf-e Kur* anachronistic, an anomaly, and furthermore, as we will see, a turning point or a beginning of serious Persian modernist prose writing. Yet again, it would be a mistake to view this work as being heterogenetic. In addition to obvious influences of Western literary traditions, which have been discussed in details in a number of studies including Michael Beard's *Hedayat's Blind Owl as a Western Novel*, *Buf-e Kur*, particularly in terms of its linguistic style and imagery, is the legitimate production of two main phenomena: characteristics of the Persian literary tradition, whose influence on this work I will discuss in the coming pages; and the achievements of this tradition in previous decades and, in particular, modernist characteristics of literary works of writers like Qa'em Maqam Farahani

(1779–1835), a prime minister during the Qajar Dynasty, Ali Akbar Dehkhoda (1879–1956), and Mohammad Ali Jamalzadeh (1892–1997), as well as those found in the writings of many intellectuals of the Constitutional Revolution period who were active in other disciplines. For example, one of the main components/achievements of the pre-Hedayat era which has been crystallized in his novella is the simplicity of its linguistic register, which has been sufficiently examined by many Iranian and non-Iranian critics. *Buf-e Kur* is also the first major work which, in terms of the language it uses and not the ideas and concepts embedded in it, *seems* to be addressing ordinary people. Of course, as we will see, the author/narrator claims that he is writing the book for his shadow or for himself; but it is also clear that there are implied readers, albeit not very many, and these interlocutors, as opposed to the audience/patrons of classical literature, are not necessarily related to the aristocracy.

As mentioned above, probably reacting to the convoluted prose which climaxed during the Safavid and continued until the early Qajar Period, the shift towards employing commonly-used words, phrases, and expressions began a few decades before Hedayat and then functioned as a sprouting seed which grew in different directions. Two famous examples are Jamalzadeh and Hedayat. They both took advantage of the popularity of the simple style, but they took completely different paths. In Jamalzadeh's stories, especially in his most famous collection, *Yeki Bud, Yeki Nabud* (Once Upon a Time, 1300/ 1921)[124] the linguistic possibilities created by the idea of writing in a simple and everyday language have been used to develop amalgams of expressions, proverbs, and sayings which were not looked upon favorably by the "respectable literati";[125] at least during the pre-Qa'em Maqam period. In many of Hedayat's stories, such as *Buf-e Kur* and some of the short stories in *Seh Qatreh Khun* (Three Drops of Blood), however, the possibilities offered to the author through simple style have been used, following the requirements of the story, to create individualistic and personal literary spaces. In fact, if we are concentrating on *Buf-e Kur*, it is because of the presence of these spaces, and of the specific effects of characteristics of the Persian literary tradition, as well as the author/narrator's acknowledging the importance of creating a self-referential universe, that this work could be called the beginning/turning point of Persian modernist writing.

Previously, I mentioned Irving Howe's definition of modern literature (which in the context of Persian literature I call modernist writing) and its two major components: "The modern refers to sensibility and style."[126] The universal characteristic of modern sensibility which, I believe, should be understood along the lines of self-referentiality, is obviously quite pronounced, while the concept of (modern) style is more related to the particular characteristics of any given literary tradition; it is this part which I am emphasizing in this assessment of *Buf-e Kur*'s place in Persian modernist writing.

Once again we should start with literary experiences which precede *Buf-e Kur* and Hedayat. Among these experiences, priority goes to Moshfeq

Kazemi's novel *Tehran-e Makhof* (The Horrifying Tehran, 1301/1923), because it is the first novel in which its didactic tone and strategies are located in new spaces (in this case, urban spaces). This approach presents a new dimension to the category of accepted/mainstream literary production. Because of its urban spaces, and because of its overall agenda to define cities—especially a metropolis such as Tehran—as locations which bring about and are full of corruption, particularly with regard to young women, this work stands a far distance from classical works such as Nezami's *Khosrow va Shirin* (Khosrow and Shirin) or Attar's *Manteq al-Tayr* (The Conference of the Birds), as well as the elevated ghazals and panegyrics of the "Return Period" and their original models (such as the ghazals of Sa'di and Hafez),[127] and effectively allows the use of ideas, language registers and spaces which until then had been considered by and large non-literary. The subgenre exemplified by works such as *The Horrifying Tehran*,[128] Abbas Khalili's *Asrar-e Shab* (Night's Secrets, 1305/1926), Ahmad Ali Khodadadeh Teymuri's *Ruz-e Siyah-e Kargar* (Dark Days of a Worker, 1305/1926),[129] Mohammad Masud's *Tafrihat-e Shab* (Nightly Recreations, 1311/1932), Jalal Al-e Ahmad's short story "*Modir-e Madreseh*" (School Principal, 1337/1958), and a number of similar examples published before and after *Buf-e Kur* clearly demonstrates this change. For example, in these works the traditional/conventional image of woman in Persian literature is replaced with images in which women have no kinship with the Ideal Beloved of classical Persian Romances. Describing one of the major sections of *The Horrifying Tehran*, in which four women who have been corrupted and forced into prostitution by the "new urban conditions" are telling their stories, Shahrokh Meskub (1924–2005) writes:

> As much as their stories seem raw and simplistic, from the point of view of the art of writing, from the point of view of the history of or the sociology of literature, they are invaluable and signal a new, dual change: on the one hand, Woman "falls" from the dream [world] into reality and, on the other hand, literature becomes aware of woman and her position and status in reality and as a social individual instead of a generalized type, and attempts to know her.[130]

This trend is not characterized solely by its move towards a new image of woman; it also includes linguistic and structural innovations which should be considered in part as reactions to the established traditions and conventions. In my opinion, as opposed to the sociological approaches to literature, an approach which in order to explicate the literary changes of this period allocates more importance to literary dynamisms—which includes the reaction to previous trends and schools—and emphasizes more the continuity of literary traditions and does not prioritize the idea that "literary production is a reflection of social and historical changes," is an absolute necessity for the understanding of Persian literature of this period. In other words, a comprehensive approach which considers socio-historical events as only one of its variables should be adopted so that we could comprehend the gradual transformations in Persian literature which began, roughly, from the Qa'em Maqam period. Indeed, it is through this approach, which includes and emphasizes intra-actions of the Persian literary tradition and its interplay with socio-historical events, as well as with other literary traditions, that one might comprehend the release of an enormous imaginative energy, emphasizing linguistic and structural innovations as well as the appropriation of spaces and characters which until then were considered non-literary. Once again, this is why *Buf-e Kur* should not be considered a work created in a vacuum; it is standing on the shoulders of its preceding experiences. The reason for it to be considered a turning point, however, is that in spite of its relatively short length, it has been able to comprise almost all the elements which contributed to the release of a new imaginative energy. The almost innumerable critiques written on this book, each of which discusses one aspect of the text and offers at least one new reading of it, are reason enough to prove this point. For example, critics such as Ehsan Tabari, the famous theoretician of Iran's Communist Party (Tudeh),[131] and Jalal Al-e Ahmad have examined literary reflections of social events and developed socio-political readings of *Buf-e Kur*. Others like Michael Beard and Nasrin Rahimieh have studied the influence of European literary and intellectual traditions and even specific writers such as Rilke and Kafka on this work. Mirabedini and Ramin Jahanbegloo have emphasized socio-historical contexts to construct their reading of Hedayat in general, and *Buf-e Kur* in particular,[132] and others such as Farzaneh Milani have constructed feminist readings of Hedayat's work.[133] Of course there have also been those who have simply dismissed *Buf-e Kur* as a work which emanated from a sick and perverted mind! Jalal Al-e Ahmad is the most famous of this category. Another ground for dismissal of the book, put forward by Najaf Daryabandari, was its inclusion in the category of decadent literature. And then, there are critics, albeit very few, who have tried to study parts of this work by underlining its interplay with characteristics of the Persian literary tradition. One such example is Youssef Ishaghpour's *Bar Mazar-e Hedayat* (on Hedayat's Grave),[134] in which he discusses the dominant images of *Buf-e Kur* and demonstrates their obvious contrarian nature with their classical counterparts. According to Ishaghpour, in *Buf-e Kur*, Hedayat has reversed the familiar sufi-*erfani* (gnostic) atmosphere of love in Persian classical works. He has done so, Ishaghpour argues, by using some of the elements of those classical images (like the miniaturistic beloved and wine), but after putting them through a metamorphosis he has given them completely different positions and functions. Here Ishaghpour's subject of examination is quite similar to that of Meskub, but his approach and analysis are completely different.[135]

The debate about bringing literature down from its lofty, aristocratic, ethereal position to earth started before the Constitutional Revolution and intensified after it, informing many critiques and readings of literary and artistic production. Many considered this a transition from heaven to earth in its limited socio-political framework; at times, this reductionist approach led to analyses which at best could be called clumsy. A famous example is Forugh Farrokhzad's utterance about Persian classical romances. In an interview with Iraj Gorgin about the characteristics of modern poetry, having said that she believes it is the environment that creates and redefines concepts, she continues:

> Let me give you a simple example, about love and the character of Majnun,[136] who has always been the symbol of perseverance and faithfulness in Love. Well, in the opinion of someone like me who lives differently, his character is ridiculous, especially when the science of psychology comes and dismantles him and analyses him and shows me that he was not a lover but rather a sick person who wanted to torture himself.[137]

This reaction completely misses the idea of literariness, aesthetics, literary conventions and their evolution, as well as the whole category of "reader response." I do not believe any serious reader of Persian literature—let alone a serious critic—has ever bought into the idea that true lovers (past or present, and in any given conditions) are those who end up in deserts living with wild animals while crying blood instead of regular tears!

Let us return to *Buf-e Kur* and its rhizomatic function, meaning the potentials it created, each of which could—and some of which did—become a literary trend.[138] *Buf-e Kur* is a short novella which is organized around the story of a young man whose portrayal, at first, seems to have no affinity with that of classical characters in Persian literature. Here, a short reference to Michael Beard's book on Hedayat, *Hedayat's Blind Owl as a Western Novel*[139] in general, and his article, "Influence as Debt: *The Blind Owl* in the Literary Marketplace" might also be helpful. In conversation with my questioning of general utterances about the influence of Western literary traditions on Persian fiction and in response to specific questions about the nature of this influence, Beard offers a number of arguments in his article. In particular, he makes reference, convincingly in my opinion, to the impact of "European innovations" in terms of character development on Hedayat's work. He writes:

> A second provision to add is that we can provide a partial answer to Khorrami's question about the components of European narrative. I would list as European innovations the emphasis on visual detail and the definition of character as a product of social conditions, traditions which we often trace from in Balzac as development of nineteenth-century Europe.[140]

This influence, and not necessarily imitation, I believe, is especially true in the case of *Buf-e Kur*, and traveling from there in the case of many other modernist Persian fictions.

This novella which comprises two rather distinct parts is organized around a particular goal, stated by the narrator, which is to describe or to know himself, or as he puts it, to introduce himself to his shadow which is cast on the wall.[141] In the first part of the book, which is dominated by a completely surreal atmosphere, this quest is pursued through the narrator's monologues, and mainly silent interactions with mirage-like characters such as an ethereal woman and an old ugly man—with remote similarity to the narrator—as well as with unstable objects and scenes which appear and disappear, all in a dimly-lit environment. In the second part of the book, scenes are provided with more light; the mirage-like quality of the characters has been removed, and they seem to share more kinship with tangible, familiar reality. Of course, they have all gone through a kind of deterioration, both physically and psychologically, except for the old man who functions as a prototype in both sections, trying to impose total uniformity, a kind of uniformity that is seen, for example, in Eugene Ionesco's *Rhinoceros* (1959).

The narrator of the story is clearly defined as an outcast, and although in his description local elements—for example, a specific place—have been used, his overall traits are quite similar to characters of other modern(ist) stories and thus reminiscent of the universality of outcastness in modernist writing. Along the same line, from the very beginning, the author/narrator directly indicates his efforts for creating a self-referential universe:

> I will attempt to write all that I remember, all that remains in my mind from the interconnectedness between the events, maybe I can come to a general judgment about it—No, perhaps it is for reassurance, or essentially so that I can believe it myself—because for me it absolutely does not matter if others believe it or not, my only fear is that I will die tomorrow and still not know myself—for in the course of my life experiences I came to this understanding that there existed a dreadful chasm between myself and others, and I understood that as much as possible one should remain inaudible, as much as possible I should keep my thoughts to myself, and if now I have decided to write, it is only to introduce myself to my shadow—a bent shadow on the wall, and it is as if the more I write, it devours it with an even greater appetite—It is for him that I wish to carry out an experiment: to see if we can come to know each other better—because from the time that I cut myself off from others, I have wanted to know myself better.[142]

But the narrator does not remain committed to this aim. On the one hand, while using mostly common, everyday words and phrases, he either distorts them or uses them to create unfamiliar juxtapositions which serve to create self-referentiality, uniqueness, and individuality, all of which defamiliarize the familiar. On the other hand, however, these efforts are attenuated through excessive judgments about his environment. These judgments, and, in general, references to his environment—which clearly constitute a critique of a collectively-accepted ensemble—as well as the clash of the story's self-referentiality with a version of a universalist nihilism undermine the narrator's stated aim. The modernist self-referentiality is further moderated by the presence of a causal plot and an overall storyline and its structural precision, elements which are not common in Persian modernist writing.

However, no matter how successful the author/narrator of *Buf-e Kur* is in his efforts to create a self-referential universe, it is clear that the announcement of the idea proved to have been very timely—an idea which was taken up by authors who occupy a significant place among Persian modernist writers, that is, the non-discursive writers whose works resist discursive categorizations.

Throughout this section, I have used the phrase *Persian* modernist writing to indicate that although I believe modernist writing could be defined through its universal components (self-referentiality, the presence of modern and unique sensibility, etc.), these components are functioning within various literary traditions and often lead to completely different outcomes.[143] With regards to non-discursive Persian works, this issue shows itself particularly in regard to the attributes of the narrators or protagonists (who in these works are often the same) and, as a partial result of this, in the architecture of the stories created around these narrators or protagonists. To place this point in the context of tradition-specific definition of modernist writing, I am suggesting that while, for example, in French literature, one could speak of the anti-hero of a modern novel as an inversion or perversion of the Romantic hero, in Persian modernist writing there is no such dynamism. Perhaps the closest substitution is the inversion or perversion of the *sufi/aref* hero in Persian literature. This comparison is useful because it points to the different processes of the development of *I*, and its extremely important position in self-referential literary works, in various literary traditions. To continue with this comparison, the French Romantic hero considers himself a prophet or even a god, equal to God, and at times even challenges him;[144] but the *aref* hero sees himself as part of the whole and believes that only if he dissolves himself in the whole can he become one with God. This comparison explains the less-individuated protagonists of non-discursive modernist Persian literature, which in turn influence the process of creation and the architecture of the self-referential universe.

Personalizing space, liberating language

One of the representative works of the non-discursive trend which undoubtedly should be placed at the heart of Persian modernist writing is the short story by Shamim Bahar (b. 1317/1938), "*Abr Baranash Gerefteh Ast*" (The Cloud Feels Like Raining).[145] This story was published in *Andisheh va Honar* (Thought and Art) journal in 1345/1966.[146] Shamim Bahar published his works, which include seven short and long stories, from 1342–1351 (1963–1972), and after that he withdrew from literary circles and scenes. "The Cloud Feels Like Raining," I believe, has a unique position in the context of Persian modernist writing because of its author/narrator's complete loyalty to a modernist literary solitude. Here I am not referring at all to the socio-philosophical concept of modern man's solitude in the context of modernity, although the effect of this reality on literature is undeniable. I am referring to modernist literary solitude as a way to express a work's self-referentiality.

The story of "The Cloud Feels Like Raining" is simple, even mundane. It is a letter that Manuchehr, the first-person narrator, has written to his friend, who lives abroad. Manuchehr writes about Giti, his friend's fiancée and describes the few days they had spent together. Giti had come to Tehran to attend her father's funeral. While describing a number of banal, everyday events, the narrator also tells his friend, in a passionless tone, that at one point he felt very close to Giti and even decided to ask her to marry him, though in the end, he did not. Finally, Giti returns, and story ends with a short account of Manuchehr's last visit with Giti before her departure back to Europe.

Like most narrators of modernist stories, it does not seem that Manuchehr's identity is part of a collective one. He does not pursue collective goals and his social and professional lives (he is an events reporter) are for the most part depicted as unimportant, inconsequential, even frivolous. Like many narrators of modernist works, he, too, seems to be an outcast. Inter-estingly though, and in contrast with *Buf-e Kur*'s narrator, he underlines this characteristic by not addressing it directly. In fact, this indifference makes him more modernist. The story, too, contrary to many Persian modernist stories which followed this one, does not have either a fluid, unfixed space or a complicated temporality. In other words, the narrator has not employed any of these common tools to personalize his universe, but undoubtedly he is aware of this process. Using the topos of an expatriate traveling back and nostalgically desiring to see her old city, throughout the story he speaks of the neighborhoods Giti wanted to see; then it is implied that each neighborhood and space is a sign that must become personalized; that the city of Tehran must become personalized, and that this process needs to be addressed quite consciously. The seeds of the narrator's method of personalizing are seen in this work, but their grown implemented examples are clearly depicted in Bahar's last work, *Seh Dastan-e Asheqaneh* (Three Romantic Stories), to which I shall return later.

The most striking quality of "The Cloud Feels Like Raining" is the narrator's explicit attempt to find a particular language through which he could form the signs and codes of his personal world. From this perspective, this story should be considered one of the distinguished examples of Persian modernist writing. The narrator is so persistent in this project that at times he becomes, narratologically speaking, compulsive or even paranoid. Mindful of the fact that any things or elements brought to the story could inadvertently suggest a collective universe, the narrator pathologically tries to avoid general and common elements and descriptions—especially those related to nature—and seems to consciously avoid using any form of metaphor or symbol, fearing that they might refer to commonly-accepted notions, ideas, or spaces. His paranoiac efforts to avoid the contamination of his personal and self-referential world show itself best at the levels of sentences and phrases. On many occasions, the narrator begins a paragraph but then, after one or two sentences, as if he has felt that his words and sentences are being appropriated by commonly-accepted signs and codes, or even that they just lend themselves to readings based on collective semiologies, he suddenly abandons them, discredits them, and continues the story from another angle. This does not mean that the story is following the "stream of consciousness" technique. In "The Cloud Feels Like Raining" there is causality; the narrative direction of the story is quite pronounced the progressing logic of the story and consequently its progression are perfectly clear. Yet the narratological paranoia is also at work. Here are a few representative passages of the story:

> Yesterday, which was a Friday, Giti returned … She didn't have a good time when she was here. First it was her father's death and then her mother's situation and things like that although her not staying had nothing to do with these things …
>
> …
>
> I want to ask how you are doing because although your letters arrive regularly you don't write about yourself and you keep writing about I don't know theater and things like that …
>
> …
>
> Giti was continuously talking and in the beginning I didn't understand what she was saying and I was too shy to ask her what she meant but then I saw that it was impossible and so I began asking and things like that …
>
> …
>
> And what you wrote was just about literature and games like that and this and that so finally I too went to the airport and I had actually looked up to see which flight she was on when I arrived I saw an army of people there all in black clothing and I realized they were her family members who had come there to like welcome her and what faces that I was scared I mean crying and crying and things like that … [147]

The "and things like that" refrain is a clear indication of the narrator's trial and error approach to the issue of narration based on a personal system of signs. This phrase and others such as "but you don't understand this" and "anyway" as well as the occasional use of ellipses in the story which serve the narrator to abandon a topic and start another one indicate both the narrator's disconnect with his environment (and the resulting question of why should one continue talking/writing) and his fear that saying more might lead to commonly-accepted readings. They are seen throughout the story and are the most important representations of the author/narrator's modernist sensibility, and sensitivity.

Here a comparison between "The Cloud Feels Like Raining" and a few others written before and after it would be helpful. As mentioned before, in the opening pages of *Buf-e Kur*, Hedayat announces that he is writing this novella for himself (or his shadow) and does not care about others whom, later on, he calls "the rabble." The surreal and strange space of the first part of *Buf-e Kur* also reinforces the idea that the narrator has been very conscious of depicting himself away from others.

> As luck would have it, my house is located outside the city, in a quiet and peaceful place, far from the commotion and clamor of people's lives—its borders are completely distinct and it is surrounded by ruins. Only from the other side of the ditch do the dilapidated mud houses appear and the city begin—I do not know what tasteless or mad man from time immemorial built this house; when I close my eyes I not only see all of its nooks and crannies, but I also feel their entire weight upon my shoulders—a house that could only have been painted on ancient pen cases.[148]

But the way Hedayat characterizes the people as well as the presence of symbolism and parody, which acknowledge the existence of commonly-accepted elements, effectively undermines his claim that he is only out to construct his own world. In other words, the linguistic and structural architecture of *Buf-e Kur* partially betrays the modernist ambition of the work. Shamim Bahar, however, manages to come closer to the modernist goal of self-referentiality, both linguistically and spatially. The narrator of "The Cloud Feels Like Raining" has realized that to achieve modernist self-referentiality he cannot ignore personalized description of spaces. Revolutionary and/or Surrealist (André Breton used to called Surrealism a Revolution) descriptions are not helpful either, because, like symbolism, they are pursuing a sublime truth and have not abandoned Universalist claims. The only solution left is to re-experience existing places, but this time without accepting their usual functions and descriptions. This direction in an urban setting leads to efforts such as "The Cloud Feels Like Raining," where locations—neighborhoods, streets, shops, etc.—are described in such a way that they challenge collective strategies defined based on their collective functions and descriptions. From a technical point of view, it is interesting to note that many such works rely on similar tools to move their characters and in general the narration through collectively-defined spaces. "The Cloud Feels Like Raining" is not the best example, but there are still quite a few instances of apparently random, disinterested approaches to locations and spaces.

> I took the raincoat of one of the colleagues and came down and waited for her who arrived in a taxi she wanted to get off but I signaled and I got on and then I told the taxi driver to go to Shemiran I mean just like that no other place came to my mind.
>
>   In the taxi she was quiet at first then she started talking about her father and the car accident and about their house which was in Shemiran when she got to this point she suddenly said that she had seen Shemiran

and she wanted to see other places she told the taxi driver to go back to the city and we returned to the city and the rain was not letting up she told the driver let's go to Tupkhaneh perhaps no other name came to her we went to Tupkhaneh Square and she said let's get off anyway we got out and just like that under the rain we started walking in the street to so-called see Tehran ... [149]

This aspect of Bahar's modernist writing is seen in a more precise, calculated, and detailed way in *Three Romantic Stories* (1351/1973). From the point of view of modernist writing, one would think that *Three Romantic Stories* should have been written before "The Cloud Feels Like Raining"; especially since it is not easy to arrive at the calmness resulting from discovering one's own language in it Also, its constant experimentation with form and language is indicative of a search which is still unfinished. However, from the perspective of settling once and for all one's relationship with his environment, as well as finding schemes through which the narrator could travel through the city in a random and disinterested manner, it is an excellent example. Indeed, the narrator of *Three Romantic Stories* manages to simply go through the city and register his observations without having been influenced by any particular aim; thus he constructs a personal narrative of contemporary history and its people. As expressed in the title, the story has three sections; each is named after one of the Iranian epic/romantic characters. In previous pages I referred to the tradition of not just rereading Iranian epic/romantic myths but of rewriting them, as well as to Hedayat's approach to the calcified images in the Persian literary tradition. Here I want to emphasize that in Persian modernist writing, the phenomenon of reaction to what has been settled has become extremely important, to the extent that it should certainly be considered one of the major characteristics of modern Persian fiction. In the next section of this study I shall discuss other examples which depict this trait.

Like Bahar's other stories, *Three Romantic Stories* does not have a straightforward narrative course and the *fabula* ("story stuff") is not that important. The interesting part, once again, is the author's struggle to find a personal modernist style. The first part of the story, "Farhad," is the story of the narrator and two young women who live abroad and have just come back to Iran. One of them, Shirin, seems to be a relative of the narrator whom he has not seen for long time; the other is Shirin's friend, Sheida.[150] The narrator tells the story to a friend in a phone conversation. The register is completely conversational, without any punctuation. Here is a paragraph taken at random from the first section of the story:

I don't remember well now but probably I had started very stupidly talking about my car and these two Shirin in front and Sheida in the back were shaking their heads calmly then I said let's go have dinner without really I was not paying attention I gave a long lecture about different places that oh yes I said I knew a very cool Mexican place and I said a bunch of good things and when I got to it has only waitresses and of course they know me there because I have been there often and so they call me Mr. Farad[151] I am an idiot I didn't realize I ordered wine and they were quiet[152]

In the second part titled *"Giv"*,[153] however, the language suddenly changes and the author begins with a lofty language and complete, even exaggerated, punctuation.

Naked; cleanly washed, the hairy tired body. Imagine it coming out of water without any memory; foams; in fragments: disheveled twisted hairs scattered in grey curls, and the sound of the passage of clean water through unseen pipes. In the mild and humid warmth, sister's henna-colored towel around the waist and on the shoulders, imagine it, in a moment there is no longer that person who turns the faucet on and presses the sponge in the feast, and perhaps it is a different person, a witness kneeled down in the hallway, ear to the door: the choked sound of fleeting foamed water, the sound of the water pouring from the faucet, the sound of the water pouring from the faucet, the sound of turning off the faucet, the little sounds of scattering powder and the rotating of a wet sponge, the sounds of someone washing the bathtub, someone bent over the light green tub, staring at the dull nickel faucets.[154]

In addition to this lofty language, there is an unbelievable degree of attention paid to the material items in the immediate environment, as if the narrator has suddenly been struck by the modernist universal epiphany that what he has seen and known so far should be redefined and re-described; this time only for himself. Many paragraphs in this section begin with the refrain of "imagine it"; then, slowly, this project which starts from material items expands and brings in other, apparently randomly-selected, components such as acquaintances and strangers to create a personal narrative. The place of the story moves out of the house. It goes to streets and neighborhoods, and another technical refrain shows up: "I remember in Tehran, the taxi driver had stopped to get a passenger ... " "I remember in Tehran, a young man was sitting next to the taxi driver ... " "I remember in Tehran, I was in a taxi coming up from the old Shemiran road ... " "I remember in Tehran, at night, I was sitting on the back seat of a taxi and was going to Shemiran, half drunk ... "[155] In the text, all these paragraphs (beginning with "I remember") are separated with a space as if the narrator is trying to emphasize their fragmented nature. Another feature of this segment is that the paragraphs do not start from the beginning of the line but rather towards the end of the line; perhaps to suggest that these vignettes of memory emerge quite accidentally and that the narrator is making no effort to determine a beginning or an end for each one of them. The language has now moved away from that lofty poetic register and has become a combination of ordinary elegance (in descriptions) and conversational style when a dialogue is recounted. These linguistic features justify a reading of this text which suggests that in the process of writing his personal narrative of his life, his world, and *the* world, the author/narrator gradually realizes that the project he has started is much more expansive than a traditional memoir. In this project all the elements which construct his personal history, and his mind, such as time, events which previously seemed to be significant, as well as those which had been ignored before—perhaps because of the influence of collective strategies—and then their redefinitions, should be re-examined.

> I remember in Tehran the taxi driver was an old man who was nagging, the gentleman comes out of the door and gets into his Buick it has AC he goes to his courtyard it has AC he goes to the beach it has AC he goes I don't know where it has AC he ain't like us Sir. With a smile I asked who are you talking about father, I asked; the nightly snow was still coming down in fragments and the street its trees were covered by snow was full of mud under the tires of the taxi. The driver turned and looked at me, purple eyes, he paused and said all of them Sir all of them.[156]

And it is only reasonable that this struggle, sooner or later, will lead the author to the perennial question of what is the responsibility of literature and of the writer, and consequently to the question of how one should write. The third part of the story, "Bahman," which is a love letter to Giti (the recurring character of Bahar's stories) starts with the following passage:

> Ordibehesht[157] fifty-one (1973)
> I was working on an article that I had to write; I have promised it and they are waiting for it—I prepared my notes and began writing and I didn't write—what I wrote was not everything I wanted to write and the topic I didn't know where to begin was simply that to tell a story in art— in all storytelling arts from, as you say, anecdote writing to theatre, always theatre, to even cinema for which I still don't have patience—we have started from short allegories, in order to educate, and have come through all these twisted roads until we have reached an art whose point is nothing but the essence of art. Then it is logical if from this end of the line—if we don't accept that this is a dead-end—we return, and we are returning, albeit unconsciously, to long allegories whose names, instead of educational, is probably struggle; and also a rediscovered frankness, removed from all artistic games—and I remembered that I had heard it not from your mouth—from someone else, who—and it was in my memory; everything, and it was for you that I wanted to write, I wanted to talk with you, and it is for you that I am writing—if I thought before to write and didn't write, if I wrote a draft and didn't finish, if I wrote it but didn't send it; now I will write it and I will send it; with love and with difficulty, with difficulty—[158]

Once again it is clear that the key research phrase about modernist writing is the struggle to define a self-referential universe whose Persian version should confront and reposition calcified characteristics of this literary tradition such as images, myths, tropes, and topoi and define itself in terms of its linguistic particularities.

We see a surprisingly similar struggle in the works of Alimorad Fadainia (b. 1925), another writer from more or less the same generation. In his long story, *"Hekayat-e Hijdahom-e Ordibehesht-e Bist-o Panj"* (The Story of Eighteenth of Ordibehesht of [13]25/1946) published in 1349/1970, we see the same usage of the taxi device. Here, too, the protagonist gets into a taxi and goes through various locations as part of the process of creating his unique universe. His language is more personal than Shamim Bahar's in that his references are extremely unfamiliar and on many occasions the text becomes quite inaccessible. Manuchehr Atashi (1931–2005) a poet and occasional critic, has described this story very succinctly.

> [The author] is always in a taxi from Shemiran to Molavi, from the west of the city to Tehranpars.[159] The author whispers an account of the story of his self and the recapturing of moments, memories, fears and unchangeable rules while traveling on these two lines, on a cross! Anyway, writers no longer write in a clear manner. When there is no goal outside the text for a fragmented text written in a taxi, when the events outside have no roots in social and historical realities and cannot be interpreted and explained by any philosophical language, when words refer to themselves and for their own sake and do not accept to be part of a collective thought or sensitivity then expecting a classical novel is unreasonable. The author does deal with *the outside of his being.*[160]

The similar usage of this device, a taxi, and other similar techniques such as the mixing of different registers found in these two stories cannot be accidental. Not surprisingly, even the title of Fadainia's story refers to this individualism. Ordibehesht 18, 1325 is Fadainia's birth date. In a sense Bahar's "The Cloud Feels Like Raining" is also a very personal title. At the end of the story Bahar, repeating once again that it is not important for him whether his friend—and by extension, readers; Others—understands him or not, writes:

> Anyway first I mean then I didn't say anything and Giti too was totally quiet until the maid called out that the breakfast is ready and I said is there any other book that I have to read I wanted to sort of make a joke before she left Giti said why did you get so angry and she knew why then she said have you heard this poem by Nima Yushij she knew that I had not and as soon as she started I realized that this was not Hamlet and it was not things like that and it was something that made me feel comfortable until today noon I remembered a few lines of it if I wrote it for you you would understand but then I forgot.[161]

The title of Bahar's story is from a famous verse by Nima Yushij:

My house is cloudy but
The cloud feels like raining

The context-less part of the line—which the narrator does not share with his friend—used as the title, is another strong indication of the individual nature of his writing. "The Cloud Feels Like Raining" and what it is referring to make sense only to the narrator. It seems as if when that epiphany occurs, the first thing to do is to find a means which could move the individual through familiar spaces which, because of rejecting collective goals and strategies, have now become unfamiliar, so that he could write his own narrative. This is exactly the Situationists' *dérive* which they defined in terms of the creation of non-collective, truly individual life.

From a stylistic point of view and in relation to the idea of linguistic/narrative struggle, other examples in Persian modernist writing are easy to find. One of the exaggerated versions of this struggle is Abbas Na'lbandian's play, *Puf.* Based on the information that Reza Ghassemi has posted on his website,[162] the play was written during the early years of 1350/1970. Because of the use of a very sexually explicit language and imagery throughout, especially in describing sex scenes, this play was banned both before and, naturally, after the 1979 Revolution. In the context of present study, this play should be considered one of the best examples of efforts to normalize a language which traditionally was considered "writing obscenity"[163] or "pornography." This normalizing process, I maintain, is still in the context of the struggle of a modernist writer to find a personal language and universe.

Examining works of Persian literature which have emphasized the usage of explicit language, especially in regard to sexual scenes and topics, from classical to modern period, is obviously not in the scope of this study. Suffice it to say that in many works representing different genres and types, from classics such as Sa'di's *Hazliyat* (facetiae) and Zakani's *Resaleh-ye Delgosha* ("The Joyous Treatise") to popular texts such as *Hosein-e Kord-e Shabestari* (Hosein the Kurd of Shabestar) as well as more contemporary texts such as *Puf,* this "obscene" language has been widely used, yet censorship applied by modern governments in particular together with social norms have never allowed these works to become part of the mainstream. In the context of Persian modernist writing, however, experimenting or simply using this language and imagery should be deemed significant in that it has helped to expand the idea of acceptable languages and spaces in Persian literature.[164] From this point of view, *Puf,* a rarely-read work, certainly plays its part.

In the first part of the play explicit sexual acts between a man and a woman, while a kid is in the room, are described in a most vulgar language. The kid is playing with plastic body parts and is trying to put them together. The second part begins when the sex ends and simultaneously the kid has placed the last leg on the plastic man, after which it stands up. The language suddenly changes into a lofty, then an archaic one. The back-and-forth between language registers continues and at the end they are mixed and placed at the same level. One of the punch lines towards the end reads: "Do you see? The only solution is for good to fuck evil."[165]

The names of the characters also are a strange combination. There are ordinary names like Shahla, Jahan, and unnamed characters like first kid, second kid, boy, and also names reminiscent of ancient Iran like Shapur, Cirus, Khosrow, Kaveh, and then there are made-up names such as Kez, Gonag, Kil.[166] The play, which is less than 20,000 words long, touches upon many themes and spaces, and at times it becomes too vague and unstructured. But one thing is clear and that is its dominant technique which is the mixing of different narrative styles, languages, and traditionally-accepted literary values in order to discredit them. Towards the end of the play, which is described by the author as a *shadinameh* (comedy), one of the main characters, Kil, who had been identified through his extremely vulgar language, presents a completely different linguistic side of himself.

Kil

Why do men cry? Why does this path go inside itself? Why do stars die, and we do not see and we do not know? Why, in this strange exile, we try to grab the heavens? Why does a pigeon, lonely on a roof, stare? Why does a cloud which is passing by, rain on us so graciously?[167] Why does time break the back of a man by sorrow? Why does a woman abandon the glory of love because of despair? Why does Good, which is a bird, fly away from us? Why is not there a path from this purgatory to any paradise? Why do trees wither in darkness? Why does a door close? Why does a brokenhearted person cry while drinking wine? Why does a yellow leaf break the Spring? Why does a moth burn? Why does a rabbit jump up from sleep? Why does wind take away a wisp of hay? Why does a mad man laugh with himself? Why does a wall stop me from going? Why does a fist pound a child? Why does a mouth curse? Why is a thorn lonely? Why doesn't a guest knock on a door? ... Why don't the dead tell us something about themselves? Why doesn't an affectionate fog embrace the forest? Why does nobody say: Love! Why is a horse afraid? *[pause]* Puf![168]

Kez, the other main character of the beginning of the play and who had been described as an ugly, vulgar, sex-craving, and low woman appears in a completely different light.

He [Kil] fades away. Kez slowly appears in the same place he was. A long white cloth is wrapped around her. She looks beautiful. Nik and Genag are completely nude.

Kez

Do you see? The only solution is for good to fuck evil.[169]

The play ends with a short passage which bears the same title as the beginning passage: "The Story of Creation."

> A desert. There is nothing. Not even a thornbush. A blinding sun. Utterly blinding. Absolute whiteness.
> Silence.
> Three minutes pause.
> Then, very slowly and languidly, lasting for about four minutes, black flower buds bring their heads out from different places from the ground. They grow towards the sky. The flower buds, their stems, leaves and petals are all black. Absolute black.
> The buds open. They turn into black flowers. Absolute black.
> Suddenly, light disappears.[170]

Abbas Na'lbandian could certainly be considered one of Hedayat's true successors. Like him, while his efforts to find a unique/individual path as well as a self-referential description of the world around him are obvious, his sensibility towards his environment is accompanied by a clear judgment. And like him, this sensibility is informed by a desire to use art to change or at least critique the world.[171]

Similar characteristics are seen in the works of many other Iranian modernist writers; each, of course, with his or her own nuances. Bahman Forsi is another such good example, whose works, like those of many other writers of this period, have not received enough attention. In many of his works, Forsi, too, mixes different registers and styles, ignores linear narration, employs fragmentations and actually makes a conscious effort to not use classic literary devices which could bridge these fragments. At the beginning of *Zir-e Dandan-e Sag* (Under a Dog's Teeth), a collection of short stories which was published with the help of Shamim Bahar, Forsi wrote:

> I speak of
>   the behavior of blood,
>   the shouting of bones.
>
> Who is friend.
> Who is stranger.[172]

These few short lines do not necessarily summarize the themes and style of the collection but reveal its Hedayat-like atmosphere. In stories which in many cases come close to the genre of memoir, while including a sketch of the world surrounding the narrator, Forsi, like Hedayat, consciously or unconsciously transfers a sense of critique of the world and the common values of its people. But like Na'lbandian, he uses linguistics and formal devices which emphasize the modernist literary self-referentiality. To read these works in their literary contexts, one of the best ways is to examine the interaction of the text with general systems of codes and signs. Works such as *Under a*

Dog's Teeth, Vesal dar vadi-ye Haftom (Union in the Seventh Valley) by Na'lbandian, and of course, *Buf-e Kur*, demonstrate a closer dependence to these systems than a work such as "The Cloud Feels Like Raining" or Alimorad Fadainia's "The Story of Eighteenth of Ordibehesht of [13]25," because the overall narrative strategy of the last two is much more informed by the goal of materializing self-referential worlds and that is why relating to them at times becomes quite difficult. Indeed, many works by authors like Bahman Forsi, Abbas Na'lbandian, Bahram Sadeqi, and Sadeq Hedayat have a closer kinship with social-literary tendencies which, for example, were formulated and promoted by social-artistic modernist movements such as Khorus Jangi.[173] Having said this, it should also be noted that during the period these works were being produced, the critique of the surrounding world was gradually succeeding in liberating itself from the yoke of political and sociological discourses and in finding a way through literary forms and styles to express a general dissatisfaction and malaise. In other words, reading these works, one realizes that a transition from literary counter-discourses which challenged the narratives of dominant discourses in various arenas to narratives which cannot be identified with any totalizing, familiar discourse has taken place. From this specific perspective, I call them non-discursive works.

Following the path of this transition and identifying particular works which could represent different stages of this trajectory—as well as the examination of directions which have branched out of this path—is one of the most useful ways of studying Persian modernist writing. This approach is fundamentally different from the one used by many critics and teachers of literature who, mainly in order to simplify the structural design of their critique or courses, instead of following the evolutionary process of characteristics of aesthetics, forms, and literary concepts, try to use historical turning points or chronology to mark different stages of the trajectory of Persian literature. This approach usually ends up requiring the insistence on the idea that social changes directly lead to literary changes, and that basically the former is a prerequisite for the latter. At times when they come across works which do not confirm the historical narrative of the period during which they have been produced, they place them in the categories of exception and out of the norm. In fact, at times, the incompatibility of these "diachronistic" works with the literarized socio-historical approach is so obvious that the proponents of this approach have no recourse except to ignore such works which could potentially undermine the construction of grand narratives about different historical periods. A very famous example of such narratives is the account of the 1953 *coup d'état*, which, they argue, created an atmosphere of despair in the whole society; thus the literary works produced during this period all reflect this despair. Following the same approach, another popular narrative is about the two decades of the 1960s and 1970s, during which, it is said in a rather grossly generalized manner, that intellectuals embraced the idea of "return to the self" and to their historical past, etc.[174] Such essentialist generalizations give the impression that all literary works of this period represent the same ideas and desires. It is not difficult to find a literary text or an intellectual who could symbolize this narrative. For the proponents of the return-to-the-self narrative, Al-e Ahmad (1923–1969) has been the main writer whose works, including his non-fiction *Westoxification* (1963), represent this notion and therefore the spirit of his age. But the simple fact is that not only are the grand narratives, by definition, incapable of presenting a comprehensive image of an era's literary production (or any other field of human activities), but even the methodology which aims at constructing such grand narratives is problematic. In this specific case, it is clear that while the tendency of "returning to the past" is indeed one of the intellectual tendencies of this period, it is also true that this tendency existed during other periods as well, especially among the literati. More importantly, along with this tendency during the 1960s and 1970s, there are many other trends which have no kinship with the idea of "returning to the past." There is a large body of works by modernist and non-modernist writers such as Bozorg Alavi, M. A. Behazin, Taqi Modarresi, Bahram Sadeqi, Sadeq Chubak, Ebrahim Golestan, Hushang Golshiri, Reza Baraheni, Shamim Bahar, Abbas Na'lbandian, Bahman Forsi, Simin Daneshvar, Alimorad Fadainia, and so on, which were produced and published during the 1960s and 1970s and are either in direct opposition to this grand narrative, or are indifferent to it. I believe such narratives have been formed mainly by sociological, historical, and generally non-literary discourses. Many of the proponents of this approach have not paid close attention to literary intellectuals and, in order to justify the generalizing nature of their thesis, have used selectively-chosen literary works or passages.[175] And this is why for example, the exemplary texts describing the desire of the intellectuals of the two decades of 1960s and 1970s are "mediocre writings such as *Westoxification* and *On the Service and Betrayal of the Intellectuals*,"[176] the non-literary works of a journalist/writer like Jalal Al-e Ahmad, while works of renowned writers such as Sadeqi, Baraheni, Shamim Bahar, and Golshiri are largely neglected.

The point here is not to imply that in order to study the process of the evolution of Persian literature, this tradition and its production should be examined in a vacuum and should disregard social, historical, and political events, or the intellectual achievements of other disciplines. In fact, and particularly regarding the last section of the present study, I maintain that in order to construct legitimate readings of works which I have categorized as "beyond modernist works," literary discourses should be analyzed with an eye not only on social, historical, and political events (as elements of a background) but on the intellectual productions of other disciplines.[177] For example, the historical uprisings culminating first in the 1979 Revolution and the events after it, and then the Iran–Iraq War which, in addition to resulting in the adoption of new policies by the discourses in power, leading to the creation of new, unfamiliar spaces, provided a novel context for Persian literature. At the same time, the trajectory of modernist Persian writing, whose most famous turning point is characterized by the publication of *Buf-e Kur*, along with other characteristics of the Persian literary tradition—particular usage of pre-Islamic myths, formation of literary counter-discourses through challenging the definition of actual by the official discourse, that is, prison literature, and on the level of language, by departing from "current linguistic usage,"[178] etc.—prepared the situation for a new jump; a jump which would incorporate all these elements and in a sense would create a new Buf-e Kurian moment.

In many of these *beyond-modernist* works, the fictional *I* is rather an inversion of the *aref* (gnostic) in Persian literary tradition, and, as suggested before, this is something that we can see in many modernist works as well. Yet these beyond-modernist works differ from purely modernist works such as Bahar's "The Cloud Feels Like Raining" or Fadainia's " ... Ordibehesht" in that they are not nearly as self-referential as the latter because they are very much interacting with existing systems of codes and signs—such as myths—and thus have a closer kinship with works like *Buf-e Kur* or *Yakolia and Her Solitude*. These beyond-modernist works also benefit from literary experiences which reject current or commonly-accepted forms, language registers, and histories, and therefore lead to an increase in formalist, linguistic, and historiographical possibilities. Another characteristic of these works (given the constant presence of significant socio-political events, a somewhat bizarre characteristic) is that it seems their narratives have been constructed at a distance from discursive confrontation and commotion. Indeed, it seems that discursivity is not part of their strategy or agenda. This is not to say that it is difficult for a critic to develop socio-political readings of these narratives, but close textual examination of them indicates that such readings will effectively have to ignore large sections and elements of these works. To provide an example I am devoting the last part of this study to a close reading of Bijan Najdi's "*Shab-e Sohrab Koshan*" (The Eve of the Slaying of Sohrab).

Listening as a deaf, speaking as a mute, changing the myths

Why is it that as soon as we see the title: "The Eve of the Slaying of Sohrab" we tend to think we are going to read a text which not only has no affiliation with the discourse in power but even includes opposing elements in it? Certainly, one of the reasons is that beginning around tenth century, with the rise of the power of the Ghazni Turks, the existing Islamic discourse tried deliberately and consciously, specifically in the field of literature, to replace pre-Islamic myths and figures with Islamic ones.[179] A clear confrontation began to take shape and, depending on the nature and policies of the sources of power in different periods, the balance of this confrontation underwent many changes and at times even became irrelevant. It is safe to say that in the contemporary history of Iran, this confrontation has never been as pronounced as it became after the 1979 Revolution. From the very beginning, the discourse in power tried to ignore pre-Islamic characteristics and codes of Iranian culture, and even to eradicate them. Shortly after the consolidation of power, it went so far as to make the unwise attempt to remove the *Shahnameh* from bookstore shelves and to ban it. Indeed, for a short period of time, the only way to purchase a copy of the *Shahnameh* was through the black market.

A second reason for the identification of the title of Najdi's book with counter-discursivity is that, particularly during the modern period of Persian literature, many literary counter-discourses and counter-narratives have successfully employed Iranian myths and in fact appropriated them. Some of the best examples of such efforts are found in Bahram Beyzai's plays for screen and stage which not only rewrite stories of the *Shahnameh* but at times use the fable-interwoven story of Ferdowsi's life and his confrontation with newly-arrived, ideologically-defined representations of power such as Sultan Mahmud and his subalterns. Bahram Beyzai is by no means an exception, and examples of such a usage of the *Shahnameh* and its characters are simply too numerous. Of course, it should also be noted that on some occasions efforts were made by margins of the current discourse in power to incorporate these myths in their narratives, but they have been utterly unsuccessful.

A third reason is that the main ingredient of many stories of the *Shahnameh*, including the stories of Sohrab and Siyavash, is the opposition to the existing order and its grand narrative. These oppositions have no religious connotations, therefore it is not easy for the current discourse in power to appropriate them.

To summarize, I argue that a large number of readings of contemporary Persian fiction begin with the internalized assumption that the discourse in power has been totally discredited by the counter-narratives of prison reports, by the counter-narratives of prison literature, by literary counter discourses of new historiography, etc. Having been confronted by these narratives and discourses, the discourse in power has lost the battle of confronting signs and images and myths and even literary forms. Today, it is enough to say Sohrab, or to use irony, or to create a new image whose elements are not related to each other based on the traditional links, or to use a non-linear logic, or to ignore the idea of existence of a single source and center of power, or to ignore a message-oriented approach ... it is enough to use any of these elements for a narrative to be thought of (by the discourse in power) as being part of a counter-discourse. And Najdi uses all of these, not to be counter-discursive, but to construct a new architecture, with new and changing spaces.

Before describing these spaces, it should be noted that it would be a mistake to try to find a specific set of commonly-accepted intellectual/philosophical sources for Najdi's works. That is not to say that it is impossible to find links between the sensibility of Najdi's works and certain philosophical ideas, but such influences should be attributed to the employment of materials which have been used mainly in literary counter-discourses and counter-narratives. Indeed, in one sense, Najdi's works should be considered as one of the possible continuations of the most significant literary trajectory in Iran's twentieth century, defined by works of writers such as Hedayat, Chubak, Sadeqi, Golshiri, Baraheni, and Dowlatabadi. Therefore, some of the elements of counter- or anti-discursivity, internalized by this trajectory are obviously implied in Najdi's work, but the presence of the fantastic—that is to say the depiction of "unreal" scenes and spaces as possible realities[180]—clearly ignores the traditional strategies of the counter-discursive trajectory.

To understand this new strategy, we might think about a combination of Lefebvrian notion of recognizing, capturing, and living authentic literary moments—which, I maintain, could be created through literature—and Flaubert's view, which considered art and literature as a sanctuary in which to take refuge from the ordinary life of the everyday. From this point of view, these works represent the purest form of countering the discourses of power by being indifferent to it. This indirect rejection of collective and powerful discourses is materialized through the creation of literary spaces and environments in which one could live, not just in its Romantic-Realist (Flaubertian) version, but in a very tangible manner. This means that narrators of these stories (and probably also many readers of the stories) succeed in using these fluid, possible realities to create their unique, non-collective realities. That is why these texts unwittingly frighten the dominant discourses.

To describe these spaces we should begin from major structures of the story. In the case of "The Eve of the Slaying of Sohrab" this is not as easy task. We have three versions of the story which are not just rewrites of the same content but completely different and free adaptations of the *Shahnameh*'s "Rostam and Sohrab" story. In fact, they are completely different stories—different characters and different settings—whose only similarities are a few recurring narrative elements. The first version does not have a particular title; it is called "*Ravayat-e Avval-e Shab-e Sohrab Koshan*" (The First version of The Eve of the Slaying of Sohrab). The second one, "*Ravayat-e Dovvom-e Shab-e Sohrab Koshan*" (The Second Version of The Eve of the Slaying of Sohrab) has its own title: "*Keshtzar-e Ostokhanha-ye Sohrab*" (The Field Where Sohrab's Bones are Planted). The third one is simply called "*Shab-e Sohrab Koshan*" (The Eve of the Slaying of Sohrab). The first two versions were published in a collection entitled *Dastanha-ye Natamam-e Bijan Najdi* (Bijan Najdi's Unfinished Stories). Judging by certain interruptions in the narratives and, on one occasion, indecision about the name of a character, as well as minor editorial inconsistencies, they certainly need final retouching. But the general structure and narrative progression are quite developed, and they can actually be called almost finished. The third, the completely finished version of the story, was published in 1373/1994 in *Yuzpalangani keh ba man davideh-and* (Cheetahs Who Ran with Me), one of Najdi's most celebrated collections of short stories.

As mentioned before, these three versions are quite different. Contrary to the irrelevant note of the publisher of *Unfinished Stories* ... they are not to be read as "the mental efforts of the artist to complete the development of his creativity."[181] These completely different adaptations depict literary components which, having been carefully selected and developed, are then left alone to move freely and to create a variety of installations and unique spaces.

There is no trace of traditional "complication" and "resolution" in any of these three narratives. In all three, especially the third one, the links between different sections of stories are quite fragile—at times very thin. The main element of unity is the modern approach/reading to the mythic story of Rostam and Sohrab.

The first version is more bizarre than the other two. In the first part of the story, a young man with sunglasses and a small bag is standing on a road outside a city. A car stops in front of him, and he gets in. This is the only "ordinary" part of the story. The young man's name is "Braseh" which undoubtedly has been created through rearrangement of the letters in the name Sohrab.[182] Shortly after the car moves away, a surreal environment is described in which the car is surrounded by birds who hit themselves against the windshields and body; the car is soon covered with blood and bloody wings and feathers. Strangely, it seems that this event had been foreseen by Braseh, who seems quite calm and unfazed. In fact, the driver has completely lost control, and Braseh is handling the situation. After the car stops, the driver gets out, and, while using an empty engine-oil can to pour water from the nearby river on the radiator, talks to the car:

> A hot steam ran towards the man's face. He said: "What is it, old man? You have really heated up! … You're feeling better now."
> With the palm of his hand he caressed the fender.
> "It is burning here, isn't it?"
> Over the battery, the dried-up acid had turned moldy.
> "You have lost all your hair."[183]

The personification of the car continues: "The man sat on the fender. He hooked his hands together and stared at the smoke-colored end of the road and listened to the breathing of the car."[184] And then he asks Braseh a strange question: "Last night you had defeated him. Do you know this?"[185] And after Braseh's affirmative answer, he asks: "Then why do you want to start again?" As he is walking towards the Porsche, Braseh replies: "Because this is how it is written."[186]

The similar transliteration of Braseh and Sohrab and these few lines are not sufficient to remind the reader of Ferdowsi's story of Rostam and Sohrab, but when the next paragraph of the story begins with the description of the painting of Rostam and Sohrab in a coffeehouse, a plausible reading of the short conversation between the driver and Braseh begins to take shape.

Recounting the battle of Rostam and Sohrab, the battle of a father and a son who face each other without knowing about their relationship, Ferdowsi describes Rostam, the father, as old, somewhat in the way the driver describes the Porsche; and Sohrab, the son, as fresh, strong, and fearless. Their battle lasts two days. The first day, after they break their swords and spears, they begin wrestling, and Sohrab defeats Rostam and sits on his chest to cut off his head. Rostam tricks the young hero by telling him that the custom is that one should defeat his opponent twice before killing him; Sohrab accepts this and goes back to his camp, promising to continue the battle the following day.

That night, while the young hero is celebrating, the old hero, tired, wounded, and desperate, goes to his camp and tries to think of a solution for the second day of the battle. The story is well-known. The following day, Rostam succeeds in placing Sohrab's back on the ground for a very short period of time and uses the opportunity to swiftly cut Sohrab's side with his dagger and kills him. It is noteworthy that in another famous story from the *Shahnameh*, the story of Rostam and Esfandiyar—the Iranian mythological counterpart of Achilles—once again, the first day of battle ends with Rostam being wounded, covered in blood and both himself and his horse being targeted and hit many times by Esfandiyar's arrows, which certainly included birds' feathers to make them fly better. All that said, I believe it would be a mistake to try to derive a very neat and particular meaning from the identification between Rostam and the Porsche. This is one of Najdi's schemes to show the presence of myths in the ordinary and even mundane spaces of everyday life. And, as mentioned before, this blending of myths with contemporary realities is the main ingredient on the backdrop of these three narratives.

One of the themes transferred from the first version to the next two is the theme of recreation of the story of Rostam and Sohrab. In the second segment of the first version, there is mention of a painting which is nailed to the wall of a coffeehouse. The painting interacts with the outside world in a most direct manner.

> Rostam went and sat on a painting whose four corners had been nailed to the wall. There, part of the head and shoulder of Sohrab, who had a seashell-colored face, were on his knees.[187]

In the second version, this representation, which aims once again to blend myths with everyday reality, is achieved through much more traditional means. A grade-school teacher in a village wants to put together a school play based on the story of Rostam and Sohrab. He asks two of his students to play the two roles. The narrative line of this story is constructed based on the reaction of these two and their family members, and on their preparation for the play. Usage of this approach is very much reminiscent of many of Beyzai's post-revolution screenplays—especially those which retell stories from the *Shahnameh*. Of those, *Siyavash-Khani* (Performing the Epic of Siyavash) has a particular affinity with the second version of Najdi's story, in that the blending of myths and everyday reality is materialized through focusing on the reactions of those ordinary people who are supposed to perform the story, as well as on the elements of the environment in which the play/story is going to be performed. However, the difference is that Beyzai follows this strategy so far that the individuals who are going to play the parts internalize their mythic counterparts to the point where it is possible for the tragic story to actually take place. Or perhaps they have always had those mythic elements inside them, and this performance is just an opportunity for them to reveal their existence.[188] In this screenplay/play we read that a group of performers have

traveled to a village and they are trying to find necessary characters to perform the Siyavash-Khani. They do that every year, and every year the first
obstacle is that they cannot find willing members of the community to play
the roles of negative characters. For them, this is not a story; the roles they are
playing represent what they are. This process reaches its apogee when they
decide to choose someone to play Siyavash. They ask seven 15-year-old boys
to place their hands over a fire and the one whose hand does not burn will be
Siyavash. This, of course, refers to the test of fire which is part of the original
story. Only Siyavash, who is pure, can go through the fire without being
harmed.

In the second version of "The Eve of the Slaying of Sohrab," however, the
relationship between contemporary elements and myths remains on the level
of a narrative line which stays in the background. I will return to this point
later.

In the third version of the story, the narrative begins with a *pardeh-khan*[189]
(storyteller), and the motif of the pardeh is introduced from the very beginning.

> The canvas painting was so large that the Seyyed could hang it between
> two aspen trees outside the village square on a hill. He tied the ropes
> of the two upper edges of the canvas to the branches, and on the lower
> edges, on the ground, he set two cobblestones. A soft breeze which was
> walking in the village and through the trees was slowly waving the faded
> picture of Esfandiyar on the canvas. On the same side of the canvas
> which was attached to the tree was Rostam's hand and his dagger raised
> as high as a blade of grass. The Seyyed told Rostam: "Wait for people to
> come."[190]

In this description, as well as the one from the painting of the first version,
the distance between literary and non-literary realities is unmistakably
removed. In the first version, Rostam walks and climbs on the painting, and
in the third version the storyteller directly speaks to the image of Rostam
who, as we shall see, acts as a live human being. Here, this technique is one of
the early indications that efforts are going to be made to change the myth.
While in the second version this objective is indirectly implied, in the first and
the third versions it is directly mentioned.

This objective should be considered as symbolizing attempts to destabilize
established narratives which, by extension, could potentially undermine
dominant discourses. From this point of view, this component of the story has
a kinship with Baraheni's attempt to rewrite history mainly by giving voice to
the voiceless. In Najdi's case, too, rewriting myths is accomplished through
the revealing of narratives which are usually ignored in traditional mythological
narration. In fact, in all his versions of the myth of Rostam and Sohrab,
Najdi has developed a meta-narrative layer which contains reflections of the
main characters of the story, and even of Ferdowsi about this tragedy. Again,
in the first and the third versions of "The Eve of the Slaying of Sohrab," the

process of forming this layer is easily recognizable. Ferdowsi, Rostam, Sohrab, as well as mythic characters from other *Shahnameh* stories, dismiss the conventions and diachronically step into the *univers romanesque* and react to the events of the story.

The third version begins with the description of a painting of the "Rostam and Sohrab" story, the gathering of the people of a village in Northern Iran, and then the storyteller's recounting of the tragedy. As is customary in *pardeh-khani*, the storyteller tells half of the story and then stops and collects money from people who are enthusiastically waiting to hear the end, promising that he will finish the story the following day. In the audience there is a young boy, Morteza, who is deaf and mute. As far as the unifying narrative line of the story is concerned, he is the main character. This empowerment of a mute who could certainly be identified with Sohrab in terms of his powerlessness, also symbolizes the process of giving voice to the voiceless. Morteza goes to the coffeehouse where the storyteller is spending the night and tries to take the painting from him to prevent him from finishing the tragedy the next day, thus stopping the mythic death of Sohrab. The storyteller and Morteza engage in a confrontation; a kerosene lamp falls; the coffeehouse goes up in flames, and both the storyteller and Morteza/Sohrab die. But the painting remains. At this point, suddenly the mythic characters and their poet, who had apparently hoped that the myth would be changed, enter the fiction's universe.

> When one of the beams of the ceiling fell down, Ferdowsi turned his head and told his generals: "Go put out the fire!"
>
> Without pulling the spear from his eye, Esfandiyar mounted his horse.[191] With the dagger thrust between his ribs, Sohrab saddled his horse and rode around the pool so many times until Siyavash looked away from the blood poured under his feet[192] and emerged, in front of his horse, from the darkness behind the stairs of Tus. They all waited for the old man. As soon as Rostam arrived, his white hair receding to the middle of his head and with uncombed beard, they all dismounted.
>
> Rostam left his fatigue on the stirrups of his horse. They helped the old man to mount. On this side of Ararat, they tethered their horses to the aspen trees and removed their armor from their bodies and placed it on the saddles. They all hung their footwear from the stirrups and went inside the coffeehouse naked.[193]

There is a clear-cut difference between Baraheni-type works and Najdi-type works. Baraheni expresses ambitious aims which, I maintain, represent a dominant trend of a period of contemporary Persian literature. Proponents of this trend want to solve tangible social problems through literature. In these works, rewriting history is done to capture and portray the most fundamental social, political and cultural characteristics of Iran's contemporary society and to offer suggestions to create fundamental change, or at least to improve social conditions. Such vast and ambitious goals are not seen in Najdi-type works. To begin with, in these works, there are very few signs which would indicate the narrator's concern about a particular geography. There is also no sign of political and/or ideological aspirations. There is no effort to capture and present the cultural essence of a particular time and place, and obviously there is no attempt to suggest solutions either. In fact, elements which could clearly describe the agreement with or opposition to different discourses have not been developed at all. All these are reflected in the literary characteristics of the work. The processes of characterization and character development are largely non-existent. The story has a reasonable progression, but clearly there is no linear logic which would lead to a defined ending. The movement/progression of the story is produced mostly through the reader's experiencing different spaces; spaces which effectively ignore dominant discourses even if some of their components are informed by discursive confrontations. This fact directs readings of Najdi-type works towards—and based on—experiencing almost independent environments in which the relationships between their components are not following any collectively-accepted logic. These relationships take shape based on the individual and extraordinary outlook of the author/narrator to his objective and subjective surroundings.

I use the phrase "almost independent" to reiterate that in Najdi's stories we can still see markers indentifying counter-discourses; these markers are significant in setting the context within which those spaces are created. The important point is that these markers do not form well-known narratives of counter-discourses, and in fact there is no sign of any traditional approach to narration. The central component of the stories are their descriptions which construct an uncontrollable universe; descriptions that underline attempts to reject the unchangeability of grand narratives and suggest possible worlds and realities where unusual interactions between their elements are not only possible but quite ordinary and expected.

In the third version of the story, since the protagonist is deaf and mute, these "unusual" interactions seem even more natural. In one of the early parts of the story, when Seyyed—the storyteller—is preparing to begin, we read about Morteza:

> Morteza opened a path through the men who were stretching their heads toward the painting. He moved away from the people so that he could walk back to the veranda of his home and sit on the edge of the veranda and listen to the quiet of the barking of a dog who was running in the yard, so that he could go to the coffeehouse and sit on a bench and look at the sound of the water inside the glass in front of him and ... [194]

Using non-standard linguistic and semantic combinations such as "looking at the sound of water" and "listening to the quiet of the barking of a dog" is quite similar to the synesthesia technique which became particularly fashionable in Persian literature with the rise of *She'r-e now* (New Poetry). Defining elements of the surrounding environment with irregular, extraordinary attributes rejects the established function of these elements. To accomplish this task, Najdi also relies on heavy usage of oxymoron and paradox to the point where they could be considered among the dominant techniques in his works. Once again, because of the physical limitations of its main character, the final version of "The Eve of the Slaying of Sohrab" provides the best conditions for the author to use these techniques and to create unique spaces. Let us review some of them. When Seyyed, the storyteller, describes the painting, Morteza who cannot hear, "pulled his mother's sleeve and by closing and opening his eyes said: What has happened? Mother showed him the canvas and with her fingers and quiet lips said: That father and son want to kill each other."[195] In the evening when they arrive home, and mother performs ablution, "Morteza's mother showed him the sound of the *azan*."[196] ... "The faces of the village men looked as if they were expecting bad news."[197] ... "Raindrops were soft, like morning which came from far away and poured on the shingles, like his mother's dress."[198] These examples and many similar ones which are found throughout the second and third versions of "The Eve of the Slaying of Sohrab" are early indications of situations where the relationships between different elements are not defined based on established functions of these elements. In such situations: "a narrow alley [goes] along the mooing of the cows,"[199] "the darkness [is poured] on the darkness of the well,"[200] "the mild taste of salt coming from the Caspian [fills] the day,"[201] "Rostam [climbs] up and [sits] on the painting whose four corners are nailed to the wall."[202] "The children [pull] the sand up to their knees and made the school's courtyard as naked as it usually [is] in summer."[203] ... "An hour later ... they [are] returning to their homes through quiet alleyways and palm trees and [are] running like the sweet smell of dates,"[204] and finally, "At noon, when children left, the classrooms left their doors open so that they would be filled up with ordinary Fridays and so that they could blow away the scent of children's bodies towards the broken windows."[205]

These are a few randomly selected descriptions which cover most of the pages of the second and third versions of "The Eve of the Slaying of Sohrab," and allocation of such a vast textual space is a clear indication of the position and significance of these spaces in the story. In other words, the narrative characteristics of "The Eve of the Slaying of Sohrab" should be considered elements which serve to construct such spaces; they are not mimetic representations of the so-called everyday reality. At the same time, and because of the presence of conventional storytelling components, the concept of fragmentation is not an appropriate concept to describe the narrative style of the story. These spaces are somewhat related, yet they should be experienced as autonomous—and not independent—spaces. Indeed, literary devices and techniques such as synesthesia, oxymoron, and paradox are used by the narrator to create this autonomy and unconventional interactions between elements of these spaces to the point where it makes perfect fictional sense to say: "the Sunday[206] courtyard which was wiggling with children."[207]

Through these phrases and out-of-the-ordinary linguistic installations, a particular agency for the components of the surrounding environment is defined which includes the consistent and exaggerated personification of things and concepts. This technique is the most effective method to reject the sources of discourses which in their grand narratives emphasize the traditional significance and functions of these elements. The grand narratives of dominant, ideological discourses, which cannot tolerate the slightest Otherness, are thus countered and indeed threatened by this method which simply points to the possibility of rearranging the position and relations of constituting elements of the environment.

The narrator of "The Eve of the Slaying of Sohrab," however, oblivious to this effect, is simply trying to complete the structure of these autonomous places, and along this direction, in addition to rejecting the traditional interactions between elements of the surrounding environment, attempts to interrupt time and space, these two major constituents of continuum. In different segments of the first and third versions, Ferdowsi and other characters of the *Shahnameh* suddenly appear in various scenes without undermining the logic of the fiction. Indeed, by insisting on his goal to create extraordinary relationships among the elements of the environment, as well as the use of a mythic background, the author/narrator has successfully justified the atemporal presence of these characters.

From the viewpoint of the narrative line, the presence of most of these characters serves to achieve the ultimate goal of changing the mythic events of the story of Rostam and Sohrab. In the first version, towards the end of the story, after Rostam climbs up the painting so that he could once again perform his eternal role, he meditates:

> Why did I have to kill Braseh? For centuries Braseh and I lived in paintings and in (the sounds of) *naqqalis*[208] which split the darkness with their battle-axes so that they could show Braseh approaching the battlefield.
>
> Braseh and I fell to the ground for hundreds of years.
>
> And I, a thousand times, a thousand times, threw the weight of my hand, my dagger and my body on him and spilled his blood without taking his immortality; and always next to him I cried tears of blood.
>
> Braseh and I were your honor and dignity; the dignity of your water, and wheat and earth. And now we die; we die now.
>
> While leaving the coffeehouse, Rostam stood in the frame of the door, floating in the grey and cold light of the day, and turned his face toward the wall. There was nothing on the painting.[209]

And at the end of the final version of "The Eve of the Slaying of Sohrab," too, after Morteza's confrontation with Seyyed to prevent the killing of Sohrab and after the coffeehouse starts burning, people arrive and:

> They stood around the heated scent of the tiles and the sound of the burning of the thatched roofs. When one of the beams of the ceiling

fell down, Ferdowsi turned his head and told his generals: "Go put out the fire!"

Without pulling the spear from his eye, Esfandiyar mounted his horse. With the dagger thrust between his ribs, Sohrab saddled his horse and rode around the pool so many times until Siyavash looked away from the blood poured under his feet and emerged, in front of his horse, from the darkness behind the stairs of Tus. They all waited for the old man. As soon as Rostam arrived, his white hair receding to the middle of his head and with uncombed beard, they all dismounted.[210]

Both Seyyed and Morteza perish, but the painting is not burned.

Over a slow rain, the night struck itself against the Azan. The generals wore their armor over the wet nakedness of their skin. The old man put the painting around the neck of his horse. Riding their horses all the way to Tus, they did not look back, and they wept.[211]

It is quite possible to construct a general reading of these stories based on the idea of symbolic interpretation of ideas such as infanticide and its relation to patriarchy, etc. Such a reading, before anything else, is not at all compatible with the powerful scene at the end of the second version of the story. The last scene of "The Field Where Sohrab's Bones Are Planted" is a description of the last preparations for the school play based on the story of Rostam and Sohrab, whose main characters are played by Bahador as Rostam and Aram as Sohrab; and, just as expected from Najdi, this becomes an excuse to create slightly-related, fluid, autonomous spaces whose contents are not at all related to the supposed main point.

Outside school, Uncle Tarak repeated again: "Remember, don't raise Aram over your head the very first minute and throw him like ... Do you understand?"

Bahador promised yet again.

Bahador's mother had gone to school before them, and they led her, in her white dress, to the tall seat of Rostam's mother.

As soon as Rostam's mother sat on the chair she tried to hide her nails which she had trimmed very short under the tassels of her long scarf. She did not even remember the crooked joints of her fingers. Until that day she had ... the wet diapers of all four daughters of the mayor and the pleated pajamas of the sons ... who suddenly disappeared like columns of sand during last winter's draft of soldiers ... On that Friday afternoon, Bahador's mother really wanted to be as far away from the washtub and water so that scattered soap foam couldn't wet her eyes. When the sound of drums came from far away, the children pulled the sand up to their knees and made the school's courtyard as naked as it usually was in the summer.

Even the women who squatted behind the row of chairs ran as they did during the days of Ashura[212] so that the music of drums wouldn't feel lonely, like a stranger going through the alleyway without being welcomed.[213]

Readings of these stories which focus on the idea of rewriting the *Shahnameh*'s "Rostam and Sohrab" will have to ignore many such sequences as being gratuitous. But if the reading emphasizes the autonomous nature of these spaces, then all these seemingly unrelated descriptive sequences, unusual phraseology and bypassing of the common approaches to time and space emerge as indispensable pieces of a profoundly personal/individual version of the author/narrator's universe, and, I maintain, the most rewarding readings of these stories are possible only by passing through and experiencing these autonomous environments.

The presence of these environments is reminiscent of one of the most important features of Persian classical poetry, especially as it is reflected in the ghazals of Hafez. In his ghazals, too, the reader experiences autonomous spaces which are almost never connected to each other through a progressing narrative. In many of his ghazals, the autonomy, and even independence, of these spaces and their fluid, unstable position in the context of the ghazal's narrative reaches a point that one could easily rearrange the order of verses without necessarily harming the poem. There is another often-cited point about Hafez's poetry which could be useful in reading Najdi's stories. Perhaps the most important reason for which Hafez is considered the unquestionable master of the Persian ghazal is that he was fortunate enough to come at the end of an evolutionary process in Persian classical poetry which had made significant progress, both technical and conceptual, during different stages of its evolution. His poems are written and indeed must be read with close attention to this background. As a matter of fact, it is practically impossible to relate to Hafez without familiarity with preceding literary scenes, techniques, narratives, and discourses. In the case of Najdi's works, and many other non-discursive works, lack of familiarity with the trajectory of modern Persian fiction has resulted mostly in ignoring the achievements of the modernist trend in Persian fiction. Najdi's literary spaces must be read with close attention to a background which is defined through the evolution of modern discourses, narratives, counter-discourses, and counter-narratives of Persian literature.

To be more specific and to summarize: from prison reports to prison litera-ture, to the rewriting of history and myths, and to giving voice to the voiceless, the trajectory of Persian literary discourse, especially after the 1979 Revolution, has developed imaginaries which counter the dominant dis-courses. More importantly, this trajectory has emphasized the usage of certain literary devices and techniques, and at times has created new ones which are identified with these imaginaries. It is necessary to know these devices and characteristics to be able to relate to non-discursive works such as Najdi's, and indeed, to many other "inaccessible" works of modern Persian fiction. Additionally, it should be noted that characteristics of this trajectory have taken shape in the larger context of the Persian literary tradition, one of whose main features, from the golden age of Persian poetry until today, is defined through its positionality in regard to the confrontations of discourses and counter-discourses.

Identifying these devices and techniques is achieved partly through an analysis of the reaction of the discourse in power. Previously I referred to a famous example of such reactions using *Adabiyat-e Dastani* and its propagandist approach and emphasis on defining "whoever, and whatever, is not with us is against us." This approach effectively disables the discourse in power to appropriate counter-discursive and non-discursive literary achievements, for example, literary spaces. Now, if we take into account the fact that the process of discrediting the discourse in power has basically been completed, then the vast importance of counter-discursive or non-discursive works could be understood. In other words, the discourse in power has lost the battle of controlling signs and codes and even forms of literary expressions. And it is worth repeating that "today, it is enough to employ pre-Islamic myths and mythic characters such as Sohrab, to use irony, to create a new image whose elements are not related to each other based on the traditional links, to use a non-linear logic, to refute the idea of one single source and center of power, to ignore a message-oriented approach, for a narrative to be considered as being part of a counter discourse."

Najdi takes advantage of all these facts, not to be counter-discursive but to erect new architectures and spaces which are not based on the specifications, or the needs of the discourse in power. The narrator of Najdi's stories, like those of Mandanipur, Julai, Fadainia, Bahar, and many others, is building a real world to live in. In this statement the word "real" is not to imply the old idea of using literature to escape reality. Spaces built in these works are real, meaning they occupy a substantial area of the narrator's, and perhaps the readers', inner and outer life. Using new codes and signs different from the codes and signs which belong to semantic systems of dominant discourses, or employing the old ones in a novel way, these spaces take shape differently and are defined differently. The ensemble created from these signs, codes, spaces, and from interactions among them, is in fact a story of what is happening in Iran; a story which is told in many unique, personal, and individualized languages.

Notes

1 To read more about this very old, yet still quite relevant debate, see Fredric Jameson's "Third-World Literature in the Era of Multinational Capitalism," where he argues for the idea of Third-World literature as national allegory. There have been many counter-arguments including Aijaz Ahmad's "Jameson's Rhetoric of Otherness and the 'National Allegory.'"
2 Erickson, *Islam and Postcolonial Narrative*, p. 12
3 Ibid.
4 Ibid., p. 13.

5 Rob Shields, "Henri Lefebvre," in *Profiles in Contemporary Social Theory*, eds Anthony Elliott and Bryan Turner, London: Sage Publications, 2001, p. 228.

6 Ibid.

7 Sadeq Chubak, *Cheragh-e Akhar* (The Last Alms), Tehran: Javidan, 1976 (2nd edn), p. 77.

8 Ibid.

9 To read more about the characteristics of Sadeq Chubak's style, see M. R. Ghanoonparvar's *Reading Chubak* (especially the Introduction), and Reza Baraheni's "Naqd-e Qesseh" (The Critique of Story), in *Jonun-e Neveshtan* (The Madness of Writing).

10 Chubak was somewhat literarily obsessed with the idea of creating interpretable images, and at times he repeated/polished similar images in different works. In Chubak's "*Arusak-e Forushi*" (A Doll for Sale), we find an amazingly similar image to the one in "The Hubcap Stealer":

> Leaning against the wall in the street, people had gathered around something. It was a little boy, crumpled and covered with snow. A few coins around him were scattered on the snow. A snow-covered doll with laughing face and closed eyes was lying next to him, and people were watching.

Quoted from Hosein Payandeh's *Dastan-e Kutah dar Iran* (Short Story in Iran), vol. 1, Tehran: Nilufar, 2010, p. 324.

11 Chubak, *The Last Alms*, p. 77.

12 Ibid., p. 80

13 Ibid., p. 79.

14 Ibid.

15 Ahmad Shamlu, "Negah Kon" (Look), in *Havay-e Tazeh* (Fresh Air), in *Collected Poems, vol. 1*, (1940–1964), Giessen: Kanun-e Entesharati va Farhangi-ye Bamdad, 1988, pp. 246–251.

16 Mehdi Akhavan-Sales. *Andisheh va Honar* (Thought and Art), special issue about A. Bamdad [Ahmad Shamlu], no. 2, 1964. Quoted from *Shenakht Nameh-ye Shamlu* (Knowing Shamlu), ed. Javad Mojabi, Tehran: Qatreh, 1998, p. 243.

17 Ibid., my emphasis.

18 Ibid., my emphasis.

19 Ibid.

20 Marjan Riahi, "After a Kiss", published in *Another Sea, Another Shore: Persian Stories of Migration*, edited and translated by Shouleh Vatanabadi and Mohammad Mehdi Khorrami, Northampton, MA: Interlink, 2004, p. 2.

21 Riahi, "After a Kiss," pp. 2–3.

22 For example, see Marjan Riahi's collection of short stories *Eshareh-ha* (Suggestions), Tehran: Mashianeh, 1999.

23 Irving Howe, *Decline of the New*, New York: Harcourt, Brace & World, 1970, p. 5, cited from the German poet Gottfried Benn.

24 In *Dastan-e Kutah dar Iran* (Short Story in Iran), Hosein Payandeh basically advocates the same argument that Persian modernist fiction has gone through its particular evolutionary process. He further specifies that Persian classical poetry has greatly influenced modern short Persian fiction. I believe his argument could easily be applied to the works of many recent Iranian writers such as Marjan Riahi. To read more about Payandeh's take on Persian modernist writing, see his Introduction to *Short Story in Iran, vol. 2 (Modern Stories)*, Tehran: Nilufar, 2010.

25 Riahi, "After a Kiss," p. 3.

26 Tahereh Alavi's "Halat-e Avval" (Original Position) was published in the collection *Zendegi-ye man dar Seshanbeh-ha Ettefaq Mi-oftad* (My Life Happens on

Tuesdays), Tehran: Qasideh-sara, 1380/2001. The translation of this story is included in *Another Sea, Another Shore: Persian Stories of Migration.*

27 Alavi, "Original Position," p. 124.

28 In addition to spaces such as planes or airports which invoke rather directly the notion of transition, we must also take into account the genre of science fiction which makes use of many transitional spaces. In Persian literature, this genre has never been popular, but the examination of the very few science-fiction stories which have been produced could add another dimension to the usage of such spaces.

29 Hasan Mahmudi, *Khun-e Abi bar Zamin-e Namnak: dar Naqd va Mo'arrefi-ye Bahram Sadeqi* (Blue Blood on Damp Ground: Critiquing and Introducing Bahram Sadeqi), Tehran: Asa, 1998, p. 9.

30 *Yalda* is the longest night of the year. Celebrating this occasion is an ancient Iranian custom.

31 Bahram Sadeqi, "*Sarasar Hadeseh*" (Action-Packed), in *Sangar va Qomqomeh-ha-ye Khali* (The Trench and the Empty Canteens) Tehran: Ketab-e Zaman, 1349/1970, p. 128. This story has been translated by me and has been published in a collection of short stories titled *Sohrab's Wars: Counter-Discourses of Contemporary Persian Fiction*, Costa Mesa, CA: Mazda, 2008.

32 Ibid.

33 Ibid., pp. 129, 130.

34 Ibid., p. 132.

35 I believe one of the reasons for Sadeqi's absence in literary mentality of other geographies—in terms of their interaction with Persian modernist writing—is that relating to Sadeqi's work requires very high level of linguistic skills. In particular it is necessary to be familiar with clichés representing prevalent discourses in Iran so that one could understand Sadeqi's tone.

36 Sadeqi, "Action-Packed," p. 135.

37 Azar Nafisi makes a similar observation about Bahram Sadeqi's use of a tone similar to that of a feuilleton. See Azar Nafisi, "Andar Naqsh-e Bazi dar Dastan: Bar-dashti az 'Aqa-ye Nevisandeh Tazeh-kar Ast'" ("About the role of playing in story: A Reading of 'Mr. Writer is a Novice'"), *Kelk* (*Pen*), no. 5, 1369/1990, pp. 31–43. See: www.madomeh.com/1391/10/18/22/ (accessed May 5, 2014). In Sadeqi's work, this tone, or style of narration, is used as part of the ironizing process.

38 Sadeqi, "Action-Packed," p. 133.

39 Ibid., p. 144

40 In "Honar-e Dastan Nevisi-ye Bahram Sadeqi" ("Bahram Sadeqi's Art of Story Telling"), *Kelk* (*Pen*), nos 32 and 33, 1371/1993, pp. 113–119, Gholam-Hosein Sa'edi underlines the importance of ambience and context in Sadeqi's work. He writes: "In Bahram Sadeqi's work, events are not important at all. Disputes are meaningless and nil. Confrontations result in almost nothing. What is important is ambience." See http://parah.blogsky.com/1391/09/04/post-194/ (accessed May 5, 2014).

41 In Shi'i Islam, the title Hojjat al-Islam is given to seminary students who have completed the first major level of their studies. This title is below the rank of Ayatollah.

42 Sadeqi, "Action-Packed," p. 143.

43 Ibid., p. 156.

44 Ibid.

45 Ibid., p. 157.

46 Ibid.

47 What I intend to convey from the phrase "mass society" is the definition that Irving Howe has offered in "Mass Society and Postmodern Fiction." This essay is part of his *Decline of the New.*

> By the mass society we mean a relatively comfortable, half-welfare and half-garrison society in which the population grows passive, indifferent, and atomized; in which traditional loyalties, ties, and associations become lax or dissolve entirely; in which coherent publics based on definite interests and opinions gradually fall apart; and in which man becomes a consumer, himself mass-produced like the products, diversions, and values that he absorbs.
>
> Howe (1970, p. 196)

There is an uncanny similarity between Howe's understanding of mass society and Debord's description of the Society of the Spectacle. And both writers wrote these descriptions in the latter part of the 1960s.

48 To read more about these categories and their subsequent developments, in addition to Lefebvre's works on *Critique de la vie quotidienne*, consult Rob Shields' and Edward Soja's works on Lefebvre, which include subsequent developments of these categories as well as critiques of them.

49 As a point of departure to read more about this topic, see "Unitary Urbanism at the End of the 1950s," an unattributed article, Translated by Paul Hammond and published in *Internationale Situationniste* #3, 1959. See www.cddc.vt.edu/sionline/si/unitary.html (accessed May 5, 2014).

50 Edward Soja, *Third Space*, Oxford: Blackwell, 2000, p. 11.

51 Rob Shields, "Henri Lefebvre," in *Profiles in Contemporary Social Theory*, eds Anthony Elliot and Bryan Turner, London: Sage Publications, 2001.

52 Mohammad Asef Soltanzadeh, "Damad-e Kabol" (The Bridegroom of Kabul), in *Dar Goriz Gom Mishavim* (We Disappear in Flight), Tehran: Agah, 2000, pp. 113, 114. The English translation of this story has been published in *Sohrab's Wars*, trans. and ed. Mohammad Mehdi Khorrami, Costa Mesa, CA: Mazda, 2008.

53 The word *Shah* means king; *Shah* or *Shah Damad* (the word *damad* means bridegroom), is used to refer to the bridegroom. *Vala* has many meanings including esteemed and honorable. It could also be a variation of *Bala* (equal). The phrase *Shah Vala or Shah Bala* is used to refer to the best man.

54 Soltanzadeh, "The Bridegroom of Kabul," pp. 127, 128.

55 Mazar is short for Mazar-e Sharif, a city in Afghanistan. This city is a pilgrimage destination for Shi'is because many of them believe that Ali, the first Imam, is buried there.

56 Soltanzadeh, " .. to Mazar," also published in *Dar Goriz Gom Mishavim* (We Disappear in Flight), p. 154.

57 Ibid.

58 A term used usually for religious leaders.

59 Apparently, one of the ways to measure whether the beard is long enough or not is to grab the beard from under the chin and it should be long enough to cover the width of the palm.

60 Soltanzadeh, "... to Mazar," pp. 158–159.

61 Vladimir Nabokov, *Lectures on Russian Literature*, New York: Mariner Books, 2002, p. 103.

62 Ibid.

63 Nabokov actually suggests a distinction between "sentimental" and "sensitive." Ibid.

64 Shahriyar Mandanipur, "*Chakavak-e Aseman Kharash*" (The Skyscraping Lark) published in *Abi-ye Mavara'e Behar* (The Blue Beyond the Seas), Tehran: Markaz, 1382/2003, p. 1.

65 Ibid., p. 11.

66 Ibid., pp. 22–23.

67 Ibid., pp. 24–25.

68 Of course the fact that the theories of the Situationists could be used in artistic realms should not come as a surprise because this movement was defined and developed not only based on the existing political and social critique of the capitalist society but on primarily artistic movements such as Surrealism, Dadaism, and Lettrism.

69 In the business world this is quite common; major companies develop products which are supposed to compete with their main products. This practice basically preempts the competition.

70 Tahereh Alavi, "*Mesl-e Hamisheh*" (As Always) was published in the collection *Zendegi-ye man dar Seshanbeh-ha Ettefaq Mi-oftad* (My Life Happens on Tuesdays), Tehran: Qasideh-sara, 1380/2001.

71 The manteau is a long dress which women wear with a scarf and pants to cover themselves from top to bottom. After the 1979 Revolution, The Islamic Republic required women to wear Islamic Hijab.

72 Alavi, "As Always," pp. 47, 48.

73 Ibid., p. 51.

74 Guy Debord, "Perspectives for Conscious Changes in Everyday Life" (1961), Berkeley, CA: Bureau for Public Secrets, www.bopsecrets.org/SI/6.everyday.htm (accessed May 5, 2014).

75 Ibid.

76 Raoul Vaneigem, *Le Livre des plaisirs* (The Book of Pleasures), Paris: Éditions Encre, 1979. p. 27. "Il n'y aura pas d'émancipation du prolétariat sans émancipation réelle des plaisirs."

77 Our central idea is that of the construction of situations, that is to say, the concrete construction of momentary ambiences of life and their transformation into a superior passional quality. We must develop a methodical intervention based on the complex factors of two components in perpetual interaction: the material environment of life and the comportments which it gives rise to and which radically transform it.

   Guy E. Debord, "Report on the Construction of Situations" (1957), www.bopse crets.org/SI/report.htm (accessed May 5, 2014).

78 Forugh Farrokhzad, *Remembering the Flight: Twenty Poems by Forugh Farrokhzad*, tr. Ahmad Karimi-Hakkak, Port Coquitlam, BC: Nik publishers, 1997, p. 7.

79 Mohammad Hoquqi (ed.), *She'r-e Zaman-e ma (4): Forugh Farrokhzād* (The Poetry of Our Time (4): Forugh Farrokhzad), Tehran: Negah, 1372/1993.

80 Shahriyar expressed this opinion in his interview with Naser Hariri. Quoted from Mohammad Hoquqi's *The Poetry of Our Time (4): Forugh Farrokhzad*, p. 36, n. 1.

81 Farrokhzad, *Remembering the Flight*, pp. 61–63.

82 Mohammad Mehdi Khorrami, "The Aesthetics of Lone Moments in the Poetry of Forugh Farrokhzad," in *Iranian Languages and Culture: Essays in Honor of Gernot Ludwig Windfuhr*, eds Behrad Aghaei and M. R. Ghanoonparvar. Costa Mesa, CA: Mazda, 2012.

83 Farrokhzad, *Remembering the Flight*, p. 93.

84 Naser Hariri, *Goft-o Shenud-i ba Ahmad Shamlu, Doktor Reza Baraheni* (A Conversation with Ahmad Shamlu, Doctor Reza Baraheni), Babol: Ketabsaray-e Babol, 1365 (1986), p. 48.

85 Quoted from Culler's *The Literary in Theory*, p. 107.

86 Ibid., p. 106.

87 Jacques Rancière, *The Politics of Literature*, Cambridge: Polity Press, 2011, p. 31. This book was first published in French in 2006.

88 Culler, *The Literary in Theory*, p. 229. Both Rancière and Culler rely on Barthes' *The Rustle of Language* to summarize the concept of "The Reality Effect" in a very similar manner.

89 To read more about Reza Ghassemi's take on *"jarian goriz"* writers, see www. rezaghassemi.com/gariangoriz.htm (accessed May 5, 2014).

90 Jonathan Culler, *Structuralist Poetics*, Ithaca, NY: Cornell University Press, 1997, p. viii.

91 To read more about the notion of inaccessibility in Southern literary tradition, see Mohammad Mehdi Khorrami, "The Image of Modern Persian Fiction in the Broken Mirror of Neo-Orientalism," in *Oriental Languages in Translation*, vol. 3, Cracow: Polish Academy of Science Press, 2008.

92 *Tarikh-e Sistan*, Bahar Edition, pp. 7–8, quoted from Shafi'i Kadkani's *Sovar-e Khial dar She'r-e Farsi* (Imagery in Persian Poetry), p. 239.

93 Shafi'i Kadkani, *Imagery in Persian Poetry*, p. 480.

94 Mohammad Fotuhi, *Naqd-e Khial: Naqd-e Adabi dar Sabk-e Hendi* (The Critique of Imagination: Literary Criticism in Indian Style), Tehran: Sokhan, 2nd edn, 2006, p. 72.

95 To find examples one needs only to look at the rather long list of those who identify themselves with the Reformist trend (especially strengthened after the June 2009 Presidential election). This list includes people such as Abdolkarim Soroush, Abbas Abdi, Mohsen Kadivar, Mohammad Reza Khatami, Hashem Aqajari, Mir Hosein Musavi, Mehdi Karrubi, and Hosein Ali Montazeri, almost all of whom at some point were either actively involved in forming some of the most reprehensible aspects of the Islamic Republic or were guilty of begin approvingly silent—while in positions of power—in regard to the crimes commited by the regime.

96 For a more detailed discussion on Mostafa Mastur's case, refer to Chapter 2 of this study.

97 See http://nagdonazar.blogfa.com/post-30.aspx (accessed May 5, 2014).

98 The term "values writers," and by extension, "values books," is used by the proponents of the regime to refer to writers who according to them adher to Islamic values.

99 The events of the past 30 years have shown that such non-conformist organizations have short lives. So, by the time this study is completed, one cannot be sure whether or not this organization will still exist and if so whether or not it has been coerced into practical silence.

100 *Adabiyat-e Dastani*, no. 97, 2005, p. 11.

101 Such ceremonies are quite common in the case of "values books."

102 According to Paul Sprachman, Mohsen Soleimani (who was involved in the project of translating "values works") suggested three books to him and asked him to pick one; he decided to go with Dehqan's book. *Adabiyat-e Dastani*, no. 102, 2006, p. 42.

103 *"Jashn-e Runama'i-ye Safar beh Geray-e 270 Darajeh"* (The Ceremony for the Unveiling of *Journey to Heading 270 Degrees*) *Adabiyat-e Dastani*, no. 102, 2006, p. 43.

104 The story of Ahmad Dehqan has reached ridiculous levels. His last novel *Parseh dar Khak-e Gharibeh* (Wandering in a Strange Land) was criticized on the same bases, and this time, Abbas Ja'fari Moqaddam, another official critic, accused him of promoting anti-Sacred Defense literature. He went so far as to say that such a writer should stand trial!

He added: "From the very beginning of the story 'Wandering in a Strange Land' we see that the author does not have a good and polite outlook and when he speaks about the Sacred Defence he uses base and absurd words; at times he even talks nonsense. The truth about the Sacred Defence does not exist at all in this story."

He said: "In my opinion, the mule in this story is a symbol and warriors often use the term 'brother' to refer to the mule. In fact, at one point in the story, one of the characters tells the warriors, 'the mule has more sense than you'. If we had a proper literary movement in this country, the author would have to stand trial." See http://khabarfarsi.com/ext/711620 (accessed May 5, 2014).

105 I have discussed this matter at length in *Modern Reflections of Classical Traditions in Persian Fiction*, Lewiston, NY: Edwin Mellen Press, 2003.

106 To read more about this phenomenon in a comparative paradigm, see Kamran Rastegar's *Literary Modernity Between the Middle East and Europe: Textual Transactions in Nineteenth Century Arabic, English and Persian Literatures*, London: Routledge, 2007.

107 Culler, *The Literary in Theory*, p. 229.

108 As I will discuss in future pages, another rare example of studies which rely more on literary concepts to explain the evolutionary process of modern Persian poetry is Ahmad Karimi-Hakkak's *Recasting Persian Poetry: Scenarios of Poetic Modernity in Iran*, Salt Lake City, UT: University of Utah Press, 1995. The emphasis on the evolution of literary concepts is a necessary reminder that histories of literature based on artificial categories—decades, historical events, etc.—are quite reductive and can no longer provide answers to the complexities of Persian modernist writing.

109 Obviously it took a while for all these elements to become crystallized in modernist works. What is clear, however, is that by the time the First Congress of Iranian Writers was held in 1946, poets and fiction writers of such works (e.g. Hedayat and Nima) were presented as representatives of a significant aspect of Persian literature of the day.

110 The majority of scholars believe that. Shamisa is one of the few who argues that all ghazals of Hafez have some kind of unity. See *Seyr-e Ghazal dar She'r-e Farsi* (The Development of the Ghazal in Persian Poetry), Tehran: Ferdows, 1983.

111 First published in Czech in 1956.

112 Ehsan Yarshater has planned a multi-volume project under the title of *A History of Persian Literature*. According to the Introduction to the first volume (*General Introduction to Persian Literature*), he has envisaged 18 volumes which would cover different periods and products of Persian literary production up to the present day.

113 *Iranian Studies*, vol. 2, no. 1, winter 1969, pp. 39–41.

114 Gérard Genette, *Figure III*, Paris: Editions Du Seuil, 1972, p. 18. My argument here is informed by Gérard Genette's discussion concerning differences between various types of historiocity found in literary studies which attempt to have a historical dimension. I am not using the terminologies of "*histoire de la littérature*" and "*histoire littéraire*" in the same way that he has used them. In fact I believe the phrase "*histoire de la litterature*" is much closer to what I called a Formalist history of literature. The point, however, is not the appellation but rather the content or the subject of such a history, which I believe Genette has identified very clearly.

115 Gérard Genette, *Figures III*, Paris: Editions Du Seuil, 1972, p. 18.

116 Ibid.

117 Mohammad Reza Shafi'i Kadkani, *Musiqi-ye She'r* (The Music of Poetry), Tehran: Agah, 3rd edn, 1370/1991, p. 21.

118 See, for example, Shafi'i Kadkani's *Sha'er-i dar Hojum-e Montaqedan: Naqd-e Adabi dar Sabk-e Hendi* (A Poet Attacked by Critics: Literary Criticism in Indian Style), Tehran: Agah, 1375/1996.

119 For a thorough discussion about the emergence of new directions and definitions of literary criticism and literature, consult Ahmad Karimi-Hakkak's *Recasting Persian Poetry: Scenarios of Poetic Modernity in Iran*, Chapter 3.

120 To this list I should add Claus Pedersen's "Pre-Modern and Early Modern Persian Literature: Written while Travelling?" which argues that in order to

understand the evolutionary trajectory of modern Persian literature one should also consider specific characteristics of Persian literary tradition, as opposed to simply relying on a universal model. *Persian Literary Studies Journal* (PLSJ), vol. 1, no. 1, Autumn–Winter 2012, pp. 75– 86.

121 Culler, *Structuralist Poetics*, p. viii.

122 Ibid.

123 To read more about debates surrounding different versions of *Buf-e Kur* and their publication dates, see the Preface to a 2011 translation of this book by Naveed Noori (www.entesharate-iran.com – accessed May 5, 2014).

124 Mohammad Ali Jamalzadeh (1892–1997) published his most famous collection of short stories, *Yeki Bud Yeki Nabud* (Once Upon a Time), in 1921. The introduction to this collection is considered by many to be the first articulation of the requirements of modern Persian fiction.

125 One of the directions along which this discussion could be developed is the influence of folk and popular literature on modern, and then modernist, Persian writing. For example, stories such as *Hosein-e Kord-e Shabestari* (Hosein the Kurd of Shabestar) or *Amir Arsalan-e Namdar* (The Illustrious Amir Arsalan) are excellent examples of linguistic registers which were considered an absolute horror by the official and elevated literati. There is no doubt that once simplicity and colloquialism became accepted registers which were commonly used, these older sources had their share of impact on the works of modernist writers.

126 Howe, *Decline of the New*, p. 3.

127 Karimi-Hakkak gives a brief description of the poets of the Return Movement:

[They] believed that Persian poetry had grown in elaborateness over time so much that it had lost its original simplicity of diction and clarity of expression. Particularly in recent centuries, they thought, this poetry had given way to bombastic wordplay of the so-called Indian School in Persian poetry. Writing early in the twentieth century, Bahar was summing up the opinion of several generations of Iranian poets associated with the Return Movement when he characterized the Indian School as one marked by "weakness of words and poverty of meaning" which sought strength in "an excess of images … and fanciful visions lacking in eloquence and true beauty … "

Karimi-Hakkak, *Recasting Persian Poetry*, p. 27.

128 *The Horrifying Tehran* was published as a serialized novel in the newspaper *Setareh-ye Iran* (Iran's Star) and two years later as a book. Quoted from Hasan Mirabedini's *One Hundred Years of Fiction-Writing in Iran*, vol. 1, p. 57

129 For more information about these texts, see Mirabedini, *One Hundred Years of Fiction-Writing in Iran*. vol. 1, p. 61.

130 Shahrokh Meskub, *Dastan-e Adabiyat va Sargozasht-e Ejtema'* (The Story of Literature and the Tale of Society), 2nd edn, 1378 (1st edn 1373), Theran: Nashr-e Farzan, p. 139. The same passage, with some modifications, has been quoted in Mirabedini, vol.1, p. 55.

131 After the 1979 Revolution, Ehsan Tabari was arrested; after spending a few months in prison he was brought on television where he recanted Marxism and converted to Islam. He was 67 years old when he was arrested.

132 *Sadeq Hedayat: His Work and his Wondrous World* (ed. Homa Katouzian) and *Sadeq Hedayat* (ed. Ali Dehbashi) are two major sources which contain articles from a number of scholars who have written on Hedyat and who represent a wide variety of different approaches to his work.

133 Farzaneh Milani, *Words, Not Swords: Iranian Women Writers and the Freedom of Movement* Syracuse, NY: Syracuse University Press, 2011, pp 50–67.

134 This short book was first published in French in 1991. The Persian translation by Baqer Parham was published in Ali Dehbashi's *Sadeq Hedayat* in 1380/2001, Tehran: Nashr-e Sales.

135 To read more about the influence of Persian classical literature, see "Sadeq Hedayat and the Classics: The Case of *The Blind Owl*" by Marta Simidchieva, in *Sadeq Hedayat: His Work and his Wondrous World*, ed., Homa Katouzian, London: Routledge, 2008.

136 Here, Farrokhzad is referring to the story of Leyli and Majnun which has been rendered into verse by many poets, including Nezami, a twelfth-century Iranian poet.

137 *Forugh Farrokhzad: Javdaneh Zistan, dar Owj Mandan* (Forugh Farrokhzad: Living Eternally, Staying at the Zenith), complied and edited by Behruz Jalali, Tehran: Morvarid, 1377/1998, p. 169.

138 M. R. Ghanoonparvar's book on Sadeq Chubak, together with his discussion of Hedayat's influence on Chubak, is a very good example demonstrating one of the literary directions which grew out of *Buf-e Kur*, or rather what *Buf-e Kur* represented.

139 Michael Beard, *Hedayat's Blind Owl as a Western Novel*, Princeton, NJ: Princeton University Press, 1990.

140 Michael Beard, "Influence as Debt: *The Blind Owl* in the Literary Marketplace," in *Sadeq Hedayat: His Work and his Wondrous World*, ed. Homa Katouzian, p. 62.

141 Noori, p. 4.

142 Ibid., pp. 3, 4.

143 In addition to Michael Beard's work on Hedayat, Michael Hillmann's *Hedayat's "The Blind Owl" Forty Years After*. (Austin, TX: Center for Middle Eastern Studies, University of Texas at Austin, 1978), "Hedayat, Sadeq (ii)," *Encyclopedia Iranica Online*, 2012, (available at www.iranicaonline.org), and his *"The Blind Owl as a Modernist Fiction,"* in *Daftar-e Honar* (Eatontown, NJ: Anjoman-e Farhangi va Ensaandusti-ye Iraaniyan, Vol. 3 No. 6, Sep. 1996) have made significant contribution to this discussion. In particular, in *"The Blind Owl as a Modernist Fiction,"* Hillmann refers to the presence of the universal and local aspects of literary modernism. In the present study, my emphasis is on identifying components of the local aspect as well as their developments in the course of the evolution of Persian modernist writing.

144 One needs only to think about, for example, Lamartine's famous line describing Man as a fallen god:

"Borné dans sa nature, infini dans ses voeux / L'homme est un dieu tombé qui se souvient des cieux"
(Limited in his nature, infinite in his desire / man is a fallen god who remembers heaven)

and Victor Hugo's many passages in which he considers himself somewhat as an equal to God and even engages in conversations with him.

145 The title of the story is taken from a line from one of Nima Yushij's poems. The translation of the title is by Sheida Dayani, a PhD candidate at New York University.

146 General information about Shamim Bahar is taken from Mirabedini's *One Hundred Years of Fiction-Writing in Iran*, pp. 714–717. According to Reza Ghassemi's website, the text was completed in 1344/1965, see www.rezaghassemi.com/dastan_122.htm (accessed May 5, 2014).

147 See www.rezaghassemi.com/dastan_122.htm (accessed May 5, 2014). Ellipses are mine.

148 Noori, p. 5.

149 See www.rezaghassemi.com/dastan_122.htm (accessed May 5, 2014).

150 Obviously the choice of names is not accidental. They are reminiscent of the romantic epic story of Khosrow, Shirin, and Farhad. This story has been written and rewritten by a number of Iranian poets and writers. The most famous version belongs to Nezami Ganjavi, the twelfth-century poet.

151 Farad is abbreviated form of Farhad which is used, sometimes in conversational Persian.

152 See www.rezaghassemi.com/sehdastan_shamim_bahar.pdf, p. 6 (accessed May 5, 2014).

153 Giv is the name of a mythic hero in the *Shahnameh*.

154 See www.rezaghassemi.com/sehdastan_shamim_bahar.pdf, p. 14 (accessed May 5, 2014).

155 Ibid., pp. 25, 26.

156 See www.rezaghassemi.com/sehdastan_shamim_bahar.pdf, p. 27 (accessed May 5, 2014).

157 Ordibehesht is the second month of Spring in the Iranian calendar.

158 See www.rezaghassemi.com/sehdastan_shamim_bahar.pdf, p. 32 (accessed May 5, 2014).

159 Shemiran is in the north of Tehran, Molavi is in the south, and Tehranpars is in the east. Atashi uses the metaphor of a cross to refer to the narrator's traveling from north to south and west to east.

160 *Tamasha* Magazine, vol. 1, no. 31, Mehr 29, 1350.

161 See www.rezaghassemi.com/dastan_122.htm (accessed May 5, 2014).

162 See www.rezaghassemi.com/Pouf.pdf (accessed May 5, 2014).

163 As noted before, Hasan Mirabedini has used the term *harzeh negari* (writing obscenity, lewdness) to refer to some such works. See *One Hundred Years of Fiction-Writing in Iran*, pp. 367–375.

164 Through not directly examining this topic, Kamran Talattof's recent book, *Modernity, Sexuality, and Ideology in Iran: The Life and Legacy of Popular Female Artists* (Syracuse, NY: Syracuse University Press, 2011) provides another important dimension to this topic.

165 See www.rezaghassemi.com/Pouf.pdf, p. 55 (accessed May 5, 2014).

166 Since in Persian short vowels are not written, it is difficult to be certain of the pronunciation of these made-up names.

167 It is difficult not to remember the title of Shamim Bahar's "The Cloud Feels Like Raining."

168 See www.rezaghassemi.com/Pouf.pdf, p. 54 (accessed May 5, 2014).

169 Ibid., p. 55.

170 Ibid., p. 56.

171 Perhaps it is also worth mentioning that, like Sadeq Hedayat, Na'lbandian, too, committed suicide.

172 See www.freewebs.com/abotorab/zire%20dandane%20sag.forsi.pdf, p. 3 (accessed May 5, 2014).

173 *Khorus Jangi* (The Fighting Cock) is the name of a modernist movement and its journal which started in the late 1940s and early 1950s, and had an extremely important influence on the formation and promotion of modernism in art and literature. This movement has not received enough attention especially in non-Persian studies of contemporary Persian literature. Arta Khakpour's Dissertation (New York University, 2014), *Each Into a World of His Own: Mimesis, Modernist Fiction, and the Iranian Avant-Garde*, is a great step towards remedying this deficiency.

174 To read more about this topic and this generalized periodization, see Mirabedini, *One Hundred Years of Fiction-Writing in Iran*, pp. 275–278 and p. 406.

175 Another point about these generalizing grand narratives—modern Persian literature started because of the Constitutional Revolution; all intellectuals of the

1950s and 1960s were a group of depressed intellectuals whose sole answer to problems of the time was a superficial romantic desire to return to the past—is that for a variety of reasons, including the lack of a continuous academic system of criticism, they have never undergone a rigorous evaluation and updating process. The examination of the calcification of these narratives is certainly a worthwhile project.

176 Karimi-Hakkak puts it best when he writes: "[Al-e Ahmad], under the guise of his writing style, introduced to young people who were thirsty for any writing or semi-reasoning against Monarchic Despotism, a number of undeveloped and superficial concepts. In my opinion, his goal was more to use these concepts as mental weapons against the country's socio-political apparatus rather than to corrupt empty and impressionable minds. In other words, *Westoxification* and *On the Service and Betrayal of the Intellectuals* were mediocre works which, in an open atmosphere, could have been the beginning of an enlightening and constructive debate aimed at achieving a better understanding of our people's cultural identity." Quoted from Mirabedini, *One Hundred Years of Fiction-Writing in Iran*, p. 1205.

177 I am purposefully avoiding the expression postmodernism because this term, especially in regard to Persian literary criticism, has been used so indiscriminately that it has basically lost its meaning. To put it differently, I believe this concept has its own genealogy and as long as this genealogy has not been defined clearly in the context of Persian literature it is prudent and less confusing to not use this term.

178 Viktor Erlich, *Russian Formalism: History-Doctrine*, The Hague: Mouton and Co, 1965, p. 252.

179 To read more about this topic, see Shafi'i Kadkani, *Imagery in Persian Poetry*, p. 492.

180 To read more about this structuralist approach to the genre Fantastic, see Tzvetan Todorov's *Introduction à la littérature fantastique* (Introduction to the Literature of Fantastic), Paris: Editions du Seuil, 1976.

181 Bijan Najdi, *Dastanha-ye Natamam-e Bijan Najdi* (Bijan Najdi's Unfinished Stories), Tehran: Markaz, 1380/2001, p. 1.

182 In Persian short vowels are not written, so the transliteration of the name Sohrab is S-H-R-A-B which has the same letters as the transliteration of Braseh.

183 The first version of "*Shab-e Sohrab Koshan*" (The Eve of Slaying Sohrab), in *Bijan Najdi's Unfinished Stories*, p. 126.

184 Ibid., p. 127.

185 Ibid.

186 Ibid.

187 Ibid., p. 127.

188 Bahram Beyzai, *Siyavash-Khani* (Performing the Epic of Siyavash), Tehran: Roshangaran, 1996.

189 The *pardeh-khan* is a traditional, and usually traveling, storyteller who uses a *pardeh*—a painting of either religious and/or mythic events depicted on large pieces of canvas—as a kind of visual aid for when he is telling the story.

190 Bijan Nadji, "The Eve of the Slaying of Sohrab" in *Yuzpalangani keh ba man davideh-and* (Cheetahs Who Ran With Me), Tehran: Markaz, 1373/1994, p. 35.

191 Esfandiyar is Achilles' counterpart in the *Shahnameh*. His eyes are his weak point, and Rostam kills him with a double-tipped arrow in his eyes.

192 Siyavash is another hero from the *Shahnameh*. At the order of the king of Turan, his head is cut off and his blood is poured down in a tub at his feet. The descriptions of Siyavash with blood poured under his feet and Esfandiyar with a spear in his eye clearly are there to emphasize the continuation of these myths from mythic to present time.

193 Nadji, "The Eve of the Slaying of Sohrab," pp. 45, 46.

194 Ibid., p. 38
195 Ibid., p. 39.
196 Ibid. The *azan* is the call to prayer. When it is time for prayer, the Azan is recited from the mosque.
197 Nadji, "The Eve of the Slaying of Sohrab," p. 38.
198 Ibid.
199 Ibid., p. 43.
200 Ibid., p. 37.
201 Ibid., p. 36.
202 Nadji, "The First Version of The Eve of the Slaying of Sohrab," in *Bijan Najdi s Unfinished Stories*, p. 127.
203 Nadji, "The Field Where Sohrab's Bones Are Planted" in *Bijan Najdi's Unfinished Stories*, p. 135.
204 Ibid., p. 131.
205 Ibid., p. 130.
206 In Iran, the week begins on Saturday. Thus Sunday is a school day; Friday is the day off.
207 Nadji, "The Field Where Sohrab's Bones Are Planted," p. 129.
208 *Naqqali* is another form of traditional storytelling. The *naqqal* (storyteller) usually performs in traditional coffeehouses and uses well-known mythic and heroic stories as sources for his monologue-based performance. On some occasions these monologues are accompanied by music or a painting as well.
209 Nadji, "The Field Where Sohrab's Bones Are Planted," p. 128.
210 Nadji, "The Eve of the Slaying of Sohrab," p. 45.
211 Ibid., p. 46.
212 Ashura refers to the days during which Hosein, the third Imam of the Shi'is, and his small group of followers were slain by the army of Caliph Yazid. The battle took place on the plain of Karbala in 680 CE.
213 Nadji, "The Field Where Sohrab's Bones Are Planted," p. 135.

Conclusion

Discourse—and by extension counter-discourse—is yet another concept which because of excessive usage, has lost its capability to have a single definition. Like many other similarly encompassing concepts, however, more important than having a fixed definition, this concept is most useful when considered in its fluidity. In other words, especially when this concept is used in the course of the study of a particular evolutionary process, instead of attempting to offer a definition of, for example, a literary or political discourse, it is more advisable to concentrate on elements of discursivity, counter-discursivity or non-discursivity. In this project I have concentrated on literary themes, devices, particular writings, and utterances which function in a framework informed by interaction between various areas of human activities, so that I could identify characteristics and, more importantly, directions of modern Persian literary counter-discursivity and non-discursivity. I believe the directions, trends, and particular works which I have analyzed in this project offer a relatively comprehensive image of contemporary and modernist Persian fiction in Iran. Inevitably, this image remains at the level of a sketch, simply because presenting a detailed description of that image is an ambitious task which cannot be accomplished until many such preparatory studies are carried out.

It should, nonetheless, be noted that it is much easier to both initiate and recognize counter-discursivity in societies where naked dictatorship and totalitarianism have made it unnecessary and superfluous for the official discourse to be sophisticated and convincing. This is because the official discourse produces and keeps its traditional sovereignty through its armed forces and its system of mostly pre-modern punishment. In such situations, the tools and means for initiating subversiveness are more abundant and, naturally, more easily attainable.

Throughout the first part of this study I referred to many speeches, or letters, or instructions by various officials of the Islamic Republic. Often this was done simply to emphasize that the mere repetition of these utterances is enough to demonstrate their stupidity and consequently to infer the ease with which narratives of the official discourse could be challenged. As mentioned above, the totalitarian aspect of the regime and its reliance on sheer force to impose itself requires no discursive sophistication or disciplinary expertise. That is why the leaders of the Islamic Republic have never hesitated to speak about matters requiring expertise, such as Iran's current literary situation, and the quality of its productions. They even provide instructions and suggestions for its improvement. One might even find it positive that such statements emerge one after another and provide enough ammunition to challenge the official and/or dominant discourses. In one of his more recent meetings with those in charge of "Hozeh-ye Honari's [The Arts Center's] Offices of Literature of Resistance and Literature of the Islamic Republic," Khamenei offered an "analysis" of the current conditions of Persian literature which later on, as is customary in such autocratic settings, was lauded by conservative newspapers, including *Kayhan*:

> On Monday, His Grace, Grand Ayatollah Khamenei, the great leader of the Islamic Republic, in an audience with those involved in the offices of art and literature of resistance and Hozeh-ye Honari's literature of the Islamic Republic described two important and significant characteristics of artistic activities: 1) Creating a great movement which inspires and incites activities in the field of the literature of resistance and the Islamic Revolution; and 2) Preventing the actualization [literally, fruition] of the desire of some of the rancorous trends of the Islamic Revolution which strive to isolate the concepts [sic] and truths of the Islamic Revolution. [His Grace] emphasized: "This effective and progressive movement made imported literature unnecessary to the country."[1]

And of course, Khamenei makes sure that he does not forget to include a cliché-ridden critique of intellectuals who, according to the religious/backward, (*Al-e Ahmadian*) definition, have always been against the traditional values and thus end up in traps made by the evil West.

> His Grace, Ayatollah Khamenei referred to certain trends of so-called intellectualism which attempt to hide and keep hidden the great and magnificent epic of the Islamic Revolution and even issues related to it; and even to show a [false] distorted image of it. [His Grace] emphasized: "Efforts by committed artists to reveal and document the great cognitive and spiritual potential that emerged from the Islamic Revolution changed the wrong approach and tradition which exist in the works of intellectuals who rely only on translated works. [These efforts] led to a self-sufficiency in relation to the production and presentation of extremely valuable and magnificent products in various fields of art and literature."[2]

Before finishing this "illuminating analysis," he repeats the mantra that in comparison to other revolutions, the Islamic Revolution has more "depth, strength, and efficiency" but it has not been documented and examined sufficiently, and this is why "it is necessary to produce more historical books, novels, and things like that." And finally he ends by offering the usual quasi-instructions about how to improve these already great works of literature of resistance and literature of the Islamic Revolution. *Kayhan* quotes these instructions directly:

> "Planning to present good written works in other artistic forms, methodical and expansive distribution of [various] forms of these works," "The necessity to translate distinguished works of literature of resistance and Revolution into foreign languages," "Bringing the literature of resistance and Revolution into the universities," "The necessity to celebrate and encourage the valuable works and active individuals in the field of the literature of resistance and Revolution" were some of the points that His Grace, Ayatollah Khamenei emphasized during this meeting.[3]

As I mentioned before, one of the basic approaches to initiate a challenge to the unsophisticated, "armed" official discourse is simply its repetition, which demonstrates its stupidity. This approach is very much inspired by Gustave Flaubert's description of *sottisier*—stupid quotations—in his unfinished *Bouvard et Pécuchet*. The idea is quite simple: there are texts "whose stupidity [requires] only the passage of a little time to come to light".[4] Yet, it is crucial to realize that the stupidity of a work or speech does not mean that it is ineffective, especially when, because of their constant repetition, these narratives, or at least some of their elements, gradually come to be considered natural and normal. And one of the worst consequences of such a naturalization process is that it creates, in an indirect manner, a series of assumptions which play a significant role in defining the grounds for debate. To clarify, for example, in the quotation mentioned above, the phrase "imported literature" is used as if it is an obvious phenomenon, indeed an accepted matter, while in fact this phrase represents only an artificial, meaningless concept which has no place in a serious literary debate.

Using such phrases and in general such language is also a reminder of the relationship between discourse and language which, although seems obvious, requires us occasionally to allude to and even to emphasize the fact that:

> "A dominant discourse is the imposition, not so much of certain truths ... as of a certain language ... , which the opposition itself is obliged to employ to make its objections known." (Descombes, *Modern French Philosophy*, p. 108) We may call it an "establishment language" (Bourdieu); a *"langue obligatoire"* (an "obligatory language"; Michel de Certeau); *"langage normalizé"* ("normalized language"; Kristeva)—among numerous alternative designations.[5]

Through its variations, this normalized and naturalized language defines realities from various disciplinary perspectives, including history and historiography.

In other words, the seemingly idiotic phrases and concepts carry within themselves in a most innate fashion, naturalized and absolutist assumption; and through them, in a most "natural" way they construct their false narratives. Such narratives are based on conventionalized falsehoods about major historical events (e.g. all religions are somehow religions of peace), or about more specific topics such as the existence of an Islamic version of the history of Persian literature, one of whose major questions is whether or not Ferdowsi was Sunni or Shi'i; or about contemporary events and realities like the situation of political prisoners in Iran both before and after the 1979 Revolution.

As argued in the section about prison reports, at early stages, confrontation with such false historiographies is usually formed through thematic counter-narratives. The contrasting narratives do not necessarily challenge the infrastructure of the dominant discourses, but their counter-hegemonic aspect plays a preparatory role in the formation of literary counter-discourses. Additionally, by underlining particular segments of history which the official discourse has tried to ignore and "make us forget," such reports at least disturb the official discourse and, from a thematic point of view, begin a denaturalization process.

It should be noted, however, that in such works one usually recognizes a streak of instrumentality which shines through concrete efforts which aim at scoring counter-narrative and counter-hegemonic points. Yet it is also clear that in terms of challenging the hegemony of the official discourse, the literary evolution is defined in part through an increasing distancing from instrumentality reflected in these crude thematic confrontations. And in general, this distancing is actualized through defamiliarized language and forms which function against backgrounds produced based on giving voice to the silenced and thus are based on rewrites of history.

To this sketch, one more element should be added: like many other literary traditions, canons of Persian literature are correctly or incorrectly associated with subversion and counter-discursivity. Implied and actual readers are more inclined to relate to works which, for whatever reasons, could potentially be identified with counter-discursivity. This is not limited to works which rely on contrasting themes but on those which employ linguistic and formalistic and even experimental innovations; they all receive the benefit of the doubt. These innovations are crucially important because they emphasize a point which is usually ignored by thematically-defined post-colonial theories and, more generally, by theoretical paradigms which rely on non-literary discourses. Terdiman explains this phenomenon very succinctly:

> Counter-discourses function in their form. Their object is to represent the world *differently*. But their projection of difference goes beyond simply contradicting the dominant, beyond simply negating its assertions. The power of a dominant discourse lies in the codes by which it regulates understanding of the social world. Counter-discourses seek to detect and

map such naturalized protocols and to project their subversion. At stake in this discursive struggle are the paradigms of social representation themselves.[6]

What is missing from this analysis is the unplanned presence of subversive elements which are read as counter-discursivity. Indeed, in the last part of this study I have emphasized these works which I believe make up the largest component of Persian modernist fiction. Planned, or unplanned, nonetheless, to offer the potential to represent difference, these works emphasize certain literary techniques and devices such as irony which make subversive readings of various forms and contents of reality possible. These readings, at times, are identified with counter-discursivity without this necessarily having been the intention of the author/narrator or the text. This is especially true in societies where, to use Debord's terminology, the concentrated form of spectacular power is in charge of protecting the official discourse. In these situations, anything other than "us" is considered against us/the official discourse, and there is no discrimination based on the intention. In fact, this is indicative of the backwardness of such official discourses which, because of their calcified nature, cannot appropriate different codes, spaces, and devices. This is exactly why it is practically impossible for the naked dictatorial forms of power to use non-violent approaches to neutralize what they consider to be counter-discourses. One obvious consequence of these conditions is that many activities (in this case, literary ones) are forced into the margins of the society; but the number and quality of these activities is so high—because "us" has become so rigid and small—that margins become the main locations where one can find the most exciting literary events. It bears repeating that many of these activities (e.g. new literary productions) are not concerned about their positionality vis-à-vis the official and at times dominant discourses; yet, as mentioned above, this does not shield them from the wrath of the various institutions of the Islamic Republic.

To repeat what I alluded to in the introduction to this study, one of the most succinct statements which crystallizes the policies the Islamic Republic devised to eradicate serious littérateurs and their literary productions and simultaneously promote repetitive and insipid literary narratives of the official discourse is Sa'di's words: "What kind of bastards are these people? They have let loose the dogs and made fast the stones."

In spite of all this, the Persian fiction of the past three decades, like many other time periods in the history of Persian literature, has been successful in construing independent voices which, in turn, have erected alternative narratives and discourses and in an irreversible fashion managed to install themselves in the society's collective/historical conscience. These narratives have either challenged directly or simply ignored the many prevalent readings of and about historical events, individuals, social spaces, myths, and traditions (artificial and otherwise). More importantly, in doing so, Persian modernist fiction has succeeded in carving new areas for artistic activities.

To complete the context, it should also be noted that new technological innovations have provided new opportunities to escape censorship, and that many literati have taken advantage of them. Indeed, notwithstanding the fact that dictatorships also take advantage of new technologies, alternative forms of dissemination have become very viable options for those who try to flee censorship and self-censorship. However, these success stories should not give the impression that in this discursive battle, counter-discourses have always been the absolute victor, without any casualties. First, we should not forget that at times many Iranian writers and potential writers, because of unimaginable difficulties created by the Islamic Republic, have simply given up. Many of them have been forced to accept that their works will never be able to reach their natural audience. This includes the very few who have succeeded in publishing their works in other languages—without these works having been published in their original language, Persian. Reza Baraheni, Shahriyar Mandanipur and Mahmud Dowlatabadi are but a few famous examples. This phenomenon naturally has its own consequences, including the fact that the authors have begun to consider different readers and different literary traditions within which they will function. Of course for Persian literature this is nothing new, and this tradition is quite familiar with the concept of literary production outside the "mainland." Persian literary productions during the Safavid, Qajar, to some degree Pahlavi dynasties, and of course the Islamic regime are clear examples. And at least one issue has been settled: Persian literary production in exile and in migration is playing an increasingly more significant role in the definition of Persian literary tradition.

No one can predict what will happen in terms of the future of this discursive battle. The fact that throughout the history of Persian literature, counter-discursive and non-discursive narratives from Hafez's poems to Hedayat's fiction, and from Baraheni's and Dowlatabadi's thematic confrontations to truly modernist efforts of authors such as Golshiri, Bahar, Na'lbandian, and Najdi, have been extremely successful in defining not just new spaces but, more importantly, in defining the mood of the period. This success, however, has led to a kind of unwarranted optimism which ignores defeat stories—periods of dark ages, found in many literary traditions, caused by antiquated policies of suppression and censorship implemented by the discourses in power. This optimism, to use the often-quoted Antonio Gramsci's phrase, can only be described as the "optimism of the will," and I do believe the danger lies in ignoring the "pessimism of the intellect." Emphasis on either one of these two concepts to predict the future of Persian literary tradition is misguided; this future is yet to be written.

Notes

1 See www.kayhan.ir/920224/3.htm#N301 (accessed May 5, 2014).
2 Ibid.
3 Ibid.

4 Terdiman, *Discourse/Counter-Discourse*, p. 206.

It is worth noting that in the context of post-1979 discursive battles, this approach has been used most efficiently in regards to religious texts. In fact, segments of many *Tawzih al-Masa'el*s written by Ayatollahs and Grand Ayatollahs, have been quoted and/or translated and published by opponents of the Islamic Republic, without any commentary, just to show the depth of stupidity of these writings.

5 Terdiman, *Discourse/Counter-Discourse*, pp. 62–63.

6 Ibid., p. 149.

Bibliography

Abrahamian, Ervand. *Iran Between Two Revolutions*, Princeton, NJ: Princeton University Press, 1982.

———. *Tortured Confessions: Prisons and Recantations in Modern Iran*, Berkeley and Los Angeles, CA: University of California Press, 1999.

Adamiyat, Fereydoon. *Andisheh-ha-ye Fathali Akhundzadeh* (The Thoughts of Fathali Akhund Zadeh), Tehran: Kharazmi, 1970.

Afar, Janet, and Anderson, Kevin. *Foucault and the Iranian Revolution: Gender and the Seductions of Islamism*, Chicago, IL: University of Chicago Press, 2005.

Ahmad, Aijaz. "Jameson's Rhetoric of Otherness and the 'National Allegory,'" *Social Text*, No. 17, Autumn, 1987, pp. 3–25.

Akhavan-Sales, Mehdi. "Nameh-i az M. Omid" (A Letter from M. Omid), in *Shenakht Nameh-ye Shamlu* (Knowing Shamlu), ed. Javad Mojabi, Tehran: Qatreh, 1998.

Alavi, Tahereh. "*Halat-e Aval*" (Original Position), in *Zendegi-ye man dar Seshanbeh-ha Ettefaq Mi-oftad* (My Life Happens on Tuesdays), Tehran: Qasideh-sara, 1380/2001.

Al-e Ahmad, Jalal. *Gharbzadegi* (Westoxification), Tehran: Ravaq, 1978.

Alishan, Leonardo P. "Ahmad Shamlu: The Rebel Poet in Search of an Audience", *Iranian Studies*, 18, no. 2/4 (1985): 375–422.

Alizadeh, Parvaneh. *Khub Negah Konid, Rastaki Ast* (Look well; It is true), Paris: Khavaran, (3rd edn) 1376/1997.

Aqai, Farkhondeh. *Jensiyat-e Gomshodeh* (Lost Sexuality), Tehran: Alborz, 1990.

Ardavan, Sudabeh. "*Azadi Par … *" (Freedom, Gone …), an interview, April 2011: www.equal-rights-now.com/April2011/sodabeh%20azadi-.htm (accessed May 5, 2014).

Ariyanpur, Yahya. *Az Saba ta Nima* (From Saba to Nima), Tehran: Ketab-e Jibi, 1351/1972.

Asad, Talal. "Reflections on Cruelty and Torture", in *Formations of the Secular: Christianity, Islam, Modernity*, Stanford, CA: Stanford University Press, 2003.

Asadi, Houshang. *Letters to My Torturer: Love, Revolution, and Imprisonment in Iran*, Oxford: Oneworld Publication, 2010.

Ashouri, Daryush. *Hasti-shenasi-ye Hafez* (The Ontology of Hafez), Tehran: Markaz, 1377/1999.

Auerbach, Erich. *Mimesis: The Representation of Reality in Western Literature*, tr. Willard R. Trask, Princeton, NJ: Princeton University Press; 50th anniversary edn. 2003.

Azad, F. *Yad-ha-ye Zendan* (Prison Memories), Paris: L'Association pour la défense des prisonniers politiques et d'opinion en Iran, 1376/1997.

Bahar, Mohammad-Taqi (Malek al-Sho'ara). *Sabk-Shenasi ya Tarikh-e Tatavvor-e Nasr-e Farsi* (Stylistics or the History of the Evolution of Persian Prose), 3 vols, Tehran: Parastu, 2nd edn, 1337/1958.

Bahar, Shamim. "*Abr Baranash Gerefteh Ast*" (The Cloud Feels Like Raining), *Andisheh va Honar*, vol. 5, no. 8, 1345/1966, www.rezaghassemi.com/dastan_122.htm (accessed May 5, 2014).

——. *Seh Dastan-e Asheqaneh* (Three Romantic Stories), *Andisheh va Honar*, special issue, vol. 7, no. 3, 1352/1973, www.rezaghassemi.com/sehdastan_shamim_bahar.pdf (accessed May 5, 2014).

Bahrami, Bahram. "Daramadi bar *Ruzegar-e Duzakhi-ye Aqa-ye Ayaz*" (A Prologue to *Les Saisons en enfer du jeune Ayyaz*), www.vazhe.com/ayaz101.htm (accessed May 5, 2014), June 2000.

Baker, Suzanne. "Binarisms and Duality: Magic Realism and Postcolonialism," *Journal of the South Pacific Association for Commonwealth Literature and Language Studies*, no. 36. (1993).

Bakhtin, Mikhail. *The Dialogic Imagination*, ed. Michael Holquist, tr. Carl Emerson and Michael Holquist, Austin, TX: University of Texas Press, 1986.

——. *Problems of Dostoevsky's Poetics*, Minneapolis, MN: University of Minnesota Press, 1984.

Baradaran, Monireh. *Haqiqat-e Sadeh* (Simple Truth), Hannover: 1376/1997.

Baraheni, Reza. *Chah beh Chah* (Well to Well), Tehran: Nashr-e no, 1362/1983.

——. *Jonun-e Neveshtan* (The Madness of Writing), Tehran: Rasam, 1980.

——. *Les Saisons en enfer du jeune Ayyaz*, tr. Katayoun Shahpar-Rad, Paris: Pauvert, 2000.

——. *Qesseh Nevisi* (Writing Fiction), Tehran: Nashr-e No, 1362/1983.

——. *Zel Allah: She'r-ha-ye Zendan* (God's Shadow: Prison Poems), Tehran: Amir Kabir, 1358/1979.

——. "*Golshiri va Moshkel-e Roman*" (Golshiri and the Problem of Novel), in *Royay-e Bidar*, Tehran: Qatreh, 1373/1994.

Barthes, Roland. *Essais Critiques*, Paris: Editions du Seuil, 1964.

——. *Le Plaisir du texte* (The Pleasure of the Text), Paris: Editions Du Seuil, 1973.

——. *Poétique du récit*, Paris: Editions du Seuil, 1977.

Bashiri, Iraj. *The Fiction of Sadeq Hedayat*, Lexington, KY: Mazda Publishers, 1984.

Beard, Michael. *Hedayat's Blind Owl as a Western Novel*, Princeton, NJ: Princeton University Press, 1990.

——. "Influence as Debt: *The Blind Owl* in the Literary Marketplace," in *Sadeq Hedayat: His Work and his Wondrous World*, ed. Homa Katouzian, London: Routledge, 2008.

Behazin, M. A. (Etemadzadeh, Mahmud). *Bar-e Digar va in Bar ...* (Once Again and This Time ...), www.iranian.de/Main/khaterate%20be%20azin.pdf (accessed May 5, 2014), 1370/1991.

Behnud, Masud. "*In Ranj Nameh-ha ra beh Ayandegan ham Beresanid*" (Give These Letters of Pain to the Next Generation as well), 1382/2003, www.pyknet.net/1382/page/09tir/p407jabari.htm (accessed May 5, 2014).

Behrooz, Maziar. *Rebels With A Cause: The Failure of the Left in Iran*, London: I.B. Tauris, 2000.

Benjamin, Walter. "Theses on the Philosophy of History," in *Illuminations*, ed. Hannah Arendt, tr. Harry Zohn, New York: Schocken Books, 1979.

Best, Steven, and Kellner, Douglas. "Debord and the Postmodern Turn: New Stages of the Spectacle," *Substance* no. 90 (1999): 129–156, www.uta.edu/huma/illuminations/kell17.htm (accessed May 5, 2014).

——. "Debord and the Postmodern Turn: New Stages of the Spectacle," www.uta edu/huma/illuminations/kell17.htm (accessed May 5, 2014).

Beyzai, Bahram. *Dibacheh-ye Novin-e* Shahnameh (*A New Prologue to the* Shahnameh). Tehran: Roshangaran, 1370/1991.

——. *Siyavash-Khani* (Performing the Epic of Siyavash), Tehran: Roshangaran, 1996.

Bhabha, Homi. "Of mimicry and man: The ambivalence of colonial discourse," in *The Location of Culture*, London: Routledge, 1994.

Boroujerdi, Mehrzad. *Iranian Intellectuals and the West: The Tormented Triumph of Nativism*, Syracuse, NY: Syracuse University Press, 1996.

Brenner, Rachel Feldhay. "'Hidden Transcripts' Made Public: Israeli Arab Fiction and Its Reception," *Critical Inquiry*, Autumn 1999, vol. 26.

Browne, Edward Granville. *The Press and Poetry of Modern Persia*, Cambridge: Cambridge University Press, 1914.

——. *A Literary History of Persia*, Vol. 4, Cambridge: Cambridge University Press 1959.

Bryant II, Carter Harrison, *Rezá Baráheni's The Infernal Days of Áqá-ye Ayáz: A Translation and Critical Introduction*, Dissertation, The University of Texas at Austin, TX, 1982.

Cavanagh, Clare. "Lyric and Public: The Case of Adam Zagajewski," in *World Literature Today*, vol. 79, no. 2, May–August 2005.

Cheheltan, Amir Hassan. *Tehran, Shahr-e bi-Aseman* (Tehran, a City without Sky). Tehran: Negah, 1380/2001

Chelkowski, Peter, and Dabashi, Hamid. *Staging a Revolution: The Art of Persuasion in the Islamic Republic of Iran*, New York: New York University Press, 1999.

Chubak, Sadeq. "*Arusak-e Forushi*" (A Doll for Sale), in *Ruz-e Avval-e Qabr* (The First Day in the Grave), Tehran: Javidan, 1968.

——. *Cheragh-e Akhar* (The Last Alms), Tehran: Javidan, (2nd edn) 1976.

Clinton, Jerome. (tr.) *The Tragedy of Sohrab and Rostam*, Seattle, WA: University of Washington Press, 1987.

——. "Court Poetry at the beginning of the Classical Period," in *Persian Literature*, ed. Ehsan Yarshater, New York: Bibliotheca Persica, 1988.

——. *In the Dragon's Claws: The Story of Rostam and Esfandiyar from the Persian Book of Kings*, Washington, DC: Mage Publishers, 1999.

Culler, Jonathan. *Literary Theory*, Oxford: Oxford University Press, 1997.

——. *Structuralist Poetics*, Ithaca, NY: Cornell University Press, 1997.

——. *The Literary in Theory*, Stanford, CA: Stanford University Press, 2007.

Daneshvar, Simin. *Savushun* (Requiem), Tehran: Kharazmi, 1348/1969.

Davaran, Habibollah, and Behbahani, Farhad. *Dar Mehmani-ye Haji Aqa* (At Haji Aqa's Gathering), Tehran: Omid-e Farda, 1382/2003.

Debord, Guy. "Report on the Construction of Situations and on the International Situationist Tendency's Conditions of Organization and Action" (1957), tr. Ken Knabb from the *Situationist International Anthology* (revised and expanded edn, 2006), Berkeley, CA: Bureau for Public Secrets, www.bopsecrets.org/SI/report.htm (accessed May 5, 2014).

——. "Perspectives for Conscious Changes in Everyday Life" (1961), Berkeley, CA: Bureau for Public Secrets, www.bopsecrets.org/SI/6.everyday.htm (accessed May 5, 2014).

——. *La Société du spectacle* (The Society of the Spectacle), Paris: Buchet-Chastel, 1967.

——. "Comments on the Society of the Spectacle," tr. Malcolm Imrie, (1988), www.notbored.org/commentaires.html (accessed May 5, 2014).

Dehbashi, Ali (ed.). *Sadeq Hedayat*, Tehran: Nashr-e Sales, 1380/2001.

Dowlatabadi, Mahmud. *Jay-e Khali-ye Soluch* (Missing Soluch), Tehran: Agah, 1358/1979.

Epps, Bradley. *Significant Violence: Oppression and Resistance in the Narratives of Juan Goytisolo, 1970–1990*, New York: Clarendon Press, 1996.

Erfan, Ali. "Les Damnées du paradis," in *Les Damnées du paradis* (The Damned Souls of Paradise), Paris: Editions de l'Aube, 1996.

Erickson, John. *Islam and Postcolonial Narrative*, Cambridge: Cambridge University Press, 1998.

Erlich, Viktor. *Russian Formalism: History-Doctrine*, The Hague: Mouton and Co., 1965.

Eslami, Maziyar, and Farhadpur, Morad. Paris-Tehran: *Sinama-ye Abbas Kiarostami* (*The Cinema of Abbas Kiarostami*), Tehran: Farhang-e Saba, 1387/2008.

Farahani, Qa'em Maqam. *Munsha'at* (Correspondences), ed. Badr al-Din Yaghma'i, Tehran: Negah, 1389/2010.

Farrokhzad, Forugh. *Bargozideh-ye Ash'ar-e Forugh Farrokhzad* (A Selection from Forugh Farrokhzad Poems), Tehran: Morvarid, 6th edn, 1357/1978.

——. *Remembering the Flight: Twenty Poems by Forugh Farrokhzad*, tr. Ahmad Karimi-Hakkak, Port Coquitlam, BC: Nik Publishers, 1997.

Felman, Shoshana. "Bejanmin's Silence", in *Critical Inquiry*, Winter 1999, vol. 25.

Ferdowsi, Abolqadem. *The* Shahnameh: *The Persian Book of Kings*, tr. Richard Davis, New York: Penguin Classics, 2006.

Fineman, Joel. "The History of the Anecdote," in *The New Historicism*, ed. H. Aram Veeser. New York: Routledge, 1989.

Forsi, Bahman. *Zir-e Dandan-e Sag* (Under a Dog's Teeth), 1343/1964, www.freewebs.com/abotorab/zire%20dandane%20sag.forsi.pdf (accessed May 5, 2014).

Fotuhi, Mohammad. *Naqd-e Khial: Naqd-e Adabi dar Sabk-e Hendi* (The Critique of Imagination: Literary Criticism in Indian Style), Tehran: Sokhan, 2nd edn, 2006.

Foucault, Michel. *Surveiller et punir*, Paris: Gallimard, 1975.

——. *Discipline and Punish: The Birth of the Prison*, tr. Alan Sheridan, New York: Vintage Books, (2nd edn) 1995.

Gallagher, Catherine, and Greenblatt, Stephen. *Practicing New Historicism*, Chicago, IL: University of Chicago Press, 2000.

Genette, Gérard. *Figures III*, Paris: Editions du Seuil, 1972.

Ghanoonparvar, M. R. *Prophets of Doom: Literature as a Socio-Political Phenomenon in Modern Iran*, Lanham, MD: University Press of America, 1984.

——. *Reading Chubak*, Costa Mesa, CA: Mazda Publishers, 2005.

Golmohammadi, Puriya. "*Goft-o-gu ba Farideh Mahdavi Damghani*" (A conversation with Farideh Mahdavi Damghani), 1384/2005, http://isil.blogfa.com/post-3.aspx (accessed May 5, 2014).

Golshiri, Hushang. *Bagh dar Bagh* (Garden Within Garden), Tehran: Nilufar, 1378/1999.

——. An Interview, "*Hayula-ye Darun, Goft-o-gu ba Golshiri*" (A Monster Inside: A Conversation with Golshiri), *Bidar*, no. 1, (1379/2000).

Golsorkhi, Khosrow. "Last Defense" (1973), video: www.youtube.com/watch?v=buTlBLGdUfo (accessed May 5, 2014).

Hajizadeh, Farkhondeh. *Khalaf-e Demokrasi* (Contrary to Democracy), Tehran: Vistar, 1377/1998.

——. *Gozaresh-Qesseh-ye 1* (Report-Story #1), Tehran: Vistar, 1380/2001.

Hariri, Naser. *Goft-o Shenud-i ba Ahmad Shamlu, Doktor Reza Baraheni* (A Conversation with Ahmad Shamlu, Doctor Reza Baraheni), Babol: Ketabsaray-e Babol, 1365/1986.

Hedayat, Sadeq. *Haji Aqa,* Tehran: Amir Kabir, 1344/1965.

——. *Neveshteh-ha-ye Parakandeh*, Tehran: Amir Kabir, 1344/1965.

——. *Karvan-e Eslam: Al-Be'sat Al-Islamiah Il-Al-Belad Al-Afranjiah* (The Caravan of Islam: The Emergence of Islam in European Countries), Irvine, CA: Iran Zamin, 1985. This book was originally written in 1930.

——. *Buf-e Kur* (The Blind Owl), tr. Naveed Noori, n.p.: Entesharat-e Iran, 2011.

Hillmann, Michael. *Hedayat's "The Blind Owl" Forty Years After*, Austin, TX: Center for Middle Eastern Studies, University of Texas at Austin, 1978.

——. *A Lonely Woman: Forugh Farrokhzad and Her Poetry*, Washington, DC: Mage Publishers, 1987.

——. "*The Blind Owl as a Modernist Fiction*," in *Daftar-e Honar*, Eatontown, NJ: Anjoman-e Farhangi va Ensandusti-ye Iraniyan, vol. 3 no. 6, 1996.

Hoquqi, Mohammad (ed.). *She'r-e Zaman-e ma (4): Forugh Farrokhzad* (The Poetry of Our Time (4): Forugh Farrokhzad), Tehran: Negah, 1372/1993.

Howe, Irving. *Decline of the New*, New York: Harcourt, Brace & World, 1970.

iran-e-azad.org. "Stoning to Death in Iran: A Crime against Humanity Carried out by the Mullahs' Regime – Stoning women to death in Iran: A Special Case Study," (n.d.), www.iran-e-azad.org/stoning/women.html (accessed May 5, 2014).

——. "Stoning to Death in Iran: A Crime against Humanity Carried out by the Mullahs' Regime", (n.d.), video, www.iran-e-azad.org/stoning/video.html (accessed May 5, 2014).

Irfani, Suroosh. *Iran's Islamic Revolution: Popular Liberation or Religious Dictatorship?* London: Zed Books, 1983.

Jalali, Behruz (ed.). *Forugh Farrokhzad: Javdaneh Zistan, dar Owj Mandan* (Forugh Farrokhzad: Living Eternally, Staying at the Zenith), Tehran: Morvarid, 1377/1998.

Jamalzadeh, Mohammad Ali. *Yeki Bud, Yeki Nabud* (Once Upon a Time), Tehran: Shahab, 1379/2000.

Jameson, Fredric. "Third-World Literature in the Era of Multinational Capitalism," *Social Text*, no. 15, 1986.

——. *Postmodernism, or, the Cultural Logic of Late Capitalism*, Durham, NC: Duke University Press, 1991.

Julai, Reza. *Nastaran-ha-ye Surati* (Pink Sweetbriers), collection of short stories, Tehran: Markaz, 1377/1998.

——. *Baran-ha-ye Sabz* (Green Rain), collection of short stories, Tehran: Juya, 1380/ 2001.

Kamshad, H. *Modern Persian Prose Literature*, Cambridge: Cambridge University Press, 1966.

Karimi-Hakkak, Ahmad. "Revolutionary Posturing: Iranian Writers and the Iranian Revolution of 1979," *The International Journal of Middle East Studies*, 23, no. 4, 1991.

——. *Recasting Persian Poetry: Scenarios of Poetic Modernity in Iran*, Salt Lake City, UT: University of Utah Press, 1995.

Katouzian, Homa (ed.). *Sadeq Hedayat: His Work and his Wondrous World*, London: Routledge, 2008.

Kazemi, Moshfeq. *Tehran-e Makhof* (The Horrifying Tehran), Tehran: Serial / Setareh-ye Iran 1301–1302/1922–1923.

Khamenei, Ali. *"Nemitavan Bazar-e Ketab ra Azad Gozasht"* (One Cannot Let the Book Market Free), July 20, 2011, www.bbc.co.uk/persian/iran/2011/07/110720_l0 6_khamenei_book_limits.shtml (accessed May 5, 2014).

Khomeini, Ruhollah. *"... Beh Nevisandegan-e Mote'ahhed"* (... to Committed Writers), *Adabiyat-e Dastani*, no. 69, 2003.

Khorrami, Mohammad Mehdi. "Neo-Orientalism: *Mokhtasari dar Bareh-ye Chehreh-ye Honar va Adabiyat-e Iran dar Amrika"* (Neo-Orientalism: A Brief Observation Concerning the Image of Iranian Art and Literature in America), *Asr-e Panjshanbeh*, nos 5–6, (1377/1998), pp. 38–43.

——. *Modern Reflections of Classical Traditions in Persian Fiction*, Lewiston, NY: Edwin Mellen, 2003.

——. "The Image of Modern Persian Fiction in the Broken Mirror of Neo-Orientalism," in *Oriental Languages in Translation*, vol. 3, Cracow: Polish Academy of Science Press, 2008.

——. (ed. and tr.) *Sohrab's Wars: Counter-Discourses of Contemporary Persian Fiction: A Collection of Short Stories and a Film Script*, Costa Mesa, CA: Mazda Publishers, 2008.

——. "The Aesthetics of Lone Moments in the Poetry of Forugh Farrokhzad," in *Iranian Languages and Culture: Essays in Honor of Gernot Ludwig Windfuhr*, eds Behrad Aghaei and M. R. Ghanoonparvar. Costa Mesa, CA: Mazda Publishers, 2012.

——, and Ghanoonparvar, M. R. (eds) *Critical Encounters: Essays on Persian Literature and Culture in Honor of Peter J. Chelkowski*, Costa Mesa, CA: Mazda Publishers, 2007.

Khorramshahi, Baha al-Din. *Hafez-nameh* (The Book of Hafez), Tehran: Entesharat-e Elmi va Farhangi, 1383/2004.

Khosrokhavar, Farhad, and Roy, Olivier. *Iran: Comment sortir d'une revolution religieuse* (How to Come Through a Religious Revolution), Paris: Editions du Seuil, 1999.

Kiakojouri, Azam. "Prison expressions," *Iranian.com*, November 2003, http://iranian.com/BTW/2003/November/Prison/Images/farhang.pdf (accessed May 5, 2014).

Larijani, Ali. *"Iranian Qabl az Eslam ... "* (Iranians before Islam ...), November 7, 2010, www.balatarin.com/permlink/2009/9/30/1780356 (accessed May 5, 2014).

Lefebvre, Henri. *Critique de la vie quotidienne* (Critique of Everyday Life), Paris: L'Arche, 1947.

——. *Critique de la vie quotidienne II, Fondements d'une sociologie de la quotidienneté* (Critique of Everyday Life: Foundations for a Sociology of the Everyday), vol. 2, Paris: L'Arche, 1961.

——. *Critique de la vie quotidienne, III. De la modernité au modernisme (Pour une métaphilosophie du quotidien)* (Critique of Everyday Life, Vol. 3: From Modernity to Modernism [Towards a Metaphilosophy of Daily Life]), Paris: L'Arche, 1981.

Mahmudi, Hasan, *Khun-e Abi bar Zamin-e Namnak: dar Naqd va Mo'arrefi-ye Bahram Sadeqi* (Blue Blood on Damp Ground: Critiquing and Introducing Bahram Sadeqi), Tehran: Asa, 1998.

Mandanipur, Shahriyar. *"Chakavak-e Aseman Kharash"* (The Skyscraping Lark), in *Abi-ye Mavara'e Behar* (The Blue Beyond the Seas), Tehran: Markaz, 1382/2003.

Mashayekhi, Mehrdad, and Farsoun, Samih (eds). *Political Culture in the Islamic Republic*, London: Routledge, 1992.

Mesdaghi, Iraj. *Nah Zistan nah Marg: Khaterat-e Zendan* (Neither Life Nor Death: Prison Memoir), Stockholm: Alfabet Maxima, 2004.

Meskub, Shahrokh. *Dastan-e Adabiyat va Sargozasht-e Ejtema'* (The Story of Literature and Tale of Society), Tehran: Nashr-e Farzan, 2nd edn, 1378/1999.

Milani, Abbas. *Lost Wisdom: Rethinking Modernity in Iran*, Washington, DC: Mage Publishers, 2004.

Milani, Farzaneh. *Words, Not Swords: Iranian Women Writers and the Freedom of Movement*, Syracuse, NY: Syracuse University Press, 2011.

Milosz, Czeslaw. *The Captive Mind*, New York: Vintage International, 1981.

Mirabedini, Hasan, *Sad Sal Dastan Nevisi-ye Iran* (One Hundred Years of Fiction-Writing in Iran), vol. 3, Tehran: Cheshmeh, 1377/1998.

Mirsepassi, Ali. *Intellectual Discourse and the Politics of Modernization: Negotiating Modernity in Iran*, Cambridge: Cambridge University Press, 2000.

Mohajer, Naser (ed.). *Ketab-e Zandan* (The Prison Book), Berkeley, CA: Nashr-e Noqteh, (vol. 1) 1998, (vol. 2) 2001.

Mohajerani, Ataollah. *Behesht-e Khakestari* (Grey Paradise), Tehran: Omid-e Iranian, 1382/2003.

Montazeri, Hosein-Ali. *Memoirs*, 2000, www.amontazeri.com/farsi/frame3.asp (accessed May 5, 2014).

——. *Tawzih al-Masa'el*, Qom: Markaz-e Entesharat-e Daftar-e Tablighat-e Eslami, 1984.

Na'lbandian, Abbas. *Puf*, (before 1354/1975), www.rezaghassemi.com/Pouf.pdf (accessed May 5, 2014).

Nabokov, Vladimir. *Lectures on Russian Literature*, New York: Mariner Books, 2002.

Nafisi, Azar. "Andar Naqsh-e Bazi dar Dastan: Bar-dashti az 'Aqa-ye Nevisandeh Tazeh-kar Ast'" ("About the role of playing in story: A Reading of 'Mr. Writer is a Novice'"), *Kelk* (*Pen*), no. 5, 1369/1990, www.madomeh.com/1391/10/18/22/ (accessed May 5, 2014).

Najdi, Bijan. *Yuzpalangani keh ba man davideh-and* (Cheetahs Who Ran with Me), Tehran: Markaz, 1373/1994.

——. *Dastanha-ye Natamam-e Bijan Najdi* (Bijan Najdi's Unfinished Stories), Tehran: Markaz, 1380/2001.

Natel Khanlari, Parviz. *Tarikh-e Zaban-e Farsi* (The History of Persian Language), Tehran: Nashr-e No, 1366/1987.

Nezami Aruzi, Ahmad. *Chahar Maqaleh* (Four Articles), ed. Mohammad Qazvini and Mohammad Mo'in, Tehran: Armaghan, 1331/1952.

Noqreh-Kar, Masud, and Aslani, Mehdi. *Jangal-e Shokaran: Nameh-ha va Vasiyyat Nameh-ha* (The Hemlock Forest: Letters and Last Wills), Paris: Arash Magazine, 2006.

Okhovvat, Mohammad Rahim. *Ta'liq*, Esfahan: Naqsh-e Khorshid, 1378/1999.

Parsinejad, Iraj. *A History of Literary Criticism in Iran, 1866-1951: Literary Criticism in the Works of Enlightened Thinkers of Iran: Akhundzadeh, Kermani, Malkom, Talebof, Maraghe'i, Kasravi, and Hedayat*, Bethesda, MD: Ibex Publishers, 2003.

Parsipur, Shahrnush. *Khaterat-e Zandan* (Prison Memoirs), Stockholm: Baran, 1996.

Payandeh, Hosein. *Dastan-e Kutah dar Iran* (Short Story in Iran), 2 vols, Tehran: Nilufar, 1389/2010.

——. *Dastan-e Kutah dar Iran* (Short Story in Iran), vol. 3, Tehran: Nilufar, 1390/2011.

People's Mojahedin Organization of Iran. *Crime against Humanity*, Foreign Affairs Committee of the National Council of Resistance of Iran, 2001, www.mojahedin.org/links/books/crime_against_humanity.pdf (accessed May 5, 2014).

Pedersen, Claus. "Pre-Modern and Early Modern Persian Literature: Written while Travelling?" *Persian Literary Studies Journal* (PLSJ), vol. 1, no. 1, Autumn–Winter 2012.

Perry, John. "The Origin and Development of Literary Persian," in General Introduction to Persian Literature, ed. J. T. P. de Bruijn, London: I.B. Tauris, 2009.

Pirnazar, Jaleh. "The Image of the Iranian Jew in the Writings of Three Modernist Writers," *Iran Nameh*, vol. XIII, no. 4, 1995.

Qazvini, Mohammad. *Bist Maqaleh* (Twenty Articles), eds Ebrahim Purdavud, and Abbas Eqbal, Tehran: Donya-yi Ketab, 1391/2012.

Qur'an, tr. Abdullah Yusuf Ali, www.biharanjuman.org/Quran/quran_translation.html (accessed May 5, 2014).

Qur'an, tr. Mohammed Habib Shakir, www.biharanjuman.org/Quran/quran_transla tion.html (accessed May 5, 2014).

Qur'an, tr. William Pickthall, www.biharanjuman.org/Quran/quran_translation.html (accessed May 5, 2014).

Rafi'zadeh, Shahram. "*Mojavvez-e Hezaran Ketab Batel Shod: Gozareshi az Siyahtarin Doran-e Ketab*" (Permissions for Thousands of Books annulled: A Report of the Darkest Time for Books), November 23, 2006. www.roozonline.com/persian/news/newsitem/archive/2006/november/23/article/-ccdbb5b06d.html (accessed May 5, 2014).

Rahimieh, Nasrin. "A Systemic Approach to Modern Persian Prose Fiction," *World Literature Today*, no. 1, Winter, 1989, pp. 15–19.

Rancière, Jacques. *The Politics of Literature*, Cambridge: Polity Press, 2011.

Rastegar, Kamran. *Literary Modernity Between the Middle East and Europe: Textual Transactions in Nineteenth Century Arabic, English and Persian Literatures*, London: Routledge, 2007.

Rejali, Darius. *Torture and Modernity: Self, Society, and State in Modern Iran*, Boulder, CO; Westview Press, 1993.

Riahi, Marjan. "*Beh Donbal-e yek Buseh*" (After a Kiss), in *Another Sea, Another Shore: Persian Stories of Migration*, eds and trs Shouleh Vatanabadi and Mohammad Mehdi Khorrami, Northamptom, MA: Interlink, 2004.

Roshangar, Majid. *Az Nima ta Ba'd* (Nima and After), Tehran: Morvarid, 1984.

Rypka, Jan. *History of Iranian Literature*, Dordrecht: D. Reidel, 1968.

Sa'edi, Gholam-Hosein. "*Honar-e Dastan Nevisi-ye Bahram Sadeqi*" ("Bahram Sadeqi's Art of Story Telling"), *Kelk* (*Pen*), nos 32 and 33, 1371/1993. http://parah.blogsky.com/1391/09/04/post-194/ (accessed May 5, 2014).

Sa'id, Edward. *Orientalism*, New York: Pantheon, 1978.

Sadeqi, Bahram. *Sangar va Qomqomeh-ha-ye Khali* (The Trench and the Empty Canteens), Tehran: Ketab-e Zaman, 1349/1970.

Safa, Zabihollah. *Tarikh-e Adabiyat dar Iran* (History of Literature in Iran), Tehran: Ferdows, 12th edn, 1371/1992.

Sarkuhi, Faraj. "*Tigh-e 'Sansor-e Akhlaqi' bar Gardan-e Adabiyat-e Iran*" (The Sword of "Moral Censorship" on the Neck of Persian Literature), August 18, 2011, www.bbc.co.uk/persian/arts/2011/08/110818_l41_book_classical_censorship_comme nt.shtml (accessed May 5, 2014).

Sarshar, Mohammad Reza. "*Aya Kafka Sahyunist Bud?*" (Was Kafka a Zionist?), *Adabiyat-e Dastani*, no. 105, 1385/2006.

Sepanlu, Mohammad Ali. "*Enqelab dar Payam-e Ash'ar Ta'sir-e Ziyad-i Gozasht*" (The Revolution Greatly Influenced the Message of the Poems), a conversation with

Fars News, 2005 www.farsnews.com/newstext.php?nn=8411080498 (accessed May 5, 2014).

Shafi'i Kadkani, Mohammad Reza. *Sovar-e Khial dar She'r-e Farsi* (Imagery in Persian Poetry), Tehran: Agah, 1350/1971.

——. *Musiqi-ye She'r* (The Music of Poetry), Tehran: Agah, 3rd edn, 1370/1991.

——. *Sha'er-i dar Hojum-e Montaqedan: Naqd-e Adabi dar Sabk-e Hendi* (A Poet Attacked by Critics: Literary Criticism in Indian Style), Tehran: Agah, 1375/1996.

Shakeri, Ahmad. "*Goft-o-gu ba Mostafa Mastur*" (Conversation with Mostafa Mastur), *Adabiyat-e Dastani*, no. 101, 2005.

Shamisa, Sirus. *Shahed Bazi dar Adabiyat-e Farsi* (Pederasty in Persian Literature), Tehran: Ferdows, 1381/2002.

Shamlu, Ahmad. "*Negah Kon*" (Look!), in *Havay-e Tazeh* (Fresh Air), in *Collected Poems, vol. 1*, (1940–1964), Giessen: Kanun-e Entesharati va Farhangi-ye Bamdad, 1988.

Shayegan, Daryush. *Au-delà du miroir, Diversité culturelle et unité des valeurs* (Beyond the Mirror, Cultural Diversity and Unity of Values), Paris: Editions de l'Aube, 2004.

Sheida, Behruz. "*Taraj-e Tan, Jerahat-e Jan*" (Raiding the Body, Injuring the Soul), (1381/2002), http://asre-nou.net/1381/bahman/2/m-sheidai.html, (accessed May 5, 2014).

Sherwood, Richard. "Viktor Shklovsky and the development of early Formalist Theory on Prose Literature," in *Russian Formalism: A Collection of Articles and Texts in Translation*, eds Stephen Bann and John Bowlt, New York: Barnes & Noble, 1973.

Shields, Rob. "Henri Lefebvre," in *Profiles in Contemporary Social Theory*, eds Anthony Elliott and Bryan Turner, London: Sage Publications, 2001.

Shirazi, Pari. *Filmnameh or Mental Cinema: A New Literary Genre in Persian Literature*, Dissertation, New York University, 2001.

Shklovsky, Viktor. "On the Connection between Devices of Syuzhet Construction and General Stylistic Devices," in *Russian Formalism: A Collection of Articles and Texts in Translation*, eds Stephen Bann and John Bowlt, New York: Barnes & Noble 1973.

Slemon, Stephen. "Magic Realism as Post-Colonial Discourse," *Canadian Literature*, No. 166 (Spring 1988): 9–24.

Soja, Edward. *Third Space*, Oxford: Blackwell, 2000.

Soltanzadeh, Mohammad Asef. "*... Ta Mazar*" (... to Mazar), in *Dar Goriz Gom Mishavim* (We Disappear in Flight), Tehran: Agah, 2000.

——. "*Damad-e Kabol*" (The Bridegroom of Kabul), in *Dar Goriz Gom Mishavim* (We Disappear in Flight), Tehran: Agah, 2000.

Spitzer, Leo. *Linguistics and Literary History: Essays in Stylistics*, Princeton, NJ: Princeton University Press, 1967.

Talattof, Kamran. *The Politics of Writing in Iran: A History of Modern Persian Literature*, Syracuse, NY: Syracuse University Press, 2000.

——. *Modernity, Sexuality, and Ideology in Iran: The Life and Legacy of Popular Female Artists*, Syracuse, NY: Syracuse University Press, 2011.

Tavakoli-Targhi, Mohamad. *Refashioning Iran: Orientalism, Occidentalism, and Historiography*, New York: Palgrave, 2001.

Terdiman, Richard. *Discourse/Counter-Discourse: The Theory and Practice of Symbolic Resistance in Nineteenth-Century France*, Ithaca, NY: Cornell University Press, 1985.

Thompson, Edward Palmer. Interviewed by Mike Merrill in *Visions of History*, eds Henry Abelove, Betsy Blackmar, Peter Dimock, and Jonathan Schneer, New York: Pantheon Books, 1984, pp. 5–25.

Thompson, Kristin. *Eisenstein's* Ivan the Terrible*: A Neoformalist Analysis*, Princeton, NJ: Princeton University Press, 1981.

Todorov, Tzvetan. *Introduction à la littérature fantastique* (Introduction to the Literature of Fantastic), Paris: Editions du Seuil, 1976.

Vaneigem, Raoul. *Le Livre des plaisir* (The Book of Pleasures), Paris: Éditions Encre, 1979.

White, Hayden. *The Content of the Form: Narrative Discourse and Historical Representation*, Baltimore, MD: The Johns Hopkins University Press, 1987.

Wisehöfer, Josef. *Ancient Persia from 550 BC to 650 AD*, tr. Azizeh Azodi, London: I.B. Tauris, 2001.

Yarshater, Ehsan (ed.). *Persian Literature*, Albany, NY: Bibliotheca Persica, 1988.

Yazdi, Ebrahim. *"Ahkam-e E'dam ra Khod-e Khomeini Sader Kard"* (Khomeini Himself Issued the Execution Orders), an interview with Dr. Ebrahim Yazdi, 2005, www.khandaniha.eu/items.php?id=274 (accessed May 5, 2014).

Zagajewski, Adam. *Solidarity, Solitude*, New York: The Ecco Press, 1990.

Zamyatin, Yevgeny Ivanovich. *We*, (1921), tr. Clarence Brown, New York: Penguin, 1993.

Zarshenas, Shahryar. *"Adabiyat-e Ya's va Bimari-ye Sadeq Hedayat"* (Literature of Despair and Sadeq Hedayat's Sickness), *Adabiyat-e Dastani*, no. 60, 2003.

——. *"Feminism va Barkhi Nomudha-ye an dar Adabiyat-e Dastani"* (Feminism and its Reflections in Fiction), *Adabiyat-e Dastani*, no. 72, 2003.

——. *"Sadeq Chubak va Naturalism-e Freud Zadey-e Lompani"* (Sadeq Chubak and Vulgar Freud-Stricken Naturalism), *Adabiyat-e Dastani*, no. 86, 2004.

Index